# Malaysia: Prospect and Retrospect

# MALAYSIA

## Prospect and Retrospect

*The impact and aftermath*

*of colonial rule*

RICHARD ALLEN

LONDON

*Oxford University Press*

NEW YORK   KUALA LUMPUR

1968

*Oxford University Press, Ely House, London W.1*

GLASGOW NEW YORK TORONTO MELBOURNE WELLINGTON
CAPE TOWN SALISBURY IBADAN NAIROBI LUSAKA ADDIS ABABA
BOMBAY CALCUTTA MADRAS KARACHI LAHORE DACCA
KUALA LUMPUR HONG KONG TOKYO

PRINTED IN GREAT BRITAIN BY
HAZELL WATSON AND VINEY LTD
AYLESBURY, BUCKS

*To*
*B.T.W.S.*

# Contents

PREFACE                                                 xi

1   THE RECENT PAST                                  1
The Paradox of Confrontation.

2   COLONIAL ORIGINS                               6
Imperial Prelude. Dutch and British Rivalry in
Indonesia. Britain's New Horizons.

3   THE MALAYAN SETTING AND EUROPEAN
EXPANSION                                  17
Malacca: The Malay Sultanate; the Portuguese;
the Dutch. The British in Penang, Malacca and
Java.

4   THE NINETEENTH CENTURY (1)                 30
Raffles and Singapore. The Anglo-Dutch
Compromise. The Malay States and the
Intervention Controversy. The Straits Settlements a
Crown Colony. The Sarawak Adventure.

5   THE NINETEENTH CENTURY (2)                 42
Tin and Chinese Immigration. The Accidents of
Intervention.

6   THE EVOLUTION AND CONSOLIDATION OF
BRITISH RULE                               52
The Resident System. The Federated Malay States.
The Unfederated States. Rubber and Indian Labour.

7   BRITAIN'S FINAL EXPANSION, AND DEFEAT   64
The Rival Sultans and the Exploitation of North
Borneo. The Enlargement of Sarawak and Decline
of Brunei. The Background to the Japanese
Assault. The Occupation and Co-Prosperity Sphere.

8   NATIONALISM AND THE POST-WAR RECKONING   79
The Indonesian Republic. The Chinese Communists

in Malaya. Malayan Union and Federation. The
United Malays National Organization. Singapore's
Separate Evolution. Sarawak and North Borneo
become Crown Colonies. Start of the Communist
Insurrection.

9   THE EMERGENCY         91
Communist Strategy and Tactics and the
Government's Response. British Leadership and
Methods. The Broadening of the Malayan
Nationalist Movement; the Malayan Indian
Congress and the Malayan Chinese Association.

10   INDEPENDENCE         104
New Malay Leadership. The Multi-Racial Alliance.
Self-Government in Malaya and Singapore.
Abortive Talks with the Insurgents. Freedom and
the New Constitution. The Opposition and the
Changed Political Scene.

11   MALAYA AND HER NEIGHBOURS (1)     117
The Structure and Pattern of Government in Kuala
Lumpur and the Chief Personalities involved.
President Sukarno and the Evolution of Indonesia.

12   MALAYA AND HER NEIGHBOURS (2)     131
Indonesian Nationalism overshadows Malaya. The
Association of Southeast Asia. The Malaysia Plan.
Singapore's Constitutional Progress; the Peoples'
Action Party and Lee Kuan Yew.

13   MALAYSIA IN THE BALANCE     144
The Cobbold Commission in the Borneo Territories.
Malaysia approved. Attitude and Policy of Brunei.
The Singapore Referendum.

14   THE GROWTH OF DISCORD     157
The Philippines' Claim to North Borneo. The
Brunei Revolt. The Manila Summit. Maphilindo.

15 THE STORM BREAKS 172

The United Nations Inquiry. The Establishment of
Malaysia. Anti-British Sabotage in Indonesia. The
Start of Confrontation. Attitude of the United
States. Djakarta's Allies.

16 THE CONFLICT SPREADS 189

Indonesian Subversion and Attacks on the Malay
Peninsula. Indonesia leaves the United Nations. Her
Leftward Drift. Separation of Singapore from
Malaysia.

17 THE TURNING TIDE 209

The Republic of Singapore. Dissensions between
Kuala Lumpur and the Borneo States; Sabah
brought into Line. The Growth of Malay Suspicion
of the British. The Djakarta Uprising of 30
September 1965. Its Critical Consequences.

18 THE BALANCE-SHEET OF UNREST 229

Malaysia's and Singapore's Continuing Prosperity.
Indonesia and the Sequel to the Communist
Defeat. The Djakarta Triumvirate and the Ending
of Confrontation. Sukarno's Enforced Eclipse.

19 MALAY NATIONALISM AND THE NEW ERA 250

The Younger Generation of Nationalists. Singapore
Champions the Non-Malays. Kuala Lumpur's
Continued Disillusionment with Britain. Sarawak
Called to Order. Campaign to make Malay the Sole
Official Language. Visit of President Johnson to
Kuala Lumpur. The Continuing Threat of
Communism.

EPILOGUE: THE PATTERN AND PROBLEMS OF
SUCCESS 274

Content and Character, in Retrospect, of British
Rule. Malaysian Government and Leadership in
the New Era. The Prospect of Southeast Asia. The
altered Power Structure of the Commonwealth.
America's New Role.

CHRONOLOGY OF PRINCIPAL EVENTS
CONCERNING MALAYSIA SINCE 1600                    286

BIBLIOGRAPHY                                       294

INDEX                                              301

MAPS                                               331

South-east Asia                                    333
Federation of Malaysia I: and Singapore           334
Federation of Malaysia II: Sarawak, Brunei, and
    Sabah                                          335

# Preface

This book is intended for all who may be interested in the recent development of one of the most vigorous new nations of Asia, a multi-racial country which has been faced with crises of the gravest kind. It is also for those more generally concerned with the consequences of British imperial action in one corner of that continent. At the same time, for a generation of Americans who have seen their country become deeply and painfully involved in Southeast Asia, some knowledge of Malaysia and its evolution is essential to their understanding of the area. The people and territories of this federation and Singapore form a link with the other countries with which the United States has been more directly concerned—with Indonesia and the Philippines, whose people are of related race and who have had ambitions to take over parts of Malaysia as their own, with Thailand who had at one time suzerainty over most of the Malay Peninsula, and with Vietnam where a communist insurrection has threatened to engulf the country as a similar insurrection threatened some years ago to destroy Malaya.

This is not a study of the more specialized aspects of the subject. I have felt it right to refrain from undertaking anything more ambitious than a short general and political survey. I have sought to give a continuous account, touching briefly on the early period, in the hope that this may prove useful not only to the general reader but also to undergraduate students in Britain and America in the Commonwealth and Southeast Asia fields. References and footnotes in the text have been kept to a minimum but the more extensive bibliography I have included may help to fill some of the obvious gaps.

It is tempting to recall that some great works of scholarship have been produced by men of the British overseas services in the past. Sir George Sansom, whose death in April, 1965, was regretted by all students of the Far East, was one of the finest modern examples but possibly one of the last, of a long distinguished tradition going back to Richard Burton, to Raffles, and beyond. Apart from the outstanding personal qualities of

such men, the more leisurely, stable pace of the world before
1914—and to a lesser degree up to the 1930s—gave to older
generations positive opportunities for scholarly achievements of
this kind. Those were the days of specialist regional staffs who
spent much of their service in small, quiet, outlying posts in the
countries to which they had dedicated their lives. From the
1930s onwards there was, however, constant stress and change.
For those whose service has lain chiefly in large cities during
the last three decades, opportunities for study or even reflection
have been rare. There has been constant pressure to deal at
speed with insistent day-to-day problems. In the former out-
posts of the Empire, remote or otherwise, there has ceased to
be the kind of close association with local life which enabled
British people to contribute so much to the knowledge of these
lands. In the Diplomatic Service the specialist staffs devoted to
one area have been replaced by language students who spend
only a fraction of their career in the particular countries. For
all recently in the public service there have thus been inevitable
barriers to thorough study. On the other hand, dealing under
pressure with the administrative and diplomatic problems
posed by immediate issues may not be entirely without value
from the standpoint of understanding the movement of events
as these were actually happening.

I have dealt primarily with Malaysia, concentrating on the
period from the Japanese invasion. A sketch of earlier history
is, however, essential. It is tempting to compare the story of
Burma, where the writer spent some years at one of the most
taxing periods of Anglo-Burmese relations. Both these countries
were at one time ruled from British India. Yet British government developed in each on very different lines and there has
been a sharp contrast in the course they have followed since
independence. Full justice can, however, only be done to this
comparison in a separate study.

There is a well-justified complaint in the new nations of
Asia that the writing of their history has been mostly Europe-
centric. All too often it has been presented from the standpoint
of the colonizing power. This is a situation which Asian historians are quickly remedying themselves. Perhaps meanwhile another book may be forgiven which is necessarily
coloured to some extent by British training and experience

though it seeks to prove no thesis in this controversial field. I have sought to give full weight to Asian viewpoints on the British record. Some of these can be healthily corrective of undue pride, prejudice and preconceived ideas.

I am in the first instance indebted to my former Foreign Office chief, Sir Esler Dening, now Chairman of the Council of the Royal Central Asian Society, whose experienced judgement taught me the elements of understanding of Southeast Asian questions; to the Ford and Rockefeller Foundations for supporting this project; and to Dr. George Taylor of the University of Washington, whose kind encouragement brought me the opportunity of new and fascinating work in the United States. My special thanks are also due to Mr. Brian Stewart, formerly of the Malayan Civil Service and of the British High Commission, Kuala Lumpur, who first aroused my interest in Malaysia and whose guidance and hospitality shaped the whole course of our stay there.

Too much space would unfortunately be needed to record my gratitude to all who so generously helped and advised me during our travel and research in the area. Amongst many others in Western Malaysia, may I particularly mention Mr. Justice Suffian and his brother Enche Mohammed Nor, Haji Mubin Sheppard, Professor Wang Gungwu of the University of Malaya, Mr. C. G. Ferguson, Adviser on Rural Development, and Mr. J. P. M. Clifford, former Deputy Director of the Federal Land Development Authority.

In Singapore I received much valuable enlightenment from Mr. George Thomson, Director of the Political Studies Centre, Mr. Charles Letts of Jardine, Matheson, and Mr. Willard Hanna of the American Universities Field Staff; and in Eastern Malaysia from the former State and Financial Secretaries in Kuching, Mr. Anthony Shaw and Mr. John Pike, from the British Deputy High Commissioner there, Mr. F. W. Marten and his First Secretary in Jesselton, Mr. Rex Hunt, from Mr. John Slimming, and from Mr. Hywel George, Resident in Tawau. I would like to add my very sincere appreciation of the kind help received from the British High Commissioner to Brunei, Mr. F. D. Webber.

My warm thanks are also due to a number of distinguished Indonesians in Djakarta who were willing to discuss the problems of their country with me at a moment of specially difficult relations; to the British and American Ambassadors, Sir Andrew Gilchrist and Mr. Marshall Green; to Colonel Wakefield, British Consul in Surabaya; and to the New Zealand Minister, Dr. Lohore, to whom I owe my journey by car through Java and Bali.

I am grateful for the patience and advice of Professors C. D. Cowan and John Bastin of the School of Oriental and African Studies of the University of London, of Mr. A. S. B. Olver, formerly Director of Research at Chatham House, of Sir Robert Thompson of the Rand Corporation and of Mr. C. D. Overton, the Librarian of the Commonwealth Office. Field-Marshal Sir Gerald Templer was good enough to permit me to consult him on particular points.

In the United States, Professors J. O. Wolters of Cornell University and Gordon Means of the University of Washington have made many valuable suggestions. I am also indebted to Mr. Charles Baldwin, the former American Ambassador to Malaysia, for his helpful comments on certain aspects of the text, and to Mr. Arley Jonish, Librarian of Whitman College, for his friendly guidance on points of detail.

Finally I owe much to the ready and cheerful efficiency of my two research assistants in Kuala Lumpur, Mrs. Dunsmure and Mrs. Finlay, to the staff of the Ford Foundation there; and to the inspiration and counsel of my wife who was kindly enabled by the Foundations to accompany me.

# CHAPTER ONE

# The Recent Past

New Year 1966 found Indonesia and Malaysia locked in the strange conflict called Confrontation in the Island of Borneo and the Straits of Malacca. It was war and not war. It had wrecked or displaced the lives of thousands, from the descendants of jungle head-hunters living in longhouses to young men from Scotland, Kelantan, or New South Wales, from London, Penang, Auckland, and Nepal. Nearly all found it hard to grasp by what stroke of fate and for what purpose they were there. In this conflict, which served to distract attention from her internal troubles, Indonesia also saw herself as the champion of the world's progressive forces against the relics of British imperialism striving to hold a puppet federation in its grip. For Malaya and the Borneo territories which together composed Malaysia, the image was very different. They had won independence but kept the friendship and support of their former rulers. They could draw not only on their help but on that of other members of a Commonwealth they had freely joined. For them, President Sukarno's Confrontation was the bid of an ambitious autocrat to impose his domination in areas over which the Indonesians had exercised a suzerainty in the distant past.

Most of the fighting had occurred along the thousand-mile border between Indonesia and Malaysia. Much of the area is utterly wild and remote; and access to it—chiefly by river and forest trail—far harder for the Indonesians, from their distant ports in Kalimantan, the southern part of the island, than for the Commonwealth forces. Only at the farthest ends of the line, in the Residency of Tawau in Sabah and in the gold-bearing region of Bau in Sarawak, was there easy approach to the adversary. Tawau, where there was access by water, was one of the areas of maximum Confrontation.

The town of Tawau is the remotest corner of what had once been British Southeast Asia, an extension of the Empire from the frontiers of Bengal through Burma and the Malay Peninsula to the fringe of the southern Philippines, undertaken mostly in the nineteenth century. Little more than two years before, Sabah had been the Crown Colony of North Borneo. Earlier still—before the Second World War—it was ruled by a British Chartered Company which had been launched in the Victorian heyday, in part by an American adventurer and a German Baron in the service of the Austrian Emperor. Then in the late summer of 1963 it had become a somewhat hesitant partner in the new federation of Malaysia. This enlargement of the Federation of Malaya, independent since 1957, also covered Sarawak, the Borneo colony originally created as a private realm by the Brooke Rajahs and, for a time, Singapore, the focus and chief port of the whole area. The twenty-eighth Sultan of Brunei, a state surrounded by Sarawak, whose ancestors had claimed to be overlords of both territories, had displayed his freedom somewhat paradoxically by refusing to join Malaysia and remaining under British protection. His princely oil revenues would still be at his own disposal.

Tawau itself is typical neither of Malaya nor of Burma, once Britain's two principal dominions in Southeast Asia. Malaya faces the Malacca Straits and the South China Sea; Burma, the Bay of Bengal. But Tawau looks towards the Philippines and Indonesia across the Sulu and Celebes Seas. With the former, brisk smuggling sustains an age-old interdependence. The latter has meant, amongst so much else, trade in copra and spices from the Moluccas which the English coveted and lost to the Dutch in the seventeenth century.

On the other side of the bay from Tawau lies the half-Indonesian, half-Malaysian island of Sebatik. Here at the turn of the year the two opponents were gauging each other's intentions across an unreal line drawn by the colonial powers. The town, its port and hinterland were a vivid kaleidoscope of races, mingling Chinese, Filipinos, Indonesians and Malays. Indonesians had been some of the most useful settlers under British rule in labour-starved North Borneo. Since Confrontation they could no longer immigrate. Yet many of the 9,000 Indonesians already in the town thronged the docks and streets. Indonesian boats from the Celebes and Moluccas continued to run the gauntlet of their own patrols to barter their copra, cloves, and pepper against consumer goods desperately scarce at home. Fifty of these boats had been sunk by their own people, yet the game still seemed worthwhile. There was runaway inflation in Indonesia and government strangulation of the country's resources. Malaysia had for them the attraction of a sound and plentiful economy with a strong internationally valid currency.

The Tawau Residency is a land of colourful paradox. The Resident in charge of civil administration was still British. Yet in military command there was a Malaysian Brigadier and under him a variegated complex of British, Malay, Gurkha, Australian, New Zealand, and 'native' units. In Kalabakan, twenty miles away, the Scots Guards, on the eve of replacement by the English Green Jackets, watched the Indonesian jungle. Their pipers were no less full-blooded than in the chilly hills of Scotland, but they were naked to the waist in the tropical heat. Scots and Irish troops were busy training the Home Guard raised by the Welsh manager of the Wallace Bay Timber Company, the Company seeing no cause for stopping operations on so flimsy a pretext as Indonesian raids. These had been encountered in some force by Malay and other allied units in the area, but few of the raiders had escaped the attention of the Commonwealth forces.

At this point in time such had been the strangely inconclusive sequel to empire in one area where Britain used to rule. She had stepped down, yet was still deeply and expensively involved. In spite of upheavals in Djakarta, the Indonesian capital, which had blurred the image and sapped the authority of President Sukarno, the possibility of escalation remained a disturbing prospect. It was already tragically in process in Vietnam.

At the opposite pole to Borneo, former British Burma was retreating into isolation. Since her military revolution of 1962 she had almost totally effaced the structure and imprint of the colonial system. Internally she was enforcing socialism of a uniquely Burmese kind. Banks and shops had been nationalized. Virtually the last traces of Western capitalism and even of Asian private trade as it had existed for centuries had been swept away. Consumer goods were frugally rationed and dispensed by People's Stores purged of a profit motive. Even food, of which she is a surplus producer, was regulated and controlled.

Externally, on the other hand, Burma posed few problems. Some of her minorities were in arms against the government, but this was an old problem going back to the early years of independence and even further to the days of the Burmese Kings. It had not disturbed the neutrality Burma had elected to observe between the Communist and Western worlds. This had at least the image of a strict, fine balance. The aid Burma received and the scholars she dispatched were divided equally between each half of the world. Whatever anxieties she had caused to West and East, neither up to that moment had felt obliged to seek a forcible solution to their differences on Burmese soil.

In the centre of former British Southeast Asia the peninsula of Malaya and Singapore were prosperous, vital, and progressive. Tin, rubber, palm oil, and incipient industry were a rich field of overseas and local national investment along the lines traditional in the West. The entrepôt trade of the ports and especially of Singapore continued in spite of an Indonesian boycott. The European still played his part in management and even in some specialized government jobs. He had not yet—as so often in the developing world—been made to feel unwelcome. The cost of Confrontation, shared with their Commonwealth associates, had added no unbearable burden to these countries with a buoyant revenue.

By mutual agreement, Singapore had joined Malaya and the former colonies of Borneo in Malaysia in 1963. Singapore had much to gain economically from this step. Less than two years later, however, the aims and methods of her leaders had seemed to the dominant Malays of Kuala Lumpur, capital of the federation, to be incompatible with their own. Separation was then in effect forced upon Singapore, which had to set up as a minute nation on her own. This was little to the taste of her ambitious Prime Minister, who had set his heart on a Malaysian nation in which the non-Malays would play a full and equal part. Mutual reproaches between him and Kuala Lumpur were the order of the day. Singapore was a predominantly Chinese city, but nevertheless had a Malay population bigger than that in all northern Borneo. Yet the Singapore Chinese, and those in Malaya and Borneo together, had formed some 40 per cent. of the population of all the Malaysian territories.

So far as Singapore was concerned, the frustration of her hopes of full co-operation had made her determined to seek eventual re-association with Malaysia, starting with economic co-operation along the lines of a common market. Meanwhile her government aimed at making of Singapore a showpiece of 'Malaysian Malaysia' as her people conceived it. They were confident that Malays would be increasingly attracted by what Singapore had to offer in the way of richer education and greater scope for careers than in the peninsula and that this would strengthen their hand when the time came to discuss re-admission to Malaysia. The Prime Minister of Malaysia himself conceded that the door for Singapore's re-entry into Malaysia might one day be reopened.

Such in broadest outline had been the latest evolution of these former British countries. If we are to understand the patterns and meaning of today's events we have to make an excursion into the past. How did Britain ever come to be concerned with overseas empire in so distant a corner of Asia? Why did a system of colonization which flourished remarkably in its time almost completely disappear? What of any value has it left behind?

# CHAPTER TWO

# Colonial Origins

By the last third of the twentieth century Britain has reverted to the role of a predominantly European power. She is back in a sense where she used to be in Shakespeare's later years, when the great Mogul, Akbar, ruled in India and the Ming Emperors in China.

The intervening phase of empire, now over, has been regarded by some as a majestic deviation from earlier and equally precious traditions which gave Britain her greatest literature, her finest cathedrals, and her most distinguished seats of learning.[1] According to this view, she is once again her essential self. It is thus no bad moment to take stock of Britain's spectacular expansion over nearly 350 years and the ultimate effects which this has produced. In doing so, however, we cannot deal with any one corner of the world without some attempt to explain far wider issues.

Why should one of Europe's off-shore islands, no larger than New York State and half the size of France, have sought for a few centuries so special a destiny and one with such far-reaching consequences for other lands and peoples? What factors, for better or worse, projected the British race, system, and ideas—and the simple yet chaotic English language—so far across the globe? How, from such small beginnings, could a situation have arisen of alleged world domination by the White Anglo-Saxon Protestant peoples?[2]

Today as in the past Britain and her fellow 'Anglo-Saxons' face two currents of latent or active hostility. One is from highly sophisticated rival nations with a great past or massive potentialities for the future which have long resented the Anglo-Saxon place in the sun. The other is from formerly dependent lands.

[1] This was the implied attitude of the Little Englanders of the nineteenth century, such as Gladstone.
[2] W.A.S.P.s for short. This is the general theme of E. Digby Baltzell's *The Protestant Establishment.*

To the irritation of many, in the nineteenth century Britain seemed cast in the role of international banker, schoolmaster, maritime policeman, and sanitary inspector. With all her attachment to ancient forms she had become in a sense the world's first modern nation. One of the principal objectives of Germany in two world wars—and of Japan in the second war— was to win a comparably commanding position. Today the United States has assumed Britain's mantle and become the dominant factor in this Anglo-Saxon world. Understandably it is now the principal target of leaders of other great national traditions like President De Gaulle. Even at the expense of his allies and the causes they uphold in common with his country, he has shown himself determined to reassert the greatness of France who in her age of power was the decisive factor in ensuring the independence of the hard-pressed American colonies.

Even those who condemn 'colonialism' do not normally blame Britain for the foundation of her colonies of settlement in America or the antipodes. There her sons went to develop, and make their homes in largely empty lands. These were colonies in the classic and legitimate sense of the term. Yet by reason of the colossal success of the United States, this nation so strongly anti-colonial by tradition is today pilloried as the arch-Imperialist, not only by the Communist bloc, but by European nations and by the former colonies in Asia and Africa to whom she has proffered such generous help.

What is more immediately critical is the latent resentment towards their former rulers of some of these newly independent African and Asian nations. Unlike the colonies of settlement, they were populous lands of different climate, custom, and complexion on which alien rule was imposed. Some of them, in Asia, had civilizations far older than that of the colonizing power. In the overseas territories governed by Britain, what did British rule achieve that was of permanent value and where did it fail? What has it left behind? How did the Asians and Africans regard the coming, the dominance, and the departure of the British?

It seems to be gratuitously assumed by certain critics that colonization was some evil new device invented and practised by Western Europeans of strange complexion invading warm lands from overseas. By some irony, Russia—which seeks to profit from both currents of anti-Anglo-Saxon resentment—escapes the strictures of most Afro-Asians because she colonized Central Asia not by crossing the oceans but merely by moving eastwards across one continuous land mass.

Yet all who have studied it are aware that colonization is as old as the world. It has been practised in all forms in every age and continent and by almost every race upon those weaker or less advanced. The empires of the Mongol invaders of China and India and that of the Ottoman Turks were examples of colonization just as valid as the empires of the European powers.

Another truth of history on which the more vocal emerging nations are perhaps humanly silent is that colonization is not always evil in its results. With Western Europe, England was colonized by Rome. A thousand years later she was colonized again and far more thoroughly by the Normans. In England as in China the colonizers eventually fused with the conquered peoples. But initially the Norman kings imposed an alien dynasty, language, and system of government. They took stock in Domesday Book of their new estate and moved their people into the lands and benefices of the defeated natives. In this admittedly grim process England was disciplined and integrated and hammered into one nation centuries before this happened in neighbouring lands.

In the case of those Asian territories on which Britain imposed her rule, the Asians themselves can best determine whether they received any comparable benefits to compensate them for the temporary loss of their independence.

It will always be something of a mystery why Britain explored and settled and established her pattern of government and society overseas more widely and effectively than any other nation. It was not starvation or overcrowding, as in China and India, which drove the English[1] in the late sixteenth and seventeenth centuries out of their fertile island to seek adventure, conquest, wealth, and a new life in distant lands, though

[1] Wales was in effect annexed to England by the Tudors. The conquered part of Ireland was also regarded as part of England. Scotland remained a separate Kingdom until the Act of Union of 1707. She was excluded from England's empire by the Navigation Acts even under the Stuart Kings.

their law of primogeniture doubtless played its part by settling family estates upon the eldest son and leaving the younger children to find their fortune in other fields. At the same time, the British expansion was not a consequence of the Protestant Reformation, sometimes alleged to have released a well-spring of energy in northern peoples, although the married Protestant clergy admittedly produced fine stock. If the Reformation had been the principal impulse, how could Portugal, a pillar of the Catholic Church, have achieved so much with her tiny population? The religious strife begotten by the Reformation accounted in the imperial field for the New England colonies, Pennsylvania, Maryland, and little else. The sea was the natural element of an island free from the tensions imposed by land frontiers with ambitious neighbours. Yet seafaring traditions are by themselves no adequate explanation. The English share these with the Japanese, the Scandinavians, the Genoese, and the Maoris, none of them notable as colonizing peoples.

A more valid explanation is England's relative weakness and lack of resources in the face of the great continental powers. In the reign of Henry VIII, Spain had twice the population of England and Wales. France's population was five times as large.[1] In 1509, in a table of precedence of European monarchs established by the Pope, the still Catholic King of England was placed after the King of Portugal and just ahead of the King of Sicily. A hundred years later, in the early 1600s, England still had no claim to be a European great power. In the Elizabethan Age, despite the courage of her sailors and the frequent ineptitude of her adversary, it had been the Queen's adroit and cautious diplomacy rather than England's innate strength that had saved her from destruction at the hands of Spain, then virtually mistress of southwestern Europe and the western hemisphere. With the gradual eclipse of Spanish power, France rapidly rose to the leadership of the whole continent. Even Holland, while still struggling to be free from Spain, for a time outdistanced England as the foremost commercial, financial, and maritime nation of Europe.

In the Tudor Age, England after years of civil war had at last turned to wider horizons. But that age had revealed the dangers of seeking to play from weakness a major role. To match

[1] Lord Strang, *Britain in World Affairs*, p. 26.

the military power of the continental nations, her people had to build up their strength by using such advantages as they possessed. One was a commercial flair, fostered by the traditional wool trade with Flanders; the other a familiarity with the surrounding sea. In time they also discovered in themselves a knack of adaptation to life in distant lands and a gift for imparting to others their peculiar forms of social and political organization. As trading posts and colonies were acquired, these were tied economically to the mother country. Under the mercantilist system which prevailed until the American Revolution, although there were important elements of mutual advantage, overseas possessions were basically designed to foster Britain's wealth. Yet in spite of an impressive gain in stature through the development of her colonies, her navy and merchant marine, and her trade, it was not until the eighteenth century, after the victories of Marlborough and the Peace of Utrecht in 1713, that Britain began to be counted as a European great power. Even by the time of the French Revolution her population was still less than one-third of that of France.

Holland embarked on a major career of trade and navigation around 1600, at roughly the same time as Britain and for similar reasons. Soon the two countries found themselves in deadly competition.

The Low Countries were by no means first in the field of distant maritime adventure aimed at lucrative trade. In Asia, Portugal and Spain had preceded them. The English East India Company was founded in 1600, two years before the United Dutch East India Company and long before any British colony had been successfully established in America. Britain had been inspired to take this step by the voyages to the Orient of Fitch and Drake and Lancaster and the stories they brought back of the wealth of Asia, and especially of the Indonesian Archipelago. First among these sources of wealth which attracted European trading adventurers were, not precious metals, but the spices of the Moluccas. These had earlier been accessible through the Levant and the Mediterranean and had been one of the main goals of merchant bodies such as the English Levant Company, but this trade had declined with the triumphs of the Turkish Empire.

In Europe the age of gross feeding and tainted food was largely over. The Renaissance had done its work. Taste had become more subtle and demanding. In 1572, when Drake called at Ternate in the Moluccas during his voyage of circumnavigation, the Sultan presented the British with a cargo of spices in defiance of the Portuguese who had maltreated him. The exceptional prices commanded by such cargoes in Europe whetted the appetites of the British and the Dutch. For some time Lisbon and Portugal had enjoyed the profits of the middleman. Now the path lay open to developing this fabulously rewarding trade direct.

By 1600, as we have seen, England had done more exploration of the Atlantic, the Pacific, and the Indian Ocean than had Holland. Yet 'Elizabethan enterprises had been energetic, explosive . . . indiscriminate and ill-regulated'.[1] The Dutch had at first been engrossed by the fight for independence on their own soil and elsewhere. They had both Spain and Portugal as enemies since the two countries had been united under Philip II in 1580. By 1600, however, this formidable combination was in decline. It was tacitly accepted that Holland could no longer be conquered. Although her independence was not formally recognized until the Treaty of Westphalia in 1648, this sturdy new nation now prosecuted what was for her a life and death struggle against the Iberian powers with rigorous determination and increasing success. In consequence of the union with Spain, Portugal's Asian possessions fell wide open to Dutch attack. In the early seventeenth century, Holland concentrated her pressure on Portuguese strongholds in the Spice Islands of the Moluccas. She eventually succeeded in almost completely displacing the Portuguese. She then sought to erect a system of restriction and monopoly which would give her control of the production, transport, and marketing of the spices on the most favourable terms.

As merchants and navigators the Dutch soon displayed a massive persistence and methodical organization considerably in advance of the British. Their position as leading commercial carriers and financiers in Europe gave them a head start when it came to operating in the East. After an initial period of unregulated voyages, the Vereenigde Oostindische Compagnie

[1] Strang, op. cit., p. 47.

(the V.O.C.) was established in 1602 for a time with a capital far larger than that of the English East India Company. The number of ships dispatched from Holland was also far greater than the number sent from England. The London Company operated for many years in a characteristically casual, hand-to-mouth fashion with a variable capital, the profits being more or less completely distributed after each voyage, before going over to the joint-stock system.

For political reasons, there was also a fundamental difference in intensity of approach which made the Dutch the stronger competitors. England was not fighting, as they were, to become a nation; and her government's policies had changed with the replacement of the Tudors by the Stuarts. The Spanish wars of Elizabeth had been a strain on England's strength; and King James I, who succeeded the old queen in 1603, was bent on peace.

Valuable though spices were, James saw no point in fighting Portugal and Spain[1] to drive them completely out of the Moluccas. He would have been quite content for the English to acquire a share of the spice trade by doing a deal with them. England rejected the Dutch claim to set up a spice monopoly in a region where they had arrived first while Holland was still a dependency of Spain. The Dutch, on the other hand, contended that they were sending bigger and stronger fleets to Indonesia than the English, that they were bearing the heat and burden of the day while the British were seeking to profit by their efforts and sacrifices.

From 1609 to 1619 there was a ten years truce between the Low Countries and Spain, during which the Dutch aggressively pressed forward with measures to enforce their spice monopoly. In 1619, faced with the prospect of renewed hostilities with their main enemy, the Netherlands decided to come partially to terms with England. An agreement was concluded between the governments providing that the two companies should share

[1] Previous to the Spanish occupation of the Philippines and the union of Portugal with Spain, there had been some dispute between the two countries over whether Spain had a claim to any part of the Moluccas. Portugal considered Spanish pretentions an infringement of the Treaty of Tordesillas of 1494 and in effect won her case. In the early seventeenth century—the countries being united—the Spaniards from the Philippines supported the Portuguese in the Moluccas against the Dutch.

the spice trade, subject to setting up an equally-balanced defence fleet and defence council.

The Dutch Governor-General in the Indies, however, violently objected to the terms of the agreement and sought to invalidate it, contending that England had no proper claim to anything in the Spice Islands. In consequence, it appears, of instructions given by him to the Governor of Amboyna not to allow the English to reduce his authority, the latter, in 1623, arrested the members of the English 'factory' or trading post. Most of them were executed after proceedings judged in England to have been a travesty of justice. This was the notorious Massacre of Amboyna.

The savage hostility displayed towards them by their former Protestant allies was a profound shock to the English. Other factories had already been established by them at Bantam in West Java and at Macassar in the Celebes which continued to operate until the latter part of the seventeenth century. But the decision had already been taken in London before the Amboyna tragedy to abandon the principal contest with the Dutch and withdraw from the Spice Islands. The last stage in England's discomfiture was when her factory was turned out of Bantam in 1682. The English then retired to Bencoolen on the west coast of Sumatra where the Dutch had not yet established their grip. Eventually the Netherlands came to dominate, not only the spice trade, but large areas of the Indonesian Archipelago. In that vast area England had to content herself with some minor dealings in pepper in Western Indonesia and the handling of such cargoes of spices as she could acquire from those smuggled out of the Eastern Islands in defiance of the Dutch controls. Most of Britain's spice trade reverted to the Levant route and the capital of the English Levant Company was ploughed into the English East India Company. Such, in broadest outline, was the course and inglorious termination of England's first intervention in Southeast Asia.

The English East India Company had already established trading posts at certain key points in India. These were at Surat and Bombay on the west coast, at Masulipatam and Fort St. George, Madras, in the southeast; and finally, in the northeast, at Fort William up the Hooghly where the city of Calcutta was founded in 1697. It was on the Indian sub-continent that the

Company concentrated its efforts after its almost total eviction from the Netherlands Indies. India was not their first choice as a field of endeavour. No one can say whether Britain's Indian Empire would have arisen in the form it did if the Dutch had been weaker or more accommodating in the Archipelago.

In their respective areas, the Dutch and English were interested above all in trade. Essentially they wanted dividends not domination. Until about the middle of the seventeenth century both Companies sought to trade profitably while avoiding as far as possible any territorial entanglements. The Company directors and shareholders of these two commercial nations rightly foresaw the heavy consequences which would ensue from actually subjugating and ruling proud and restive Asian peoples. The last thing they wanted was the expense and sacrifice of 'colonial' wars. Military operations swallowed up their profits, leaving the Dutch Company bankrupt by the end of the eighteenth century and the English Company virtually under government control. In the event, it was approximately between 1660 and 1685 that England's position in Asia first shifted from that of a trading nation, with 'factories' on or near the coast, to that of an incipient ruler of territories and subjects. These were the years of the reign of Charles II.

The Elizabethans blazed the trail for Britain's first empire. Yet the building of it was chiefly the work of our Stuart monarchs. Often so inept in internal government, their vision was far keener overseas. For all his failings Charles II proved to be one of England's greatest Imperial statesmen. This remarkable, profligate, half-French king, who died a Roman Catholic in the faith his subjects had abjured, was freely and sometimes unjustly abused for his internal policies. Nevertheless, in his lifetime two colonies in America were taken over from the Dutch and two more founded. The Hudson's Bay Company was established. A new Charter was granted to the East India Company, establishing it on a far solider and more effective basis. Bombay, which the King had acquired as part of the dowry of his Portuguese Queen, was leased to the East India Company for a nominal rent.

What in these years caused so fundamental a transformation in Britain's status in Asia? The principal factor is usually acknowledged to have been the precarious authority of the Mogul Empire at a time of resurgent Hindu resistance to Muslim rule. Yet the Great Moguls remained dominant in India until the eighteenth century. Later the weakness of the Empire increased as its vassals carved out autonomous fiefs for themselves and, when they deemed it to their advantage, called in the European merchants at their door for competitive support against their rivals. But at this stage in Asia merchants were generally despised. They could remain on condition of fulfilling the requirements and paying the contributions demanded by the local authorities. Yet the latter felt no obligation to defend them or support one company against another. Against this shifting background, the European traders felt obliged to establish the machinery of government and to extend administrative control ever more widely in order to ensure the security and stability of their settlements. 'At the beginning of this period the President of Surat is the local manager of a trading concern; at the end of it he is President of Bombay, head of an executive government, with law courts, a standing army and a system of taxation of its own.'[1] This was the first step upon a road along which succeeding governments and monarchs of Britain were to travel far indeed. Few more deceptive half-truths have been uttered than that trade follows the flag, although this was valid up to a point in Britain's colonies of settlement. In India and indeed in most parts of Asia it was exactly the reverse. Trade was established and the flag followed. Once hoisted, it tended to remain indefinitely and change the destiny of a particular land until displaced by force of circumstance.

From the last years of the seventeenth century until 1815, Britain was intermittently at war with France. This was, it is said, the second Hundred Years' War between them, the first having ended in the fifteenth century with the loss of England's mediaeval empire carved out of France by the descendants of her Norman kings. The new wars eventually ended less favourably for France. Yet in the course of them France ensured that Britain was deprived of the American colonies, the most creditable and advanced achievement of her overseas endeavours.

Much of the struggle was in and around India. Britain

[1] Lord Elton, *Imperial Commonwealth*, p. 81.

achieved considerable success in Asia in the eighteenth century even during the war of the American Revolution. The upshot was to leave her mistress of Bengal and firmly installed in the hinterland of Madras and Bombay. Calcutta had become, under Warren Hastings as Britain's first Governor-General, the capital of all the East India Company's holdings in India. After his departure in 1785 a decision was taken in Calcutta which was momentous for the Malay Peninsula. In 1786, just over a century after the loss of the Bantam factory in Java, Britain acquired the island of Penang in the Straits of Malacca.

# CHAPTER THREE

# The Malayan Setting
# and European Expansion

The island of Penang off the west coast of Malaya was in the dominions of the Sultan of Kedah, a vassal of the King of Thailand.

The inhabitants of these Malay states, as the British found them in the late eighteenth century, had passed through a long and chequered evolution. In pre-historic times they had been part of the southward drift of various peoples from what is now western China. Elements of the Malay races had come down early from Yunnan before Chinese culture had penetrated that region. Later some had migrated from the Malay Peninsula into and beyond the Indonesian Archipelago, which had at one time been linked by land bridges with the mainland of Asia and with Australia. Other groups which emerged historically from these southward migrations from the general area of western China were the Burmans[1] and the Thais—the latter not until the thirteenth century. There were also earlier and more primitive inhabitants in the Peninsula. These, however, were 'driven back into the dark jungles and the mountains by the superior culture and force of the Malay invaders'.[2] There they tended to cling to their aboriginal, nomadic life.

The Malays of the Peninsula evolved as an amalgam of various more or less related racial groups. Many came from Sumatra and other Indonesian islands to which their ancestors had migrated in pre-historic times. In the pre-Christian and early Christian era they absorbed, like most Southeast Asians, strong Indian commercial, cultural, political, and religious in-

[1] Including both the dominant Burmese race and the hill peoples; the Karens, the Shans (of the same racial stock as the Thais), the Kachins, Chins, etc. [In the U.S.A. Burmans and Burmese have opposite meanings.]
[2] Rupert Emerson, *Malaysia*, p. 12.

fluences. They also maintained links of trade and policy with Imperial China. In the religious, political, and social development of Indonesia and Malaya, indigenous animism, then Hinduism and Buddhism, played a significant part. Hinduism evolved as a court religion and contributed significantly to the political organization of these countries. Ultimately Islam became the dominant religion, though elements of the earlier religions and especially of Hinduism remained.

Somehow the Malay peninsula never achieved in ancient times the high Hindu and Buddhist culture of Java, which was superseded by Islam, or the Hindu culture which Bali has retained. It lacked the rich volcanic soil of Java producing multiple rice crops making the land attractive for settlement and capable of supporting the density of population which is a prerequisite of sophisticated development. The soil of the peninsula is relatively poor. Population was extremely scanty until the immigration of other races and the general improvement in living conditions of modern times. Much of the interior remained uncultivated jungle. The impact of civilizing influences was confined to the small towns at the estuaries of the rivers, and the parts around the coast. In any event, the imported elements of Indian culture, religion, statecraft, and social organization were modified by the genius, traditions, and folkways of the indigenous people into something of strong local character in each region. On the one hand, the states of Indonesia and Malaya evolved forms of monarchy with symbols, ceremonial and ideology reminiscent of the Hindus. On the other, the status of women—to take but one example—was far higher and more independent there and elsewhere in Southeast Asia than it had traditionally been in India.

By the middle of the eighth century A.D., the maritime empire of Srivijaya which had emerged in Sumatra had developed a sea-based power structure extending to much of the Malay Peninsula and other parts of Southeast Asia. Srivijaya's capital was at Palembang, within easy reach of the Malacca and Sunda straits. At the height of its power, Palembang was in a position to control the movement of shipping and trade through both these vital channels; and the island and port of Singapore at the tip of the Malay Peninsula was a key factor in the exercise of this maritime power. In the last quarter of the thirteenth century the power of Srivijaya in the Peninsula was broken by the first Thai Kingdom which had adopted Buddhism. The Thais succeeded for a time in imposing their suzerainty over most of the Peninsula. The extreme south, however, including the island of Tumasik or Singapura was claimed by successive East Javanese Kingdoms. That of Majapahit and later Mataram endured in dwindling strength and area until after the arrival of the European invaders in the sixteenth century.

Meanwhile, Islam was gaining a foothold in the Malay world. It was brought by Arab merchants and teachers directly from Arabia and the Persian Gulf, and later by Gujeratis from northwest India and other Indians who had been converted to the new religion. In 1292, Marco Polo, when he visited Pasai in northern Sumatra on his return from China, found that some people in this region had been converted to the 'Law of Mohammed'.[1] Little over a hundred years later, at the end of the fourteenth century, the foundation of the port-kingdom of Malacca became a factor of vital importance in the spread of Islam in Southeast Asia. Situated in the southwest of the Malay Peninsula, Malacca was a focal point in the region, ideally placed for the diffusion of new ideas.

According to the consensus of historical opinion, Malacca was founded by the last ruler of Singapore. He had been a minor prince of Palembang, married to a Majapahit princess, who had escaped from the Javanese. He moved northwards from Singapore in the face of a Thai directed assault in retribution for his murder of the Thai governor of the island. He settled in Malacca, then an insignificant village. With the sea gypsies and other followers he built up a large and increasingly powerful settlement. As Malacca grew in strength it sought to shake off Thai suzerainty. To reinforce his position the ruler sent an Embassy to China in 1405 and received Imperial recognition.

The new settlement inherited Srivijaya's commercial power. It was in a better position than Palembang to control the Malacca Straits. It sought to force all ships passing through them to put into Malacca to pay dues and take out passes. These monopolistic practices were later continued by the European powers. They bore harshly on local people by check-

[1] S. Q. Fatimi, *Islam Comes to Malaysia*, p. 8.

ing the natural flow of trade. We have already seen their initial impact in the Spice Islands.

In later life the founder of Malacca took a Muslim wife and was converted to Islam. The Malacca monarchs eventually adopted the Islamic title of Sultan, borne to this day by nearly all the rulers of the Malay states. Malacca became the most important entrepôt of Southeast Asia, not only because of its geographical position but because it was at the junction of the monsoons. Here Indian textiles were exchanged for the spices of Indonesia. In a vaster field, the products of China and the Far East were traded for those of Europe and Western Asia. As a political power, Malacca established her dominance over the Malay states of the Peninsula and the east coast of Sumatra. As she did so, Islam, for which she became the centre of diffusion, penetrated these territories also. Further afield, Brunei, the first Muslim state to appear in Borneo, came to accept Islam partly through its trading connexion with Malacca. Sarawak and most of Sabah were parts of the Sultanate of Brunei.

Trade was conducted with northern Java and the Javanese were numerous and important at Malacca. This intercourse promoted conversion to Islam. The whole of Java eventually became Muslim, as did the greater part of Indonesia.

Malacca was the first independent and substantial state of the Malay Peninsula in the modern age. Its wealth and fame soon attracted the onslaught of the first Europeans to penetrate the Indian Ocean. In 1511 Malacca was captured by the Portuguese who had recently established themselves in western India at Goa. They sought to win souls for the Catholic faith. They also sought to make money by seizing an intermediate point from which to develop east-west trade.

The Portuguese strongly fortified themselves in Malacca and left on it a stamp of unique character which it has in part retained. But they did not win friends for Europe. They appear to have operated with a fanaticism and ruthlessness which was repaid in kind by the displaced Malays. Even their great countryman, St. Francis Xavier, said after visiting Southeast Asia that the Portuguese had learned to conjugate the verb to rape in all its tenses. Their hold on Malacca was stubbornly contested by the surrounding Malay states. In spite of their efforts much of the local trade continued, though with some break in the normal pattern. Their chief enemies were Johore in the south of the Peninsula—whither the Malacca rulers had migrated after their defeat—and Acheh the fiercely Muslim Sultanate at the northern tip of Sumatra. Attacks from both were beaten off, but there were cases of captured Portuguese being given the choice of embracing Islam or being blown from a cannon's mouth.

To the Malays, even the Dutch seemed preferable. They were traders first and foremost. They had no proselytizing fire. They held the Christian Portuguese to be their major adversary and they did not regard Islam as an unclean thing to be stamped out at all costs. They were prepared to be friends and allies of any Muslim power so long as this served their interests. In the early seventeenth century they had established their headquarters at Batavia, now Djakarta, in Java. Malacca in hostile hands was a dangerous rival to be eliminated if the Dutch system of monopoly was to be widely effective.

For a time, both Acheh and Johore seemed prepared to make common cause with Batavia against the Portuguese. When the final attack on Malacca was launched by the Dutch in 1641, Acheh backed out at the last moment. Johore, however, collaborated with the Dutch. The Johore rulers appear to have believed that, in return for their help, the hinterland of Malacca would be restored to them, the Dutch contenting themselves with occupation of the port. They were soon disillusioned. Having secured Malacca, the Dutch took over the whole area originally conquered by the Portuguese.

After this conquest the Dutch concentrated on building up Batavia as the commercial centre of the area; and the importance of Malacca gradually declined. Nevertheless, the Dutch applied with a new tenacity and efficiency the system of control of shipping passing through the Malacca Straits which the Portuguese had inherited from the Malacca Sultanate. They also tried to extend—with some success—the system of monopoly of local produce which they had applied in the Spice Islands. They sought to secure by treaty the co-operation of the Sultans of the west and northwest of the Peninsula. Thus the Sultan of Perak was to be made to sell to the Dutch the tin produced in his state. The Sultan of Kedah was to put a stop to the entrepôt trade which flourished there between west and east as it had at Malacca. In fact, however, breaches of the Dutch restrictions by the states of the Malay Peninsula continued throughout the seventeenth and eighteenth centuries. They were encouraged by the British as Britain strengthened and extended her position in India. Other factors also contributed to the decline of the Netherlands United East India Company which had reached the peak of its power in the late seventeenth century.

The Dutch Company had found—as the British found in India—that the pursuit of trade in the framework of a mercantilist system led inevitably to conquest and colonization in the regions of key importance. This was a source of vast military and administrative expense for a country of very limited manpower. The severe monopolistic measures taken by the Dutch to control the availability and movement of spices and other valuable products of Indonesia was most successful and profitable for a considerable period. The production of spices was restricted to designated areas and crops grown outside these areas destroyed. Forced sales were exacted at artificially low prices. One consequence was that other colonial powers turned when they could to growing spices in their own territories. Another was the impoverishment of the Indonesians. The natural flow of island to island and inter-Asian trade was disrupted by the Dutch system which failed to adapt itself to the local commercial pattern and could never be effective over so vast an area. 'Illegal' trade and piracy flourished increasingly in the eighteenth century, with further loss of potential profits to the Netherlands Company. The Dutch monopoly was broken by their conflict with Britain during the war of the American Revolution. Their company fell increasingly into debt but concealed the extent of the disaster until it was virtually bankrupt. In 1799, after the invasion of Holland by the French revolutionary armies, the East India Company was dissolved and the Netherlands Government assumed control of Dutch interests in Southeast Asia.

Through most of the seventeenth and eighteenth centuries shifting strains and pressures kept the states of the Malay Peninsula in ferment and disorder. There were the exigencies of the Thais and the Dutch. There was also penetration and partial domination by fellow Muslims from Indonesia belonging to the variegated family of races loosely classified as Malays. In different regions and with varying fortunes Minangkabaus from western Sumatra and Bugis from the Celebes fought for power against the local princes, the Europeans, and each other.

The Minangkabaus came originally from the pepper-growing southwestern regions of Sumatra and their structure of society, unique among the Malays of the Peninsula, is based on matrilineal descent. There had been Minangkabaus in the area behind Malacca before the coming of the Portuguese. Their fiefs were originally under the suzerainty of the Malacca Sultans. Subsequently many were for a time vassals of Johore. Eventually, after many vicissitudes, they formed at the end of the eighteenth century a loose confederation of nine small realms which became the single state of Negri Sembilan—literally the Land of the Nine Nations. Even in modern Malaya its ruler still has to be elected with the approval of the principal chieftains.

The Bugis were skilled navigators and pirates, brave fighters and shrewd merchants, adept at evading and impeding Dutch controls. After the Dutch capture of Macassar in southern Celebes in 1667, many moved elsewhere. They intensified their guerilla warfare on the seas. This did increasing damage to Dutch trade as the United East India Company lost strength, and indeed hastened the whole process of decline. In their wanderings they descended on the Malay Peninsula and acquired control—for a time or more permanently—in certain southern and western Malay states. Some of the Malay Sultans and political leaders of today are proud to acknowledge Bugis descent.

Early in the eighteenth century the Bugis became the effective rulers of Johore as Underkings controlling a Sultan of the royal house originally descended from the Sultans of Malacca. After being expelled by the Portuguese, these princes and their successors had laid with some success the foundations of a new empire further to the south which might eventually have rivalled Malacca's. For a time they asserted their ascendancy not only over the Minangkabau chiefs but over parts of Sumatra, over Pahang to the east and over the Riau Archipelago, Lingga and other islands to the south of Singapore.

The capital of this extensive kingdom—destined to disintegrate in the early nineteenth century—was moved from the mainland to Riau after the destruction of the earlier capitals along the Johore river. In the later years of the eighteenth century the Riau Archipelago and neighbouring islands came under Dutch control until Holland's power in the region was temporarily eclipsed by Britain's as a result of her subjugation in the French Revolutionary Wars.

In the further course of the eighteenth century, the Bugis ascendancy spread northwards to the tin-producing states of Selangor, Perak, and Kedah. In Selangor they established a dynasty of their race. Only the remoter and poorer states of Trengganu and Pahang seemed to be free from Bugis power. The Sultan of Kedah was driven out of his capital by the Bugis. When the British first became conscious of the desirability of securing a territorial foothold in the Malay area, the Kedah ruler was less concerned about the possible exigencies of his overlord the King of Thailand than about these Bugis pretensions. He was casting around for outside help to throw them out.

Like so much of Britain's expansion overseas, her initial commitment in Malaya was undertaken in an exasperatingly casual manner judged by any logical standards. It certainly owed little to deliberate government planning. It was a case, as so often, of an individual perceiving an opportunity and eventually persuading a reluctant hierarchy that there might be something in pursuing it. Some later British moves in Malaya were, as we shall see, even more arbitrary but no less characteristic. Here and elsewhere it was at times a case of an individual taking action far beyond the sober plans of those at home and committing the authorities so fully that it was virtually impracticable for them to withdraw.

Yet in the last resort the process of British expansion in Asia in the late eighteenth and early nineteenth centuries was governed less by particular events or people than by a whole trend of circumstance. However resourceful the man on the spot, however hesitant or positive the policies of government, both tended to be the unconscious instruments of forces which were transforming western society. In the sixteenth and seventeenth centuries, Europeans had conquered vigorous and flourishing Asian nations essentially through the possession of superior weapons. There had been no great disparity in strength and it was often a close call. By the late eighteenth century, however, the Industrial Revolution had started in Britain and through it Europe multiplied her strength. Yet by this time Asian society had largely lost the dynamic impulses of the past. This disparity of power between east and west was further accentuated in the case of Malaya by the partial disintegration of the states of the Peninsula through constant civil strife and anarchy. In this new phase, the west was bound to make a fresh and disturbing impact upon the east. Europe was destined to transform the still largely static and traditional societies of Asia and introduce to them the ferment of ideas accompanying modern economic and political life. This could have occurred in many ways. In practice it was effected in most cases by colonization, or by economic and political dictation. The process was sometimes harsh, arbitrary, unethical. Yet many of the sweeping changes it brought were beneficial and necessary. It was in any case the inevitable prelude to the eventual emancipation of the Asian peoples from those who had imposed their will upon them.

As we have seen, the restrictions which the Dutch sought to impose on the Malay states were constantly evaded in the seventeenth and eighteenth centuries. Britain continued to conduct a large private trade with Kedah. In 1771, Francis Light, a young British merchant captain trading for a firm in Madras, reported that the Sultan of Kedah was prepared to grant to the British his 'seaport . . . with a fort lying near it' if the British would help him against 'the people of Selangore' (i.e. the Bugis). An envoy of the British East India Company who visited the Sultan in the following year was unable to promise such aid and was dismissed.

In the course of the next fifteen years, the war of the American Revolution was fought and Britain found herself hard pressed by the French in Indian waters. There were no good harbours on the east coast of India and British warships and merchantmen were constantly hampered in their operations by having to bring their ships round from the Bay of Bengal to Bombay on the west coast for refitting. Some other harbour had to be found adjacent to the general area where a squadron might be stationed to guard Madras and the Bay of Bengal during the northeast monsoon. It was also needed for victualling, careening, and refitting ships engaged in the China trade. Thus Captain Light was enabled to return to the charge and revive with success the scheme he had originally put forward.

In August 1785 a new Sultan of Kedah authorized the East India Company to make a settlement and harbour on the island of Penang on condition that he should receive substantial annual compensation in dollars[1] for the loss of his trade monopoly. A more important condition required the Company to bear the burden of any hostilities from enemies arriving by sea; and, in the case of an attack from the interior, it should lend Kedah men, arms, and money, the latter to be repaid. The Thais, having just driven the Burmese out of their country had plans to subjugate the Malay Peninsula. The Sultan's fear was that their nominal suzerainty over Kedah was to be converted into effective domination.

In their reply the Company was evasive over compensation and (as before) over the help they might furnish. On the first point they said that they would 'take care that the King of Quedah shall not be a sufferer' in consequence of the British settlement. If an attack came from the interior, the matter would be 'referred for the orders of the East India Company'.[2] When Light visited the Sultan in the following year His Highness was comprehensibly reluctant to hand over Penang until a specific assurance had been received from the Company on the point of protection. Nevertheless Light, with the support of two of the Company's ships, formally took possession of Penang on 11 August 1786. Light was to be Superintendent of the settlement, the Dutch were not to be made jealous, and Asians were to be taught to regard the British as their friends and protectors. The island was fertile and there was some hope of growing spices and other valuable crops.

Light spent eight years in Penang. It was practically uninhabited when he came, yet British protection, which was not extended to the Sultan, was an attraction for many Asians in the area. Furthermore the British, unlike the Dutch, placed no

[1] Spanish dollars at this period. They were worth slightly more than the old par value of the U.S. Dollar (4/4 as against 4/2 in Sterling).
[2] See Sir Richard Winstedt, *History of Malaya*, p. 164.

restraints on trade. The population rose with the advent of Chinese, Malays, Tamils, and many others. In 1794, the year Light died there, he reported that the Chinese numbered about 3,000 and were 'the most valuable part of our inhabitants'. Then (as now) they were 'indefatigable in the pursuit of money'.[1]

Before this, however, in 1790, the Sultan determined that he would not part with Penang unless the British promised him the assistance against the Thais which he had stipulated. He attempted to retake the island with his own forces and was defeated by Light. The sequel was a treaty providing for the payment of an annuity to the ruler as long as Britain kept Penang, and the exclusion of other Europeans. This at last gave some basis in international law to Britain's possession of Penang. Yet it hardly disposed of the awkward presumption that the British originally occupied Penang under false pretences and in effect retained it by force. In 1800 the Sultan was persuaded, in return for an increase in his annuity, to allot to Britain a further piece of territory. This was a strip on the mainland opposite the island (named Province Wellesley after the ruling Governor-General of India) which assured the island of a food supply of its own.

In 1821 the Sultan's worst fears were fulfilled. The Thais invaded Kedah and turned him off his throne for twenty years. He received no help from the British during these operations and became a refugee and dependent in Penang.

Penang only fulfilled in part the hopes of its founders. These had risen so high by 1805 that it was given the status of a major administrative centre or Presidency of India. But it could not afford the expense of such elaborate bureaucracy. Two years later a regular legal system was introduced for the first time. This followed two decades of haphazard improvisation in most public fields. Land had been alienated in the most casual way and legal decisions had broadly followed the customary law of the local Asians. The Malays felled the forests and cleared the ground and concentrated on rice growing, especially in Province Wellesley. The Chinese and Europeans concentrated on commerce and on cultivating certain cash crops, including nutmeg, indigo, and sugar, most of which proved an initial disappointment. A further set-back was that the timber of the

[1] Victor Purcell, *The Chinese in Southeast Asia*, p. 244.

island proved unsuitable for shipbuilding. On the other hand, free trade was something new in Southeast Asia and the results were at first encouraging. The volume of it grew rapidly but then levelled off and for a time lost ground as Britain developed new and more strategic bases for commercial operation in Southeast Asia.

The Dutch in Malacca had looked on the rise of Penang with a jaundiced eye. They forbade their people to migrate there. Only a few years later, however, the Dutch were embroiled in the French revolutionary wars, their country occupied and their ruler expelled. Like a later ruler of Holland in 1940, he took refuge in England. From there he ordered his people overseas to hand over Dutch colonies to the British in the hope that Britain might restore them when the wars were over. In this manner Malacca was taken over by Britain in 1795 after only token resistance. The new masters destroyed her massive Portuguese fortifications. This historic city might have been completely abandoned. It was saved by the vigorous intervention of a young civil servant from Penang, a student of the Malay culture and language, Thomas Stamford Raffles.

Batavia was more resolute in refusing to obey the Dutch ruler's orders to hand over to the British. In 1810 Raffles came to prominence in this connexion. He embarked at Malacca with Lord Minto the Governor-General of India to conquer Java. He became its Lieutenant-Governor for nearly five years and afterwards wrote the first scholarly history of the island. His rule there is generally regarded, even by the Indonesians today, as signifying a liberalization of some of the harsher aspects of Dutch rule. On the other hand the policies Raffles pursued—many of them subsequently reversed—were in part those which the more enlightened Dutch administrators had themselves wanted to apply.[1] He sought to substitute a land rent for the heavy burden of contributions in kind by the local cultivators. He diminished the feudal powers of the Javanese aristocracy; and aimed at some initial introduction of a money economy into the static pattern of Javanese village life. Characteristically, he was criticized by the East India

[1] Such as H. W. Muntighe and Dirk van Hogendorp—see John Bastin, *The Native Policies of Sir Stamford Raffles in Java and Sumatra*, p. 13.

Company because his administration of Java did not pay its way as he had assured them it would.

At the same time, Raffles was ambitious for his country. He favoured the permanent incorporation of Java and its dependencies in the British Empire. This had, after all, been the earlier fate of the Dutch colonies in North America and was later to be the lot of Dutch Ceylon and South Africa. It was a bitter reverse when he was removed from Java and Britain restored the Netherlands Indies as well as Malacca to their former masters in the hope that Holland might thus be strengthened to resist any revival of French imperial ambitions in Europe. Although knighted for his services, this man of remarkable vision and dedication was then relegated to the outpost of Bencoolen in Sumatra, the only British 'factory' which had survived the domination by Holland of the Indonesian Archipelago. He harboured a strong grudge against the Dutch and a determination to enhance Britain's role in Southeast Asia by any means still available, now that the principal prize was lost. The Dutch meanwhile lost no time in occupying or claiming all that had formerly been theirs.

In 1818 Raffles visited Lord Hastings, who had succeeded Minto as Governor-General, at Calcutta. He obtained from him authorization to search for a new site for a British station which would command the southern entrance to the Malacca Straits. He was ordered, however, to do nothing which might upset Britain's friendship with Holland. Orders cancelling Raffles' instructions were indeed sent after him but were too late. His first goal was Riau, but the Dutch had already reasserted their control there. The second was Johore. Here Raffles turned his attention to a spot which had the same advantage as Riau, being at the precise junction of the South China Sea and the Malacca Straits. This was the island of Singapore, a substantial port in the days of Srivijaya and later ruled by the founder of Malacca before he fled there towards the end of the fourteenth century. Since those days it had been virtually abandoned. It was a desolate, mangrove-fringed, swampy stretch of land, peopled by a handful of Malays and Chinese, when Raffles disembarked there on 28 January 1819. With him was Farquhar, the former Military Governor of Malacca, who had been designated to take charge of the new settlement.

# CHAPTER FOUR

# The Nineteenth Century (1)

Singapore was then ruled by a hereditary chieftain, the Temenggong, who owed allegiance to the Sultan of Riau, Lingga, Johore, Singapore, and Pahang. The Temenggong saw personally no difficulty in Britain establishing a trading post at Singapore. On the other hand his overlord, being under the eye of the Dutch, could not be expected to consent. As it happened, the Sultan at Riau was a younger son. Powerful influence at court had contrived to put him on the throne on his father's death in 1812 during the temporary absence of his elder brother who was supported by the Temenggong and other chieftains.

Raffles' solution to this problem was to arrange to bring the Sultan's elder brother from Riau to Singapore. On arrival he was recognized by Raffles as the legitimate Sultan though his authority was in practice confined to Singapore Island. In that capacity he set the seal of his approval on a document giving Britain trading rights in Singapore in return for an annual subsidy to himself and a somewhat smaller one to the Temenggong.

The ethics of this equivocal transaction were hotly debated. The Dutch, in effect, accused Raffles of sharp practice amounting to a breach of international law and talked of an armed assault on Singapore. In the event they did not push matters to this extreme. They did, however, gain the support of the British Governor of Penang, who was jealous of Raffles and who urged on Calcutta that Singapore and Raffles should be abandoned. Whatever second thoughts about Raffles' enterprise Lord Hastings may have had, he resented this approach and ordered the Governor of Penang to send troops to help Raffles if necessary. He replied to the Dutch expressing regret and alluding to his attempt to recall the instructions given to the expedition. But he refused to abandon Singapore, because to do so would suggest 'subscribing to rights which the Dutch claimed about which the British authorities were not satisfied'.

Part of Raffles' case was that when the Dutch surrendered Malacca in 1795 they had explicitly disavowed the existence of Dutch rights over Riau, Lingga, Johore, and Pahang, clearly in order to minimize Britain's acquisitions at the time. On the strength of this, Britain had signed an agreement with the Sultan at Riau only five months before the landing at Singapore. In it assurances were given against obstruction to British trade in the Sultan's dominions. It also, however, recognized the very ruler whom the British found it convenient to disown when it was a question of acquiring Singapore.

When the Dutch resumed control at Riau they set aside the treaty favourable to Britain and compelled the Sultan to sign a new agreement declaring his harbours free only to Dutch and local vessels (except Riau and Lingga which were to be free ports). Raffles had of course no right to interfere in the domestic politics of the Johore-Lingga kingdom which had been bound to the Dutch by intimate ties for two centuries.[1] By the high standards he normally set himself it should perhaps have been irrelevant that his adversaries had been hardly more scrupulous when they judged their own vital interests to be at stake.

A distinguished American historian—himself critical of much that Britain achieved in the area—has said: 'In the history of British Malaya there is no single name that can afford even a distant rivalry to that of Sir Stamford Raffles . . . from the time of Raffles' appearance . . . may be dated a new era in Malaysian history.'[2] Contemporary accounts suggest that there was much both lovable and lofty in the character of this outstanding protagonist of Britain's imperial ambitions. Abdullah, his teacher and interpreter at Malacca and Singapore, says of him: 'He was very good at paying due respect to people in a friendly manner . . . He was solicitous of the feelings of others and open-handed with the poor. He spoke in smiles.'[3] He was also humanly capable of formidable outbursts when he felt he had been let down.

---

[1] See Winstedt, *History of Malaya*, p. 171.
[2] Emerson, *Malaysia*, pp. 71 and 87.
[3] Hikayat Munshi Abdullah, 'An Annotated Translation,' by A. H. Hill, *Journal of the Malayan Branch Royal Asiatic Society*, Vol. XXVIII, Part 3, June 1955, p. 73.

Faced with official disapproval, Raffles admitted that he persisted in occupying Singapore solely on his personal responsibility. He held that 'no man was fit for high station . . . who was not prepared to risk even more than fame and fortune at the call of judgement and his conscience'. In spite of Lord Hastings' initial rebuff to the Netherlands claims, the fate of Singapore hung for long upon a decision of the home authorities. Although the East India Company had clearly realized its value from the start, its retention was not formally assured until 1824. Not until April 1826 did the Directors of the East India Company specifically acknowledge that they were greatly indebted to Raffles for the step he had taken. Three months later he was dead, at forty-six, after weathering a series of personal reverses and disappointments.

By that time most of the prophecies he had made for Singapore with his usual eloquent self-assurance were beginning to come true. In June 1819, he had written: 'Our object is not territory but trade; a great commercial emporium and a fulcrum, whence we may extend our influence politically as circumstances may hereafter require . . . one free port in these seas must eventually destroy the spell of Dutch monopoly.'[1] Later he added: 'Our station completely outflanks the Straits of Malacca and secures a passage for our China ships at all times and under all circumstances.' 'This is by far the most important station in the East and, as far as naval superiority and commercial interests are concerned, of much higher value than whole continents of territory.'[2] In 1820 he could say: '. . . the settlement has advanced in the most rapid manner . . . the port is now surrounded by an extensive town and the population does not fall short of ten or twelve thousand souls, principally Chinese.'[3]

Raffles ascribed this swift expansion above all to three freedoms; freedom of trade, freedom from racial discrimination in economic matters, and freedom from piracy. These were for him sacred principles. In pursuing them he was a generation in advance of his time since they became Britain's official creed

[1] Charles Burton Buckley, *An Anecdotal History of Old Times in Singapore*, p. 6.
[2] ibid., p. 6.
[3] ibid., p. 67.

in the mid-nineteenth century. These freedoms had been partially initiated when Penang and Malacca were taken over. Raffles was determined that his articles of faith should be given full play in Singapore. In 1823 he discussed the constitution to be given to the settlement and laid down as the main objectives not only 'the utmost possible freedom of trade' and protection of property and person but 'equal rights to all'.[1] These freedoms were a new departure in contrast to the restrictions imposed by the Dutch. They were a powerful attraction to traders from all parts of Southeast Asia and especially to the Chinese. The equality of Asians and their rulers before the law—standard practice in British overseas territories—was also a significant novelty. In other European colonial regimes such as the Dutch, a separate legal system was provided for Europeans to that which governed their Asian subjects.

Raffles was something more than a fair administrator and an economic liberal. As he showed in his *History of Java* he was also a scholar deeply interested in the history and evolution of one branch of the Malay race who from their past glories had fallen out of step with the modern age. He believed it was Britain's essential mission to raise by education as much as by good administration the standards of those she presumed to rule. Nowhere perhaps is the spirit which pervaded this confident period of British imperial expansion better expressed than in Raffles' famous Minute on the foundation of the Institution for education in Singapore which eventually bore his name. Here he somewhat portentously asserts that

the acquisitions of Britain in the East have not been made in the spirit of conquest . . . other nations may have pursued the same course . . . but they have not, like her, paused in their career and by moderation and justice consolidated what they had gained. While we raise those in a scale of civilization over whom our influence is extended, we shall lay the foundations of our dominion on the firm basis of justice and mutual advantage, instead of on the uncertain and unsubstantial tenure of force and intrigue. Commerce is the principle on which our connexions with the Eastern States is formed . . . Education must keep pace with commerce in order that its benefits may be ensured and its evils avoided, it should be our care that, while with one hand we carry to their shores the capital

[1] ibid., p. 78.

of our merchants, the other shall be stretched forth to offer them the means of intellectual improvement.[1]

These majestic passages are not for the contemporary world and were indeed little heeded even in Raffles' time. Today many of us reject as evil the faith of men who believed there could be virtue in ruling other races for their benefit. But they are in no way spurious in their sincerity, and their author was neither an exploiter, a cynic, nor a fraud.

The long tension between the Dutch and the British in Southeast Asia had lasted for some two hundred years. It had been essentially a local feud. For much of the period the Netherlands and Britain had been close friends and allies in Europe and even for a time under the same king.[2] By a treaty with Britain of 17 March 1824, the Netherlands Government made a realistic compromise which ended for the time being most of the disputes between the two colonial powers. Under this agreement Britain surrendered Bencoolen (Fort Marlborough) from which Raffles had governed Singapore and her other minor posts along the coast of West Sumatra; while the Dutch finally surrendered Malacca, together with the small 'factories' they still retained in India. The British undertook to abstain from all future settlements in, or political intercourse with Sumatra; and the Dutch were to abstain from similar activities in the Malay Peninsula. The Dutch recognized the British occupation of Singapore, but the British undertook to make no settlement on the neighbouring islands, in which the Dutch already had an interest, or others to the south of Singapore. (This last provision was to lead to a further minor clash when later an adventurous Briton staked out a claim in northern Borneo.) The general sense of the arrangement was a division of spheres of influence. Britain left Holland a free hand in the Indonesian Archipelago and she herself was given a free hand in Malaya. Commercial relations would not be regulated on a basis of monopoly but of most favoured nation treatment.

Later in the same year, a further agreement was concluded by the East India Company with the Sultan and Temenggong

---

[1] Buckley. op. cit., pp. 789 and 790.
[2] William III of Orange who reigned in England jointly with Mary II from 1688–1702.

ceding their rights in Singapore to Britain—though they retained their rank and ceremonial position—in return for fresh
financial compensation.

Singapore kept up the remarkable rhythm of its expansion throughout the nineteenth century the pace being quick-
ened by the opening of the Suez Canal in 1869. It soon
outstripped Penang and Malacca in the volume of its trade and
economic importance and eventually in its population.[1] Singapore for many years was blessed with an absence of political
history and indeed Windstedt depicts it as being, until the
Japanese occupation of 1942, 'a scene of peaceful commercial
development, disturbed only for a few years by pirates who
molested its sea traffic and by pitched battles among Chinese
Secret Societies which in 1854 resulted in the killing of 4,000
Chinese in ten days'.[2]

Meanwhile the structure of British rule gradually evolved.
Penang, Malacca, and Singapore became known as the Straits
Settlements and Labuan was added to them for a number of
years. All shared for a few years Penang's exalted status as a
Presidency of India. Then they were reduced in 1830 to the
minor status of a Residency and in 1832 the capital was shifted
from Penang to Singapore. They were controlled with some
strictness from India, for although Singapore eventually paid
its way, the Straits Settlements as a whole were a drain on the
Indian exchequer. This was felt the more keenly in Calcutta
after the East India Company lost their monopoly of the China
trade in 1833.

In all three settlements much was haphazard in the early
stages, as so often in the initial organization of British possessions. In Penang and Singapore the different communities were
at first left largely to organize themselves under their own
leaders, known as Kapitans China in the case of the Chinese.
There was no legal system at first, the practice being to base
legal decisions on the customary law of the local Asian communities. When a legal system was introduced, in Penang in

---

[1] Between 1825 and 1864 the trade of Singapore increased five times from
£2,610,440 to £13,252,175. In the latter year Singapore's trade was
approximately three times that of Penang (£4,496,205) and more than
sixteen times that of Malacca (£821,698).
[2] Sir Richard Winstedt, *Malaya and its History*, p. 61.

1807 and in Singapore in 1826, it was based on English law as applied in India but modified by local circumstances.

For fifty years after 1824 the expansion of trade was Britain's main objective. Further intervention in the Malay Peninsula was officially discouraged. There were currents of opinion at home unfavourable to the assumption of fresh imperial burdens. At the same time, the success of the free trade system seemed to revive an old illusion. This was that commerce based on ports adjoining a disorganized area could be indefinitely pursued without the burden of seeking to control the hinterland. Yet paradoxically, and whatever the anti-colonial trends in certain quarters, Britain in fact became strenuously involved during this period in the expansion of her Southeast Asian empire. Two wars in 1824 and 1852 resulted in the annexation of the coast and lower regions of the Kingdom of Burma, adjoining Western and Southern Thailand. These new territories, like Penang, Malacca, and Singapore, were then incorporated in Britain's Indian dominions.

It has been suggested that the middle years of the nineteenth century in Malaya were for Britain 'a half century of inactivity'.[1] Viewed in the broader perspective of Southeast Asia this is hardly the case. And even in the Peninsula Britain did not by any means just leave things to take their course.

A clumsy and costly military expedition was undertaken in 1831–32 to incorporate the small state of Naning into neighbouring Malacca, in the belief that it had once been subject to Dutch sovereignty. Again, in a paradoxical pursuit of non-intervention, Britain sought to minimize interference in the Peninsula by the one country which had some historical claim to intervene, namely Thailand. She was prepared to acknowledge Thai suzerainty over Kedah in the northwest and Patani in the northeast. But the Governors of the Straits Settlements did all they could to check Thai activity, and invalidate Thai pretensions, in the states further to the south.

Two missions were sent to Bangkok to seek a general settlement and a commercial arrangement on acceptable lines. Eventually, in 1826, the Thais accepted a commercial treaty which later they were reluctant to observe. Certain provisions

[1] Emerson, *Malaysia*, p. 91.

stipulated that they would not 'obstruct or interrupt commerce' in Kelantan and Trengganu while the British would enjoy 'trade and intercourse . . . with the same facility and freedom . . . as heretofore' but would not 'molest, attack or disturb' these states. This less than candid wording could be interpreted as giving Britain a pretext for later intervention if the Thais should hamper British trade and intercourse. As regards Perak, the Thais and British undertook not to attack or disturb her. The British further agreed to protect her against attack by Selangor, her neighbour immediately to the south, while the Thais promised not to attack Selangor. On the formal side, the Thais were content in the case of Perak with a stipulation that the ruler could send the *bunga mas*—gold and silver flowers, the traditional symbol of vassalage—to Bangkok 'if he desired'. Even so, a British force was sent into Perak to evict Siamese agents. The leader of this expedition took it upon himself to assure the Sultan of Perak of aid and protection by the East India Company if he resisted Thai, or Selangor, interference. He further persuaded him to assign to Britain the islands off the Perak coast, including those of Dinding and Pangkor. Although these last arrangements do not appear to have been formally ratified, they were used many years later to justify Britain's first major intervention in the interior of the Peninsula.

The acknowledgement by Britain in 1826 of Thai rights over Kedah was deplored by the Governor of the Straits Settlements as a further reverse for the ruler who had given her Penang. The British did, however, make repeated efforts to persuade the Thais to restore the Sultan to his throne. In 1842 these were successful. The Sultan was permitted to resume his dominions on condition of once again acknowledging himself a vassal of the Thais. Kedah, however, was diminished by the loss of the small northern territory of Perlis. This had succeeded in establishing a separate status under its Rajah which it has since maintained.

Meanwhile, in the middle years of the nineteenth century, a new factor was emerging to produce a disturbing ferment in the already unsettled conditions of the Malay states.

Tin had been mined in Malaya by the Chinese from early times. In the first half of the nineteenth century, hard-working Chinese immigrants flowed into the Straits Settlements encouraged by the British authorities. The harsh conditions arising out of the Taiping Rebellion in southern China stimulated this flow and the chances of prospering overseas made an ever stronger appeal. Some of the less fortunate Chinese were brought in and initially exploited by their countrymen as indentured labour. Yet despite this inflow of ready hands there was a limit to economic expansion in the Settlements prior to the development of the interior. Trade fluctuated and the growing of cash crops proved a disappointment. Increasing numbers of Chinese, using the Straits Settlements as a base, turned to the more exciting and profitable exploitation of tin in the Malay states. This was the first step in the creation of that plural society which is the problem and challenge of Malaysia in the 1960s.

In many parts of the Peninsula this Chinese influx added fresh confusion to the chaos resulting from rivalries in the Malay world. The Treaty of 1824 had split the Johore Empire, the Riau Archipelago remaining in the Dutch sphere of influence, while the two most powerful chieftains in Johore and Pahang, formerly subject to the Sultan of Riau, founded independent dynasties of their own. The ineffective descendants of Sultan Husain who had ceded Singapore were disregarded for the succession to the throne of Johore. In their place the British supported the more vigorous family of the Temenggong of the Johore Empire. In Pahang the throne went to another great chieftain, the Bendahara, at the end of a long war with his brother from 1857–63. There were also disputes over the rulers' succession in Negri Sembilan and in Perak. The last of these proved to be of capital importance from the standpoint of Britain's future in Malaya.

Meanwhile, the intensely competitive Chinese had fierce disputes over the exploitation of particular areas. These grew into regular wars, with considerable bloodshed, waged by rival secret societies. These had originated partly in opposition to the Manchu dynasty in China, partly for legitimate mutual help. In time many became a clandestine focus of crime and violence. It is this genius for secret organization, exhibited so forcefully a hundred years ago, which has made the Chinese in the mid-twentieth century capable of becoming some of the world's most effective and dangerous communists.

In 1860 the Governor of the Straits Settlements took action in Negri Sembilan in aid of Chinese miners and commercial interests. In 1862 he brought temporarily to an end organized hostilities between other Chinese miners in Larut in Perak; and in celebration of the eventual settlement the neighbouring town was given the Chinese name of Taiping or Great Peace. In the same year, disturbed by Thai activities in Kelantan and Trengganu he blockaded Trengganu from the sea and temporarily put a stop to Thai intervention in the northeast. This and other moves were condemned by higher authority. Singapore was not linked with London by telegraph till 1871. It is clear that until then, and even for some time after, the tradition persisted of high-handed personal initiative on the spot. It derived from an age when more than a year might elapse between a seaborne request for instructions and their receipt, and had been responsible for most of the major acquisitions of the British Empire.

The divergence in outlook between Calcutta and Singapore was sharpened by the rejection of policies in which the Settlements believed. The official and mercantile communities there —both British and Chinese—whom successive Governors were obliged to consult, increasingly objected to being treated as a minor outpost of an Indian empire whose officials were ill equipped to deal with Malays and Chinese. Calcutta had also vastly different problems to their own, such as the costly and capital crisis of the Indian Mutiny. Furthermore, after losing its monopoly of the China trade in 1833, the East India Company had a decreasing interest in Singapore. When the British authorities in India proposed to impose duties and taxes—and the Indian currency—in the Settlements, resentment came to a head. This was a violation of free trade, the faith of all Singaporeans from Raffles onwards. Other factors, too, promoted this urge to change. France had established herself nearby in Indo-China and might well look further afield. The Dutch were extending their area of control. The natural resources and scope for development in the Malay States were becoming better known to enterprising British and Chinese in the Straits. The Germans were also interested in the area, particularly in certain deposits of iron ore. Yet economic advance there was checked by confusion and unrest. After 1855 there was a growing demand in Singapore for the transfer of the Settlements from the control of India to the direct authority of Her Majesty's Government. After ten years of interdepartmental dissension, on 1 April 1867 the Settlements became a Crown Colony under the Colonial Office in London. This step was a gain for the advocates of a forward policy. It was shortly to lead to far more positive British action in the Malay States.

By this time an enterprising private citizen had brought another part of the Malay world within Britain's sphere. James Brooke, son of an Indian civil servant, sailed in his own yacht to Borneo in 1839 in a spirit of adventure and scientific exploration.

Most of the area was nominally ruled by the Sultan of Brunei, whose capital lay on an estuary near the centre of the coast. In practice, the Sultan's vassals loosely controlled the outlying regions and made what profit they could from them. Piracy and subversion flourished, however, and were often beyond their control. At the time of Brooke's arrival, the Sultan's Viceroy had failed to subdue a revolt of the Malays and Land Dayaks in the northwestern area known as Sarawak. The Sultan sent his uncle to pacify the country and in 1840 Brooke was persuaded by him to help in the suppression of the rebellion. This European intervention was strikingly effective. The insurgents were forced into accepting a settlement. As a reward for his achievement Brooke was accorded the status of ruler of the small area around Kuching. He was installed as Rajah of Sarawak on 24 September 1842.

The conferment of this title may have been intended as little more than a complimentary gesture. Later, as we shall see, a similar distinction was conferred on an adventurous American intent on developing another portion of the Sultan's dominions. The American failed in his enterprise. Brooke, on the other hand, was determined to turn into a reality both his title and the functions it implied.

This was no easy task. He was involved for years in fighting, especially with the fierce, unruly Sea Dayaks or Ibans. His success against them, and against hostile intrigues at the Sultan's Court, was ensured by the support of the Royal Navy under Admiral Keppel. In 1846 Brooke persuaded the Sultan to cede to Britain his offshore island of Labuan, valuable as a coaling station for ships sailing to the Far East. In 1847 the Sultan was induced to conclude a treaty with Britain 'for the furtherance of commercial relations and the mutual suppression of piracy'. This provided for extra-territorial jurisdiction over British subjects and precluded the Sultan from ceding territory to any other nation or national without the consent of Britain. After these arrangements there gradually developed a regular movement of trade and navigation between Singapore and Malaya, the north coast of Borneo, China, and eventually Japan.

Brooke not only ruled over Sarawak. The British Government made him their first Governor of Labuan and Consul-General in Brunei. He was knighted and was for a time in high favour with British ruling circles and society. But he was no easy character. He had the uncompromising intensity of the Victorians, and he remained a life-long bachelor. He incurred the enmity of a former business agent. He was accused in British quarters of unwarrantable harshness in his suppression of the local rebels and had to answer to a court of inquiry in Singapore. Although this acquitted him, he was regarded by local Asians as having ceased to enjoy the support and approval of the British authorities. The Chinese, moreover, resented the river tolls introduced by Rajah Brooke and the fact that he ruled chiefly through the Malays. From the gold mines in Bau, the Chinese attacked Kuching in force and Brooke only narrowly escaped. Once again, however, he succeeded in restoring his position and eventually in widening his dominions at Brunei's expense. When James Brooke died in 1868, Sarawak extended to beyond Bintulu, almost half way to Brunei itself. James was succeeded by his nephew, Charles Johnston, who had served under him and who took the name of Brooke. Equally forceful in character, Rajah Charles was perhaps even more domineering and seriously tenacious than his uncle. Under him the frontiers of Sarawak were extended considerably further.

# CHAPTER FIVE

# The Nineteenth Century (2)

The first Governor appointed to Singapore by the Colonial Office was a soldier named Ord. He did not endear himself to the local communities. He was determined to mark the separate status of the new Colony by building an imposing Government House and ensuring that the dignity of the Queen's representative was properly respected.

He was bound by his instructions to include members of the local community in his Legislative Council, but some refused to serve. The local British, for their part, promoted the formation of a Straits Association in London. This took advantage of the new opportunities offered by separation from India. It included representatives of the powerful principals of the firms operating in Southeast Asia and was able to exercise considerable pressure on the London Government. It raised objections to increases in expenditure in Singapore and proposals to meet them by taxation which implied an infringement of the free port status of the Settlement.

In spite of his unpopularity, Ord did useful work in reorganizing the Civil Service. A system based on regular selection of cadets with adequate pay was designed to attract educated and responsible young men. One such cadet, who arrived in 1871, was Frank Swettenham.

The opening of the Suez Canal in 1869 and the drastic shortening of voyages from Europe brought a striking expansion of trade to the Far East with marked benefit to Singapore. Economic expansion was accompanied by increased colonial activity on the part of the European continental powers. The Dutch aimed at completing their domination of Sumatra. In 1873 they started a long war with the northern Sultanate of Acheh, having freed themselves by concessions to Britain under the Anglo-Dutch Treaty of 1871 from treaty obligations to respect its independence. A disquieting feature of this war was the attempt of the Achinese to invoke the help of European powers or of the United States. At the same period the Spaniards were seeking to extend their control over the Muslim areas of the Philippines. The French, even after their defeat by the Germans in 1870–71, were moving into a position of gradually expanding strength in Indo-China; and German interest in the area was the more disturbing by reason of the emergence of Germany as a powerful united Empire which could well be tempted to seek a place in the Asian sun. The British Government in London had no particular interest in the Malay states as such. Their dominant goal was to ensure the defence of India and the security of the trade routes to the east and especially to China. It was for these purposes that the Straits Settlements had been established. For the same reasons the London Government 'wished to prevent any other power from becoming established in Malaya or North Borneo, not to become involved in these areas themselves'.[1]

British commercial interests in the Settlements, however, and many local merchants envisaged new fields of profitable trade and investment in the Malay states, if the British Government, at its own expense, brought order out of chaos. 'The idea . . . was that the Colonial Office should authorize . . . military and naval expense. The profit would go to Straits investors (who paid practically nothing in taxation) and the cost would fall on the British taxpayer.'[2] The British Government, however, long persisted in refusing to countenance intervention. Piecemeal efforts were made to reduce local disorders but a systematic, centrally directed, plan of imperialist expansion was not part of the British scheme of things.

In a letter to the Malacca Chamber of Commerce of 21 August 1872, the Colonial Secretary, James Birch, re-defined Britain's policy of non-intervention. He admitted that the Straits Government's peace-making efforts to settle the dynastic squabbles of Selangor had failed. This had caused loss to British trade and persons, but it was

the policy of Her Majesty's Government not to interfere in the affairs of these countries unless it becomes necessary for the suppression of piracy or the punishment of aggression on our people or territories . . . if traders, prompted by the prospect of large gains,

[1] C. D. Cowan, *Nineteenth Century Malaya*, p. 269.
[2] C. Northcote Parkinson, *British Intervention in Malaya 1867–1877*, p. 62.

choose to run the risk of placing their persons and property in the jeopardy which they are aware attends them in these countries . . . it is impossible for Government to be answerable for their protection or that of their property.

Dynastic conflict was no less rife in Perak than in Selangor. The Perak Sultan having died in 1871, there were three pretenders to the throne, each seeking to justify his claim under the state's complex rules of succession. To complicate matters further, the ruler or Mantri of Larut, the richest tin mining area, aspired to autonomy. He had hopes of securing this from the old, weak candidate who had actually been installed as Sultan.

Finally, the Chinese tin miners in Larut were organized into two violently hostile Secret Societies, supported by the Malay chiefs in varying degrees according to their success or failure. There had been clashes between them in 1861 and 1865 and these recurred in 1872, with considerable loss of life. The Colonial Government had a natural fear that these disturbances might spread to Penang and Singapore, which had suffered from Chinese riots in the past.

In September 1873, Governor Ord decided to recognize the pretensions to independence of the Mantri of Larut, who supported the Chinese faction in actual possession of the tin mines, and he raised no objection to the recruitment of an eccentric Englishman called Speedy into the Mantri's service. This policy in effect discountenanced the claim of Abdulla, the former Crown Prince or Raja Muda to be Sultan of the whole of Perak. A few months later, Ord's term of office came to an end.

Meanwhile, in the course of 1873 there had been in British government circles a change of opinion to the view that some sort of action was necessary in Malaya, while pressure of opinion in the Straits Settlements in favour of intervention had increased. Local merchants pleaded that this rich area would be impoverished unless the British Government interfered to restore order and peace. The new Governor, Andrew Clarke, a Colonel of the Royal Engineers, had the advantage of personal contacts with politicians in London of both parties and the reputation of being cautious as well as able. But as Professor Cowan has pointed out[1] he had strong imperialist

---

[1] Cowan, op. cit., pp. 177, 178.

views and a detestation of bureaucratic routine which seem to have been little known to official circles at home. Some months before his departure, British government circles appear to have been definitely stimulated to a change of course contemplating some measure of intervention by remonstrances to the Colonial Office from a representative of British tin-mining interests in Selangor. These suggested as likely 'that the smaller states of the Peninsula would put themselves under the protectorate of some European power'. Failing England Germany was mentioned as the most likely.[1] However specious this argument, on the day of his departure for Singapore Sir Andrew Clarke received instructions containing the following equivocal but significant passage:

Her Majesty's Government have no desire to interfere in the internal affairs of the Malay States. But looking to the long and intimate connection between them and the British Government and to the well-being of the British settlements themselves, H.M. Government find it incumbent upon them to employ such influence as they possess with the native princes to rescue, if possible, these fertile and productive countries from the ruin which must befall them if the present disorders continue unchecked.

I have to request . . . that you will report . . . whether there are . . . any steps which can properly be taken by the Colonial Government to promote the restoration of peace and order, and to secure protection to trade and commerce with the native territories. I should wish you especially to consider whether it would be advisable to appoint a British officer to reside in any of the States. Such an appointment could . . . only be made with the full consent of the Native Government, and the expenses . . . would have to be defrayed by the Government of the Straits Settlements.

Sir Andrew Clarke decided after arriving in Malaya that his instructions were too cautious. Ord's policies had not restored order in Perak and Selangor. The situation seemed to demand urgent action. It was easier for him than for Ord to take an independent line, as he was not by training and experience a Colonial official. He promptly questioned the wisdom of Ord's support for the Mantri of Larut and his implied rejection of Abdulla's claim to the throne.

Abdulla reached an understanding with the Chinese faction

[1] ibid., p. 167.

opposed to the Mantri, the leader of which demanded a share of Perak's prospective revenue for his part in promoting the pretender's claim. He also informed the Governor—under prompting from the merchants in Singapore—that he and the Perak leaders wished to settle under the protection of the British flag. He asked that an able man should be sent to show them a good system of government so that the country might be profitably opened up.

The Governor decided that there was a case for reviewing Abdulla's claim. Was he or Ismail, the prince actually installed as Sultan, the rightful ruler? The claims of the third pretender, Raja Yusuf, were not considered at all. The strongest character of the three, he had antagonized many of the chieftains by the severity with which he had dealt with them at the behest of a former Sultan of whom he was the eldest son. The Governor also aimed at pacifying Larut by mediating between the two hostile groups of Chinese.

Clarke succeeded in bringing together the leaders of the opposing Chinese at a meeting on his yacht at Pangkor Island off the Perak coast, to which some, but not all, of the Perak princes and chieftains were invited, including Ismail, Abdulla, and the Mantri, but not Yusuf. Ismail did not appear, claiming that he had received his invitation too late. The meeting was briskly conducted by the Governor. Frank Swettenham acted as interpreter for the Malays and one W. A. Pickering for the Chinese, the latter afterwards becoming the first British Protector of Chinese in Malaya.

Agreement was achieved with, and between, the Chinese. The Malay chiefs present went through a form of election. The upshot was unanimous, if in part reluctant, consent to Abdulla becoming Sultan. An Engagement was signed on 20 January 1874 (sometimes loosely called the Treaty of Pangkor). This recognized Abdulla as Sultan and Ismail as ex-Sultan. The Sultan was to receive a British officer as Resident whose advice must be asked and acted upon on all questions other than those touching Malay religion and custom. There was also to be an Assistant Resident to control the Mantri at Larut. The cost of the Residents was to be a first charge on Perak funds. The collection and control of revenue, and the general administration of the country was to be regulated under the advice of the Residents. On the re-establishment of peace among the contending factions the previous status was to be restored at the tin mines.

Clarke and the business community leaders in the Settlements were delighted with this achievement. The Governor reported that he had exceeded his instructions but felt confident that the government would consider him justified! Very cautiously, the London authorities expressed the hope that the Governor's proceedings 'may have the effect of allaying disorders and promoting peaceful trade'.

Most of the Malays seem to have been frankly bewildered by the speed and bluntness of the Governor's approach. To express agreement was a traditional reaction on their part to anything put to them forcibly by someone in a stronger position than themselves. There was thus scope for painful misunderstanding when they realized the full implications of the document to which they had set their seal. Anglo-Saxon pragmatism had cut sharply across a situation to which they were accustomed—full of confusion and discord. The British had sought a clear-cut, practical, solution without strict regard for all the relevant factors which would have made it scrupulously just. The capital test would be how the new, enforced relationship between modern European and traditional Asian concepts could be humanly applied.

After returning to Singapore the Governor aimed at tackling in similar fashion the affairs of Selangor and Sungei Ujong, one of the states of Negri Sembilan adjacent to Malacca.

In Selangor the British authorities had for some years supported the Sultan's son-in-law, Tunku Dia Udin, who was supposed to be in charge of the state as Viceroy. But there had been civil war, as the Viceroy's position was contested by other leading chieftains and members of the Sultan's family. Supported by the Royal Navy the Governor visited the Sultan, demonstrated his approval of the Viceroy and lectured the Ruler on the importance of achieving order. A number of alleged pirates were executed. He also sought to force an agreement on the rival chiefs in Sungei Ujong, one of them being selected for British approval and support. At this stage, however, the plans of the Singapore Government for the further extension of British influence in the Peninsula still received little encouragement from the Colonial Office in London.

Meanwhile the Colonial Secretary in Singapore, James Birch, applied for and was eventually given the post of British Resident in Perak with Speedy as Assistant Resident in Larut. His appointment followed a preliminary and frustrating mission to Perak with Swettenham, the Assistant Resident in Selangor, in which he vainly attempted to secure the Sultan's regalia from Ismail so that Abdulla could be properly installed. Shortly afterwards Clarke was succeeded as Governor by another senior officer of the Royal Engineers, Sir William Jervois.

Birch was judged not to be well versed in Malay affairs. As the Governor's deputy, he does not seem to have enjoyed his chief's confidence. The post in Perak was an opportunity to justify himself. But he brought to the task an impatient, missionary zeal for reform typical of the Victorians. His courage vastly exceeded his judgement. He sought to introduce modern revenue methods before the local chieftains had been assured of allowances to compensate them for the loss of their traditional perquisites. He also aimed at overthrowing in short order practices glaringly at variance with Christian ethics. One of these was debt slavery. 'His attitude . . . was coloured by a Victorian disapproval of its immoral (as opposed to its merely oppressive) aspect. It was the slave *girls* he wanted to emancipate, allowing the Malays to draw the sort of conclusion that a modern psychologist might partly endorse.'[1] Finding his efforts at reform by persuasion inadequate, he persuaded the Governor to authorize him to govern the state directly in the Sultan's name.

Soon Birch was on the worst of terms with Sultan Abdulla, ex-Sultan Ismail, and most of the Perak chiefs, who closed their ranks, merged their differences, and eventually determined to remove the Resident by murder. By sending to one of the State Officers, the Maharaja Lela, a kris—the Malay dagger— Abdulla implicitly authorized the murder.

Birch was speared through the walls of a bath house on the

[1] Parkinson, *British Intervention in Malaya*, p. 220. The accepted Malay interpretation, repeated to the writer in 1966 by the Dato Bendahara of Perak, is that Birch was a 'womanizer'.

Perak river on 2 November 1875. He and his staff had been posting proclamations which Abdulla had been persuaded to sign. These, which were promptly torn down, announced that the British would administer Perak in the name of the Sultan.

Birch had clearly realized the danger he ran but remained convinced that he was right in persisting in his headlong and uncompromising policy of change. It is almost as if he had foreseen that his murder would be the decisive factor leading to Britain's eventual assumption of control step by step over virtually the whole of the Malay Peninsula.

After receiving confirmation of the murder, Swettenham, who had been despatched up-river, managed to return downstream to the British Residency in spite of the preparations to kill him too. The Residency was eventually relieved by a force from Penang. Believing that a general rising in Perak and elsewhere was likely to take place, the Singapore authorities summoned troops from Hongkong and India.

There was no general rising; and the British troops made an impressive incursion into Perak and other parts of Western Malaya. Selangor remained quiet. There was some fighting in Sungei Ujong. But by the end of 1875 effective resistance had largely ceased. In Perak, those closely identified with Birch's murder were hunted down and tried. Some were hanged, including the Maharaja Lela in spite of his exalted rank. Ismail handed over the Regalia. Abdulla was exiled with the Mantri and other chieftains. Raja Yusuf became Regent and eventually Sultan. After a short interregnum during which Davidson, the Resident from Selangor, took charge, a new British Resident was appointed. This was Hugh Low, who had been magistrate of the island of Labuan off Borneo. There would be no drawing back. Apart from imposing order, Britain had next to attempt to rescue the state from the bankruptcy produced by all its troubles. Low eventually achieved by his personal qualities the success which had totally eluded Birch. What had happened in Perak proved to be decisive for the evolution of the whole country.

The transition to British control in other regions was a smoother and less dramatic process than it had been in Perak. Selangor and Sungei Ujong had accepted British Residents by the end of 1874. To the south, Johore was already virtually under British control in view of the close links preserved by its rulers with adjacent Singapore. To the north, Kedah and Perlis owed allegiance to Thailand but had come under British influence through their proximity to Penang. In the eastern Peninsula, the ruler of Pahang was descended from one of the great chiefs—the Bendahara—of the former Johore dominions. He eventually assumed the title of Sultan as did the ruler of Johore, descended from the Temenggong. Only Kelantan and Trengganu, also under Thai suzerainty, were still broadly outside the sphere of British influence.

There could, however, be no further extension of British control until the London Government knew what it wanted. It had been gravely disturbed by the turn of events in Perak. The Governor had acted with ability and determination. But he had taken decisions far beyond the scope of his instructions. He was sharply rebuked and his mission terminated early in 1877. London, not Singapore, was to decide policy in future. If there was to be no withdrawal, what course should be pursued short of outright annexation?

In June 1876, London cautiously defined official intentions in very general terms. There was no proof, it was stated, that the system of Residents had failed. It had broken down in one area, but had had fair success in others. It was unnecessary to withdraw them. They could give valuable help with the administration, but they would need an armed guard. For this, 150 to 200 police should be sufficient and all troops should be withdrawn.

There should be state councils of mixed Malay chiefs and British officers (as the Governor had suggested). Thus the chiefs could themselves take a useful part in administration and the Residents should train those of sufficient capacity for this purpose. The councils would also give the Residents a chance to gauge local feeling about their proposed reforms. British officers should not interfere more than necessary in minor details. They should aim at maintaining peace and law and instituting a sound system of taxation so as to develop the country's resources.

The Governor was subsequently informed that no extension of the Resident system could be sanctioned until there had been more experience of its working. Britain's responsibilities must not be enlarged. There would be quite enough to do bringing peace and order to the states with which Britain was already connected.

Sungei Ujong was the only state of Negri Sembilan placed specifically under British protection. From 1876, however, the British Resident system was gradually extended to other parts of the area helped by the coalescence of various of its smaller units into larger groups. By 1895 the process was complete; as an organized confederacy all the groups and units in Negri Sembilan had agreed to accept the British method of control.

Such was the trend of events and opinion which led to Britain assuming a new and important imperial role. It all seems strangely casual, and would hardly have been comprehensible without going into some detail. For the next seventy years, however—until the Japanese occupation of 1942—the story can be told in broader outline. It is less dramatic, less complex, and far more down to earth.

# CHAPTER SIX

# The Evolution and Consolidation
# of British Rule

The British Government intended that henceforth Residents should be advisers only. They were not to aim at being the effective rulers of their states. In practice, however, this is what they gradually became.

Davidson, the Resident in Selangor, with Swettenham as his assistant, had little trouble in organizing a modern system of finance and a police force. Under the control of its Chinese headman, the mining centre of Kuala Lumpur gradually took shape as a small settlement which eventually became the capital of the modern federation of Malaysia. Slavery was abolished as were many ancient dues which had restricted trade. Stable and clearly regulated conditions were the source of a new prosperity.

In Perak a legacy of resentment had to be overcome. The basis of Low's success was that he managed to make friends—as always, the key to achievement in Asia. He compensated the chiefs promptly, out of revenue and by giving them government jobs, for the loss of their feudal dues. Yet even for Low the evolution of the Resident system bristled with problems.

The British Government—not for the first time in its history —issued instructions which ignored logic and reality in the tacit expectation that a workable system would be evolved by the men on the spot in spite of these. It was inevitable that the instructions would be exceeded, but their advantage was that the local officials could be called to account if their unauthorized initiatives led to trouble.

Thus the Colonial Secretary laid it down in June 1876, that Residents were 'not to interfere more frequently . . . than is necessary with the minor details of government; but their special objects should be the maintenance of peace and law, the initiation of a sound system of taxation, with the consequent development of the resources of the country, and the supervision of the collection of the revenue, so as to ensure the receipt of the funds necessary to carry out the principal engagements of the government.'

As Sir Frank Swettenham has pointed out,[1] 'nothing with any pretensions to a system had ever been formulated. That was all to come, and to be worked out by the Residents themselves.' On the face of things it was an impossible task '. . . for one white man to maintain the law—something unwritten and unknown—and preserve the peace in a foreign state of which he knew very little, initiate a sound system of taxation and get it observed, develop the resources of the country et cetera' under the rule of minimum interference laid down in these instructions.

This logically insoluble dilemma was solved in practice by Low's tact and patience. He remained twelve years, paid off the state deficit in six, and transformed it into a flourishing credit balance. He initiated the State Council system which handled all important matters of government. The Council included Chinese business men and Malay chiefs. As a member of the Council with the Sultan in the chair the Resident could only persuade. If he failed to secure agreement to a particular proposal, he had no recourse but to try again when he judged his chances to be more favourable. If he succeeded, he ceased to play any visible part. The Council took the policy decision and issued its own orders. 'The Sultan retained prestige and had an important political role as President of the State Council. As the State prospered both he and the leading Malay chiefs were aware that the new régime was not without advantages for them.'[2] In spite of the difficulties, through the State Council the Resident was able to gain local co-operation in applying the new essential measures.

In twelve years the population of Perak rose more than two and a half times. The Perak Council became a model for other parts of Malaya. The legal and judicial system of the Straits Settlements (which largely followed that established by the British in India) was introduced into this and the other Malay states. Unlike the legal régime in the Dutch and French col-

[1] Sir Frank Swettenham, *British Malaya*, p. 217.
[2] J. Kennedy, *A History of Malaya 1400–1959*, p. 183.

onies, the British codes were no respecters of race or person. Equality of Europeans and Asians before the law was introduced for the first time. Yet the fact that the Chinese and other non-Malay settlers continued to be regarded as aliens to some extent impaired the practical application of these principles of legal equality where the local Asians were concerned. Each state was divided into districts with British and Malay District Officers and magistrates. The villages were run by Malay headmen with police duties.

Tin was the capital factor in the revenue of the Malay states under British protection and the Chinese who mined it, and handled much of the retail trade, long dominated almost exclusively the economic life of the country. The Chinese miners in the Larut area prospered in peace. The first railway in Malaya, built in 1884, gave Larut access to the sea. In Selangor the second Malayan railway gave the Kuala Lumpur mines similar access to the sea through Klang. Other forms of transport became progressively more vital. Streams were cleared and roads were built.

In 1888 the state of Pahang came under British protection; and, as we have seen, in 1895 the whole confederation of Negri Sembilan, the small states of which elected one Supreme Ruler or Yang di Pertuan Besar. Pahang was the least developed area in Malaya and had been one of the least well governed. In 1887 Governor Weld persuaded the Sultan to accept a British Consular Agent and in 1888 (after the murder of a Chinese British subject) a British Resident. Here the transition was clouded by a rebellion and British military action to suppress it. The affairs of Pahang first gave prominence to Hugh Clifford, another of Britain's outstanding pioneers in the modernization of Malaya.

Immigration and foreign investment followed Britain's assumption of control. By the 1880s withdrawal had ceased to be a practical issue. On the other hand, outright annexation of the kind practised in Burma was judged to be quite unsuited to the circumstances of the Malay States. Yet the Residential system, a pragmatic compromise, developed with a minimum of control and co-ordination. It demanded review and this was undertaken between 1880 and 1895.

With money available for modern facilities, the scope of a

Resident's duties had inevitably expanded. Roads, railways, schools, disease, had high priority. A Resident was constantly travelling around seeing what should or could be done within his state. He sent the Governor an annual report and financial estimates and some information on current events in the course of the year. But before 1896 each of the Residents was very much of a free agent. There were few in Singapore who could have checked what he told them from their local knowledge.

In 1893 Frank Swettenham, then Resident of Perak, submitted to the Governor a scheme for the federation of the four protected states. The Sultans were assured by Swettenham that their powers, privileges, and autonomy would be undiminished. The scheme was accepted and introduced on 1 July 1896. Much was changed with its adoption.

The Federated Malay States evolved a common civil service, with a central bureaucracy in Kuala Lumpur. At the head of this, Swettenham, as Resident-General, supervised the administration of the states through the individual Residents. He was officially subordinate to the Governor, who was also High Commissioner for the Federated Malay States. Yet in practice he retained considerable autonomy and local power and prestige. From being a regional power in his own right the Resident became a civil servant under central control.

As government departments multiplied the Resident-General came to exercise effective legislative as well as executive power. In key positions in the central administration he had, amongst others, a Legal Adviser, a Secretary for Chinese Affairs, a Financial Commissioner, a Judicial Commissioner, a Commissioner of Police, and Directors of Public Works, Railways, Forests, etc. 'Kuala Lumpur became the legislative as well as the administrative centre, and the position of the State Councils which had been so vital a feature of the old Residency system, necessarily deteriorated before the inevitable growth of centralization.'[1]

The structure of this first Federation illustrated Britain's practical sense and lack of preoccupation with theoretical symmetry or logic. It worked effectively, yet it emasculated the State Councils which the British had created and the Sultan's prestige and authority which they had been concerned to

[1] D. G. E. Hall, *A History of South-East Asia*, p. 532.

uphold. There was, it is true, provision for consultation of the Sultans and for discussion of proposed measures in a Conference of Malay Rulers inaugurated in 1897. Yet, in practice, decisions were taken by the central administration and passed on to the State Councils for legislative action.

The Federation was not in fact a federation in the accepted sense of the word. It did not guarantee a measure of local autonomy like the federal constitution of the United States. It largely abolished state autonomy in favour of administrative co-ordination. This had admirable results in streamlining and speeding up the process of modernization. There were massive increases in population and revenue and impressive development of communications and public health measures. Yet in these earlier years little administrative responsibility was assigned to the Malays and they resented it. The achievements hardly seemed to them to justify a situation in which the supposedly indirect system of British rule had become almost indistinguishable from direct administration. 'An unsanctioned system of direct government by Residents [had] developed which, however successful . . . was completely at variance with the *de jure* position. The gulf between practice and theory was only widened by the so-called Federation Agreement.'[1]

It was not only the Malays who complained of their lack of participation in government. By the early twentieth century such participation was also sought by the rapidly growing commercial, mining, and planting communities. The Sultans, moreover, became comprehensibly restive as centralization increased. They resented in particular the extent of the Resident-General's influence on policy.

The upshot of all these grievances was the establishment in 1909 of a Federal Council, which, however, still disappointed Malay hopes. The Governor, as High Commissioner for the Malay States, presided. The four Sultans were members in addition to the Resident-General, the four Residents and four unofficial members nominated by the High Commissioner. Heads of departments could be added if they were matched by an equal number of unofficial members. The latter (mostly British with a few Chinese and Malays) were intended to represent the chief economic interests of the country: trade,

[1] Cowan, *Nineteenth Century Malay*, p. 270.

industry, and agriculture. The Council met once a year and considered the financial estimates of each state. It was supposed to legislate for the Federation as a whole and in practice it made all important decisions of policy. Laws passed by the State Councils (exclusively competent in Islamic matters and Malay custom) continued in force unless in conflict with those passed by the Federal Council. The authority of the Rulers and State Councils was again diminished and this further belied Swettenham's assurance to the Sultans at the time of federation. A change in the Resident-General's title to the more modest one of Chief Secretary seems to have done little to reduce his independence or the overriding authority of the central administration.

The principles underlying this Council were even less logical than the original structure of the Federation. According to Kennedy

The Federal Council was a curious piece of constitutional machinery. Its President was the Governor of a neighbouring Colony and its unofficial members required the approval of the British Government . . . the four Sultans sat . . . as ordinary members with no powers of veto, and its business went on whether they attended or not. Its legislation was signed by the High Commissioner. The Sultans either sat silent or ceased to attend . . . the main voices were those of the Chief Secretary and of the unofficial members.[1]

In the year 1909 which saw the establishment of the Federal Council, the sphere of British responsibilities expanded. Thailand was persuaded to transfer to British protection the four northern Malay States over which she had exercised a more or less nominal suzerainty. The inducements were the abandonment by Britain of her jurisdiction over British subjects in Thailand and a loan to build a railway-line linking Bangkok with the Malayan railway system. After their transfer to Britain, however, Kedah, Perlis, Kelantan, and Trengganu firmly declined to join the Federated Malay States. Supported by Johore they evaded the drastic centralization imposed by Kuala Lumpur. They insisted on preserving those elements of autonomy compatible with gradual modernization.

There was a long way to go. In 1909 much was still mediaeval

[1] Kennedy, *A History of Malaya*, p. 240.

in the two eastern states. Kelantan and Trengganu were hardly
more advanced than Perak had been forty years earlier. They
had preserved much that was traditional in Malay life. Kedah
and Perlis, on the other hand, in close touch with the British
settlement of Penang, had absorbed more Western influence.
In any event, the greater independence of these Unfederated
Malay States (as they came to be known) had certain advantages for the future. Each state maintained a civil service of its
own with a minimum of Europeans. Malays occupied a
substantial number of responsible posts—a tradition which
contributed to the successful assumption by Malays of wider
responsibilities when partial self-government and eventually
independence came.

After the transfer of Thai rights Britain concluded separate
treaties with each Ruler. Some, e.g. Kelantan, already had
British advisers and other officials appointed from Bangkok.
Perlis promptly accepted a British adviser. Kedah and Trengganu agreed in 1910 to more or less limited British advice and
supervision. Trengganu did not formally accept a British
Adviser till 1919 and Kedah till 1923. The title of Adviser was
a genuine definition of the functions he exercised, functions
which had been exceeded in the Federation as a result of the
Resident system.

There had been only limited British contacts with Kelantan
and Trengganu. These east coast states had not come under the
influence of Penang as had Kedah and Perlis. Consequently
little English was spoken or understood there at the time of the
cession. Even in the twentieth century, in these strongly traditionalist Muslim states, English education was for some time
regarded as being in conflict with their religion. The head-
master of the first English school to be established in Kelantan
was threatened with serious consequences if he did not get out.
The Unfederated States were essentially governed by their own
Malays with a certain amount of British guidance. As we have
seen, the strength and effectiveness of their State Councils was
the envy of the Federated States where the administration was
essentially British though with some regard for Malay privileges.
One detail which persists to this day in independent Malaysia
symbolizes this difference. The former Federated States observe
the Christian holiday of Sunday and work on Friday, the Muslim

holy day. The others insist on observing Friday as their day of rest and work on Sunday.

After the cession of the four northern states Britain had gathered under her protection most of the Malay regions of the Peninsula. Only the state of Patani and the areas of Satun, Yala, and Narathiwat remained under Thailand. Despite the religious differences—the Thais were predominantly Buddhist and the Malays predominantly Muslim—as the twentieth century progressed these Malay regions were destined to be increasingly absorbed into the Thai cultural, social, and governmental system.

Johore was the last state formally to accept British protection. This was not from any antipathy to the Colonial Power. The state had had intimate relations with Singapore since this had become one of the Straits Settlements, and had been strongly influenced by the British system. But it was not until 1914 that the Sultan formally accepted a British General Adviser.

The greater autonomy retained by the Unfederated States prompted the rulers of the Federated Malay States to seek to revitalize their own State Councils. The British authorities for their part hoped that the Unfederated States could be induced to reconsider their objections to joining the federation if the federal system were rendered more attractive. The eventual consequence was a reorganization of the Federal Council in 1927. The Sultans thenceforward formed no part of it but held separate annual meetings with the High Commissioner and Chief Secretary and were usually consulted by the Residents before Council meetings. The number of Council members was increased to thirteen official and eleven unofficial. In the second category Malay participation was strengthened.

Later still, in the 1930s, the Residents in the four Federated States were freed from the supervision of the Chief Secretary and this formerly key figure was given the even less resounding title of Federal Secretary. The states recovered control of agriculture, health, and public works. From this time the State Council put forward its own budget proposals for consideration by the Federal Council and again became responsible for legislation. Federal officers for finance and legislation were made members of all the State Councils.

The system of British rule, first in the Straits Settlements then in the Federated Malay States and finally in the Unfederated States, had evolved in a haphazard and not very tidy fashion. In the political field the general pattern which this chapter has described continued until the Japanese invasion of December 1941.

In the economic field Malaya exploited in the twentieth century a source of wealth more profitable even than tin. This was rubber. Seeds of the wild rubber tree were smuggled out of Brazil in 1877. They were planted first in the Botanical Gardens at Kew near London and then in those at Singapore. For long, Malayan planters (chiefly of coffee) took little interest. By 1910, however, the motor industry had stimulated a boom. Ten years later, Malaya exported more than half the world's production of natural rubber and the generally high level of prosperity of the country masked such resentment as existed towards British rule. The expanding demand for labour on the rubber estates was met by the recruitment of Indian labourers, mostly Tamils from the south. This introduced fresh human problems into what was already a multi-racial society. By this time Malaya had become part of the modern world.

Before the advent of the British, the states of Malaya had little in common save religion, some racial customs and character-istics, and slightly varying forms of the same language. There were obvious differences of pace and approach between the Federated and Unfederated States when confronted with modern evolution. There was a sharp divergence even inside each group. Trengganu lived in pious seclusion without a coastal road to link its towns even after the First World War. On the other hand Johore, on the threshold of Singapore, had a ruler who entertained British Royalty with dashing sophistication. Among the Federated States, Pahang with its huge areas of jungle was in complete contrast to Perak with its dynamic Chinese entrepreneurs who eventually constituted half the population.

In spite of the divergences, under British rule all the states gradually acquired a sense of common destiny. This owed little to any set plan or purpose of a colonial power which prided itself on distrust of theory and logic. British administrators judged that they were there essentially to bring public order, and reliable, clean-handed administration, fair justice, decent treatment for the under-privileged, balanced budgets, and cautious exploitation of resources, preferably by free enterprise. This might—and did—produce prosperity beneficial to British trade. Yet Britain's advantage was never regarded as the sole and paramount objective. In this economic expansion the Chinese played an important, often a leading role. Their immigration attained massive proportions under British rule. The Indians were also quick to seize the profitable opportunities offered. Most had been brought in originally as estate labourers but many played an increasingly significant part as dealers, shopkeepers, clerks, teachers, trade-unionists, doctors, lawyers, and eventually politicians.

The Malays formed the bulk of the rural population. They grew the rice and most of the basic foods on which the towns depended. For the British Colonial officer, one of his principal tasks was to ensure that the Malays, whose land it was, had a proper share in the country's economic growth. But the Malay *kampong* was a traditional world, offering a quiet resistance to the exertions and changes of modern life. Secure against arbitrary oppression and unchecked disease the rural Malays multiplied and their human standards rose. But the pace of advance was inevitably slower and more hesitant than that of the other communities. The Malay villager was largely indifferent to the secular education so eagerly sought by the Chinese and Indians. Qualification in English as a key to success had little appeal for him. He was content with his Malay vernacular schools and with the local religious leaders (the *Kathis* and *Imams*) to teach him the Qur'ān. He distrusted hospitals and Western medicine. As there was little demand for these things in the rural areas, the British did less about them there than might have been desirable. They had little of the strict paternalism with which the Dutch applied their admirably careful Ethical System in Indonesia.

The British fully realized that the new order could only be effectively implemented with Malay approval and participation since some form of self-government would have to be granted to the country eventually. They sought to bring educated Malays into gradually more responsible government jobs; and eventually succeeded. Yet the Malay rulers and their families, the aristocracy and upper classes, only gradually accepted the modernization of their country. They long felt that to send their sons overseas for modern education was a betrayal of their traditions and religion.

The liberal and humanitarian elements in Britain were influential in her policies in the nineteenth century. In the early years they had led her campaign against slavery and the slave trade. Such people were reluctant to accept the comfortable assumption (propounded on occasions by their Continental rivals) that colonies were essentially for the benefit of the mother country. Britain's mercantilist creed of the eighteenth century had in any event been dispelled by the salutary shock of the American Revolution and the subsequent discovery that a far more profitable relationship could be developed with a flourishing independent people than with recalcitrant subordinates. American independence had also implanted the conviction that in all British overseas territories government by consent—and possibly separation—would come one day. By the nineteenth century Britain saw no merit in restrictive systems such as those which had kept Spain supplied with precious metals from her colonies in the New World, or the Dutch (before the adoption of more liberal policies in the later nineteenth century) with cheap cash crops cultivated by forced labour under the Culture System in Java.

It is often alleged by critics of colonialism that colonies were acquired specifically to contribute to the wealth of the colonial power. This is hardly borne out by Britain's imperial history. Many of her colonies were eventually a source not of profit but expense. For most of the colonial period, Britain sold her manufactures to Malaya, and Malaya exported her raw materials at world prices in a general pattern of free trade. The normal commercial returns from these transactions were on the whole advantageous to the business communities in both countries. Yet no special or exclusive economic links were imposed for the benefit of the mother country, save to the marginal extent of the imperial preferential tariff introduced in 1932. There was no direct financial gain to the British Government, though in the recent years of Britain's currency restrictions Malaya was a valuable source of U.S. dollars for the sterling area.

Such was the level-headed and not always very imaginative pattern of Britain's domination in Malaya. By such methods and without really intending to do so she effectively laid the foundations of a nation where there had been none before. National consciousness was slow in emerging. It was largely dormant until after the Second World War. Yet eventually the demands it presented were punctually met. In the final analysis, Britain's part in the creation of what eventually emerged as one of the most hopeful independent forces in mid-twentieth century Asia, would be held by many in Malaya to extenuate, and by some to justify, the rule which she had imposed upon them.

# CHAPTER SEVEN

# Britain's Final Expansion, and Defeat

The Second World War shattered the structure of European colonial rule throughout Southeast Asia. The British régime was swept away as was that of the Dutch and French in the territories which had become theirs. Before we consider how this happened and what were the consequences some account is due of the evolution of British rule in the territories of northern Borneo which came to be associated with Malaysia in recent years.

Under the second Brooke Rajah, the frontiers of Sarawak had advanced from the southwest at the expense of Brunei. Further to the north and east, territory ruled or claimed by Brunei fell eventually into other hands. In 1865 the Sultan leased a considerable proportion of North Borneo to an American adventurer, a former seaman named Charles Lee Moses, who set himself up as United States Consul in Brunei and who promptly sold his rights in Hong Kong to a group which called itself "The American Trading Company of Borneo".[1]

The American Trading Company whose leading figure Torrey had, like Brooke, been made a Rajah by the Sultan eventually sold its interests to the Austrian Consul in Hong Kong, Baron von Overbeck, who went into partnership with an Englishman called Alfred Dent of Dent Brothers in the City of London. They found that, apart from the alleged overlordship of the Sultan of Brunei, the Sultan of Sulu claimed suzerainty over the parts of the territory adjacent to the Philippines. The latter was forced in the 1870s to submit to the Spanish colonial authorities in Manila. Consequently, after Overbeck and Dent received from the Sultan of Brunei in 1877 a nominal title to much of the northern and eastern area, they negotiated a separate agreement with the Sultan of Sulu confirming their right to rule the parts claimed by the latter. In return for

[1] K. C. Tregonning, *A History of Modern Sabah 1881–1963*, pp. 5 and 6.

annuities to both Sultans the partners acquired some 30,000 square miles of territory. Later Overbeck sold out to Dent, having sought in vain to interest the Austrian Government in his project. The latter then floated a British North Borneo Provisional Association in 1878. This later became the British North Borneo Company which received a Charter from Queen Victoria in 1881.

Objections to this new phase of British expansion were raised from three quarters. The Spaniards, having conquered the Sultanate of Sulu, claimed all the territories which had been subject to it. They were, however, persuaded to abandon their Borneo claims in 1885 in return for British recognition of Spanish sovereignty over the Sulu Archipelago. By an Anglo-American convention of 1930, the U.S. Government which replaced Spain as the sovereign power in 1898 recognized North Borneo as being under British protection. Yet there was to be further controversy over this British agreement with the Sultan of Sulu after the Philippines became independent.

The Dutch alleged that the activities of the British company were a breach of the Anglo-Dutch Treaty of 1824. London had, however, already overriden similar Dutch objections to the Brooke acquisition of Sarawak and Britain's acquisition of Labuan, on the grounds that these areas were outside the scope of the agreement, being north of the Equator. The Dutch had eventually accepted the Anglo-Brunei Treaty of 1847 and therefore felt constrained to accept the British presence in North Borneo after the Company received its Royal Charter.

In the case of Rajah Brooke there was an element of jealousy. He regarded northern Borneo to some extent as his preserve. There was also a valid legal objection so long as Overbeck, a foreigner, was in control. For the Sultan of Brunei was precluded by the Treaty of 1847 from ceding territory to a nation or person who was not British without Queen Victoria's consent.

In spite of this, Dent's enterprise was not rebuffed. The 1880s saw a scramble by European Powers for colonies in the Pacific as well as Africa. Britain feared that one of her rivals might move in if she neglected her opportunity and in granting the Company a Charter the British Government imposed a measure of control. The external relations of North Borneo came under Britain, whose authority was also required for any alienation of territory. Slavery was to be abolished, native religion and custom maintained. In the administration of justice due consideration must be paid to local law.

The seal of respectability had been set on British acquisition of North Borneo. After this it was hardly possible for London any longer to restrain Sarawak from expanding further at the expense of Brunei. An additional large area covering the Baram basin was taken over by Rajah Charles in 1882. But the disintegration of Brunei heralded a danger of foreign intervention. France and Germany in particular were expanding east of Singapore and might be tempted to exploit the situation. To avert this risk, in 1888 Britain brought Brunei, Sarawak, and North Borneo officially under her protection. So far as Brunei was concerned, the Sultan agreed by a further treaty with Britain in this year that the foreign relations of the state should be conducted by the British Government and that the extra-territoriality of British subjects and foreigners under British protection should be safeguarded by the establishment of consular courts to try their cases.

In the half-century before the Second World War, the structure of government in each of these British-protected Borneo territories evolved on very different lines. The local Malays—predominant in Brunei itself—had to some extent a privileged position in them all. But these were not necessarily people of Malay stock, though, like the Malays of the Peninsula, many were of Indonesian origin. Virtually any person of the native races could qualify as a Malay by embracing Islam. Thus, classified with the Malays were Muslim Melanaus, Kedayans, Illanuns, Suluks, Bajaus, and in general many from the coastal races. Inland, the border with Netherlands Borneo followed well marked natural features such as mountains and rivers. Yet the up-country native tribes such as the Kenyahs, Kayans, Kelabits, Muruts, tended to straddle the frontier and frequently migrated from side to side.

In Brunei, in spite of the presence of a British Consul-General, the rulers continued to govern in their own arbitrary fashion. After the appointment in 1906 of a British Resident under the authority of the Governor and High Commissioner in Singapore, some progress was made with the enforcement of law and order, the extension of communications and economic development. Yet Brunei long remained something of an insolvent backwater. With this background and pretext further portions of the Sultan's dominions were incorporated in Sarawak and North Borneo until these were reduced to an insignificant enclave of 2,226 square miles surrounded by British-dominated territory. Brunei's poverty was, however, eventually transformed into affluence by the discovery of a valuable oilfield on her territory in 1929.

In Sarawak, the Rajahs, benevolent autocrats almost to the end, recruited a well-trained civil service, staffed chiefly by British officers and local Malays, to carry out their policies. As elsewhere in Southeast Asia, the Chinese who had immigrated in increasing numbers dominated in most economic fields. The country had poor soil and very limited mineral resources: some gold, antimony, and coal in the west, and some oil near the Brunei border. Except for the permitted activity of the Borneo Company—the Rajah's bankers—the Brookes set their face against economic exploitation of the country by outside business interests. The rubber tree had proved tolerant of poor soil in Malaya. It was developed to a limited degree as a smallholder crop in Sarawak. Yet the big plantations which brought wealth to the Peninsula were discouraged in Sarawak. An even more valuable, though chancy and exacting crop—pepper—was tenaciously developed in Sarawak by smallholders, especially the Hakka Chinese and the local Malays.

The Rajahs were also concerned to protect the natives (a term still used without opprobrium in Borneo for the indigenous races) from the destruction of their traditional ways. The land on which they had traditionally practised shifting or partly settled cultivation was reserved for their use. There was a severe limitation on the quantity of land which smallholders such as the prolific and enterprising Chinese could acquire and their land hunger produced serious political and social problems in a later age. In general the Brookes judged that the primitive but gifted native peoples would be happier with a minimum of contact with European civilization. For the Ibans and Land Dayaks, the Kenyahs, Kayans, and others of Sarawak this meant in practice a minimum of education, of medical facilities and of participation in the running of the country. There was widespread illiteracy; and until well into the twentieth century messages to Dayak headmen were often conveyed by pieces of knotted string.

The third British Rajah, Vyner Brooke, who succeeded during the First World War, was a more genial personality than his father. Under him (as Charles Brooke had feared) there was some relaxation in the austerity of the Sarawak régime though during nearly all his reign the general principles of Brooke rule were maintained. But in 1941 there was a fundamental change. To celebrate the centenary of the dynasty, the Rajah promulgated in September of that year a constitution under which he ceased to be an absolute ruler. Social and education services and general living standards were to be improved and the people were to be entrusted with self-government when educated in the responsibilities of citizenship. A Supreme Council was set up through which the Rajah had to exercise his executive functions. An existing consultative body, the National Council (Council Negri) was expanded and re-vitalized. It had both official and nominated unofficial members. Without its advice and consent no legislation could be enacted. In its original form this gallant experiment in democracy hardly had a trial. Three months later, the Rajah having departed, the Japanese arrived.

In North Borneo, some of the Governors appointed by the Chartered Company were able Colonial officers from Malaya. But they long suffered from the lack of an adequate and properly trained civil service and at times from arbitrary dictation and interference by the London Board. After Alfred Dent, another adventurous figure called W. C. Cowie became the dominant figure in the Company. He had done business in the area in earlier years and had been granted trading rights by the Sultan of Sulu. Under his influence, and based on his limited personal knowledge, some rash and expensive projects were launched, designed to open up the country. There was no belief, as in Sarawak, in the virtue of holding back modern economic progress in order to protect the interests of the indigenous races. Yet ultimately their welfare was not neglected and it remained a debatable point between those loyal to the methods of the Rajahs or of the Chartered Company which system was more beneficial or prejudicial to the indigenous races. One capital miscalculation was, however, made by the Chartered

Company in its early stages. It was wrongly assumed that there were numerous natives in the interior. In fact much of North Borneo was empty and the territory has always suffered from the lack of an adequate labour force. To a very limited extent this was remedied by recruitment from the Philippines, from Hong Kong, and from Indonesia.

North Borneo had one advantage over Sarawak, namely an area of rich volcanic soil. Partly for this reason its economic resources proved to be strangely varied. As late as 1885 almost a third of the country's exports were edible birds nests—the gelatinous structures built by swifts and highly prized as a delicacy by the Chinese—and jungle produce such as rattans and gutta percha. From that time timber—both soft and hard wood—gradually developed as North Borneo's major resource, though a profitable potential was neglected since most of it was exported in log form instead of being processed locally. Timber became a significant economic factor in Sarawak too. A valuable timber by-product, exploited in both territories, was cutch, a khaki dye extracted from mangroves.

In the 1880s it was also found that some of the best tobacco—a cigar leaf of high quality—could be grown in North Borneo. A boom in tobacco was checked in 1891 by the decision of America, the principal buyer, to protect the tobacco grown in her Southern States by imposing heavy duties. The local industry eventually dwindled to insignificance.

Rubber came later to North Borneo than to Malaya. When it did, it was grown on large scientifically developed plantations as well as on smallholdings. One of Cowie's rash and badly executed projects had been a railway, originally intended to cross the country, which had been built down the west coast and some distance inland. This came into its own when the land on either side proved fit for rubber and big inducements were successfully offered to investors in the early twentieth century. In spite of serious fluctuations in price after the First World War and during the Depression, exports from North Borneo and to a more limited degree from Sarawak rose to an impressive volume.

The middle years of the twentieth century gave certain Asian nations the chance to redress the many humiliations which

Asia had suffered at the hands of Western Powers. Alone among these nations Japan had achieved the status of a Great Power. After the startling impact of Commodore Perry in 1853 she had mastered the techniques of the West with patient tenacity and thoroughness. This seemed in sharp contrast to the emotional reverence for custom of most oriental peoples. Yet in spite of modernization she clung to her strongly nationalist traditions with a religious basis in the Shinto faith. At the end of the nineteenth century, she defeated her vastly greater neighbour China which had remained wedded to the ancient ways. Early in the twentieth century Japan was victorious over the Russian Empire and destroyed the myth of the white man's invincibility. After this, and the annexation of Korea in 1910, for the best part of a generation she consolidated her initial gains as an imperialist power. Though rapacious where China was concerned, she was on the whole correct and co-operative with the West. She was for many years—and throughout the First World War—an ally of Britain, then the dominant European Power in the Far East. After the war she was awarded the mandate of the German Pacific islands. Subsequently, in 1922, she accepted the Washington Treaties which guaranteed her security and established naval parity between the United States and Britain although they fixed a lower ratio for the Japanese Navy. This disparity was, however, resented by the extreme nationalists, as were the restrictions, real or imaginary, imposed by America and Britain on Japan's potential dominance in China and the Pacific. The military gained ground, as did patriotic societies of a fascist type.

Beginning in September 1931, Japan launched a further campaign of expansion on the mainland. This eventually engulfed Manchuria and a great part of China despite the new and more effective leadership given to the Chinese nation by Chiang Kai-Shek after the years of chaos and discord following the downfall of the Manchu Empire. After the Japanese occupation of Nanking in 1940 the Nationalist Government of China retreated westwards and established its capital at Chungking. Further Chinese resistance was now largely sustained by supplies through the British territories of Hong Kong and Burma. This gave Japan a special motive for trying conclusions with her former ally, Britain, who was also her principal commercial

rival. The moment was opportune. Britain and her friends
were strained to the utmost by a war in Europe which had led
to the German occupation of France and Holland, the other
two principal colonial powers in Asia. The United States,
however, was envisaged as the chief antagonist, because she had
become the strongest Western Power in the Pacific. She was to
be kept in play by Japanese diplomacy until the moment
seemed ripe for the final test.

Meanwhile Japan prepared for this inevitable trial of strength
with the West by allying herself with Germany and Italy in
1936 and 1937. In 1940 she secured a dominant position in
Thailand. In the same year, France under German dictation
was forced to give Japanese troops entry into French Indo-
China. The following year brought the crisis to a head. In
April 1941 Japan secured the neutrality of Russia. In June the
German invasion of Russia further protected her against Soviet
intervention. In July she occupied the whole of Indo-China.
The United States, which had denounced its commercial
treaty with Japan in 1939, retaliated with further economic
restrictions. By this stage Japan had resolved to employ against
America the move which had given her a decisive initial advantage against Russia in 1904: the sudden knock-out blow
without previous warning. This occurred on 7 December
with the attack on Pearl Harbor. A day later by the calendar
(because of the international date line running through the
Pacific) but in fact two hours earlier, Japanese troops landed at
Kota Bharu in Kelantan and in the Thai area immediately to
the north. The British battleships sent to intercept the landings
were sunk. The Japanese soon established command of the air
as well as the sea. Working from the north and through the
jungles, they gained the element of surprise. The British
strategic planners had rashly concentrated their preparations
on the prospect of a sea-borne assault on Singapore.

In any event the collapse of British Malaya could at best
have been delayed. For over two years Britain had been forced
to concentrate all her best forces and equipment against the
overwhelming menace of Germany who had brought the
continent of Europe under her control more effectively than
Napoleon had ever done. Germany, in occupation of the whole
French coast, had come within an ace of invading and subduing

Britain herself. So far as England was concerned, Malaya was an area remote from the central conflict. She had to be defended with such forces and weapons as could be spared. For Australia, it was a vital area at her back door. She sent the best she could there, but, as the enemy moved into the Philippines, Indonesia, New Guinea, and the neighbouring Pacific islands, she was absorbed with the menace of Japan around her whole vast coast-line. Such troops as there were in Malaya faced the *élite* of the Japanese forces and a formidable concentration of weapons. Command of the sea and air enabled these to be used with double effect.

For the first thirty years of the twentieth century, power in Japan had lain on the whole with those elements which respected the constitutional, legal, and ethical heritage of the West. But under militarist rule there was a rejection of Western ideals; and the more liberal elements—including the Imperial House—lost much of their power. This helps to explain the disturbing contrast between Japan's earlier punctiliousness— her desire to be esteemed as a new Great Power observing the rules of modern nations—and the startling cruelty with which the victorious Japanese troops handled the Asians and Europeans whom they now conquered. Mutilations, tortures, and public humiliation were reminiscent of far more ancient and primitive traditions. Only the oldest Malay citizens could perhaps have recalled something comparable from the days of their grandfathers. Japan had earned great prestige among her fellow Asians by successfully defeating their white Colonial masters. Yet in Malaya and other territories there was soon a feeling that the old masters had shown more regard for local susceptibilities.

Finally, while British civilians were interned more or less in accordance with the procedure of other nations, prisoners of war were treated without respect for the safeguards of the Geneva Convention which the Japanese had not signed. This again was a reversion to an essentially non-European tradition. The Japanese regarded it as an unforgiveable disgrace if their own soldiers allowed themselves to be captured alive. From this narrowly nationalist outlook, prisoners of war were beings beyond the pale. In one other respect the Japanese seem to have borrowed one of the less endearing concepts of their western allies. The activities of their special police—the Kempeitai—had a sinister resemblance to that of the German Gestapo.

While the war lasted, the internationally-minded Japanese were at a discount. Some had a minor role under the military, but with a minimum of influence.[1] Yet they clearly recognized when the tide had turned. It was the renewed strength of their voice which brought the war to a sudden end.

The Japanese forces swiftly overran the Philippines, Indonesia, British Borneo, and Burma with a skill and courage comparable to that which they had shown in Malaya. But by the middle of 1942 they had been checked, in the east by the American naval victories in the Pacific, and in the west by the defeat of their air assaults on Ceylon. Their new empire had reached its greatest extent and for the next three years they were concerned with defending it and attempting to organize their conquests in the manner most profitable to Japan. Although there were individual collaborators who aimed at using the conquerors for their own ends the Japanese approach to the Asians won virtually no popular political support for their policies. In the economic field they sought to establish what they described as a Greater East Asia Co-Prosperity Sphere. Malaya with its tin, rubber, and iron ore was one of the richest prizes for inclusion in this ostensibly imaginative scheme. It might have achieved remarkable success had it been run with a free hand by Japan's business leaders who had raised her to the status of one of the world's leading commercial and industrial nations. Under military control it degenerated into a clumsy weapon for extracting as much as possible in the shortest time for the Japanese war effort.

With the British eliminated, the Chinese in Malaya were the principal victims of Japanese hostility. Many were killed of those who had supported Nationalist resistance to the Japanese during the campaigns in China. Others, who put business first,

---

[1] One was Marquis Tokugawa, descendant of the last family of ruling Shoguns. According to the Deputy State Secretary, Johore—one of many Malays to whom he showed kindness and friendship—he was instrumental, as war-time Director of the Singapore Museum, in saving its collections with their irreplaceable relics of Raffles and British imperial activities.

allegedly traded for commercial advantage some measure of help to the Japanese occupation authorities.[1] Others again were supporters of the Malayan Communist Party. This had been illegal before the war because of its refusal to disclose the information about its foreign connexions which the Colonial authorities made a point of requiring as an insurance against subversion before it could be registered as a society. From June 1941 (after Britain and Russia became allies) the communists supported the war effort. They were largely Chinese and during the occupation they played a major part in such armed resistance as the Allies managed to conduct through a body known as the Malayan Peoples' Anti-Japanese Army.

As enemies of Britain's foes they inevitably received support and supplies of weapons and equipment from Southeast Asia Command, the Allied organization based on Ceylon under the orders of Admiral Mountbatten. The British military groups or individuals left behind to organize resistance, or later parachuted in for this purpose, collaborated with the M.P.A.J.A., some of whom were officially commended by the British forces. All this was to have far-reaching consequences, the ultimate objective of the M.P.A.J.A. being of course to establish a communist régime in Malaya, not to assist Britain to restore colonial rule.

Another significant development in which the Chinese—as town dwellers—were largely involved, was a revival of a practice which had started during the depression. It was a move out of the towns to the fringes of the jungle by hungry people seeking a chance to grow food. And now they particularly sought to evade the close Japanese control in the urban areas. This created a squatter problem which had to be drastically resolved after the war when the communist menace had replaced that of Japan.

The occupying forces, perhaps comprehensibly, made a point of humiliating Europeans in the eyes of the Asians. To be half European was also a penalty and the Eurasians suffered

[1] According to K. R. Ramanath, an Indian journalist and Editor of the *Sabah Daily Express*, who himself experienced the Japanese occupation in Singapore, the Chinese who were prevailed upon to assist the Japanese there managed to run many Indian firms out of business and take over their interests.

accordingly. In the case of the Indians the Japanese encouraged, with some response, support for the anti-British
Indian Nationalist Army of Subhas Chandra Bose. They also
obtained some co-operation in their police work from certain
Indians, and rather particularly from the Sikhs who had
traditionally been prominent as guards, night watchmen, and
policemen. The non-co-operative Indians suffered with the
rest. Many were assigned to forced labour, as were the prisoners
of war. The most dramatic of these forced labour projects—
and that most wasteful of human life—was the building of the
railway linking the Thai network with the lines in southern
Burma. This, like most of the other projects, was dictated by
purely strategic objectives. The line had little or no economic
value in normal times and was abandoned after the war.

The Japanese policy was on the whole to favour the Malays.
Yet the Malays, like everyone, suffered from the compulsory
levies of supplies and the general economic breakdown. Tin-
mining equipment and rubber-processing plants had been
damaged by the retreating British troops. So far as these were
restored, it was hard for them to operate effectively with the
loss of international markets and even Japanese markets for
tin and rubber and great shipping difficulties due to the effective American submarine campaign. Again, the mismanagement characteristic of Japanese military rule produced failures
of distribution and serious shortages of the foodstuffs and consumer goods normally imported with the foreign exchange
earned by Malaya's exports.

General suffering also resulted from the lapse of the creditable
health standards built up by the British. Medical supplies and
equipment were commandeered for the Japanese forces from
the hospitals. The preventative measures taken by the Colonial
authorities against malaria and other tropical diseases were
dropped.

The more moderate attitude of the Japanese towards the
Malays seems to have been inspired by their general policy
of seeking political collaborators from the nationally dominant
race. This had achieved some success in the Philippines,
Indonesia, and Burma. They had assumed direct control of the
Straits Settlements. In the Malay States, however, they left the
Sultans on their thrones, after rebuking those who were con-

sidered to have displayed sympathy for the British cause. In some cases they altered the order of succession of the Rulers, apparently in order to secure candidates who would be more pliant to their demands.[1] The state governments continued to function but were placed under the supervision of Japanese agents.

The Japanese tried—unsuccessfully—an innovation which may have been intended to build up a Malay/Muslim counterpoise to the Chinese and Indian half of Malaya's population. They combined the administration of Sumatra and Malaya under the authority of Singapore. The experiment was given up in 1944. While it lasted, however, it abolished the divisions artificially imposed by the colonial powers. It may have given new life to the awareness of common interests between the peoples of Malay race in Indonesia and Malaya. This was to be a significant factor and problem in the post-war development of both regions when the colonial system was in retreat.

In 1943 the Japanese established local Malay councils with advisory functions. Some of their members were elected by village headmen, some nominated by the occupation authorities. Again the results were negative. In Burma and Indonesia there had existed long before the war anti-colonial, nationalist fervour which the Japanese were able to turn to their account. In 1943 they erected a puppet government in Rangoon which purported to be the independent Republic of Burma. Yet after a time it was rejected by certain Burmese national leaders who had consented to serve in it. In Indonesia, as their defeat approached in 1945, the Japanese sponsored Sukarno's nationalist Republican campaign.

The pre-conditions for a comparable exercise in Malaya simply did not exist. The first loyalty of most Malays was to their state and Sultan. The pre-war attitude of some Malay rulers could be illustrated by the alleged inquiry of a foreign visitor. 'Don't you want your independence?' 'Independence? What do you think we pay the British for?' The concept of Malaya as a nation was still in embryo. There was as yet no

---

[1] For example in the case of Perlis. The present Raja and former Yang di Pertuan Agong of Malaysia, who was Crown Prince when the Japanese took over, was excluded by them from the succession and restored after the British returned.

general sense of unity, no leaders of the Malay people were acceptable to the country as a whole. There had not emerged a clearly defined rejection, based on national pride, of Malay dependence on British rule and British organization.

The occupation was no less harsh in Britain's Borneo Territories. When Sarawak was suddenly attacked, none of the Brooke family happened to be in the country. The various peoples were so accustomed to the safe paternalism of Brooke rule that their mood was one of apathy and disbelief. There was little resistance on the part of the indigenous peoples or of the Malays and Chinese. The official left in charge of the government, and who carried out the surrender to the Japanese, was subsequently killed by them. For some three years little stirred; no groups or individuals seem to have been able to operate effectively for the Allied cause. Then, early in 1945, a group of special British military agents—among them the future Director of the Sarawak Museum—were parachuted into one of the wildest mountain areas bordering on Indonesian Borneo. They succeeded in winning the co-operation of the local tribes who had relished a revival of head-hunting—banned under the Brookes—at the expense of stray Japanese. With their help, a guerilla campaign was mounted which before the surrender had managed to free extensive areas from enemy control.

In North Borneo the occupation was one of those which took the heaviest toll. The Japanese reversed the general system of the Chartered Company. 'Whereas the Company had controlled the territory from the coast, and with instinctive British concentration on sea-borne trade, had developed the ports while neglecting the interior, the Japanese moved in strength inland and controlled the area from the centre.'[1]

Links were established between guerillas in the Philippines under American guidance and resistance elements on the North Borneo coast. Among the latter the Chinese played a courageous and prominent role, together with Suluks, Bajaus and other people of the islands. These Chinese were not communists like so many of the resistance fighters in Malaya. The communist party had never been allowed to gain a footing in North Borneo. An uprising in October 1943, the temporary

[1] Tregonning, *History of Modern Sabah*, p. 216.

capture of Jesselton with the killing of many Japanese, and plans for a further outbreak six months later, led to an exceptionally savage campaign of repression which notably reduced the population of the West Coast.

One of the final tragedies was the sacrifice of a large group of prisoners of war. All but six were lost of two thousand Australian prisoners who had been sent to Sandakan from Singapore. Early in 1945, after the Allied forces had reached the northeastern Indonesian islands, the Japanese anticipated an Allied landing at Sandakan. This never took place but most of these unfortunate men were marched off into the interior. Some died before they started, far more of them on the way, and a few at the end of the trail.

The occupation in Brunei was less dramatic. The Sultanate was treated by the Japanese in similar fashion to the occupied Malay states. The original Japanese landings in northern Borneo on 16 December 1941 had been just to the west of the Brunei border, near the oil installations at Miri and Lutong in Sarawak. The final Japanese defeat in all these Borneo territories began just the other side, in Brunei Bay, when the Allied forces landed on Labuan Island on 10 June 1945.

# CHAPTER EIGHT

# Nationalism and the Post-War Reckoning

It was a shattered world to which the Colonial Powers returned. Japan had achieved dominance by Asians in Asia but on her own harsh terms; and she had forfeited the credit it could have gained her. By 1945 the subject peoples had seen the collapse in relatively short order of the European colonial governments and of the fascist/militarist domination of Europe by Germany and the Far East by Japan. For those Asian nationalists who had struggled against alien rule this was an immense encouragement. Yet they also became aware of the emergence of Soviet Russia as a world power of the first rank. This leader of international communism and vociferous enemy of colonialism (despite Russia's own imperialist record) was acclaimed by the victorious democratic nations. For many simple people, communism acquired fresh glamour and prestige. Understandably, many failed to realize that it implied a new imperialism no less oppressive than those which had been defeated.

Nothing could be the same again. Asians generally were determined to be masters of their own affairs. There were, however, marked differences of outlook, timing, and approach between the different peoples.

Despite their ties of race, there was wide divergence between Indonesia and Malaya. Nationalism had awakened in the latter but chiefly in the form of sporadic Malay violence and hostility towards the Chinese. In the former it was passionately alive. President Sukarno conceived of the Indonesian Revolution as an historic event of comparable importance to the American, French, and Russian Revolutions. He acquired strong authority under a constitution drawn up in 1945. He had already set himself to create in the disparate peoples of the Archipelago a sense of nationhood based on a common Malay language. This became his great historical achievement. Half Javanese and half Balinese himself, he saw the focus of the nation in these areas of highest traditional culture, and particularly in Java. At the same time he sought to stir up a revolutionary fervour impregnated with Pan-Malay ambitions which went far beyond the borders of his country. At one point he declared his faith in the reunion of Singapore and Malaya with Indonesia as in the days of the Empires of Srivijaya and Majapahit. This vision continued to haunt him and colour his thinking for the next twenty years.

The Allies had planned with some care the future of the territories they fought to liberate. Yet their time-table was disrupted and their plans confused by Japan's sudden surrender in mid-August 1945, after striking Allied advances in the Pacific and the devastation caused on her home territory by mounting air raids and the first atomic bombs.

In Southeast Asia, after the resounding defeat of the Japanese in Burma, the British Commonwealth forces under Lord Mountbatten planned their assault on Malaya. United States forces from the Pacific were to pursue the reconquest of Indonesia. But the surrender and the prospective occupation of Japan required a concentration of American forces and planning in that area. Consequently the responsibility for accepting the surrender of the Japanese in Indonesia and southern Indochina and dealing with future developments there was suddenly assigned to the British who found it hard to cope promptly with both the Malayan and Indonesian commitments. A delay of some weeks occurred. The occupation forces did not arrive in either territory until September. In Indonesia the nationalist forces had time to gather strength and establish control in certain areas. The country was proclaimed an independent Republic on 17 August 1945, three days after the capitulation. The Japanese punctually surrendered. Afterwards, however, some of the British and Indian troops were roughly handled by the Indonesian nationalists, notably in Surabaya. The Dutch military and colonial authorities eventually returned to Djakarta and some other parts of Java, and to many of the Outer Islands. In view of the strength of the nationalist movement, Britain sponsored—with very qualified success—negotiations between the nationalist leaders and the Dutch.

In Malaya the predominantly Chinese Malayan Peoples Anti-Japanese Army attempted to fill the gap between the collapse of Japanese authority and the arrival of the British forces. They sought to establish a communist régime and in the period of confusion ruthlessly paid off old scores against their opponents. This heightened the tension between Malays and non-Malays which the Japanese had fostered. When the British military administration was set up, it was at first proposed to give handsome terms to these resistance fighters to facilitate their return to civilian life. Some had earned such credit that they took part in the Victory Parade in London. Eventually, however, less generous and perhaps more short-sighted counsels prevailed. The M.P.A.J.A. were required to hand over their arms. On discharge each man received the equivalent of U.S. $116 (M$350) in gratuity. As might have been foreseen, by no means all arms were surrendered. The communist leaders did not relax their efforts or disband their organization. For the time being they profited by the fact that the post-war colonial government eventually legalized the communist party and accepted the revival of the trade unions. The British Labour Party sent out a mission to try to organize the Malayan unions on sound, non-communist lines.

In the first months the military authorities accomplished as best they could the task of restoring confidence, order, production, and supplies in an impoverished and demoralized land. Food had to be imported, disease brought once more under control. For the vital tin and rubber industries much fresh capital was needed. Labour had to be reorganized and redistributed against a background of communist-fomented unrest, and trained executives and technicians found for the key posts.

When civil government was restored political parties started to take shape. For the non-Malays—and largely for Chinese of the professional class—the Malayan Democratic Union emerged as a counterpoise to the newly legitimized Malayan Communist Party. A Malay Nationalist Party was founded in November 1945. It was significant of the disturbing interest which Indonesians were beginning to take in the affairs of the Peninsula that it was started with Indonesian encouragement and support. Its leader, Dr. Burhanuddin, allegedly aimed at the inclusion of Malaya in Indonesia.

The British were not unwelcome after the Japanese. Nevertheless, having seen the débâcle of 1942, the peoples of Malaya had lost faith in British strength and wisdom. At this juncture, when it was essential to restore their local credit, the London Government embarked in 1946 on a new course in Malaya. In the light of Britain's reverses this had been carefully worked out during the war. Unfortunately, it was one which aroused wide resentment in Malaya and was sharply criticized by authoritative voices in Britain.

Yet there was much in theory to justify the change. Britain was proceeding administratively and politically on the assumption that Malaya would soon evolve towards independence. Her planners ascribed Malaya's weakness in face of the Japanese attack largely to her administrative fragmentation. In 1942 there had been ten different governments—those of the Straits Settlements and of the four Federated and five Unfederated Malay states. All had to be brought into line on major questions such as defence. Greater centralization and unity were essential if the country was to be organized more effectively in future. The new scheme brought Penang and Malacca and all the Malay states under one centralized administration: the Malayan Union. Although one of the objects of the Union was to give the Chinese in Malaya a bigger say in affairs, Singapore was excluded in view of its predominantly Chinese population. Its inclusion would have given the Chinese an ethnic majority in the country as a whole, which would by this stage have been quite unacceptable to the Malays. Singapore was to remain for the time being a British colony.

Administratively the Union was a more drastic and far-reaching application of the system already existing in the Federated Malay States. The Unfederated States had refused to join this original scheme of centralization. They were now to be forced to do so. The Federated Malay States had been largely due to Frank Swettenham's initiative. Yet Swettenham himself—then in his nineties—came out strongly against Malayan Union, as did others in Britain who had been prominently associated with Malaya. They objected because the Union embodied a new and revolutionary departure which they considered unjust to the Malays. Britain's obligations had been to the Malays and their rulers and not to the immigrant races. Their protests stimulated opposition within Malaya. The acquisition of citizenship was to be simplified for people of any race, and all citizens would have equal rights. Except for the retention of their Land Reservations, the Malays would be deprived in their own Malaya of the special position which had historically and legitimately been theirs before the arrival of the Europeans or the other Asians. Moreover the Sultans were in effect to lose all political power, though they would continue to participate in advisory councils on Muslim affairs.

The government was to be very similar to that of a British colony. There would be a Governor assisted by Executive and Legislative Councils, performing the functions of a Ministerial Cabinet and of an embryo Parliament or Congress. The State Councils would continue, but only for minor matters. Citizenship could be claimed by all persons born in Malaya or Singapore, or by those who had lived there for ten of the fifteen years before 1942. Henceforward citizenship could be obtained after five years' residence. A special representative of the British Government, Sir Harold MacMichael, who visited Malaya in the autumn of 1945, briskly persuaded the Sultans to sign away their powers. He had been authorized to confirm or withhold British sanction of their position as rulers. One reason, it appears, for the comparatively swift acquiescence he secured is that some of the Sultans had in fact shown pliancy towards the Japanese. They were initially relieved at escaping disagreeable consequences and retaining their rank and privilege even though they lost their power.

Developments during the war had played their part in bringing about this cavalier treatment of the Malays. When the future was being considered during the Japanese occupation the British were deprived of all but the most meagre clandestine contacts with Malaya. In England people were aware that a number of Malays had accepted the conquest with a certain passivity. The non-Malays on the other hand—and particularly the Chinese—had suffered more severely at the hands of the Japanese and had in some respects played a more prominent and exposed role in combating enemy oppression. The fact that the core of the Chinese resistance fighters were communists fighting for essentially Marxist objectives was overshadowed by the effective help they had given at the time to the Allies.

The new policy's justification was not only the creation of

more efficient government machinery. It aimed at greater national integration with a view to eventual self-government for Malaya on the pattern foreshadowed in other British Asian territories. Unfortunately certain human factors had been ignored.

The non-Malays showed little enthusiasm for Malayan Union, despite the generous opportunities it offered them for the exercise of political influence and admission to the government service. The Chinese in Malaya were chiefly preoccupied with the restoration of their businesses rather than with politics. Had they shown greater interest in the Union, the British Government might well have continued to uphold it. As it was, they woke up to its desirability when it was too late. Their lack of interest was partly explained by the fact that some 40 per cent. of them had been born outside Malaya. On the other hand, the proposals gave great offence to the Malays. For the first time Britain found herself faced with a powerful movement of Malay nationalism which rejected her policy and sought self-government on its own terms. An inspiring figure with great gifts of eloquence took the lead. This was Dato Onn bin Ja'afar, who became Chief Minister of Johore and was related to the Sultan's family. His breadth of vision and cosmopolitan sophistication may have been partly due to this distinguished background which included some elements of Caucasian heredity.

In pursuance of his campaign Dato Onn founded in March 1946 the United Malays National Organization, or U.M.N.O., which has remained to this day the principal instrument and mouthpiece of Malay nationalism. Anti-U.M.N.O. feeling crystallized around Dr. Burhanuddin and his Malay Nationalist party which with other smaller groups formed the People's United Front (Pusat Tenaga Ra'ayat or PUTERA). In 1946 U.M.N.O. was chiefly concerned with combating Malayan Union and preparing the Malays for the responsibilities of ruling themselves. In their immediate objectives the Malay nationalists in U.M.N.O. were successful to the extent that Malayan Union was never fully put into operation.

It was a measure of British political sense that the London authorities were prepared with some promptness to reverse their former plans. During a period of provisional government more acceptable solutions were discussed with the Malays and other races. These were implemented from February 1948, in the form of a new and wider Federation than that of 1896. It covered the same territories as the defunct Union and continued to exclude Singapore. In a sense this was a triumph for the policy Britain had always favoured of bringing all the Malay states under one administration. In fact, however, some of the former Unfederated States such as Kelantan retained an abiding reluctance to take orders from Kuala Lumpur. Yet the Federation embodied far-reaching and significant concessions to the Malay point of view.

The states, with British advisers, were again to have executive and legislative powers, particularly in local government, health, education, agriculture, and lands. Their governments would be headed by a Chief Minister (Mentri Besar) under the Sultan, or the Resident Commissioner in Penang and Malacca. At the centre of the federation the representative of Britain in Kuala Lumpur ceased to be a Governor. He reverted to the less commanding title of High Commissioner. In the legislature there was a considerable majority of non-official members and a predominance of Malays. The Conference of Rulers was revived but it was to meet three times a year, considerably more often than in the early days of the Federated Malay States. Constitutional amendments, appointments of certain senior officials, and changes in the immigration laws, had to be submitted to it for approval.

To meet Malay objections, citizenship was much more restricted than under Malayan Union. Broadly speaking, Malays were automatically citizens. The non-Malays could also be automatically citizens if they normally spoke Malay and followed Malay customs; or were permanently resident in Malaya, having been born in the federation of a parent born there; or again if their fathers were federal citizens at the time of their birth. Others could apply to become citizens if they were born in the federation and had lived there for eight of the twelve years before the application; or if they had lived there for fifteen of the twenty years before they applied. Aspiring citizens had to know Malay or English and undertake to settle permanently in the country.

The new rules of citizenship favoured the Malays. In general they found the new system acceptable and a good deal of heat was taken out of their nationalist agitation. Yet the drive for self-government, once launched, continued under its own momentum. The non-Malays did not like the new régime. They resented the restrictions on citizenship and the scant importance ostensibly assigned to them. The Chinese objected to the continued exclusion of Singapore. Yet the non-Malays could count on increasing their stake in the country as time went by. The development of an electoral system for most of the seats in the legislature would contribute to this. Moreover some of the non-Malays—the Chinese in particular—had a lower infantile mortality.

However little it appealed to some at the time, this modern Malayan federation, introduced under British rule, in fact took root and survived. Its general system of checks and balances, both racial and constitutional, was still in operation nearly twenty years later. In that time it had weathered two major crises—a communist insurrection and Indonesian Confrontation—the first as grim in its way as the Japanese occupation and far lengthier. Even the exciting stimulant of independence led to no major changes in its structure.

Singapore had meanwhile become something of a problem child. This was the only former Straits Settlement to have retained the subordinate status of a Crown Colony. Commercially and racially Singapore had had specially close links with her former associates, Penang and Malacca. Now, across the Johore Strait, a new and separate nation was emerging into which they had been incorporated. The strongest and most prosperous of the three Settlements, Singapore had always had a distinct personality and counted for considerably more than the other two. Apart from a predominantly Chinese population her economy had an essentially different basis to that of Malaya proper. Malaya's chief sources of wealth were export duties on agricultural and mineral products and import duties on the country's necessities. Singapore did not depend on agriculture or minerals—though there had been some growing of spices in the early years. Industrial development was in its early stages. By the late 1940s, Singapore had resumed her traditional role of an entrepôt port profiting from free trade.

Despite her divergent background and interests, Singapore did not relish the separate status or the isolation which Britain had imposed. Another minor loss was the Island of Labuan off Brunei Bay. This had had a chequered career. It was originally associated with Sarawak when James Brooke was its Governor. Subsequently it was allotted to the Chartered Company, and then in 1906 placed under Singapore. Forty years later, after the Second World War, Labuan reverted to North Borneo. Singapore did, however, retain until her own separation from Britain some specks in the Indian Ocean, the Cocos Islands, and Christmas Island. These were transferred to Australia in 1955 and 1958.

Before 1942, the government of Singapore had been that of a typical British colony. Under the Governor there were Executive and Legislative Councils, the former mostly of officials. In the latter, the nominated unofficial members matched the official ones in number. Some appointments were made by the Governor on the recommendation of special bodies such as Chambers of Commerce. There were no elected legislators. After the war the Legislative Council was allotted a majority of non-official members, nine of them elected. Yet it could still hardly be called democracy. Six of these unofficial members were elected by the British subjects, Asian and European, in Singapore, the rest by the Chinese, European, and Indian Chambers of Commerce. Apathy and opposition to colonial policy limited participation in these first post-war elections.

Japan surrendered just over two months after the Australians landed in the area of Brunei Bay. Brunei came once more under British protection. Not till September could Australian troops arrive in Kuching to take the surrender there. After seven months of military rule, Sarawak was restored to the Brookes in mid-April 1946. Two and a half months later, Rajah Vyner Brooke ceded his territory to the King and Sarawak became a British Crown Colony from 1 July 1946.

The Brookes had literally been fathers to their people; and to many in Sarawak this sudden withdrawal was startling and unpalatable. There had been less physical damage than in North Borneo and there was thus less compelling reason than in the territory of the Chartered Company for the British Government to take complete control in return for assuming the burden of rehabilitation beyond the resources of the country. The cession was in any case surrounded by controversy: it seemed to go back on the progressive Brooke Constitution of 1941. It was only passed by a narrow margin in the local legislature, and it was never accepted by the Rajah's nephew and heir, whom he mistrusted. It has also been suggested that the British Government, through the Colonial Office, exerted pressure to bring about the change. According to this presumption, the Labour Party which came to power in Britain in 1945 was unsympathetic to the monarchical trappings which a British family had arrogated to themselves in the East. They also deplored the paternalistic brakes imposed by the Brookes on modern economic development in Sarawak. The exact truth is for future historians. Meanwhile post-war Sarawak suddenly confronted a new phase with a Governor and the conventional organization of a British Colony. Provision was made, however, for the implementation of the liberal principles in the Constitution granted by the last of the Brooke Rajahs.

In North Borneo the principal towns on the east and west coasts had been almost totally wiped out. In Sandakan in the east, which had been the pre-war capital, there was nothing left. The administration was therefore transferred to Jesselton in the west which had a few houses standing. The cost of reconstruction throughout the territory dictated with little question the shape of its future. It went so far beyond the resources of the Chartered Company that the assumption of direct control by the British Government was virtually the only solution. The transition was easier than in Sarawak. North Borneo had always been essentially on a business footing, and it did not have the problem of personal loyalties to a dynasty which had lasted over a hundred years. The government bought out the rights and assets of the Company on the basis of an arbitral award. Two weeks after Sarawak, on 15 July 1946, North Borneo in its turn made a fresh start as a Crown Colony.

The Federation of Malaya was introduced in 1948 against a background of unrest. The communist bid to establish control of the country after the Japanese surrender had been defeated

by the resumption of British rule and the subsequent disbandment of the Malayan Peoples Anti-Japanese Army. As might
have been expected, the communists by no means abandoned
their objective. They sought to exploit fresh opportunities after
the legalization of the Malayan Communist Party; and the
post-war revival of trade unions. In the political field, they
participated in a Chinese dominated group known as the All
Malayan Council for Joint Action or A.M.C.J.A., which included the Old Comrades Association of the defunct Malayan
Peoples Anti-Japanese Army. The A.M.C.J.A. was also partly
based on the trade unions, through which a series of strikes were
set on foot. There was a clear attempt to disrupt the economy
through labour and political agitation. The British authorities
dealt very firmly with this and it failed. The communists then
turned increasingly to armed violence. They used it in the
form of intimidation by murder and destruction. This was
applied at key points such as roads, railways, tin mines, plantations, and police stations, so as to cause maximum chaos and
disruption. By June 1948, the government, faced with a series
of attacks amounting to armed insurrection, declared a State of
Emergency. Although less directly affected, Singapore took the
same step a few days later.

Malaya was not the only country of Southeast Asia in which,
around this period, the communists made determined efforts to
gain power. There were also outbreaks in Indonesia, Burma,
and Vietnam. All of these may have been part of a co-ordinated
plan evolved in February 1948 at a communist gathering in
Calcutta. Their success was variable and communist tactics
were adapted to every changing situation. In each of these
three countries communist subversion remained over the years
an enduring danger. In Vietnam it had developed by the
middle sixties into a major military threat to the free world.
In Malaya a victory of the communists came perilously near.
Nevertheless eventually and at great cost they suffered a total
military defeat.

Through the local intelligence organization and security services and an efficient police, the British authorities were reasonably well informed of the ramifications of the communists'
network. The police had traced those chiefly responsible for the

threat of total subversion. As matters moved towards a crisis they urged on the government the vital importance of arresting the key figures within reach without awaiting the detailed evidence of illegal activities normally required, before they disappeared into the underground. This they were forbidden to do on the grounds that there could be no interference with due process of law in advance of the Emergency Proclamation. When the police could proceed, their men had vanished. The conspiracy could no longer be crushed in its initial stages. Scruple for legality had lost the British a chance that did not recur. The 'Emergency'—as it continued to be called—developed into a long and deadly civil war.

CHAPTER NINE

# The Emergency

The State of Emergency was declared four months after the inauguration of the Federation of Malaya. Much of the attention of the British authorities had been concentrated on working out this constitutional solution, which withstood surprisingly well the heavy strain to which it was suddenly exposed. It was some time before the communist forces could deploy their strength in the guerilla campaign which spread across the country. Their normal combatant figures were not more than about four or five thousand, though they reached a maximum of 10,000 in the peak period of 1951–52. Unfortunately the British authorities were even slower to organize the counter-measures so urgently required. The British High Commissioner and former Governor, Sir Edward Gent (killed accidentally soon afterwards on his journey home for consultations) had been reluctant to believe that so grave a crisis was at hand. The danger was more keenly realized in certain higher quarters and notably by the United Kingdom Commissioner-General in Southeast Asia, Mr. Malcolm MacDonald.[1] Under the new High Commissioner in Kuala Lumpur, Sir Henry Gurney, the strategy and tactics of the enemy—both military and political —were on the whole correctly assessed. Certain useful methods of dealing with them were discovered and put into operation. Considerable progress was made in the first three and a half years in containing and turning back the tide of communist military success. Yet a civilian High Commissioner without complete authority over the whole field of military as well as political operations was necessarily hampered in prosecuting

[1] The British Government's objective after the war was not only greater administrative co-ordination (hence the ill-fated Malayan Union) but greater co-ordination of policy and ideas between those in charge of its interests in Asia. The United Kingdom Commissioner-General, stationed in Singapore, had responsibility for co-ordination in this wider field, and for advising the British Prime Minister on over-all policy.

the campaign with all the swiftness and efficiency needed. Meanwhile, communist recruitment and communist morale continued for years at a high pitch.

As we have seen, the formidable strength of communism after the war was partly due to the humiliation of the European imperialists and partly to the glamour communism acquired for some when Russia emerged victorious against Germany and Japan. But a fresh impulse was soon given to their cause. Little more than a year after the post-war struggle started, the guerillas in the Malayan jungles saw communism triumph in China, the land of their own people. For them, the encouragement and potential support of Asia's most massive nation seemed to foreshadow a similar triumph in Malaya. The recognition by Britain early in 1950 of the communist régime in Peking could only mean that the imperialists were weakening and saw the writing on the wall.

The successful spread of communism, in Malaya as elsewhere, demanded concurrently a negative and positive approach. On the one hand, chaos had to be created by destruction of the machinery of government and of economic equipment and resources which could not be turned to communist use. At the same time an aura of fear had to be generated by intimidation.[1] On the other hand, there had to be a subtle and dedicated battle for men's minds to make them converts to the cause. The support of non-communists had to be rallied without their really being aware that this was happening. Hence the avoidance of the self-betraying communist label and the proclamation of 'respectable' causes with a general emotional appeal such as nationalism, anti-colonialism, democratic equality, liberation. In this way, during the later stages of the occupation when the cause of Japan was losing ground, most of the Chinese in Malaya and Singapore had collaborated with the communists under the specious banner of the Malayan Peoples Anti-Japanese Army. Now, during the Emergency, the communists rallied many of the unsuspecting by a plausible manifesto promising wide freedom, democratic elections, inter-

[1] The eerie tenseness of atmosphere created by communist subversion in the plantations and jungle fringes is well described in John Slimming's *In Fear of Silence*. This young writer, then serving in the Malayan Police, was himself severely wounded in the anti-guerilla operations.

national neutrality, etc. They also made anti-British appeals designed to stir up nationalist resentment against the colonial power. To further their purpose they renamed their subversive jungle guerrillas the 'Malayan Races Liberation Army'.

The leaders of the 'Liberation' guerrillas were in fact the men who had led the M.P.A.J.A. Some of their commanders had had brief training by the British and had learned the habits and methods of this new adversary. They were armed largely with British weapons—the residue of those dropped to them in the jungle when they and the British had been fighting on the same side. They adopted the classic guerrilla tactics of seeking to establish themselves in defined areas which could be gradually enlarged and eventually linked together in a country-wide network of control.

Supply, recruitment, and intelligence were their chief problems. To solve them, they organized a 'Movement of the Masses' operating by persuasion and intimidation among the town and country Chinese. Their chief target was the half-million Chinese established on the fringes of the jungle during the Japanese occupation and earlier who had reverted to the agricultural habits of their ancestors in China. These were vulnerable to the jungle fighters and remote from government control. Most were illegally on their land and in natural antagonism to the government having 'squatted' on state land, on Malay reservations, or in forest reserves. A number of these simple farmers seem to have believed the allegation that the colonial government had agreed to hand control over them to the communist party. They were permeated by the influence and connexions of the Chinese communists who were often their kith and kin. For their part the guerrilla forces aimed at reproducing the conditions during the Japanese occupation when they could rely on help from most of the other Chinese in Malaya.

One of the government's first measures to deal with the emergency was to ban all potentially subversive associations, especially those with communist affiliations. Police and military forces were sharply increased. In the first instance this was to protect the country's vital economic assets—the mines and plantations—and the people who had stayed behind to work them at grave risk. On the export of their products depended the viability of Malaya as a modern country. The Communist Terrorists (or C.T.s), as they came to be known, sought either to destroy these assets or, where possible, to appropriate the products to themselves. When they achieved the latter they built up funds to acquire the sinews of war. They had started with arms salvaged from the air drops during the occupation. They now added those captured from time to time in attacks on the government forces.

Some of these attacks were disturbingly successful. The numbers engaged against a few thousand dedicated guerrillas eventually rose to over 120,000. There were about 20,000 regular troops, with 60,000 police and 40,000 home guard. Most of the regular units were British or Commonwealth forces including the local Malay Regiment and the multi-racial Federation Regiment. But much of the success of the campaign depended on the operations of a force of 60,000 police. On the face of things, the defenders of Malaya thus operated with a numerical advantage of some twelve to one during the critical period. Yet this advantage was nullified in practice when dealing with a mostly intangible and invisible foe; and indeed the eventually successful campaign against the guerrillas has been defined as the crafty use of a shoe-string. The enemy had a widespread and effective network for intelligence, propaganda and supply, and was constantly able to employ the weapon of surprise. This network operated not only among the settled populations and on the wilder fringes. It extended to the aborigines in the deepest jungle on whom both sides depended for intelligence about enemy movements. An officer of the government's Department of Aborigines operating during the Emergency in the backwoods of Kelantan[1] was told by a group of Temiar that he was the last European left alive in Malaya and that the Commonwealth aircraft which they saw overflying their area were all Chinese.

Nevertheless, in spite of the unfavourable factors and many government reverses, even at the worst stages of the fighting the communists were prevented from establishing any widespread areas of control. They did not manage to progress beyond the purely guerilla tactics of sudden attack and subse-

[1] See John Slimming, *Temiar Jungle* pp. 5 and 6. The author had been transferred to the Department of Aborigines after being invalided out of the Police.

quent disappearance. They never managed to mount large-scale operations of regular warfare, as the communists eventually began to do in Vietnam. Finally, these tough and fanatical guerillas were men of narrow outlook and limited education, who tended to be rigid and repetitive in their methods of communication, organization, and military action. With greater flexibility and imagination they might have achieved far more. As it was, they brought the established order in Malaya for a time to the edge of disaster. There were moments when moderate Malayans and Europeans felt deep discouragement. The communist effort seemed to be expanding, the enemy's ranks to be continually filling up; and there was no end in sight. Understandably some of the British, such as planters exposed to constant and nerve-racking danger, said: 'The Japanese chastised us with whips, but the Chinese chastise us with scorpions.'

In the initial stages the communists had one further advantage over the government. The communist effort was strictly concentrated and co-ordinated whereas Britain's unpopular attempt to streamline the administration through Malayan Union had failed. With the revival of state rights, Malaya had reverted to the more disjointed type of administration which had allegedly weakened her resistance to the Japanese. There were many to be consulted before drastic action could be taken. It followed that the Government of the Federation earned disproportionate unpopularity when forced to impose progressively more ruthless measures on the whole country. This was the case with the Emergency Regulations brought in in 1949. Under them the authorities could arrest people anywhere where there was suspicion of help being given to the communists. Many innocent persons were penalized.

The Chinese inevitably suffered more than any of the other races. Few were dedicated communists or had any keen interest in politics or a major political stake in the country. For most, the chief goal was to gain a profitable living. Many were not Malayan citizens and had no local patriotism. Malaya was just a corner of the Nanyang—of the overseas world—in which they could do better for themselves than in China. With their hard-headed realism they had little enthusiasm for getting hurt for causes alien to their normal lives. The instinct of the vast majority was very humanly to sit upon the fence until they knew which side was going to win. This was just what both the government and the communists were determined that they should not do. They were caught between the force exerted by the one and the other. They came under constant suspicion, especially from the Malays. This was partly by reason of their ties of race and family with the adversary in the jungle. It was also because so many were in fact forced to help the communists by terrorism and intimidation. Most vulnerable of all to such pressure, and in turn to the government's reprisals, was the Chinese squatter population in easy communication with the jungle. If the main communist drive was to be weakened this needed corrective action of the strongest kind. The government's counter-offensive consisted of a series of operations jointly planned by the civilian authorities, the police, the army, the information services, and the home guard. The general strategy was one of advancing northwards from the southernmost state of Johore, winning successive areas from the communists and consolidating government control of these areas before moving further afield.

It had been realized since 1948 that one of the first essentials was to cut the channels of communication, recruitment, and supply between the squatters and the guerrillas. But not till ten months after the Emergency started was a Director of Operations appointed to assume responsibility under the High Commissioner for the government's anti-insurgency activities. In 1950 this officer, General Briggs, initiated a system for isolating the communists which proved of capital importance in achieving their ultimate defeat. The squatters were to be removed from the jungle fringes and eventually this emerged as a programme for their resettlement in New Villages where they could be controlled and defended. Some 600 of these more or less compact defended settlements were eventually established as a sequel to the Briggs Plan in various parts of the country. The resettlement was immensely difficult. Mistakes were made and the results were of varying effectiveness. To secure the co-operation of the Malayan Chinese was one of the government's primary objectives. The squatters had therefore to be moved without antagonizing them too much. A number indeed welcomed the protection offered when they realized it was something upon which they could rely. The authorities had also to persuade the Malays in the state governments, who had little affection for the Chinese, to make good land and other facilities available to them so that they could earn a decent living in their new areas. Many became tin workers or were employed on rubber plantations; and the rise in industrial wages caused by the Korean war helped to compensate them for the loss of their illegal farms. So much was in fact done for the Chinese under these resettlement plans that this later led to insistence by the rural Malays that they, who had resisted communist penetration and caused far fewer problems during the insurrection, should be given at least equally generous treatment. Such was the origin of some of the government's impressive later schemes for rural development in the Malay village areas.

The three fundamental objectives to be achieved in isolating the communists from the population have recently been summarized by a former senior official of the Malayan Civil Service[1] who played an important part in carrying them into effect. The first was protection during the phase of initial installation of the new settlers. It required the provision of physical and human defences and certain basic facilities. The inhabitants of the village had themselves to be involved in its defence. But, pending the training of a local home guard, government units and police had to hold the fort with the help of good communications with the larger regional centres. Then the communist network had to be eradicated inside the village. Only rarely could this be completely and permanently effective. The communists always sought to re-establish broken links and their efforts had to be constantly checked. The second objective was more positive. The village people had to be infused with the spirit and organization of a community and develop some interest and participation in vital national issues. The third—more positive still—could only be tackled when the insurrection was in retreat. The new settlements had to be given modern, sophisticated amenities such as schools, markets, medical centres, etc., and regular contact with the outside world. In this way their people could be brought to participating through elections in regional and national political life.

[1] Sir Robert Thompson, *Defeating Communist Insurgency*, pp. 124–7.

In Malaya the programme of resettlement, concentrating on these essential objectives, achieved a significant success. 'Many new villages in Malaya . . . looked barren and depressing when first established, but now . . . are thriving small towns with all modern amenities . . . at the end of the Emergency very few families wished to leave their new homes and return to the old sites.'[1] In Vietnam a similar plan, known as the Strategic Hamlets, was initiated some twelve years later when this same former Malayan official was head of the British Advisory Mission there. It failed chiefly because these objectives were not clearly and consistently pursued. Later still, during Confrontation between Indonesia and Malaysia, a Chinese subversive movement in Sarawak called forth the same kind of measures and their success is still in the balance.

October 1951 brought the first phase of the Emergency to an end. In that month the British High Commissioner, Sir Henry Gurney, was murdered in a communist ambush on his way to one of the hill stations with his wife. The Briggs Plan owed much to his perception and support; and one of his major achievements had been to restore confidence in the British and an atmosphere of relative calm after the bitter controversies surrounding Malayan Union. He had also promoted the dawning realization that in mid-twentieth century Asia there was no future in a war for the preservation of colonial rule. Self-government for Malaya was one more indispensable key to success. Unfortunately he had lacked the autocratic unity of power, and perhaps the ruthlessness which so grim a situation dictated. His death by enemy hand well over three years from the start of the fighting was a further blow to British and Malay morale. Yet in fact the military tide had already begun to turn. There was a shift of emphasis in the communist campaign dictated by the realization that military victory had eluded them. From the later months of 1951 the insurgents seem to have concentrated as much on political work—clandestine subversion and penetration of government organizations—as upon the military struggle. At the same time the British government in London, once more headed by Sir Winston Churchill, realized that a dramatic stiffening of resolution was required.

[1] ibid, p. 125.

It decided to appoint as the new High Commissioner one of Britain's most distinguished soldiers, General Sir Gerald Templer who had recently been Vice-Chief of the Imperial General Staff. He was given effective authority over the whole field of government operations, military as well as civilian. In practice much of his effort had to be concentrated on dealing with the Emergency. The day-to-day administration of the country was largely left to his Deputy, Mr. (afterwards Sir) Donald Mac-Gillivray.

The new High Commissioner pursued with inflexible drive and determination his dual mission of winning the war and preparing Malaya for her freedom, the second an objective to which he attached capital importance. Most of those in Malaya at the time found his vigorous and peremptory prosecution of his task like a fresh breeze. It gave an immediate stimulus to morale. While respecting the co-ordinating functions of the Commissioner-General and seeking his experienced advice, he insisted on his own complete freedom of judgement and action. His dealings with persons were strongly individual. He had a feeling for those of all races who were inconspicuous and ostensibly unimportant which won many hearts. At the same time stupidity and pretentiousness were unwelcome and the timid went in awe. He sometimes judged it right to test people's fibre by a sharp approach, to which he appreciated a courageous response. He often became a hero to such men, if their nerves were strong. Some were readier to take offence and, perhaps through a sense of having been personally ill-used, felt impelled to belittle both the man and the policies he pursued.

One charge concerns his handling of the Chinese. It was strongly made in various writings by a former Protector of Chinese[1] in the Malayan service who had been while in England an unofficial adviser to the Malayan Chinese Association and who returned to visit Malaya during the Emergency. Before his visit he had created some difficulties for the Malayan authorities by voicing his criticisms in the English press. In these circumstances, his reception in Kuala Lumpur was less than sympathetic; and he later elaborated his criticisms in published works.

[1] The late Dr. Victor Purcell. See his *Malaya Communist or Free.*

His complaints were by no means confined to the Templer régime. From the early days of British intervention in Malaya up to the Second World War, special consideration had always been given to the Chinese and their problems (despite Malaya being regarded as essentially the country of the Malays), not least because of their value in the economic field. Later the Secretariat for Chinese Affairs, which had succeeded the former Chinese Protectorate, was deprived of most of its staff and powers. It was felt to be at variance with the goal of creating a common national consciousness, of encouraging all races to think of themselves primarily as Malayans. In fact this emasculation of the Chinese Secretariat was recognized by General Templer and his predecessors to have been a grave mistake. It had deprived the authorities at the time of the detailed insight into Chinese thought and activities which could have enabled them to forestall the disaster.

A further complaint from the same quarter was that the government and many of the British, faced with a Chinese enemy during the Emergency, tended to see an enemy in all Chinese. The suggestion was that the authorities, from the period before the war, had been unwarrantably biased in favour of the Malays; that they had come to regard them as the victims of alien interlopers and the only legitimate inhabitants of the country. Such critics also deplored as unduly harsh and frequently unproductive the collective punishments inflicted on the villages which had been forced to collaborate with the enemy in the course of General Templer's sharp drive to isolate the communists.

While it is true that the General's forceful personality helped to boost European morale, this advantage was more than offset by the effects of his collective punishment on the new Chinese villages, which increased enmity towards the British without effectively denying men or food to the guerillas. The General would arrive at a village with his squadron of eight armoured cars, summon the inhabitants on parade, abuse them for helping the Communists, cut their rice ration, and then rumble off. Directly he had gone the guerillas would come out of the jungle and execute anyone who had had the temerity to obey his orders or in any way attempted to co-operate with him.[1]

[1] Victor Purcell, *Malaysia*, pp. 112 and 113.

Finally it was alleged that 'When the General left Malaya in 1954 there were still as many communists active in the jungle as when he arrived two years earlier and the rebellion still had six years to run'.[1] This last allegation is hardly warranted by the facts as they have become known. By this time the communists were dispersed and had fallen back on the deep jungle. In the following year, as we shall see, they sued for peace.

One obvious justification of the Templer methods and measures in this and other fields is that the course he set was maintained after his departure and achieved in the end virtually complete success. If the defence measures in the villages were adequate, communist reprisals for collaboration with the government failed. If they were not, the unfortunate inhabitants paid the penalty in the first instance. The government forces had then to assert their ability to apply stronger sanctions than the communists and more effective protection. Not only were the New Villages made to work. Supplies were further denied the communists by the complete banning under the severest penalties of the carrying of food in certain areas. Yet other areas where the situation had been brought under control were declared 'White'. Normal life was resumed. Morale rose and strengthened determination to secure a wider enjoyment of free living by doing what the government required. The new strength of the government's campaign and the change of communist strategy due to their military set-backs, coupled with the vast improvement in morale and determination effected by the Templer régime, had transformed the situation by the middle of 1954 when he left.

There was also advance in the political, cultural, and social fields. Some of this stemmed from plans and ideas adopted by his predecessors but prosecuted under Templer with a new vigour. Others owed much to the General's personal initiative, and that of Lady Templer who initiated the co-operation of women of all races in newly-founded institutes and other organizations. Two of his many new departures were the building up of the national museum at Kuala Lumpur and the launching of the Malayan Historical Association. In his treatment of the non-Malays he by no means thought of the Chinese solely in terms of compulsion. One of his main objectives, as of

[1] ibid, p. 113.

his predecessor, was to draw them and the other non-Malays away from expectant neutrality into positive co-operation with the Malays and British in the anti-communist struggle. The banning of parties with subversive associations had left the United Malays National Organization largely in possession of the field. The other races, however, formed organizations of their own. A Malayan Indian Congress, representing the Indian tenth of the population, had existed since 1946. Early in 1949 another counterpart to U.M.N.O. was founded for the Chinese with the approval of Sir Henry Gurney. This was the Malayan Chinese Association. Despite its wide membership, the Association tended to represent the more substantial and conservative commercial and professional Chinese. Most of them were Chinese-educated rather than English-educated, and this difference in background created some divergence of outlook. Yet the founder of this new group was paradoxically one of the sophisticated English-educated Chinese, many of whom also found their home in the Association. This was Tan Cheng Lock (afterwards Sir Cheng Lock Tan) of an old Malacca family, who owed his acceptance by the Chinese-educated to his personal qualities. Like many families from the Straits Settlements his had small knowledge of Chinese and were largely Malayanized in their way of life. This was, however, a valuable factor in their dealings with the Malays. His son, Tan Siew Sin, became U.M.N.O.'s closest Chinese collaborator. Yet the cultural divergence between the leaders and the rank and file has continued to threaten the unity and effectiveness of the Association.

A Malaya torn by suspicion between the different races could not hope to survive as a free nation. It was not enough for the non-Malays to acquiesce in the government's policies and pay something towards their cost. At a moment of national extremity they had to play a full part, exposed to all the dangers of making these policies work. Under Templer there was a strong drive to promote their enlistment in the armed forces and police. This was not simple with the intensely individual Chinese. Despite their toughness and courage as a race many saw small charm in bleak and risky jobs at a fixed salary, less gainful than the humblest forms of commerce. Inducements such as generous family allowances helped to bridge this gap.

A Federation Regiment open to all races was raised, as a counterpart to the Malay Regiment confined to Malays. Again, non-Malays were encouraged to join the Civil Service, though most responsible administrative posts continued to be reserved for British or Malays.

On the eve of self-government any resentments towards the colonial rulers needed special vigilance. In spite of the recent humiliation of the white races, attitudes of European superiority died hard, and the Templer régime was determined to sweep their remnants away. Certain clubs which excluded Asians were sharply forced to open their doors. There was also an insistence that European employers should deal fairly with their Malayan labour. Genuine trade unionism revived, and the High Commissioner was on easy terms with some of the most powerful Union leaders[1] and brought his personal weight to bear where conditions of work were conspicuously bad.

The wisdom of the separation of Singapore was gravely called in question during the Emergency. It would have been far simpler to crush the insurrection had the two territories come again under one control. The communists were particularly active in Johore and had little difficulty in obtaining supplies from Singapore since the government of the island was unable to agree to the closing of the Straits between them. Singapore contributed something to the cost of the Malayan operations. But it was felt in Kuala Lumpur that the Malayan Government's task was rendered unfairly difficult by the insistence of the Singapore Government and business community on maintaining as far as possible normal conditions and the usual free and profitable flow of trade.

Political developments during the Emergency, described in the next chapter, hastened the advent of self-government both in Malaya and in Singapore. The independence of Malaya proved to be the vital element needed for the final overthrow of communist subversion.

[1] Notably P. P. Narayanan, Secretary General of the National Union of Plantation Workers, then a member of the Legislative Council. The surrender early in the Emergency of the pro-communist Secretary of the Tin Workers Union facilitated the trade union revival.

# CHAPTER TEN

# Independence

In 1951 a new leader took charge of U.M.N.O. This was Tunku Abdul Rahman, a prince of the Royal House of Kedah. The brilliant but impatient Dato Onn had resigned when his policies were rejected. These, like Britain's Malayan Union, were fundamentally out of tune with, and perhaps in advance of, Malay thinking. Although Dato Onn had been strongly opposed to Malayan Union the two plans were in fact similar in some respects. Dato Onn also envisaged a united Malaya, a common citizenship and a measure of equality of non-Malays with Malays in the government service and elsewhere. In one way he went further than Malayan Union. Dato Onn had ambitions to become the Malay Deputy to the High Commissioner and resented the Rulers' rejection of this plan. He apparently contemplated at one time not merely a reduction of the Sultan's powers but a possible evolution towards a constitution without separate state governments and with only one monarchy for the whole country. His final break with U.M.N.O. occurred when he proposed that it should have multi-racial membership. He seems to have felt that on this broader basis U.M.N.O. could be a representative body to negotiate for independence. At the same time he counted on the probable reluctance of the Chinese and Indians to join in large numbers, to ensure continued Malay dominance. This was too subtle for the U.M.N.O. rank and file. Dato Onn departed to found a multi-racial party of his own—the Independence of Malaya Party—to implement his programme. Neither this nor his later alternative—the National (Negara) Party—captured the public mind and he went eventually into political eclipse.

His successor, a lawyer, had been Assistant Government Prosecutor. He had little of Onn's intellectual brilliance or eloquence, but a shrewd sense of what the Malays wanted or could be induced to accept. With this, Tunku Abdul Rahman had a warm and tolerant personality and a gentle conciliatoriness towards all except the few who became his enemies, which made him, as time went by, a national leader acceptable to every race in the country. In the following year the Malays agreed to an easing of the conditions in which non-Malays could become citizens.

The transition in Malaya from a colonial-autocratic régime to an autonomous-democratic one came with startling swiftness and achieved remarkable success. It was all accomplished in some six years. An embryo ministerial system was tried out in 1951. The Legislative Council was still not elected. It consisted of officials and nominated members, but some of the latter were made responsible for particular government departments and in this way learned the rudiments of ministerial responsibility. In 1952 elections were introduced for local government which sowed the seeds of inter-racial political co-operation. U.M.N.O. and the M.C.A. supported each others' candidates, chiefly against Onn's Independence of Malaya Party. This worked so well that in 1953 a regular alliance was concluded between the two groups, which was joined in the same year by the Malayan Indian Congress. The Alliance then felt strong enough to set as their goal independence for Malaya within the British Commonwealth. At the beginning of 1954 they sought a genuine parliamentary system beginning with an elected unofficial majority in the Legislative Council. The British Government at first temporized, and Tunku Abdul Rahman was rebuffed when he visited London to present the Alliance case. The consequence was a boycott of public activities by Alliance members and a partial retreat by the British authorities. In July 1955, a year after Sir Donald MacGillivray had succeeded General Templer, the first federal elections were held and the Alliance secured 51 out of the 52 elective seats and an overall majority in the Legislative Council. The parliamentary system was now a reality and Tunku Abdul Rahman became Chief Minister of Malaya. Through striking changes of circumstance he retained his position as head of the government almost continuously for over ten years.

Singapore had meanwhile also elected a Chief Minister and was far on the way to internal self-government. The indifference of her citizens to the post-war constitution led in 1953 to a British Government Commission headed by Sir George

Rendel, a former Ambassador, charged with recommending alternative provisions. A miniature parliament was established —as in Malaya—on the Westminster model. Elections under the Rendel Constitution were also held in 1955. A government was formed by the leader of the Labour Front, which had most seats though no absolute majority. David Marshall, who became Singapore's first Chief Minister, was a fiery lawyer of Middle Eastern antecedents who very properly insisted on the dignity of his office being respected.[1] Some way to the left, and enjoying a measure of communist support through the trade unions, was the People's Action Party with only three seats. This was led by Lee Kuan-Yew, an English-educated Chinese with a brilliant academic record, who was to become Singapore's most outstanding and controversial statesman.

Before pursuing the campaign for independence, the Alliance Government and the new Singapore Government explored the possibility of ending the insurrection. With a worsening military position the communists were seeking peace by negotiation in the hope of switching to a more effective campaign in the political field. At the end of 1955 the Alliance leaders, with David Marshall, met the Secretary-General of the Malayan Communist Party, Ch'in P'eng, under flag of truce at Baling in northern Malaya thus ending the second phase of the Emergency. The communists pitched their demands too high and the talks broke down. Ch'in P'eng tried to insist that the Communist Party should again be legalized and its members allowed to resume political activity whatever they had done in the past. It was on this occasion that Tunku Abdul Rahman showed his gift for national statesmanship transcending political expediency. He rejected the popular and easy course of reaching a compromise with the communists, of which, however, the latter would have taken full advantage later. The government negotiators were only prepared to offer a conditional amnesty for a limited period. Those who rejected communism could go back to normal life. Those who clung to it could return to China or would be detained.

---

[1] He told the writer that after he formed his government he found that the British authorities contemplated no special office for the Chief Minister, a newly created and unfamiliar post. He then camped out under the stairs of the Government offices until this omission was rectified.

The Baling talks did more than end the second phase of the Emergency. At one point before the fighting resumed, the communists, perhaps rashly, foreshadowed the future. 'Ch'in P'eng anxious to represent the M.C.P. as leaders of the battle against colonialism, said that his forces would come out of the jungle and lay down their arms when Malaya became independent.'[1] Specious though this promise was, the adversary himself had shown where the key to future victory lay. From the start of the Emergency, the British who governed Malaya had recognized that independence was the condition of success. But for the sake of future stability they insisted on advancing at what they judged to be a cautious pace. To the more impatient nationalists this caused inevitable exasperation. Yet it was soon clear to London that the Alliance had laid the basis for a sound, multi-racial government after independence. Once Tunku Abdul Rahman's administration had proved capable of functioning effectively, further delay in implementing the transfer of power would have been a denial of sense and justice. The crucial talks were held in London and Malaya in 1956 and a date for independence set in 1957.

The future shape of Malaya as a free nation was considered by a Constitutional Commission with representatives from India and Pakistan as well as from Australia and Canada, one British member and a British Chairman. The new federal constitution was broadly based on their recommendations, with some adjustments by a working party representing the Sultans and the Alliance. Much of it followed the lines of the federal constitution of 1948.

It had, however, one unique feature. There was to be an elected constitutional monarch with a term of office of five years. This system obviated the jealousies which would have arisen if any one of the Sultans had become permanently Head of State. The Conference of Rulers continued and elected their temporary Sovereign. In practice the choice of King or Paramount Ruler (Yang di Pertuan Agong) did not necessarily fall upon the most senior or outstanding Ruler, or the one of greatest importance by virtue of the size or wealth of his state. (By some of these criteria, the Sultan of Pahang, for example, would have had a strong claim to be the first choice.) He would

[1] J. M. Gullick, *Malaya*, p. 106.

normally be one whose qualities were specially suited to the decorous limitations of a constitutional monarchy in which— as in Britain—the monarch had to be guided in his public acts by the decisions of his government, subject to his right to be kept informed, to advise and to warn. This was still a somewhat unfamiliar concept in Malaya, but it was intended that in future (except for some special functions of the Council of Rulers) all Rulers of the individual states should in similar fashion be strictly guided by the decisions of their state governments. The new Constitution also provided for the election of a Deputy King— the Timbalan Yang di Pertuan Agong—who assumed the royal functions in case of absence or illness of the King and, by reason of this, was the probable choice for the supreme position when the succession became vacant.

There was also, under the new constitution, a full-fledged Parliament, not just a Legislative Council with some elected members. Its two Houses were given the American (and Australian) names of Senate and House of Representatives. In contrast to the American Senate, however, the powers of the small Upper House (like those of the House of Lords in Britain) were severely limited. It could veto legislation (other than financial) for no more than a year. It had only thirty-three members, two elected by each of the eleven states and the rest nominated by the King on the advice of the government to represent minority interests. The Lower House had 104 members from single member constituencies. The Prime Minister was to be normally the leader of the majority party and he would choose his Cabinet from other members of that party in the House of Representatives. A similar system was provided for the states, except that some of the old colonial names were retained. Each would have a Chief Minister or Mentri Besar and Executive and Legislative Councils, the former constituting the state government.

In this new federation the responsibility of the states covered land, agriculture, forestry, and local government as well as Muslim law and custom. On the other hand, apart from the main subjects reserved for the federal government certain matters became the concurrent responsibility of the federation and the states, as in the constitution of independent India. Among these were public health and social welfare. Some special rights for Malays were to be maintained. These included the reservation of key posts in the armed forces and the police and a preponderance (of four to one) over the non-Malays in the administrative branch of the Civil Service. The conditions for obtaining citizenship were again improved for the non-Malays. Elections would not be held until 1959 so that they might benefit from these concessions. By reason of the fact that all persons born in Malaya after independence would automatically become citizens, the non-Malays had a genuine prospect of eventual equality.

Independence was proclaimed on 31 August 1957. The Ruler of Negri Sembilan had been chosen as the first King of Malaya and was installed for these Merdeka (Freedom) celebrations. The Prime Minister described them as a beginning rather than an end in Malaya's history.

British forces remained in Malaya under an Anglo-Malayan Defence and Mutual Assistance Agreement. This pledged Britain to help Malaya to expand her armed forces. Australia and New Zealand, associated with the Agreement, were also committed to supply troops to continue the fight against the communist guerillas. Finally they would help to constitute a Commonwealth Strategic Reserve if armed attack threatened Malaya or British Far Eastern territory.

The second provision was of immediate importance. With the insurrection unfinished Malaya was still in peril. In a country which was now its own master Britain and her associates continued to shoulder this expensive commitment as a matter of obligation rather than prestige. The result might have been in doubt had the Malayan forces been unsupported by their friends. If help were needed, these had a clear duty to ensure that the job was finished. At the same time the odds had shortened. This was no longer a 'Colonial' war. The appeal of the communists collapsed once they could not claim to be freeing the country from the rule of the oppressor. More and more of Malaya came under the government's control. On 31 July 1960, the concluding phase of the struggle ended when the Emergency was officially declared to be over.

At this moment, the war against communism in Vietnam was entering its most dangerous phase. It is held by some that the continuance of the Vietnam conflict could have been averted if, when subversion started after the war, the Vietnamese nationalists had been able to count, as had the nationalists in Malaya, on the punctual and constructive withdrawal of French colonial rule. As the war has in fact developed there, Vietnam has remained a focal point for the possible revival of a communist menace in the Malay Peninsula. When the guerillas were eliminated from Malaya some took refuge in the more lightly controlled Thai border areas. Despite liaison between Malay and Thai police (and some facilities for the former to cross the border) a hard core of a few hundred remains a nucleus of danger should there be a sweeping triumph of communism further north. The communists apparently put their faith in the precedent of Japan. After Japanese forces had mastered Indo-China, they were able without difficulty to occupy Thailand and Malaya. The fallacious logic of history seems to the communists to promise an assured victory in these two countries if the whole of Vietnam and her neighbours should succumb to their forces.

Even after the military defeat of the communists, much of the policy of independent Malaya was shaped by her experience of the Emergency. The Malays were determined to forestall a revival of such an outbreak from any quarter. Yet a latent threat of subversion remained in the Federation, especially among the workers and Chinese students. Further afield the government saw with suspicion and concern the prevalence of communist intrigue in Singapore in the trade unions, the Chinese Middle Schools and the new Chinese University.[1] In contrast to Britain's policy, Malaya refused diplomatic recognition to Peking China and all communist countries, lest their missions should become instigators of unrest. For similar reasons, the Kuala Lumpur branch of the Bank of China was closed. As this attitude implied, Malaya was by no means neutral in the conflict between east and west and differed in this from so many newly enfranchized colonial territories. Nevertheless, despite Malay antagonism to the Soviet-Chinese bloc and the continued presence of Commonwealth troops on their soil, there was no question of the Federation following in the wake of British or western policy. The Southeast Asia Treaty Organization had been founded at Manila in 1954, in effect to guaran-

[1] Nanyang University, founded in 1955.

tee Southeast Asia against communist erosion. Malaya as a
Muslim nation had natural affinities with Pakistan, the most
powerful Muslim country in the world, and a founder member
of the Organization. Yet Malaya declined to be associated with
an alliance which was suspect to many of her neighbours by
reason of its predominantly non-Asian composition.[1] Another
reason for Malaya's abstention was, it seems, the realization
that S.E.A.T.O. was ultimately directed against the threat of
China under a communist régime. Yet China was the mother
country of nearly half of the population and Malaya's membership of S.E.A.T.O. might well have aroused strong feelings
among her Chinese citizens. Malaya insisted that the Commonwealth troops in her country must not use Malaya as a base for
any S.E.A.T.O. operations. There was some unreality about
this stipulation since the Malayan Government made it plain
to Britain that she was free to use Singapore (on which most of
the troops were based) for S.E.A.T.O. operations as long as
Singapore was a separate territory.

By 1959 Malaya had become a more genuinely multi-racial
country than ever before. Far more non-Malays than formerly
were in a position to exercise their rights as citizens in the
elections of that year. There were more than five times as many
Chinese with the vote and the Malay proportion of the electorate had dropped from 80 per cent. to 57 per cent.[2] The Alliance
won an easy victory. They secured nearly three quarters of the
seats in the Lower House. Yet their triumph was much less
sweeping than in 1955, and at the same time the distribution
of influence and power between the races, and with it the basis
of the Alliance, had started to change significantly. The Malays
still retained political preponderance. The Chinese remained
dominant in business and finance. But the Malays were beginning to seek the advantage of wealth through wider participation in the economy. The Chinese, on the other hand, sought
to increase their political stake. They wanted a part in the

[1] The member countries of S.E.A.T.O. are: The United States, the United
Kingdom, Australia, New Zealand, France, Pakistan, the Philippines,
Thailand, only the last two being in Southeast Asia. Others who have
adopted a negative or critical attitude are Indonesia, Burma, and Cambodia.
[2] Purcell, *Malaysia*, p. 132.

running of the country in some proportion to their major share in its development. They and the Indians were also determined, by these means, to combat and remove the residual discrimination against the non-Malays. This was to be the general pattern of relations between the races for the years to come.

Before the 1959 elections Tunku Abdul Rahman temporarily resigned as Prime Minister in order to prepare his political followers for the contest. Tun Abdul Razak, the Deputy Prime Minister and Minister for Defence, took office in his place. The Tunku's task was complicated by tension within the Alliance. Some Chinese resigned from it before the 1959 elections and joined the opposition. They resented the limited number of candidates from their community permitted by the Malay leadership to stand for Parliament. Among these was a brilliant and cynical medical practitioner Dr. Lim Chong Eu who later (in 1962) founded the United Democratic Party. This was based on his own area of Penang and he became its sole representative in Parliament. Dr. Lim had been for a short time President of the Malayan Chinese Association in succession to Sir Cheng Lock Tan. The premature publication of a letter in which he threatened the withdrawal of the M.C.A. from the Alliance was deeply resented by the Prime Minister. This temporary breach of inter-racial tolerance within the Alliance was largely healed by Tan Siew-Sin, the son of Sir Cheng Lock Tan. Outstandingly acceptable to the Malays and a loyal adherent of Tunku Abdul Rahman, he took over the Presidency of M.C.A. in 1961 and was still in office five years later.

Thirty of the Representatives elected to the Federal Parliament in 1959 were at odds with the Alliance.[1] The largest opposition group was well to the right. This was the Pan-Malayan Islamic Party. It had a following in the Malay countryside of the less advanced areas and it resented the racially

---

[1] ibid., p. 138

| | | |
|---|---|---|
| Pan-Malayan Islamic Party (P.M.I.P.) | 13 seats | |
| Socialist Front | 8 ,, | |
| Peoples Progressive Party (P.P.P.) | 4 ,, | |
| Party Negara | 1 ,, | (Dato Onn) |
| Malayan Party, Malacca | 1 ,, | |
| (Chinese) Independent | 3 ,, | |

The Alliance secured 73 seats and there was 1 vacancy due to the disqualification of a P.M.I.P. candidate just before the poll.

mixed and economically more advanced west coast. Its chief strength lay in the two most traditionalist states, Kelantan and Trengganu. It had carried both in the preceding state elections, with a sweeping victory in the former and a bare majority in the latter. The P.M.I.P. had been formed under a different name in 1948 and was later joined and inspired by Dr. Burhanuddin, the former leader of the Malay Nationalist Party. It stood for strong Malay nationalism and kept alive irredentist claims, discouraged by the Alliance Government, to the Malay provinces of Southern Thailand. Tunku Abdul Rahman, himself half Thai, had received his early education in Bangkok. He was personally opposed to any such pretensions. The party also favoured links with Indonesia and the upholding of religion. 'The P.M.I.P. used Islam as a political rallying cry. . . . The credulous Malay villager was being told that he risked punishment in the next world, if not in this one, if he voted for the U.M.N.O. candidates who had compromised with the infidel Chinese, etc.'[1] The party sought special priority for Islam and Malay education and the exclusion of non-Malay Ministers from the federal government. It follows that in the P.M.I.P. states there was a general resistance to regimentation from Kuala Lumpur. The record of the party in state government was in the event conspicuously unimpressive and the Alliance recovered Trengganu in 1961.

To the left, the Socialist Front had two main components. These were the Labour Party and the People's Party or Party Ra'ayat. Both were founded before independence and both professed socialism of a more or less respectable kind. They favoured selective controls, state enterprise and equality between classes and nations. At the same time, the Front was widely suspected of some communist penetration on its extreme wing. It had (particularly the Labour Party) much support from Indian and Chinese voters. The Front was strong in Penang, Selangor, and Johore. The programme it put forward appealed to urban and industrial workers and left-wing intellectuals. It was on the whole too extreme for the moderate trade unionists who tended to support the Malayan Indian Congress in view of the large membership and influence of the Indians in the unions.

[1] Gullick, *Malaya*, pp. 138, 139.

Rather paradoxically, the Chairman of the Party Ra'ayat, Ahmad Boestamam (who was also leader for a time of the Socialist Front in Parliament), was a Malay nationalist, but of left-wing views which had little appeal to the normally conservative Malays. The Socialist who emerged as Secretary-General of the Labour Party was from a wealthy family, like certain western socialists. This was Lim Kean Siew, an eccentric and personally attractive young Chinese from Penang with a taste for polo, and, for a time, an American wife. His sister, a gifted lawyer who before independence had campaigned with Tunku Abdul Rahman for the introduction of trial by jury in Malaya, was prominent in the legal defence of the less privileged and as legal adviser to a number of labour unions. Their brother had spent some years in Peking where he had helped to form a communist-sponsored group, the Malayan Democratic Union. The appeals of his family eventually secured permission for him to return to Malaya on condition of abandoning politics completely.

The member of the House who became, after Boestamam, the effective spokesman of this heterogeneous combination in Parliament was a respected Chinese Methodist—also a medical practitioner—Dr. Tan Chee Koon, one of the few members of the left-wing opposition for whom the Tunku[1] had a considerable personal regard. The questions, written and oral, with which Dr. Tan has habitually assailed the government in Parliament seem to be regarded by them as a useful stimulus and indication of the thinking of their more responsible critics and opponents.

Also in the left-wing opposition was the Peoples' Progressive Party or P.P.P. This was largely a local body drawing its support from Perak and based on co-operation between the non-Malay communities. It has been described as 'the party of the Kinta Valley Chinese', this valley being the main area of tin mining in middle Perak. It stood for nationalization of the rubber and tin industries. Both the Socialist Front and the P.P.P. were parties of the town rather than the country. They exploited the economic grievances of the workers and the

[1] The Tunku (equivalent to Prince) is the short designation by which the Prime Minister, Tunku Abdul Rahman, is almost universally known in Malaysia today.

sectional political resentments of the non-Malays. The P.P.P. was started in 1955 by two Ceylonese Tamil brothers, both lawyers, D. R. and S. P. Seenivasagam. The latter became Mayor of Ipoh, capital of the state and its principal business and mining centre. A shy, reserved man in contrast to his more eloquent brother S. P. Seenivasagam made of Ipoh a conspicuously efficient municipality. The main criticism of his Municipal Council seems to have been their refusal to raise the local rates in order not to prejudice their political popularity. In course of time, as we shall see, the central government came to resent these independent municipalities. They appeared as a disturbing focus of political opposition and plans were set on foot to render them more amenable to the views of the prevailing government coalition.

It can be argued that the Westminister parliamentary system[1] bequeathed by Britain to her Asian territories is by no means certain of success in the circumstances of these independent nations. In a number of cases, such as Pakistan and Burma, it has broken down through new and powerful revolutionary forces uprooting the post-independence establishment. In Malaya the system has hitherto survived. Yet this glimpse of the principal opposition elements elected in 1959 reveals a significant departure from the Westminster system: the absence of any serious possibility of an alternative government by parliamentary process. This fundamental feature of the Westminster system is characteristically absent in other former British nations of Asia (though Ceylon has proved somewhat of an exception). In India, for example, as in Malaya, independence was achieved as the result of a massive freedom movement spearheaded by outstanding national leaders. The coalition of forces which won freedom has remained for many years in power. It has appeared to most citizens as the only assurance of safety in a disordered world. The parliamentary opposition in Kuala Lumpur as in New Delhi, has remained fragmentary and disunited and in a state of semi-permanent inferiority.

[1] That is the system whereby, as in Britain, the government is dependent on a parliamentary majority. There is no separation of Legislature and Executive as in the United States, where the government is in certain respects stronger and more stable being independent of parliamentary variations.

We have shown the main steps in Malaya's evolution to independence, her structure of government as a new nation, and some of her initial moves in the international field. We have also sketched some of the features and difficulties of the operation of the new parliamentary system in Malaya and in Singapore. The circumstances and achievements of the two countries in the post-colonial era will require far fuller treatment in the following chapters. So will the dominant personalities in their governments. Externally we shall be faced with the dramatic transformation of Malaya's relations with Singapore, Borneo, and Indonesia. Internally the Malayan Government will be contending with a host of problems: with raising the standards of the rural Malays at a time of sharply expanding population; with the vicissitudes of the economic situation through and after the temporary boom brought about by the Korean war; and with the creation of a national loyalty in all her citizens. One significant feature of this last policy has been the promotion of greater uniformity in the educational system through the partial assimilation of the non-Malay elements. Another, the planned introduction of Malay as the compulsory national language for all races. There has been no simple and permanent solution to the conflicts this has produced.

# CHAPTER ELEVEN

# Malaya and Her Neighbours (1)

The Malayans had inherited from Britain a system of administration which on the whole was practical, just, and effective.
With other developing resources they produced two vital raw
materials—rubber and tin—in constant world demand and of
high value in normal times. In consequence they had achieved
a prosperity and standard of living second in Asia only to that
of Japan. Having sailed with so fair a wind, and being suddenly
freed from colonial rule, they expected immediate and tangible
benefits from their new political power. Instead, there was the
disillusionment of being confronted with a host of uncomfort-
able and recalcitrant problems. Most had hitherto been shoul-
dered by Britain. Now the British were available to a limited
extent and at Malayan request in the judicial, security, defence,
and economic fields.[1] But hard solutions to all the national
problems had now to be sought by their own efforts and decisions taken on their own responsibility.

Fortunately there was a rich diversity of character and
qualities among the top leaders of the new Malaya. The
Cabinet eventually contained four Chinese and two Indians
to ten Malays.[2] In a land of continuing racial tensions, a multi-
racial Cabinet should logically have suffered in unity and
effectiveness. With the Alliance Government this was by no

[1] The principal British officers continuing to serve for a time after independence at the request of the Malayan Government were:

The Chief Justice (afterwards Lord President of the Courts of Malaysia) —
Sir James Thomson
    The Inspector-General of Police—Mr. (afterwards Sir) Claude Fenner
    The Secretary for Defence—Mr. (afterwards Sir) Robert Thompson
    Chief of Armed Forces Staff—General Sir Rodney Moore
Apart from the many British in the private economic sector, a number of
persons from the British Isles continued to serve in a senior capacity in
government corporations such as the Rubber Fund Board (Dr. L. Bateman)
and the Federal Land Development Authority (Mr. J. P. M. Clifford).
[2] The distribution after the 1964 elections.

means the case. It was almost as if the ethnic rivalries stimulated efficiency and achievement. At the same time, the differences of aspiration and outlook in so varied a team commanded constant compromise, at which the Tunku and many of his Malay associates were artists. What the Alliance Government lacked in the way of doctrinaire ideology and rigidly symmetrical planning was fully compensated by its sensible and practical flexibility.

Born in 1903 the Tunku was emphatically Malaya's senior statesman. This was an added asset in Asia where age is still respected and persons start to be rated as elderly at fifty. His Deputy Prime Minister, Tun Abdul Razak, was nineteen years younger. His two other principal lieutenants, Dato Ismail, Minister for Home Affairs and Justice,[1] and Tan Siew Sin, Minister for Finance,[2] were some thirteen years his junior. With great gifts of mind and character, reserved, phlegmatic, and calmly persistent, Tun Razak was in marked contrast to his leader in other matters than age. Yet both were shrewd and pragmatic rather than rhetorical. They lacked the gift and inclination for rabble-rousing speeches. Tun Razak's father was one of the hereditary chieftains of Pahang, of a family of Bugis[3] origin. The ancient Bugis hegemony in the Malay Peninsula may explain his expressed fear of Indonesian domination of his country in modern times. Like many of the sons of the aristocracy and rulers, he studied at the Malay College at Kuala Kangsar in Perak. This had been founded by the British for the key purpose of training a Malay *élite* for public service. Afterwards, like Tunku Abdul Rahman, he had qualified as a lawyer in England and entered the Malayan Civil Service. But in the Service, unlike the Tunku, he had specialized in administration rather than in legal work. In three years his ability had made him State Secretary, or head of the civil service in Pahang. In three years more, in 1955, he was Pahang's Chief Minister.

[1] From 1964. Dato Ismail is the son of the President of the Senate, Dato Abdul Rahman.

[2] From 1959. Tan Siew Sin—see pp. 102, 112—had also eventually succeeded his father, Sir Cheng Lock Tan, as President of the Malayan Chinese Association.

[3] The Bugis from the Celebes in Indonesia, famous as navigators, conquerors, and pirates, dominated much of the Malay Peninsula in the eighteenth century. See pp. 23–5.

Like the Tunku, Tun[1] Razak had been a collaborator of
Dato Onn in U.M.N.O. When the latter resigned in 1951 he
was instrumental in securing the Tunku's election to the Presidency as Onn's successor. He himself became, and has since
remained, the Deputy President of U.M.N.O. His coolness of
manner is felt by many to be less endearing than the Tunku's
generous cordiality. His enemies like to suggest that he is prone
to be anti-Chinese and anti-Indian. Yet he is universally recognized as the Tunku's heir apparent not only by the Malays but
by all the non-Malays who support the Alliance. Malaya thus
embarked on independence with an invaluable factor of stability denied to most post-colonial countries. In Indonesia,
India, Pakistan, Burma, and other lands a disturbing shadow is
cast on the durability of the post-independence system by the
absence of a future leadership automatically acceptable to the
nation as a whole.

Nevertheless Tun Razak's pre-eminence in the line of succession has added a special weight to his tasks and burdens. His
functions have been triple, as Deputy Premier and Minister for
Defence and also, since 1959, Minister for Rural Development.
In the field of defence he has sought to make Malaya self-
reliant and self-sufficient at a time when she has to some extent
been forced to turn to outside help in order to survive. In
building up her forces with Commonwealth training he has had
to contend with the lack of enthusiasm for the military life of
many non-Malays. There were other difficulties even with his
own people. Their long warlike traditions and personal courage
were not always readily translatable into the regimented toughness and tenacity which modern war demands. In view of his

---

[1] The most commonly used Malay titles, in descending order, are:

*Tunku* = (approximately) Prince

*Tun* = (approximately) Lord

*Dato* = (approximately) Sir (as in an English Knighthood). But the distinction is conferred a good deal more frequently and is to that extent less
highly rated.

*Tan Sri* was introduced in 1966 as the equivalent title for Federal Datos,
i.e. those whose distinction was conferred by the Yang di-Pertuan Agong
on the recommendation of the Federal Government, as opposed to those
whose titles were granted by one of the State Rulers. To avoid complication the original and more familiar title for Federal Datos has been retained.

Promotions are not infrequent. Thus Dato Ismail was promoted Tun in
1966.

multiple functions he has needed exceptionally able support from his Secretaries for Defence.[1] He received this from Sir Robert Thompson and his gifted Malay successor, Abdul Kadir bin Shamsuddin, who had organized the Cabinet Office (in effect the Prime Minister's planning staff and Secretariat) immediately before and after independence.

Tun Razak chose to give very personal attention to rural development within the framework of the first Five Year Development Plan (1956–1960). The Plan itself will be considered later in the context of the general economic development of Malaya since independence as will the work of the able Chinese, Dr. Lim Swee Aun, who became Minister for Commerce and Industry in 1962. The rural problem, however, had assumed special importance after the Emergency. Normally the other communities in Malaya tended to be more vocal than the Malays. But the Malay peasants had become restive and articulate at the spectacle of all that was done for the resettled Chinese in their New Villages during the struggle. They claimed modern facilities and comparable solicitude from a government dominated by their own race. They felt that the Malay kampong should be given the opportunity to prosper through development. The first step in this direction had in fact been taken by Sir Henry Gurney with the creation in 1950 of the Rural and Industrial Development Authority. This was to promote the welfare of the Malays through better agriculture, hygiene, and housing; and through local handicrafts and minor industries based on their particular skills and the primary materials they produced. Dato Onn was appointed the first Chairman. Indeed the Authority was created partly to give him a constructive channel for his activities at a difficult moment in his career. This was after he had resigned as Chief Minister of Johore and not long before his resignation from the Presidency of U.M.N.O.

Onn's association with R.I.D.A. meant that it suffered some neglect after his political eclipse. The drive and effectiveness of its work deteriorated and eventually a major part of the programme of rural development was placed in the hands of an

---

[1] Contrary to United States practice, this designation means the official or Civil Service head of a government department as opposed to the political head who is the Minister.

alternative body known as M.A.R.A.[1] which was more specifically linked with the policy and personality of Tun Razak. Land
development as such was later removed from the main work of
rural development and, in view of its key importance, placed
in the hands of a special body, the Federal Land Development
Authority. Here again Tun Razak remained in ultimate command. With the help of a British officer from the Malayan Civil
Service who had been retained as a special adviser on rural
matters[2] the development projects were screened and pushed
forward in the manner of a military campaign, largely inspired
by the Briggs and Templer methods during the Emergency. A
special Operations Room was organized under Tun Razak's
auspices which dramatically revealed in lighted diagrams the
achievements and shortcomings in the execution of the various
plans. This enabled the Deputy Prime Minister, who constantly toured the country, to descend swiftly on those responsible with condemnation or encouragement.

By 1960 the Malays were only a bare half of the population
of their country.[3] Most had remained close to the soil and
indifferent to the kind of gain which could only be secured
through grim exertion. Indeed it has been suggested that there
is a human bond between the British and Malays, both peoples
being by tradition allegedly more concerned with behaving
like gentlemen than with ruthlessly getting on at all costs. In
any event in a solvent and rapidly advancing society many
Malays felt themselves out-distanced by the immigrant races in
the attainment of the good life. Again, in many cases the non-
Malays, who were largely from the towns, were increasing
more rapidly, having better nutrition, hygiene, housing, and
medical facilities within their reach. Yet the Malays regarded

[1] The Malay title is 'Majlis Amanah Ra'ayat Bumiputra', meaning Council
of Trust for the Indigenous People.
[2] Mr. C. G. Ferguson.
[3] The following figures for the Federation of Malaya for 1960 were calculated from official estimates—see Gullick, *Malaya*, Appendix 2:

|  |  |  |
|---|---|---|
| Malays and other Malaysians | 3,510,000 | (50%) |
| Chinese | 2,595,000 | (37%) |
| Indians (incl. Pakistanis) | 786,000 | (11%) |
| Others | 126,000 | (2%) |
| TOTAL: | 7,017,000 | (100%) |

their rights and interests as having first claim in the land which bore their name.

Hence Tun Razak's dedicated efforts to raise the hopes and standards of the rural Malays. There was perhaps too much paternalism about the whole programme, too great a solicitude for those who could have done more to help themselves. Too many projects, such as village halls, new bridges, better access roads, may have been undertaken at considerable expense and without urgent economic need chiefly to demonstrate that it was best to support the Alliance since they had the villagers' welfare constantly at heart. But all this was not just a matter of social and economic justice. To make the Malays less economically vulnerable was a political necessity. It was the implicit condition of their acceptance of the multi-racial basis on which their country was run. This recurring theme in the history of post-colonial Malaya will be treated more fully later.

In another important field Tun Razak has pursued the improvement of standards and efficiency in the Civil Service. He encouraged the formation of special bodies such as an Economic Planning Unit and a Development Administration Unit under the aegis of the Prime Minister to promote the expert preparation and execution of some of the government's more important projects.

Dato Ismail, the Minister for Home Affairs and Justice, was the second key figure in the Prime Minister's team and the next in line of succession. A complete contrast both to the Tunku and his Deputy, he came, like Dato Onn, from Johore and had practised medicine there after studying it in Australia. With a diffident and unassuming manner, he was a man of strong integrity and courage and wide experience of public affairs before and after independence. He had joined U.M.N.O. in the year Tunku Abdul Rahman assumed the leadership, and became its Vice-President. Before the end of 1960 he had been Member, or Minister, for Lands, Mines, Communications, Natural Resources, Commerce and Industry, External Affairs, and Internal Security. He had been Ambassador to the United States and Representative to the United Nations.

As Home Minister he was charged with the fundamental questions of internal order and stability. As Minister for Justice one of his principal tasks was to safeguard the rule of law. This has proved to be in Asia a more basic element of genuine democracy than any parliamentary system. During the Emergency, regulations had been enforced permitting swift security action against subversive elements. Some of these had been retained after the Emergency ended. But Malaya was not transformed into a police state. Somehow the rule of law survived, though it had lost ground or been swept away in many of the new Asian nations. This did not of course prevent opposition critics from alleging that the Malayan Judiciary had become subservient to the Alliance Government. But it was a partial refutation of these charges that the government could be accused of such things with impunity so long as there was no breach of law.

Dato Ismail has also been concerned with the inter-racial situation in the government service. He admits that many Malays resent the privileged position reserved for them in this. Such persons feel it as an implied reflection on their capacity to compete with the other races on equal terms. They reject the fears of their weaker brethren that free competition would inevitably result in a Chinese-dominated state. They argue with much justice that the alleged incapacity of the Malays is largely due to the slow-moving rural background from which most have sprung. The health, and especially the educational facilities provided by the colonial system in the remoter areas were insufficient and their inadequacy impaired vitality and incentive. This reproach is acknowledged by many British officers of the Malayan Civil Service to have some validity, with the reservation that, through ignorance and apathy, there was a very limited demand for such facilities. The people in these small village communities tenaciously set in their ways were in fact reluctant to resort to Western medicine or modern education.

It is nevertheless true that many Malays who have emerged from this rural background and made a success of higher education have proved to be outstandingly able and progressive. Their gifts tend to lie in the political, administrative, and judicial fields rather than in commerce and finance. It is arguable that this Malay *élite* would be increased if the government service were less easily accessible to Malays. At present the prospect of so many reserved posts in the administration seems to tempt many young Malays into pursuing easy options at their University. With the stimulus of free competition there might be less emphasis on obvious choices for them such as Malay studies. There might be more Malays seeking the tough, exacting fields of knowledge which the modern world demands.

We have briefly introduced some of the leading personalities and policies of the Alliance and Opposition in the years immediately following Malaya's independence. This will need later elaboration. Many other men of character and ability played a significant part in the evolution of the country during this vital period and later. The government team in fact continued for nearly a decade with little variation, though with comparatively frequent interchange of portfolios between the different Ministers. This reflected the Tunku's loyalty to his friends and associates of all races, provided that they did not betray his trust or wreck his policies. Even controversial figures could count on his support if their loyalty to him was assured.[1] This meant, however, as the years went by, that the Alliance leaders were accused by those out of power of developing into a kind of monolithic oligarchy. The feeling of such people was that the Alliance would need large doses of fresh blood after the Tunku's departure otherwise it would face the danger of being replaced by a government of more radical complexion.

Another of the key personalities in the Cabinet has been Dato V.T. Sambanthan who became Minister for Public Works, Posts, and Telecommunications from 1959, after earlier periods as Minister for Labour and Health. From a Perak family, he was a rubber planter in one of the worst areas during the Emergency. As a loyal adherent of the Alliance he held that the Malays had treated the non-Malays with fairness and justice. His special value has been that he embodies Indian support for the régime as President of the Malayan Indian Congress. He also is keenly interested in the major challenge of rural development for the Malays. He has made his own contribution to this problem quite independently of the

[1] Senator Tan Tong Hye (T. H. Tan), a Chinese business magnate who acts as Honorary Secretary of the Alliance, is frequently classified as one of the Tunku's less popular associates.

R.I.D.A. and MARA projects. This has been through a co-operative land purchase scheme. Some of the larger estates have been bought up and divided among the participants through a fund to which each gave a small capital sum and a monthly quota.

Enche Senu bin Abdul Rahman has represented an element of Malay nationalism and has been considered by the Chinese and other non-Malays to be unsympathetic to their aspirations. A former school teacher from Kedah, he was at one time Secretary-General of U.M.N.O. After independence he was Malaya's Ambassador to Indonesia and Germany and later became Minister for Information and Broadcasting. His name has often been linked with the strongly nationalist Malay newspaper, *Utusan Melayu*, whose editor, Melan bin Abdulla, was of recent Javanese origin. This publication was usually considered to reflect, or inspire, his views.

Also from Kedah was Mohammed Khir Johari who has been Minister for Commerce and Industry, Agriculture, Health, and Education and later Secretary-General of U.M.N.O. Enche Khir is conspicuous less for intellect than for his gifts of tolerant and easy geniality. These have made him so popular with Malays and non-Malays alike that he is sometimes rated as another possible national leader of the future.

The Tunku, like Tun Razak, has assumed multiple responsibilities. He was Prime Minister and Minister for External Affairs. Later (from 1964) he also took over the Ministry of Culture, Youth, and Sports. This accumulation meant that in a Ministry as exacting and full of pitfalls as that of External Affairs (like Tun Razak at the Ministry of Defence) he needed a Deputy of outstanding ability and strength of character. The Permanent Secretary of the Ministry, Dato Muhammad Ghazali bin Shafie, was a man of this stamp.

Dato Ghazali, like Tun Razak, was from Pahang. He had a wide and varied education in Wales and England in law, economics, and political science.[1] He was also, like numbers of his countrymen, of partly Indonesian descent. Indeed, so active has the intercourse been between the two countries in modern and ancient times that one prominent Malay has esti-

[1] His interests ranged as far as a special study of Welsh law in the tribal period.

mated that no less than a third of the Malays of Malaya are of comparatively recent Indonesian origin. Circumstances after the war accentuated this trend. As Dutch control and participation in Indonesia disappeared, and President Sukarno pursued his revolutionary path, the economic situation there sharply deteriorated. That of Malaya remained buoyant. Immigration to the Peninsula from across the Java Sea and the Straits of Malacca increased. Over the generations a mental vigour and vivacity in the Indonesian tradition came to the fore in the many leading Malays of Indonesian background. Through his family, Dato Ghazali had preserved links with Sumatra and other parts of the Archipelago. He acquired in this way a penetrating knowledge of Indonesia and her peoples which was to be invaluable in the years to come. As the executor of the Tunku's policies in the external field he was to be particularly concerned with Malaya's relations with her island neighbours, the Philippines and Indonesia, and Kuala Lumpur's response to the often startling initiatives of President Sukarno.

In the early 1960s Malaya faced a crisis in her relations with her neighbours. This may have been due in part to Sukarno's sincerely held beliefs; more obviously it reflected his keen sense of national and personal dramatization. After the establishment of the Indonesian Republic in 1945, this remarkable man remained at the helm for over twenty years. In that time he weathered storms and changes which might have submerged any less forceful personality. His survival was chiefly due to his being the embodiment of the new image of his country. The creation of Indonesia as a nation had been largely his work. At the same time he displayed a genius for dramatization and sensational slogans. He made a personal crusade out of condemning the evils of colonialism and extolling the virtues of the new emerging forces. In 1955 he sponsored an Afro-Asian Conference in Indonesia which became a sounding board for such denunciations, though representatives from certain recently independent British territories struck a more objective note. Malaya was not represented being still a colonial dependency. After establishing her freedom she remained unimpressed by the Afro-Asian *mystique*. Eventually even the United States which gave generous support to Indonesia became suspect in

Djakarta of 'imperialism'. In a posture of nominal neutrality between East and West, Indonesia under President Sukarno's guidance began to lean heavily on aid from the communist countries.

The President's defiance of the established order excited the imagination of many. Others were appalled at his reckless indifference to sound economic and administrative sense. His revolutionary fervour is regarded by one distinguished Indonesian thinker[1] as typical of a Jacobin strain found in certain of his countrymen particularly from Java. An opposite strain, essentially constructive, is found in others, chiefly from the Outer Islands. Characteristic of the 'constructivists' have been three Sumatrans: Mohammad Hatta, Sutan Sjahrir, and General A. H. Nasution. These men were destined to play a notable if partly unsuccessful role in Indonesia's recent history. Without some reference to this it is impossible to clarify the post-war issues between Indonesia and Malaya.

The Indonesian Republic headed by Sukarno had been established at the end of the war with Japanese encouragement. When the Netherlands authorities were persuaded by the British to open talks with the nationalists they were prepared to negotiate with Sjahrir, leader of the Socialist Party who became the first Prime Minister of the Republic, and with Hatta of the Muslim Masjumi, who had been a member of the Netherlands Parliament, the States-General, and later also headed the Republican Government. They were not prepared to deal with Sukarno in view of his association with the enemy. The Dutch had returned to a position of some strength. They had reoccupied the Outer Islands and parts of Java and Sumatra. In some of the Outer Islands, notably the Celebes, they adopted a punitive policy of remarkable harshness which rendered harder a permanent reconciliation with their former subjects. Two agreements reached between the Indonesians and the Dutch in 1946 and 1948 broke down and were followed by Dutch military actions which finally led to their occupation of

---

[1] Soedjatmoko, head of the Pembangunan Publishing House, Djakarta, himself a Javanese and brother-in-law of Sjahrir through the latter's second marriage. Sjahrir's first wife had been Dutch. Author of *An Approach to Indonesian History: Towards an Open Future*. Editor of *An Introduction to Indonesian Historiography*.

all the chief centres of Java and the capture of Sukarno and Hatta.

At this point, in December 1948, it seemed that the former rulers of Indonesia had virtually succeeded in resuming by force their pre-war position and authority. But the clock could in fact no longer be put back. On the one hand, the Dutch were faced with strong guerilla action from the Indonesian nationalists. On the other, the issue was brought before the United Nations Security Council at the request of Australia and the United States. The latter, traditionally anti-colonial, had since the war been specially preoccupied with the communist menace to the western world. They applauded the efforts of a former colony struggling to be free. It seemed to reflect the lessons of their own history. They had also been impressed by the way the Republic had crushed a communist revolt in Java a few months earlier.

Faced with international disapproval of their efforts to re-establish their position by force, the Dutch consented, after a conference at The Hague in 1949, to grant sovereign independence to the Republic of the United States of Indonesia. They had stood out for a federal form of government hoping to preserve their political influence in the Outer Islands and those parts of Java and Sumatra not under direct nationalist control. More importantly, they counted on being able to retain their rich economic and financial stake in the country as a whole. One intractable question was shelved which contributed to the eventual destruction of many of these hopes. This was the future of Netherlands New Guinea. This vast area was claimed by the nationalists as having been part of the former colonial territory, although in fact it had nothing in common with Indonesia. The Netherlands insisted on leaving the problem over for later negotiation in order to ensure the passage through the States-General of what was in fact a major policy retreat.

The hopes which the Dutch had built on the operation of the federal form of government were swiftly wrecked by President Sukarno. In spite of the largely ceremonial role allotted to him under the new Provisional Constitution he retained vast influence and an obsessive ambition for power. 'Within a little over seven months the R.U.S.I. structure had been negotiated out of existence and replaced by the unitary Republic of Indonesia.'[1] Thus the whole country was placed largely under Javanese control. By the end of 1956 resentment over this and other measures had started a process of disintegration which later culminated in a military rebellion. Autonomous régimes were established in parts of Sumatra, Celebes, and elsewhere. To check this crumbling and reassert his leadership President Sukarno sought to substitute for the comparatively liberal régime of the early fifties a more personal form of rule known as 'Guided Democracy'. When this was rejected by the Assembly in 1959 he implemented his scheme by an act of power. The Assembly was dissolved and the authoritarian Constitution of 1945 was re-established. Executive power was thus concentrated once again in the President's hands. Parliament was streamlined to suit his purposes.

Under 'Guided Democracy', members of the Indonesian Communist Party (the P.K.I.) were incorporated in the government alongside representatives of Muslim groups (in particular of the Muslim Teachers, the Nahdatul Ulama), and the Indonesian Nationalist Party (the P.N.I.) which had all along been one of Sukarno's main supports. The military rebellion was crushed and the Armed Forces brought uneasily into line. The parties of his chief rivals for influence and respect among the Indonesians—the Socialist Party of Sjahrir and the moderate Muslim party, the Masjumi, of Hatta (elements of which had been compromised in the rebellion)—were banned. For years the President retained his dominant position by manipulating with disturbing skill the discordant elements inside and outside his Cabinet. The largely anti-Communist Armed Forces (which did, however, contain some communist elements) were counterbalanced by the increasing strength of the P.K.I.

Late in 1957, to distract his countrymen from their dissensions and the economic consequences of erratic government, President Sukarno inspired a campaign of confiscation and expulsion against the Dutch. The pretext was the failure of the Netherlands to negotiate the surrender of West Irian (as the Indonesians called New Guinea). Nearly all Dutch enterprises were nationalized. The Indonesian debt to the Netherlands was

[1] *Governments and Politics of Southeast Asia*, Ed. G. M. Kahin, Cornell, 1964 ('Indonesia' by Herbert Feith), p. 204.

repudiated and diplomatic relations broken off. With the departure of the Dutch, the economy took a new downward plunge. This was only partly checked by the temporary substitution of British for Dutch commercial representation in certain fields.[1] In 1962, however, West Irian ceased to be an issue. After armed encounters with Indonesian forces in the area the Dutch decided to abandon their costly stake. West New Guinea was transferred to the United Nations and later to Indonesia. The solution of this problem made it almost inevitable that President Sukarno would continue to pursue what had become for him almost a substitute for rational policy. Some fresh issue was likely to be invoked to stir the revolutionary fervour of his people and take their minds off present troubles—some new grievance against the outside world.

[1] This occurred with Shell and Unilever, amongst others. Both these firms had British as well as Dutch participation.

# CHAPTER TWELVE

# Malaya and her Neighbours (2)

The ties of race between Malaya and Indonesia might have promoted sympathy and understanding between their peoples. One obstacle, however, was an Indonesian sense of superiority particularly marked among the Javanese. One of the highest ancient civilizations of Southeast Asia had been due to their subtle intelligence and artistic ingenuity.[1] So marked were these qualities that even so sturdy a British imperialist as Raffles had suggested that the Javanese might be destined to be the dominant race in the region. In any event, with President Sukarno in charge of Indonesia's destinies, the prospects of easy and constructive relations with Malaya were remote. He had visited Malaya in the later stages of the Japanese occupation and expressed at that period a disquieting concept of Greater Indonesia.[2] This was inspired by the imperial role of past Indonesian rulers who had extended their dominions to the Peninsula. It came strangely from a man who was the proclaimed foe of all imperialism.

More recently, as if to ignore Malaya's equal and sovereign status in international law, he had refused all invitations from the King and government of this new nation to pay them an official visit. In the period of the Indonesian military revolt immediately following Malaya's independence, he was gravely suspicious of his neighbour's ostensible neutrality, not entirely

[1] Javanese cultural influence extended to the Southeast Asian mainland. 'During the course of the ninth century Javanese cultural patterns made a substantial contribution to both Cambodia and Champa.' John F. Cady, *Southeast Asia: Its Historical Development*, p. 75.

[2] 'I still say, despite the danger of my being accused as an imperialist, that Indonesia will not become strong and secure until the whole Straits of Malacca is in our hands. If only the West coast of the Straits of Malacca [is ours] it will mean a threat to our security', Mohammed Yamin, *Naskah Persiapan*, Vol. 1, p. 206. This and other portions were translated by the Malaysian Ministry of External Affairs in 1964 under the title, 'Background to Indonesia's Policy towards Malaysia'.

without grounds since some Indonesian rebels had received occasional supplies from and eventually found refuge in Malaya. There had in any case always been a special kinship of race and feeling between the Sumatrans, resentful of the high-handed Javanese, and the Malays of the Peninsula. Djakarta was often haunted by the spectre of Malaya's possible ambitions to detach and absorb Sumatra. Although a treaty of friendship was concluded between the two countries in 1959 it did little to put their relations on a warmer or closer footing. Virtually all that was achieved was the removal of some differences between the two forms of Malay used in Indonesia and Malaya.[1]

With her formidable neighbour[2] under such leadership, Malaya could feel little confidence in Djakarta's future intentions. In spite of the Defence Agreement with Britain, she could of course no longer rely permanently and automatically on Commonwealth protection. Yet the mere existence of such an agreement, Malaya's cordial relations with her former rulers, the retention of British co-operation in certain fields, all gave Indonesia's President a pretext for asserting that Malaya was still in voluntary bondage to the imperial system. She was accused of being a 'neo-colonial' state.

In spite of her faltering post-war economy, the Indonesia of President Sukarno aspired to the status of a major power. She had a population larger than Japan's and some pretension to exercise hegemony over Southeast Asia. Leadership of a world movement or regional grouping was her natural climate. Hence her sponsorship of Afro-Asian solidarity and resentment of Malaya's coolness towards this largely artificial concept.[3] She

[1] Many of these were merely differences in the spelling of words in romanized script resulting from the diverse rendering of particular sounds in Dutch and English respectively, e.g. Djalan = Street (Indonesia) = Jalan (Malaya).

[2] In 1962 Malaya had a population of 7,375,731. That of Indonesia was (in round figures) 100 million, i.e. more than fourteen times as large. After the formation of Malaysia, Indonesia still had ten times the population of her neighbour.

[3] It can be argued that the principal, if not the only real bond between the new nations of Africa and Asia is that they were subjected to European colonization. It is hard to discover any genuine community of ideals or traditions between the ancient, developed civilizations of Asia and the far simpler conditions which remained general in African communities until recent times. For many Africans, the Asian has appeared traditionally in the unwelcome image of the Arab slave-trader or the Indian shopkeeper.

had small enthusiasm for the initiatives of others. This was perhaps predictable in the case of the Southeast Asia Treaty Organization, which she rejected for the same reasons as Malaya.[1] There was less justice in her refusal to join the Association of Southeast Asia, a purely regional, Asian grouping launched by the Philippines, Malaya, and Thailand in 1961.

A.S.A had been established after the state visit to Malaya of President Garcia of the Philippines. There were significant divergencies in international policy between the three countries concerned. Unlike Malaya, Thailand and the Philippines were members of S.E.A.T.O. and closely aligned with the United States. It was thus not practicable to give the association a political content. It concentrated therefore on cultural and economic co-operation. It was hoped to evolve closer economic ties, together with better communications, travel facilities, etc. Unfortunately, the economic structure and needs of the three countries were so similar that there was a limit to what could be achieved. Their economies were not complementary. All were producers of raw materials for export and importers of manufactured goods from outside the area. All of them needed more capital and greater industrialization. Yet it was hard in underdeveloped and economically unsophisticated countries to achieve a regional specialization of industry. The chances of organizing some kind of common market were even more remote.

A.S.A. was not the only important regional occurrence in 1961. Two months earlier, in May, the Malayan Prime Minister made a speech in Singapore to the Foreign Correspondents' Association of Southeast Asia. In one passage of this he hinted at a change of course which was profoundly to affect his country and her neighbours. His remarks were disarmingly casual. He said:

sooner or later Malaya should have an understanding with Britain and the peoples of Singapore, North Borneo, Brunei and Sarawak. It is premature for me to say now how this closer understanding can be brought about, but it is inevitable that we should look ahead to this objective and think of a plan whereby these territories can be brought closer together in political and economic co-operation.

[1] See p. 111.

What prompted this ampler vision of the future? Singapore had been the pre-war capital of British Malaya. The Kuala Lumpur Government had favoured its post-war exclusion in order that the Chinese should not outnumber the Malays in the country as a whole. Afterwards came the bitterness and suspicion engendered by the Chinese-Communist insurrection. This had only ended the previous year. Yet the Prime Minister of Malaya was now positively seeking closer association with Singapore. More remarkable still, he was presuming to assert the need for such association with the territories of northern Borneo which were still under Britain's direct rule or protection.

The genesis of these new departures must be sought in the first instance in the territories concerned. The course of events in Singapore is particularly important and in the words of a contemporary American scholar long resident in the area, 'the most persuasive development of all' in view of the serious challenge to the P.A.P. by its extremist faction.[1] It also inevitably derived from the rapid post-war evolution of Britain's colonial policies. In the twenty years following the end of the Second World War her concept of her future role in the world radically changed. This was partly due to her diminished economic and military strength by comparison with the rise of vaster and more populous powers. It was also a voluntary and timely recognition of the new climate in Asia and Africa. On the whole Britain's recognition of the changed state of the under-developed world was prompter than that of the other European colonizers. Her policy was based on the new realization that all territories had a claim to freedom which could be viable independently of European rule. Thus, in 1957, a few months before Malaya's independence, Ghana, the former British Gold Coast, became the first European colony in Africa to attain the status of a free nation. London consequently was faced with the dilemma: how could the lengthy continuance of European rule in the northern Borneo territories be justified? What alternative possibilities would provide fairly and justly for the future of these lands, which needed continued guidance

[1] 'Unless the P.A.P. government could now make good on its primary policy objective—that of achieving merger with the Federation—it seemed certain to collapse and Singapore seemed as certain to turn violent, communist, or both at once.' Willard Hanna, *The Formation of Malaysia*, p. 8.

since they were far more backward than most of the rest of Southeast Asia?

In Singapore during 1955 it became clear that David Marshall was determined to assert his rights and those of his electors in other matters than office accommodation. He was soon insisting that Singapore should become its own master. As a first step he secured the agreement of the Colonial Office to an amendment in the Constitution compelling the Governor to accept the Chief Minister's advice.[1] In 1956 he was invited to a Conference in London to discuss self-government. The talks broke down on the connected issues of foreign defence and internal security. There had been strikes and riots, and the risk of communist subversion was a real one. Some doubt was cast on the capacity of the Marshall government to cope with these dangers. During the talks Marshall refused to accept Britain's stipulation that she should retain in case of emergency the final word in a proposed defence and security council. There was some unreality about the whole argument, since much of the economy of the island depended on the bases of the Commonwealth Armed Forces. These employed a quarter of Singapore's labour. There was thus no desire on the part of the Singapore Government that they should be removed. On the other hand, Britain, Australia, and New Zealand were comprehensibly reluctant to leave decisions about even the local employment of their forces in the hands of an inexperienced and emotional nationalist régime.

Marshall resigned and was succeeded by Lim Yew Hock, a locally educated Chinese who had been prominent in the moderate labour Unions. He had made a special study of the British and American trade union system. Lim had been Minister for Labour and Welfare under Marshall and later became President of their party, the Labour Front. The new Chief Minister demonstrated his government's ability to deal with subversion. People judged dangerous were arrested.

[1] As we have seen, under the British constitutional system, unlike the American system, the head of state and head of government are separate. As self-government is attained by a former colony, the role of the former becomes essentially ceremonial. This stage is reached when a head of government takes office backed by an elected parliamentary majority.

Bodies susceptible to communist infiltration were suppressed, including the Middle School Students' Union. Other unions and students caused disturbances and forces were brought in from Malaya to deal with these. In 1957 a further constitutional conference in London was successful. Internal self-government was to be granted to the 'State of Singapore', in 1959 when the Rendel Constitution was due to terminate. The island was to have a Malayan as Head of State;[1] and a fully elected and enlarged Legislative Assembly with a membership of fifty-one. The earlier difference over security and defence was solved by the terms of reference of an internal security council. The senior British representative in Singapore would be its Chairman. Under the new arrangements this was to be the Commissioner for the United Kingdom, most of whose functions were essentially diplomatic.[2] The council was to have three British members in all, with three from Singapore and one from Malaya who would have a casting vote in the event of a Singapore-British deadlock. It was provided that Britain should remain generally responsible for defence and foreign policy. Elections to the Legislative Assembly of the new state were held at the end of May, 1959. The constitution was put into operation a few days later. Before this, Britain had caused some resentment among the radicals by her insistence that persons of known subversive activity should not be eligible for election. These included arrested members of the left wing of the Peoples Action Party. The P.A.P. claimed to be non-communist. But like all groups of a revolutionary complexion it was anti-establishment and therefore at that stage anti-British. The

[1] With the Malay title of Yang di-Pertuan Negara. The last British Governor functioned in this capacity for several months. The post was then filled by Tun Yusof bin Ishak the founder of Utusan Melayu (see p. 125) and a former President of the Press Club of Malaya. A Malay nationalist, he had the reputation of being anti-British.

[2] Apart from his functions on the security council and certain special powers for dealing with an emergency, the role of this representative was that of Britain's Ambassador to the new state. In practice, for many years the same person fulfilled this task as well as the policy-co-ordinating duties of the Commissioner-General for the United Kingdom in Southeast Asia (see p. 91, footnote). The first occupant of this dual post was thus the Commissioner-General at the time. This was Sir Robert Scott of the British Diplomatic Service. He was succeeded at the beginning of 1960 by the Earl of Selkirk.

Treasurer of the party, Ong Eng-Guan, had become Mayor of Singapore. He had then insisted on the removal of the British flag from the City Council chamber and stopped the use of the civic regalia inherited from colonial days.

In spite of their members in prison—and possibly stimulated by the repressive attitude of the authorities—the P.A.P. scored a huge success in the elections. They won 43 out of the 51 seats in the legislature. Before they would take office, however, they insisted on the release from prison of eight of their former associates. Having secured this, Lee Kuan Yew became the first Prime Minister of Singapore. Under his leadership, the government declared it to be their objective to 'bring about . . . an early re-unification with the Federation'. This would of course imply the complete independence of Singapore from Britain. A favourable moment for this fresh change of status might be when the 1959 constitution came up for reconsideration in 1963. Meanwhile the P.A.P. favoured the adoption of Malay (which Lee spoke with considerable fluency) as an official language.

Henceforward, the P.A.P. were the dominant party in the political life of Singapore. But both before and after their triumph there was a grave fear that the extremists might take the party over. It soon became clear that these men were pro-communist in their loyalties and that if they did this Singapore would become a communist state. The struggle between them and the right wing eventually split the party. There had at one time been a fear that Lee Kuan Yew himself was a dangerous firebrand. Once in office, however, he emerged as the leader of the moderates. A man less skilled in political manoeuvre than he might well have foundered under the pressures to which he was exposed. A statement in August 1960, when his position was threatened by communist intrigue, is a measure of his somewhat devious ingenuity. He said that a clash was inevitable between the 'adventurers of the Left' and the 'colonialist imperialists'. The P.A.P. policy was to let them tear each other to pieces.

A year later, in June 1961, the militant left wing of the P.A.P. under Lim Chin Siong broke away to form their own group, the Barisan Sosialis, which campaigned for the overthrow of the government they had previously supported. By

mid-1962 the situation was even worse. There were disturbances on the labour front. The Prime Minister and the moderates
who remained in the P.A.P. seemed to be losing ground to the
communists in the trade unions. As a result of defections and
losses in by-elections, the P.A.P. no longer had an absolute
majority in the Assembly. Fortunately, they could count on
some support from other moderate groups such as the Singapore People's Alliance, latterly organized by Lim Yew Hock,
and the Singapore supporters of the U.M.N.O.–M.C.A.
Alliance. These abstained from voting on a vital motion of
confidence which could have brought the government down.

Education was another crucial problem. Like the leaders of
the Malayan Chinese Association, Prime Minister Lee was
English educated. With an outstanding Cambridge degree, he
had a fund of knowledge and swiftness of intelligence which few
Englishmen could match. He successfully set himself to learn
Chinese fluently. This was an accomplishment which Tan Siew
Sin, President of the M.C.A., never managed to attain. It was
not the only divergence between the two men. Others were to
become more acute as time went by.

Lee Kuan Yew also sent his children to Chinese schools. To
survive politically, he had to win the support of the Chinese-
educated majority, their student children, and the teachers of
those children. Such students and teachers continually agitated
for the maintenance and extension of teaching in Chinese. It
seemed to the teachers that their livelihood was at stake. They
also sought more money from the government for the, mostly
private, Chinese schools. Meanwhile, communist China encouraged them to believe that she was the sole upholder of
Chinese culture. The bourgeois lackeys of imperialism were
betraying Chinese culture. This was one of the communists'
gentler phrases for the Overseas Chinese who opposed them,
like those in the Lee government. Peking made their own textbooks readily available and these were widely used. The communists also assisted, and were assisted by, a long-established
trend which had spread northern (Mandarin) Chinese as a
*lingua franca* among all Chinese language groups.[1] This had

[1] Most of the Singapore Chinese, like those in Malaya, were from South
China. While all Chinese share a common written language which has
been the principal vehicle for the preservation of Chinese culture, the

been effectively initiated by their predecessors and adversaries the nationalist (Kuomintang) régime. These textbooks gave of course a strongly loaded version of events calculated to imbue the students with the communist interpretation of history and politics. Nanyang University, founded by a group of rich Chinese capitalists, was rather paradoxically another major source of left-wing trouble. Chinese was widely used there as a medium of instruction as well as English. The student body became a base for communist subversive agitation.

Thus in the early 1960s there was a grave risk of Singapore falling under communist control. That the risk was averted was largely due to the political skill and resourcefulness of Lee Kuan Yew. He had admittedly the support when needed of the British and Malayan authorities backed by the resources of the Commonwealth bases. This made it easier to deal with his more dangerous opponents. He could also argue that the only path for Singapore to follow was his own. Otherwise it would succumb to communism or revert to outright British control. Nevertheless, to have won this struggle without a military campaign or any substantial deployment of armed force was a major feat, given the sinister effectiveness of communist operation. Unfortunately, his knack of arousing antipathy lost him much of the credit he deserved.

In order to defeat such enemies, he had to employ a ruthlessness hardly inferior to their own. He was accused of harshness and arrogance, of resorting to individual intimidation and of a readiness to sacrifice his allies when they had served their purpose. Singapore preserved the forms of parliamentary life, though a stage was reached when the Legislative Assembly was boycotted by the extreme left. The stimulating flow of life of a bustling and prosperous business community continued. Yet much was in fact autocratic about the Lee Kuan Yew régime. The more subversive trade unions were brought forcefully to heel. Nanyang University was subjected to ultimate

---

spoken versions of Chinese in the different regions (e.g. Cantonese, Hakka, Fukienese, Hainanese, etc. in the South) are so different as to be virtually separate languages and a serious barrier to mutual understanding. These differences of spoken language were preserved by the emigrants when they settled overseas. The communists had installed their capital at Peking where Mandarin had been the language of successive Imperial dynasties.

government control and the student body purged of the worst trouble makers. Many leading members or supporters of the Barisan Sosialis were eventually arrested or re-arrested on the decision of the security council, although the Prime Minister renounced responsibility. These included some, like Lim Chin Siong, on whose release the Prime Minister had insisted when he first took office.

On the more positive side, this was a régime of sternly paternalistic socialism. An English socialist journalist, Alex Josey, became one of the Prime Minister's right-hand men in the publicity and other fields. Corruption in the public service was virtually stamped out. The better-off were severely taxed—far more severely than in Hong Kong.[1] The poorer classes benefited by a far-reaching system of social welfare. Better health, housing, and education facilities took the edge off those hardships which had sharpened the appeal of communism. Much of the discontent over Chinese education was eliminated by the organization of multi-lingual government schools in which cheap education could be had at the choice of the parents in Chinese, Malay, English, or all three. Similar provision was made for the Indian Tamils. In the case of the Chinese, these new facilities induced many parents to transfer their children from the more expensive private Chinese schools to the government schools. The latter provided new fields of activity for the Chinese teachers who had feared for their livelihood. At the same time, education in English and Malay and contact with other groups of society lessened the cultural isolation and narrowness of outlook of Chinese students who knew only their own language. It also increased their chances of profitable employment, a powerful attraction for all Chinese.

Yet in the final analysis neither the Prime Minister's skill nor the backing of the local security council could by themselves have secured the position in Singapore. The decisive factor was that it proved possible to implement his first declared objective, namely to re-unify the island with Malaya. The union proved

[1] Singapore endeavoured to counter-balance the attraction for business men and industrialists of the lower taxation in Hong Kong by providing such people with first-class facilities for investment and installation. Singapore had the advantages of ampler and more accessible space, less over-crowding and easier communications.

brief. Two years later, separation recurred. Yet the establishment and maintenance of this union during the crucial period gave Singapore a stability which later dissensions could no longer destroy.

We have seen why, after the war, Britain and the Malay leaders favoured breaking the old association between Malaya and predominantly Chinese Singapore. With eventual independence in the offing, the Chinese with a clear majority might soon have dominated the whole country. The Malays would have faced the spectre of becoming second-class citizens in their own land. But a problem of almost equal gravity soon reared its head. Before the war, Britain controlled both territories from Singapore. With separation and the progressive withdrawal of the British, the Malays awoke to the fact that, except for the slender link of the security council, the evolution of Singapore was no longer subject to control. As they now realized, through some well planned coup and faulty vigilance on the part of the authorities the island could fall into the grip of communists or political adventurers overnight. This realization became acute in the first years of the P.A.P. government. The communist danger in Malaya had subsided with the official ending of the Emergency in 1960. Just at this juncture Singapore threatened to become a fresh focus and base of operations for communist subversion.

Such was the background to what seemed to many a sudden and unpredictable change of course on the part of the Malay leaders. Yet these had by no means lost sight of the fact that the inclusion of Singapore would mean increasing the numbers and weight of influence of the Chinese in their country. '. . . the franchise in Singapore was universal for all adults, male and female, and the addition of some half a million fully enfranchised Chinese voters to the rolls might mean that the Malays would be outvoted at the elections—especially if there were any considerable Chinese immigration from Singapore.'[1] Thus the government in Kuala Lumpur could not envisage association with Singapore in isolation. It could not possibly contemplate—nor would the Malay people ever accept—a step which would give the Chinese an automatic majority in the

[1] Purcell, *Malaysia*, p. 185.

new federation. Such a change could be made only if the new Chinese element were counterbalanced by widening the scope of the new state still further and including territories which had a population chiefly of Malay or related race.

It was natural for the thoughts of the Malay leaders to turn in the direction of Britain's Borneo dependencies. Many of the conditions there were similar to those in the more primitive, eastern, parts of Malaya. They were on the trade route to China and the sea had long been a link between them and the Peninsula, with some mutual assimilation of population, customs, and ideas. On the other hand, they were largely sealed off by high and difficult mountains from the rest of Borneo. Their development, such as it was, had lain mostly seawards along the banks of the rivers. They had also shared with Malaya the same currency and the same British administrative tradition. There had been frequent interchanges of official staff.[1] More importantly, it was a region in which the Malays, and those local groups which had become Muslim and therefore counted as Malay,[2] had for centuries played a major part. The predominantly Malay Sultanate of Brunei had ruled, however nominally, large parts of the area before the arrival of the Brookes or the forerunners of the Chartered Company. Other parts had been controlled by the Sultanate of Sulu and penetrated by surrounding Muslim races or converts to Islam—Suluks, Illanuns, Bajaus, etc. and Indonesians from Central and Southern Kalimantan or other parts of the Archipelago. Apart from all these considerations, Tunku Abdul Rahman was of course aware of Britain's desire to adapt these dependencies to the new climate of Asia by providing for

[1] Thus Hugh Low was appointed Resident in Perak after being Magistrate in Labuan. For a vivid if highly coloured story, based on an actual event, reflecting something of the life of the British official in Borneo, see Somerset Maugham's 'The Outstation'.

[2] As we have seen, to be a Malay is not legally a question of race but of religion and social custom. A person of virtually any indigenous ethnic origin who embraces Islam and conforms to Malay custom can claim to be a Malay. He has *masok melayu*—entered (the) Malay (fold). Yet prejudice was liable to persist between the ethnic Malays and those of other origin who had entered the Malay community, particularly when, as in Borneo, the 'true Malays' of Brunei had dominated the less developed races. On the other hand, a person of Malay race who, for example, is brought up a Christian or converted to Christianity, ceases to be regarded as a Malay.

their future on some secure basis, involving neither premature independence nor the indefinite continuance of European colonial domination. One plan had contemplated an association confined to the three Borneo territories. These might then have evolved towards independence as one separate unit on their own. The danger here was the weakness of so restricted a combination. It would be that much more vulnerable than the larger federation now proposed by Malaya, and even more exposed to the appetites of an expansionist Indonesia. This and other aspects of the Borneo territories under and after colonial rule will be left for the next chapter.

Meanwhile, considerable progress was made with the new plan in 1961. In September there was a conference between the Prime Ministers of Singapore and Malaya in Kuala Lumpur. This was only four months after the nebulous hints conveyed in the Tunku's speech to the press. Much of importance was agreed and a working party set up to deal with details. The obvious point was settled that Singapore would have to have greater autonomy than the Malay states, especially in such matters as finance, labour, and education. The Malayan Government had small difficulty in gaining parliamentary approval for the initial stage of their plans. The Singapore Government faced a much harder and longer task of persuasion. In November, in London, the Tunku sought and received the agreement in principle of the British Government to the accession of the Borneo territories to the new federation. But it would be necessary first to consult the wishes of their people and be sure of their agreement.

# CHAPTER THIRTEEN

# Malaysia in the Balance

After the London talks on Malaysia in November 1961 a joint statement was issued by the Malayan and British authorities. This welcomed the agreement between Malaya and Singapore and announced the appointment of a commission by the two governments. Its task was to find out the views and wishes of the peoples of Sarawak and North Borneo. Brunei was one of the territories with which Tunku Abdul Rahman had advocated a closer understanding. But in view of its special status as a Sultanate under British protection, and the circumstances, personality, and attitude of its ruler, it was not included in the official scope of this inquiry. The two governments undertook, however, to seek the Sultan's views.

The Chairman chosen for the Commission was Lord Cobbold, a former Governor of the Bank of England. He had the advantage of having no previous experience of the area and therefore none of the prejudices inseparable from actual dealings with divergent and rival races. Apart from the Chairman, there were two British members, a former Governor of Sarawak and the last British Chief Secretary of Malaya. The Malayan representatives were the Chinese Chief Minister of Penang, a former school teacher called Dato Wong Pow Nee, and Ghazali, the head of the Ministry of External Affairs.

Some months earlier the Parliamentary Association of the British Commonwealth had held a regional meeting in Singapore attended by leaders from the Borneo territories, Singapore, and Malaya. After the meeting, a Malaysia Solidarity Consultative Committee was set up with representatives from each of the areas, those from Brunei having the status of observers. It prepared a memorandum explaining the main issues for the education of the local peoples. This was one of the many documents considered by the commission during the three months (February to April 1962) of its inquiries in the field.

Sarawak and North Borneo had been British Crown Colonies since the supersession of the Brooke dynasty and the Chartered Company in 1946. The change had in no sense been a revolution. In each case the British Government had built on the foundations laid by the previous régime. They merely applied more stereotyped and conventional methods of administration. Adapted to local conditions, they were those which had been common practice and tested by experience in Britain's Crown Colonies in all parts of the world. It greatly simplified the transition that the earlier systems had been operated chiefly through British colonial officers. This new phase of rule by the Crown contemplated, as elsewhere, the gradual development of representative institutions increasing the participation of local people in administering their country. This again was in the spirit and intention of the Rajahs and the Chartered Company.

In Sarawak the third Rajah had granted a constitution in 1941 to mark the hundredth year of Brooke rule.[1] This was in effect still-born, since the Japanese captured Kuching three months later. The post-war colonial constitution incorporated the Rajah's Nine Cardinal Principles envisaging eventual self-government. It went, however, even further along the road he had traced. The embryo of a local parliament, the Council Negri, formerly a consultative body, received legislative powers under the Rajah's constitution of 1941, but retained a majority of officials. Under the colonial constitution this was replaced by an elected majority. Under the Brooke constitution the governing cabinet, the Supreme Council, also had an official majority. The post-war constitutions gave the Council five members elected by the Council Negri, balanced by three officials and two nominated non-officials.

A first step had been taken on the road to self-rule. But this was a land with a mere three-quarters of a million people. Due in part to the Rajah's policies and its own modest resources, Sarawak had primitive communications, a high degree of illiteracy and poor medical facilities. Like North Borneo it had achieved only incipient economic and educational development. In much of the country, conditions for advanced agriculture, such as the double-cropping of rice, were adverse as the soil was constantly drenched by the rains of the two monsoons.

[1] See p. 68.

(The Peninsula of Malaya was spared this by the central spine of mountains which concentrated each monsoon on either side of the country.) The chief exports of Sarawak: rubber, timber, pepper, and sago were limited by all these factors.

In normal circumstances, independent nationhood for a land of this character would have been a remote prospect. With Malaysia, this was destined to come sooner than anyone could have anticipated and in special conditions which few could have foreseen. Some thought had, it is true, been given to closer local integration between the two Borneo territories after they became Crown Colonies. It was hoped that they could thus have a broader base for eventual self-determination than if they attained independence separately as weak fragments easily dominated or annexed by stronger neighbours. They would form a substantial regional unit with which Brunei might become associated. Proposals for the formation of a central authority covering all three territories and responsible initially for defence, external relations, internal security, and communications had been announced in 1958. Brunei had, however, shown herself reluctant to pursue this course. Subsequently this plan was superseded, so far as Brunei was concerned, by the constitutional arrangements agreed with Britain in 1959, which will be mentioned later. In spite of this setback, a common free trade area between Sarawak and North Borneo was tentatively established. Yet the results were disappointing. This separate local integration was not in fact to be the pattern of the future. Earlier jealousies and divergences between Sarawak and North Borneo had left their trace. In the years before the formation of Malaysia these had perhaps rendered their colonial rulers less receptive than they might have been to the potentialities of this broader local pattern.

Thanks to the imaginative lead given by the third Rajah and the post-war policies of the British Colonial Office, by 1961 Sarawak had made greater constitutional progress than North Borneo. The elective principle had been introduced into urban and rural municipalities and the major administrative Divisions. The members of the Kuching legislature were indirectly chosen by electoral and sub-electoral bodies based on these local assemblies. In North Borneo by the same date only the planning stage had been reached for future elections to District

Councils and Town Boards. These were eventually to lead to indirect elections to the legislature, but the prospect was not immediate. Meanwhile, the unofficial majority in the Jesselton Legislative Council was still nominated by the Governor. So were the unofficial members of the Executive Council, the governing cabinet corresponding to the Supreme Council in Sarawak.

Such was the general background of the Borneo colonies when the Cobbold Commission arrived. The delegates from North Borneo and Sarawak on the Malaysia Solidarity Consultative Committee claimed, perhaps humanly, that they, as moulders of public opinion in their territories, were convinced of the necessity and inevitability of Malaysia. In fact, however, for most of the people in British Borneo, Malaysia was a new and unknown or strange and disturbing prospect. For the Malays and assimilated Muslim groups, it had the attraction of closer association with their cousins and co-religionaries of the Peninsula. There was also a keen expectation of rural development on the same generous scale as in Malaya. On the other hand there was a general concern about immigration from other parts of the new federation. The simple non-Muslim natives feared that Malaysia might mean Malay domination. So did many Chinese. Yet with their strong business instinct, the more level-headed Chinese fully realized the profitable potentialities of a wider economic unit with a common market to stimulate trade and considerably more capital for investment than could ever be available under the colonial regime. The Chinese communists in Borneo as elsewhere rejected Malaysia because one of its plain objectives was to check communist expansion.

Before 1961 race relations in the two territories had been excellent. Political activity was quiet and North Borneo had hardly awakened to the exciting issues of Asian nationalism and constitutional progress. The shock of the Malaysia announcement stirred up controversy and tension. New political parties emerged and joined issue. To turn this new and dangerous effervescence into constructive channels and ensure a proper response to the Commission's visit, the two colonial governments prepared their own public statements of the issues involved. These urged the local races to consider Malaysia favourably in their own interests. They were published in

January and February, 1962, almost simultaneously with the memorandum of the Malaysia Solidarity Consultative Committee and covered much of the same ground. They were given the widest possible circulation in the far too limited time available. They allayed fears and dissipated misunderstandings. But inevitably their picture of these complex and vital issues had not penetrated to all the remoter regions when the Commission arrived.

The government papers were necessarily more cautious and objective than that of the Malaysia Committee, which so outspokenly acknowledged the 'inevitability' of Malaysia. They stressed the communist danger and argued that the larger federation would be far better equipped than any territory in isolation to overcome it. Colonial rule was obsolete and unpopular and the British Government aimed at granting independence to all its colonies when they were prepared for it. Malaysia would require a strong federal government to deal with such subjects as external affairs, defence, security, and law. The Borneo territories would, however, like Singapore, have to retain considerably greater autonomy than the states of Malaya. They should control the matters they considered of vital interest to themselves such as immigration, land and the preservation of local customs. They must, the statements continued, expect increased taxation with Malaysia. But this would have been inevitable even if they had remained colonies. It would have been far higher had they become independent on their own. Finally it was stressed that ties of culture, economy, and history made the peoples of Malaya and Borneo natural associates and that the opportunity of independence as part of Malaysia was unlikely to recur.

The Cobbold Commission found that racial harmony in the Borneo territories was in part an artificial product of colonial rule. Tensions had remained latent so long as the reins of power were in firm and impartial alien hands. But the prospect of self-government had aroused the fear of the natives at the prospect of sharing political power with the more alert and advanced Chinese and other immigrant races. As usual in Eastern Asia, the Chinese were economically dominant but not just as shopkeepers and manipulators of money. Many made a livelihood from the soil, concentrating on potentially profitable cash crops such as rubber and pepper. With their skill and frugality and the sophisticated realism of ancient traditions, the Chinese would infallibly have become the leaders had these territories attained independence on their own. And experience in Malaya had shown the danger of a Chinese communist bid for power. But association with Malaya might offer some guarantee. There at least the problem of Chinese domination and Chinese communist subversion had been met and, for the present, overcome.

From the standpoint of danger from the immigrant races, the first Sarawak elections had had disturbing results. The first political party to be formed was a group largely opposed to Malaysia known as the Sarawak United Peoples' Party. This was predominantly Chinese. A moderate leadership tended to mask the active communism of the extreme left wing. Many young Chinese felt a sense of frustration about their future prospects. With a fast growing population the Chinese were frequently barred from expanding their properties and means of livelihood by laws which reserved to the natives all land which they had ever used, however casually and improvidently. The communists had gained recruits by fanning these and other grievances. The emergence of the S.U.P.P. led in turn to the formation of Malay and native parties usually with an anti-Chinese bias, some of them associated in a local Alliance. Yet this general readiness to form a common front against the Chinese did not mean that the indigenous races were united among themselves. The non-Muslim natives, of whom the Ibans or Sea Dayaks formed the largest group,[1] did not relish the memory of being ruled by the Brunei Malays. Some even supported the S.U.P.P. in the 1963 elections because of this

[1] The total population of Sarawak at the census of 1960 was 744,529. This included:

| | |
|---|---|
| Malays | 129,300 |
| Melanaus (predominantly Muslim and assimilated to the Malays) | 44,661 |
| Iban (Sea Dayak) | 237,741 |
| Land Dayak | 57,619 |
| Other indigenous (including Bisayah, Kedayan, Kayan, Kenyah, Kelabit, Murut, Punan) | 37,931 |
| Chinese | 229,154 |
| European and Eurasian | 1,631 |
| Others (including Indians, Pakistanis, Ceylonese and Indonesians) | 6,492 |

party's anti-Malay stand. They were disturbed by the proposals that the new federation should be called Malaysia, that Malay should be the national language and Islam the national religion. This seemed to some to portend a revival of Malay oppression, hardly more welcome than the prospect of Chinese hegemony.

In North Borneo (henceforward to be known by its pre-British name of Sabah) the rivalry between the local races had not started to become acute. Special factors eased the situation there. In comparison with Sarawak the territory was smaller but more compact and some of its soil was considerably richer. Owing to the disposition of the mountains it did not suffer from monsoon drenching to the same extent. The country's principal exports of timber, rubber, and copra had rapidly expanded, and timber in particular had given Sabah a more viable economy than that of Sarawak. The Chinese were less frustrated. There was little communist subversion. Marriages between Chinese and the principal native community, the Dusuns or Kadazans,[1] had made a minor contribution to inter-racial understanding. There was another difference. The Sarawak Chinese looked broadly speaking towards Singapore, and Malaysia was to some extent a logical development. Many Chinese in Sabah, especially in the eastern towns of Sandakan and Tawau, came from and did business primarily with Hong Kong.

North Borneo had always suffered from a chronic shortage of manpower.[2] Many had come or been brought in from the Sulu Archipelago and other parts of the Philippines, as well as

---

[1] The total population of Sabah at the census of 1960 was 454,421. This included:

| | |
|---|---:|
| Dusun (Kadazan) | 145,229 |
| Murut | 22,138 |
| Bajaus and Illanuns (predominantly Muslim) | 59,710 |
| Other indigenous (including Brunei, Kedayan, Orang Sungei, Bisayah, Sulu, Tidong, Sino-Native) | 79,421 |
| Chinese | 104,542 |
| European and Eurasian | 1,896 |
| Others (including natives of Sarawak, Malays, Cocos Islanders, Filipinos, Indians, Pakistanis, Ceylonese and 24,784 Indonesians) | 41,485 |

[2] See p. 69.

from Hong Kong. But the most readily accessible source of manpower was Indonesia, which had a common frontier in Borneo with Sabah. The number of Indonesians and Filipinos in the country was to be a major problem during the next four years.

The Cobbold Commission found that about a third of the people of Sarawak and Sabah definitely favoured Malaysia. They demanded few if any special terms. To another third, Malaysia was acceptable subject to specific safeguards and conditions. The remainder objected that independence should come first or preferred that British rule should continue for the present. Not all of these were irrevocably opposed to the plan. The hard core of the opposition might amount to a fifth of the people in Sarawak and rather less in Sabah.[1]

The investigation confirmed that the Muslim and Malay elements tended to favour the new plan, but were wary of domination by Kuala Lumpur as they had been of Brunei (or Sulu) domination in the past. Again it showed that not all the other natives were fully cognizant of the issues involved. Many favoured the plan because, after years of British paternalism, they had a touching faith in Britain knowing what was best for them. Some Chinese felt that Britain was letting them down by handing them over, as they saw it, to the potential domination of less gifted fellow Asians. Apart from trust in Britain's lead, many were influenced in favour of Malaysia by the attractive personality and reputation of Tunku Abdul Rahman, the Malayan Prime Minister. This had its effect although he and the other Malay leaders were not invariably skilful on their visits to Borneo in concealing a sense of superiority over peoples who had progressed less remarkably than they had in the past hundred years. In later years when the Alliance leadership in Kuala Lumpur assumed a more masterful tone some felt their initial fears of Malay domination to have been confirmed.

On the basis of the majority which their findings revealed, the Cobbold Commission concluded that the proposed federation of Malaysia could and should be implemented at an early date in the interests of the Borneo territories and of the other proposed members of the new federation. They saw less merit in a regional association, but there was much to be said for

[1] Report of the Commission of Enquiry, North Borneo and Sarawak, 1962.

closer links between Sarawak and Sabah within Malaysia. They recommended that the constitution of Malaysia should be based on that of the existing Federation of Malaya. This would provide the much needed strong central government. The two Borneo colonies would enter the enlarged federation as additional states, but with safeguards for their identity and special interests. The Commission advocated that no amendment or withdrawal of any safeguard in the federal constitution should be made without the concurrence of the state government concerned; and that the power of amending the state constitutions should belong exclusively to the people of the state. In response to an almost universal demand from the indigenous people, they recommended that the native races should be secured at least for the time being against the competitition of the immigrant races by special advantages in connexion with the public service, scholarships, etc. They would be similar to those provided for the Malays of the Peninsula.[1] In view of the special character of the Borneo states and of the fact that their racial composition was intended to balance the Chinese majority in Singapore, the number of members representing them in the federal parliament was to be greater than that to which they would have been entitled strictly on the basis of their population. For similar reasons, reflecting Singapore's continued measure of autonomy and Kuala Lumpur's fears of Chinese strength, the representation of Singapore was to be less than that corresponding to its population.[2]

Amongst other important recommendations, the Commission proposed that the state government should retain control of land, agriculture, forestry, and native customs and usage. Special attention should also, they felt, be paid to development in rural areas, to the improvement of education and medical

[1] See p. 109.

[2] In the constitution of the federation of Malaysia Singapore with a population of approximately $1\frac{1}{2}$ million was allotted 15 seats, Sabah with less than $\frac{1}{2}$ million 16, and Sarawak with under $\frac{3}{4}$ million 24. As a compensation for small parliamentary representation, Singapore retained considerable autonomy in matters of finance, labour, and education. With the 104 seats representing the states of Malaya, this raised the total membership of the House of Representatives to 159. The Senate increased to 50, 28 elected by each of the 14 states and the rest nominated by the King.

facilities and the provision of administrative and technical training. Malay should be the national language, but English should be kept as an official language. Borneo people should be recruited increasingly for the public service and the federal posts in the Borneo states should be filled as far as possible by Borneans. But pending the emergence of highly trained Bornean administrative officials, the services of certain key British officers should be retained. There were some natural divergences between the British and Malayan members of the Commission. Since the peoples of Sarawak and North Borneo had so little governmental experience, the British advocated a transitional period of three to seven years before the final incorporation of the two states in Malaysia. The Malayans (whose view eventually prevailed) were positive that in order to minimize uncertainty and tension, Malaysia should be brought about within a year.

The recommendations of the Cobbold Commission were in general approved by London and Kuala Lumpur. In August 1962, the Malayan and British Governments announced that Malaysia would be established on 31 August 1963, the sixth anniversary of the independence of Malaya. The defence agreement with Britain would be extended to the other states of the new federation. An inter-governmental committee was set up to work out the detailed arrangements for the incorporation of Sarawak and Sabah. The final settlement was generous and conciliatory especially on those points which had aroused anxiety or controversy in Borneo. While Islam would be the national religion of Malaysia there would be no state religion in the Borneo states, which would be guaranteed full religious freedom. The official use of English would be retained for ten years. Powers normally appertaining to the federal government in certain fields, of which education was one, were temporarily delegated to the state governments. Control of immigration into the federation had inevitably to remain with Kuala Lumpur. But the Borneo states were given control over immigration into their territories from other parts of Malaysia. Sarawak and Sabah would not have a special citizenship, as would Singapore (whose citizens would automatically become nationals of Malaysia). On the other hand, people of the Borneo states who had resided in Malaysia (outside Singapore) for seven of the past ten years could apply for Malaysian nationality if they intended to live in the federation permanently.

When the Malaysia proposals had taken shape, Tunku Abdul Rahman visited the Sultan of Brunei to explain them personally. He secured the Sultan's initial approval, and that of his advisers, to the plan. Subsequently His Highness showed his interest in a possible association with Malaysia by reducing the number of his British officials and advisers and putting Malayan officials in their place. The change met with indifferent success. It was hard for Kuala Lumpur to spare their really good people from the limited number available and those seconded did not impress the Brunei authorities. It is clear from later developments that the Sultan had reservations about committing himself definitely to Malaysia even at this time. A small, proud, soft-spoken, sensitive prince, keenly conscious of being the twenty-eighth ruler of his Royal House, he had acquired exceptional skill in pursuing the advantage, as he saw it, of his country and dynasty with invariable courtesy and unswerving, if somewhat devious, determination. The constitutional arrangements evolved with Britain for Brunei were in many respects similar to those which had existed in the Malay states. The Sultan was strictly speaking required to follow the advice tendered to him by the British High Commissioner. In practice, Britain no longer insisted on the literal fulfilment of this obligation. In most respects the Sultan was able to go his own way on the understanding that in due course his essentially personal régime would be modified along more democratic lines. Rich from his substantial oil revenues, and protected by Britain, he had no need to compromise Brunei's freedom of action for the sake of outside military or financial support. There was little attraction in joining Malaysia unless he were accorded the position he considered his due as a ruler of considerably more ancient lineage than many of the Sultans of the Peninsula. He appears to have felt that he had some claim to be chosen as Supreme Ruler of the Federation on the basis of the length of his reign rather than of the date of Brunei's prospective accession to Malaysia. On such matters the Tunku seems to have given the Sultan little encouragement. The impression left in Brunei was that their ruler had been treated by the Malayan Prime Minister with a certain condescension and lack of deference. These may have been factors affecting Brunei's ultimate disinclination to participate in Malaysia. More decisive was a critical turn of events at the end of the year.

Meanwhile, in the summer of 1962, the Singapore Government faced the task of securing the acceptance by their people of the plan for association with Malaysia agreed with the Malayan Government a year earlier. This was by no means easy. It was only a few weeks after the Tunku launched the idea of Malaysia in May 1961 that the communist-inspired wing of the People's Action Party had broken away. It formed, as we saw, the Barisan Sosialis or Socialist Front in opposition to the P.A.P. moderates supporting the government of Lee Kuan Yew. Like the extremists of the Sarawak United People's Party it was fully aware that the new plan was designed to check the spread of communism. It therefore sharply attacked Malaysia from two inconsistent angles. It was a neo-colonialist plot to perpetuate British control or a bid by Malaya to build up an empire of her own. Prime Minister Lee, however, launched a counter-propaganda campaign which was conspicuously effective at the time.[1] In terms which would ring hollow three years later he argued that the merger was inevitable. The artificial barrier of the Johore causeway must be swept away. Malaya and Singapore were vital to each other's survival. Malaya produced the rubber and tin which were the mainstay of Singapore's economy. A separate Singapore and Malaya meant that they would be cutting each other's throats. With one integrated area there need be no wasteful duplication of facilities such as different rubber markets in the two territories. At the same time, Singapore with her special problems would have to be autonomous in education and labour matters. He accused the communists of seeking the kind of merger which would favour them, in which security would not be under federal government control. He showed how the communists, in spite of their military defeat and the banning of the Communist Party, were fighting by other means and making new recruits from the Chinese middle schools. He had sought in vain to persuade such people to think and act as Malayans alongside the Malays, the Indians and the rest. But the communists hoped to advance

[1] See Purcell, *Malaysia*, pp. 189–91.

their interests by continuing the anti-colonial struggle and Singapore was a useful base from which to undermine Malaya.

When the Singapore government decided to put the issue of Malaysia to a referendum it became clear that the Prime Minister's eloquence had achieved considerable success. The Barisan Sosialis urged a demonstration of protest by the casting of blank votes. In the event only a quarter of the votes cast were blank and there was a majority of over two-thirds for the Malaysia plan.[1]

The whole project was virtually unique in colonial history. A nation recently freed from colonial rule was to receive a massive addition of territory voluntarily relinquished by the same former governing power. The peoples of the new areas had shown no particular wish for early independence. But they had been persuaded that it would best serve their interests to abandon their colonial status for a form of association safeguarding their special character with a more or less distant and familiar land. With all obvious differences, it was as if Britain in the 1790s had handed over Canada to the United States by friendly arrangement.

By the autumn of 1962 a stage had been reached—or so it seemed—of general acceptance and imminent realization of Malaysia without major controversy within the area immediately concerned. In fact its birth and early years were beset with major crises. These sprang from the ambitions, the anxieties, and the resentments of Malaysia's island neighbours.

---

[1] The Singapore Government had ingeniously arranged a referendum on a basis of three choices, of which only the first (the agreed plan) was obviously attractive. The other choices—merger on the same conditions as the existing states of Malaya or on terms not less favourable than those for the Borneo territories—were of doubtful appeal. The choice of not merging with Malaya at all was not offered. See *The Federation of Malaysia*, British Information Services, New York, I.D. 1417, May 1963, pp. 64 and 45.

# CHAPTER FOURTEEN

# The Growth of Discord

From President Sukarno's attitude to Malaya since he assumed power it was simple to predict that he would contest any growth in her power and size. He had long chosen to regard alien possession of the eastern shores of the Straits of Malacca as a threat to Indonesia's security. In spite of Malaya's small-ness and modest military strength he was aware of the attrac-tion she exercised on the Sumatrans by her good organization and prosperity. The latter were traditionally resentful of Javanese domination. More recently they had rejected the in-ept policies of Djakarta which had made their country virtually bankrupt and had sacrificed the interests of the Outer Islands. Their protest had taken shape in a military rebellion which President Sukarno unjustly suspected Malaya of having helped. Now this disturbing neighbour was moving in to Northern Borneo, three-quarters of which already belonged to Indonesia.

In spite of his violent hostility to 'colonialism', before the announcement of Malaysia Sukarno had been resigned on the whole to leaving northern Borneo for the time being in British hands. Britain was still something to be reckoned with. The aura clung to her of having been the foremost European power in Asia. Moreover, she had shown understanding of the nationalist movement when she had responsibilities in Indo-nesia just after the war. Finally, many of her colonies had gained freedom more swiftly and smoothly than those of other lands. It should therefore only be a question of time before British Borneo would be able to exercise self-determination. It would then logically seek to be re-united with its natural hinter-land to the south. Yet now Malaya was seeking to make the colonial divisions of Borneo permanent by artificially linking these territories with her own land a thousand miles away. And in so doing she was abetted and encouraged by Britain, with whom she maintained a highly suspicious collaboration. Troops of the British Commonwealth were to defend and guarantee this iniquitous denial of Indonesia's legitimate rights. Yet Indonesia had potentially ten times the military manpower of Malaya, and Britain was no longer the force she had been fifteen years ago. Indonesia could afford to challenge their pretensions. Britain could perhaps be spurred into shedding her remaining responsibilities in Asia if these were made sufficiently burdensome and costly. Arguing from roughly such premises, the President could envisage a cause, a banner, and a slogan to distract the attention of his peoples from mismanagement at home, when New Guinea should have ceased to be a live issue.

Yet it was not by Indonesia that Malaysia was first called in question. Malaya had sought to mediate in the West Irian (New Guinea) dispute between the Netherlands and Indonesia. This had met with scant appreciation from Djakarta. Nevertheless, the two latter countries had retained contact and understanding. There was some evidence of this when Dr. Subandrio, the Indonesian Foreign Minister, stated in a debate on West Irian in the General Assembly of the United Nations in November 1961, that Malaya had informed Indonesia of its intention to merge with the three British territories in northern Borneo. He added that Indonesia had informed the Malayan leaders that it had no objection and wished them success. The first major challenge to Malaysia came not from this quarter but from the Philippines.

In 1961, the year in which the Malaysia plan was launched, President Garcia of the Philippines was succeeded by President Diosdado Macapagal. The former had been one of the sponsors of the Association of Southeast Asia which had promoted friendly co-operation between the Philippines, Malaya, and Thailand. President Macapagal, like many statesmen, had small interest in following in his predecessor's wake and upholding in difficult circumstances a policy he had not originated. It was politically important for him to take new initiatives demonstrably his own even if these involved the over-shadowing of A.S.A. and abandoning, in this form, President Garcia's goal of friendship with Malaya. He purported to have been disturbed by the prospective change of régime on his borders. The argument advanced was that under weaker, less efficient, or more divided, control than that of Britain, North Borneo might become a focus of subversion dangerous to a land ideologically conservative and aligned with the United States. The prospective links with Singapore and Sarawak might lead to infiltration by Chinese communist elements known to have been active there. The President may genuinely have believed this line of reasoning. On the other hand there are grounds for supposing that the argument was largely built up for the sake of political expediency.

A press campaign in the Philippines was followed by a resolution of their House of Representatives in April 1962 stating that the Republic had a legal and valid claim to North Borneo and requesting the President to take the necessary steps to recover the territory. The claim was formally presented to Britain in June 1962. Malaya was approached on the subject shortly afterwards, but pointed out that the matter was still essentially one for the United Kingdom. The British authorities, while declining to entertain any doubt as to their title, eventually agreed to talks in London on the problems of Anglo-Philippines relations. President Macapagal subsequently revealed[1] that he had made a personal study of the claim and, while at the Philippines Embassy in the United States, had been encouraged to believe in its validity by 'an American expert in Anglo-Saxon law in George Washington University'. When serving in Congress in 1950 he had sponsored an earlier resolution calling for the presentation of this claim. His efforts had contributed during these post-war years to the transfer of the Turtle Islands from North Borneo to the Philippines. Then and now he seemed determined to make of all this an issue to enhance his personal reputation.

In July 1962 the President took a fresh initiative which clearly commanded his deep personal interest. He advocated the establishment of a Confederation of Greater Malaya which would embrace the Philippines, Malaya, Singapore, North Borneo, Sarawak, and Brunei and would supersede 'the British sponsored Federation of Malaysia'. Asians, he said, should not accept a European project; an Asian one was preferable.

Meanwhile, the launching of the Philippines claim was a disconcerting surprise to Malaya in some contradiction to the

[1] In his State of the Nation Address to the Joint Session of the Congress of the Philippines on 28 January 1963.

President's wider objective of harmony between the Malay races. There had in fact been no question of the validity of Britain's title to North Borneo since before 1885. In that year Spain had renounced her sovereignty over the territories 'on the continent of Borneo formerly belonging to the Sultan of Sulu' in return for Britain's recognition of Spain's sovereignty over the Sulu Archipelago.[1] In 1898 Spain's rights devolved upon the United States, who cast no doubt on Britain's title, then or later. Although this did not pass unchallenged by certain elements in the Philippines, in an Anglo-American Convention of 1930 Washington recognized North Borneo as being under British protection and when the independence of the Philippines was proclaimed by President Truman in 1946, this convention was expressly cited.

The original document drawn up in 1878 by the Sultan of Sulu, Alfred Dent, and Baron Overbeck stated that the Sultan, on behalf of himself and his heirs and successors 'granted and ceded' to these two gentlemen 'forever and in perpetuity, all rights and powers, over all the territories and lands tributary [to the Sultan] on the mainland of Borneo . . . with all islands within three marine leagues of the coast' (that is, within territorial waters). In return, the Sultan and his heirs and successors would receive five thousand Malayan dollars a year. The annual payment was increased by three hundred Malayan dollars when the Sultan, in 1903, specified the islands affected, the names of which had not been included in the original agreement. While still under American sovereignty, the Philippines had refused to continue to recognize the Sultanate's authority over the Sulu Archipelago and had assumed power in place of the Sultan and his successors. Britain, however, had continued to pay the annuities to the Sultan's heirs, of whom nine were officially recognized to exist in 1939. When not claimed, the money had been put in a deposit account at the disposal of the beneficiaries.

The stand taken, and arguments advanced by the Philippines had certain inconsistencies. On the one hand they contended that the Sultan had no right to dispose of the territory at all, since Spain and not he was sovereign in the area at the time. Britain contested this point with the argument that Spain had

[1] See p. 65.

been unable to control the Sultan up to the time when the cession was made. Spain had, it was true, made treaties with the Sultan in 1836, 1851, and 1864, but Britain had refused to recognize them because of Spain's lack of effective power in the area. The alternative contention put forward by the Philippines was that, if the Sultan did have a right to dispose of the territory, he did not intend to sell it outright but merely to lease it. They asserted that the word *padak* used in the Malay text of the original document was less sweeping and specific than the words 'grant and cede' in the English translation, though it was not disputed that the arrangement was defined as being 'for ever and in perpetuity'. As regards Washington's recognition of the British protectorate over North Borneo, Manila maintained that it could not be bound by undertakings entered into, before independence, with a colonial power. Rather strangely, despite the Philippines acquisition of sovereignty over the Sulu Archipelago and their earlier assumption of the position of the Sultan's heirs, the Republic claimed to be acting 'on behalf of the descents of the Sultan of Sulu'.[1]

Before the promised discussions between the British and Philippines Governments could take place a grave crisis had arisen in Brunei. This was directly traceable to the tension and discontent which the Malaysia project had aroused in certain quarters. From it and the other factors in dispute, there developed between the Malay nations a phase of intensified suspicion and resentment which was to last for three and a half years.

In 1959 relations between Brunei and Britain had been placed on a new footing, intended as a modest advance towards constitutional democracy. After the treaty of 1888, the British presence in Brunei had for some years been a Consul-General, but the Sultans had continued to rule in a highly personal fashion with the advice of a State Council. As we have seen, in 1906 this personal regime was qualified by the Sultan's acceptance of a British Resident appointed from Sarawak who tendered advice and had general supervision over the administration except in regard to Islam and Malay custom.[2] The Resident was in turn under the authority of a High Com-

---

[1] George E. Taylor, *The Philippines and the United States*, p. 266.
[2] See p. 66.

missioner for Brunei. Pre-war this had been the Governor of the Straits Settlements; from 1946 it was the Governor of Sarawak. The arrangement was similar to that which had existed in the Malay states. The new constitutional system introduced by the Ruler in agreement with the British Government in 1959 emphasized the separate and special status of the Sultanate by the appointment of a British High Commissioner solely concerned with Brunei, the existing British Resident being promoted to this more exalted post. As High Commissioner, he had to advise the Sultan on defence, external affairs and internal security as well as on ordinary administration. Under Brunei's first written constitution, the State Council was replaced by an Executive Council and a Legislative Council. The latter (an embryo parliament) had members indirectly chosen by elected district councils (as in Sarawak) balanced by official or nominated members. The Executive Council (responsible for the actual work of government) included unofficial members appointed by the Sultan from the Legislative Council as well as officials performing ministerial duties. The British High Commissioner was a member of the Council and acted as the Sultan's minister for external affairs and defence. One response to the new constitution was the development of political controversy. In particular there emerged a People's Party (Party Rakyat) which eventually, in August 1962, captured all the elective seats in the Legislative Council. What was ostensibly a clear manifestation of the people's will proved to have consequences of the most disturbing kind.

The organizer and chairman of the party was Sheikh A. M. Azahari, a colourful anti-colonialist, partly Arab and partly Malay by race. He had studied in Indonesia during the Japanese occupation and had afterwards fought with the Indonesian nationalist forces. He had returned to Brunei in 1952 and had set up in business as well as politics. His early political ventures were inauspicious. In 1953 he was briefly imprisoned for holding an unlawful meeting. Yet his considerable gifts of oratory achieved the subsequent success of the Party Rakyat. In the opinion of local circles he could without difficulty have become Chief Minister had he possessed greater stability, administrative competence, and qualities of leadership. A more important factor was that his stay in Indonesia and the indoctrination he seems to have received there had made him an opponent of Malaysia sympathetic to the policies of President Sukarno. His party had established links in Djakarta with Partindo, a group favourable to the President which had broken away from the Indonesian Nationalist Party in 1958. He had also been in touch with the Indonesian Consulate in Sabah. This was later penalized by the British authorities for conducting subversive activities through the local Indonesian associations. It eventually became clear that his objective was to bring the three British Borneo territories under the rule of the Sultan of Brunei as the independent unitary state of northern Borneo (or Kalimantan to use the Indonesian name for the island). This plan was a significant variant on that of the British authorities for a looser association of the three. It appears to have enjoyed Indonesian support for the comprehensible reason that a smaller and weaker combination than the proposed federation of Malaysia could be more readily absorbed into Greater Indonesia. Kuala Lumpur subsequently gained the impression that Azahari had been authorized by the Indonesians to hold out the prospect of the Sultan becoming ruler of the whole of Borneo. Whether, if his plans had succeeded, the Indonesians would have made their offer a reality is open to some doubt.

Despite the obvious contradiction between the goals of the Party Rakyat and the indications given to Malaya of Brunei's interest in joining Malaysia, Azahari for a time enjoyed a measure of the Sultan's favour and even financial help. This attitude may have reflected His Highness's doubts about the wisdom of Brunei joining the Malaysian federation. At the same time, he may well have been attracted by the enhanced dignity of the role reserved for him in the Party's plan. This corresponded in some respects to the position his ancestors had occupied in northern Borneo. It also promised him a status of visibly greater eminence than that which would be his as a newly joined member of the Conference of Rulers in Kuala Lumpur. He may have hoped that the change could be peaceably effected with the consent of the British. Only four years earlier they had put forward the idea of Brunei's association with Sarawak and North Borneo as a step towards the independence of all three territories. Perhaps they were not irrevocably committed to supporting the formation of Malaysia.

In fact, by the summer of 1962 any prospect of Britain abandoning her support for the inclusion of the Borneo territories in Malaysia was totally unrealistic. The Cobbold Commission's report was broadly accepted by London and Kuala Lumpur, and the inter-governmental committee started discussing the detailed arrangements for the status of the territories in Malaysia. Azahari himself seems to have had no illusions about the possibility of realizing his schemes except by force. Towards the end of the year, the police and many individuals became aware of unusual activities which might portend a subversive outbreak. According to British residents, green cloth was in short supply, tailors were working overtime, uniforms of an unauthorized pattern were discovered in Lawas across the Sarawak border, their servants absented themselves unexpectedly on the plea that they had to go for 'training'. Little or no action appears to have been taken by the Brunei authorities on the warnings conveyed to them by the senior British officers in the police; and the British High Commissioner was on leave when the situation looked like coming to a head. The possibility of serious developments had however been conveyed to the Earl of Selkirk, the United Kingdom Commissioner-General for Southeast Asia in Singapore. Disturbed by what he had heard, at the end of November Lord Selkirk visited Brunei and convinced himself that the situation was in fact dangerous. After his return to Singapore, a Gurkha unit was alerted for action in the event of emergency.

A few days later, on the morning of 8 December 1962, a major insurrection broke out in Brunei and the neighbouring areas of Sarawak and North Borneo. Azahari and his principal lieutenant, an officer of the Party Rakyat called Zaini, were not there to take the lead, having moved to Manila. By the evening of the first day, the Gurkha troops were able to arrive and occupy entrenched positions in the main square of Brunei city. They were followed by British and other units. Meanwhile the rebels had established a strong-point in the city gaol. Earlier in the day, the High Commissioner's secretary had persuaded successive cordons of rebel troops to let her drive through to his residence. She found that his deputy, who was living there, had been tied by rebel guards to the balcony of the house. Again this determined young lady was able to get her way. The rebels had apparently had instructions not to harm the British, and those at the house included some young people whom she had known in normal life. They agreed to her taking her official superior away. Both eventually found refuge in the police station, where the business of the British High Commission was transacted as best it could be for the following days. One of the rebel objectives was evidently to capture the Ruler in his palace, but they met with successful resistance from loyal guards. After the outbreak, the Sultan's attitude seems to have been one of uncertainty and hesitation. He was, however, visited by a representative of Lord Selkirk and was prevailed upon to join the party already established in the police station.

Meanwhile, Azahari had announced himself from the Philippines as 'Prime Minister' of the 'Revolutionary State of North Kalimantan'. He established what purported to be a diplomatic mission representing this state in Djakarta, where his representatives were given official membership of an Afro-Asian Journalists Conference. He described his 'forces' as the 'North Borneo Liberation Army' and said he had ordered them to carry out 'general sabotage' particularly against the Shell Company's installation at Seria, the principal source of Brunei's wealth. According to the information of the Brunei authorities, Azahari, though not himself a communist, had established contact with the pro-communist wing of the anti-Malaysia Sarawak United People's Party.

It took the British forces ten days to recapture the various places which the rebels had managed to occupy. These included Seria, Tutong, and Kuala Belait in Brunei, Weston in North Borneo, Limbang in the Sarawak salient between the two areas of Brunei, Lawas in the Sarawak area separating Brunei from North Borneo; and the neighbourhood of Miri in Sarawak, another oil area adjacent to the western border of Brunei and linked by pipeline to Seria. In some of these centres there was heavy fighting, but the rebels were ineffective in pursuing their objectives. Although they held Seria for three days, the damage they did to the oil installations was negligible. After losing the points they had held, many of the rebels took to the jungle and their final elimination was a slow process, especially after they started to receive outside help. Their total number was estimated by the British military authorities at about 2,000, of whom some 250 were captured in the fighting.

On 17 December the defeat of the revolt was officially announced by the United Kingdom Commissioner-General. Despite the comparative ease with which it was suppressed it had been, for those in the country, a harsh and menacing experience. In Seria prisoners taken by the rebels had been used as a human shield when resisting attacks by government forces. In Limbang the captured British District Officer and his wife had been threatened with hanging. The shock caused by the whole series of events was reflected in the drastic measures taken by the authorities. In the early stages, the Party Rakyat was banned and warrants issued for the arrest of Azahari and his associates. Many were imprisoned in Brunei itself. None were subsequently brought to trial. This is ascribed by some to a desire in the highest government circles to avoid embarrassing revelations. Zaini, who was influenced by the British to give himself up and elected to return to Brunei in the hope of leniency, was arrested there and was still in prison three years later. Release of the offenders considered no longer dangerous was repeatedly delayed. The Sultan suspended the constitution and governed for the time being through an Emergency Council.

Apart from these internal consequences, the Brunei revolt had notable repercussions in the international field. The opponents of Malaysia exploited the fact that the Brunei People's Party had captured the democratic, popular, vote. The representatives of the people had been defeated by troops of the colonial power with the approval of the Malayan government. Could there be clearer proof that the Kuala Lumpur regime, despite its pretence of independence, was a puppet of its former imperial masters? Arguments of this nature shortly became Indonesia's basic theme. Tunku Abdul Rahman was, however, also in combative mood. On 11 December he stated that Azahari's 'army' had originated in Indonesian Borneo. The Indonesian government called this provocative; they were not implicated in the revolt. The Tunku retorted that he had not referred to the government but to Indonesian elements who on their own admission had encouraged and helped Azahari. On 19 December President Sukarno declared that the Indonesians sympathized with the people of northern Borneo in their struggle for independence as they did with the peoples of Algeria, Angola, or the Congo. At the turn of the year the British Government sought and failed to obtain from Djakarta a clear assurance that Indonesia would not support the rebels in guerilla warfare. At the end of January, Antara, the Indonesian government news agency, quoted one of the top Indonesian Generals as saying that the Indonesian army was awaiting the order to move in support of the insurgents. Two divisions of 'volunteers' were ready to enter British Borneo to 'halt the massacre of the people by the British'.

In February, the controversy sharpened and the Indonesian leader gave it a definition which had already become memorable in connexion with the West Irian campaign. According to President Sukarno, Malaysia was an attempt to save rubber, tin, and oil for the imperialists. Indonesia supported the insurgents because they were fighting for independence against Malaysian neo-colonialism. If the Malaysia plan was pursued, Indonesia would have no choice but to face it with political and economic 'Confrontation'. Later he told the Indonesian troops that, having carried out their duties successfully in West Irian they still had to defend their country which was being undermined by other threats. On the same day a Malayan fishing vessel was captured and removed to Sumatra; the Indonesian naval forces would, it was said, burn any Malayan fishing boat caught in Indonesian waters. In March, anti-Malaysia propaganda started issuing from a radio station on Indonesian territory called 'The Voice of Freedom Fighters of Northern Kalimantan'. From July similar subversive material was broadcast by a station in northern Sumatra calling itself the Radio Malaya Independence Movement. In justification of Confrontation, accusations multiplied. Malaya was hostile. She was attempting to 'encircle' Indonesia. She had earlier tried to annex Sumatra in collusion with the rebels there. She was opposed to the 'new emerging forces' of the world, etc. Kuala Lumpur conducted its own defence. Amongst other points it stressed the strong influence of the Partai Komunis Indonesia on the Djakarta government. No objection had been raised in

Indonesia to British bases, or the Anglo-Malayan Defence Agreement, before the announcement of Malaysia. The first challenge had then come from the communists, in a resolution of the P.K.I. in December 1961. Faced with these hostile manifestations, the Malayan government felt it essential to start expanding her armed forces and to take internal security precautions. Ahmad Boestamam,[1] who had been imprisoned during the Emergency but had more recently been leader of the Socialist Front in Parliament, was arrested for having been connected with the organizers of the Brunei revolt and in touch with the Indonesian Embassy and the P.K.I. He admitted that he sought the 'unification of Indonesia, the Philippines, the Borneo territories, South Thailand, Malaya, and Singapore into Greater Malaysia'.

Meanwhile the Vice-President of the Philippines had held inconclusive but amicable talks with the British authorities in London at the end of January. The two governments had decided in advance that, as members of the Southeast Asia Treaty Organization, they were both vitally concerned with the security and stability of Southeast Asia and that 'recent developments' made the talks desirable. The final announcement stated that the Philippines delegation had given the details of their government's claim; that the British had explained why it could not be accepted; that both had agreed to exchange copies of the documents on the legal position, and to co-operate over piracy, armed raids, smuggling, and illegal immigration. During the talks President Macapagal reiterated the Philippines claim but urged that the North Borneans should decide, preferably by a referendum under United Nations auspices, whether they wished to be independent, part of the Philippines, or 'under another state'.

February also saw a determined attempt launched by Vice-President Pelaez of the Philippines (who was also Foreign Minister), on his return from London, to reach a friendly settlement of the Malaysian dispute under Philippines auspices. This eventually took shape in three gatherings at Manila, the first at official level, the second of Foreign Ministers, and the third a 'summit' meeting between the national leaders of Indonesia, Malaya, and the Philippines. Meanwhile, prepara-

[1] See p. 114.

tions for the implementation of Malaysia continued. At the end of February, the inter-governmental committee on the constitutional arrangements for the Borneo territories in Malaysia published their report. Early in March, the Malayan Government announced that it had agreed with the Sultan of Brunei the terms for Brunei's entry into Malaysia. Three months later, however, in June, negotiations in Kuala Lumpur on the detailed conditions for Brunei's accession broke down. The final point of dissension does not appear to have been any question of the Ruler's precedence but rather that of the allocation of his oil revenues. Although production had been declining, Brunei was still, after Canada and Trinidad, the third largest oil producer in the British Commonwealth. Of her yearly revenue of some U.S.$ 40 million, one half came from oil. Kuala Lumpur claimed that the oil revenue should be paid into the Malaysian Treasury ten years after the creation of Malaysia. The Sultan wished to keep these funds indefinitely for internal development. At further talks in London which the Sultan attended in person, every effort was made by the British authorities but without success to persuade him to join the new federation. The position in Sarawak and North Borneo was far more positive. Elections held in these territories in June and July gave the pro-Malaysia parties a big majority in the two legislatures.

Meanwhile the talks between Indonesian, Malayan, and Philippines officials had been held in Manila in April. At the end of May, the Tunku had an ostensibly cordial meeting with President Sukarno in Tokyo. According to the account of these events published by the Malayan Government,[1] the President was informed that the Tunku was going to London shortly to sign the agreement by which Malaysia would be established from 31 August. He asked if the date could be changed or postponed, but was told that this would not be desirable and did not raise any objection. At the preliminary conference of Foreign Ministers in June, attended by Tun Razak and Dr. Subandrio, Vice-President Pelaez urged the acceptance of his President's proposal for a Malay confederation, which had now become enlarged to include Indonesia. The Vice-President

[1] Malaya-Indonesia Relations, 31 August 1957–15 September 1963; Government Press, Kuala Lumpur, 1963.

pointed out that such a combination, with a population of 140 million, in one of the richest and most strategic areas of the world, would constitute a 'powerful bastion against aggression from any quarter', and ensure peace and security. Within such a framework the Philippine claim to North Borneo could be settled 'justly and expeditiously'. Pending the meeting of their leaders this met with no immediate response. The Ministers agreed, however, that the three countries shared responsibility for maintaining peace and stability in Southeast Asia; and that machinery should be set up for regular consultation between them on matters of common concern. They also maintained that they had succeeded in a spirit of 'close and brotherly association' in reaching agreement on how to solve both the Malaysia problem and the Philippine claim. This encouraging consensus did not however endure. On 9 July the final agreement for the establishment of Malaysia was signed in London. President Sukarno then claimed that the Tunku had broken an alleged understanding between them at Tokyo. He also asserted—without support from the facts and ignoring the Cobbold Commission—that the Foreign Ministers had agreed that Malaysia should not be established until the peoples of Sarawak and North Borneo had been consulted. He told a crowd in Djakarta on 27 July, that Malaysia was a British project and that Indonesia was determined to crush it. Only in response to a last minute appeal by the Philippine President would he agree to come to the Manila meeting.

Here once again Indonesia's temperamental leader displayed a mood of charm and *bonhomie*, while remaining alive to the dramatic possibilities of making a scene on the international stage. It was promptly agreed to send a letter to U Thant, Secretary-General of the United Nations, asking him to 'ascertain the wishes' of the people of Sabah (North Borneo) and Sarawak prior to the establishment of Malaysia. There was no question of anything as far reaching as the referendum which had been favoured for the former by President Macapagal. The task of the United Nations was essentially to make sure that the two peoples had had a genuine opportunity to exercise self-determination within the terms of the Charter. Had the recent elections been properly conducted and had they taken into account the desires of the inhabitants regarding

Malaysia? The Tunku was prepared to envisage a short post-ponement of the date for the inauguration of Malaysia to permit this new inquiry to be held. The three leaders endorsed the findings of their Foreign Ministers. They agreed that a 'just and expeditious settlement' of the Philippine claim to North Borneo would be sought. In a Manila Declaration, they undertook that their countries as 'new emerging forces' and states which had become sovereign 'after long struggles from colonial status to independence' would maintain fraternal relations and strengthen their co-operation in the economic, social, and cultural fields. They would also struggle against colonialism and imperialism and take initial steps towards the establishment of an association which would realize President Macapagal's vision of a Malay confederation. The title would be a strange-sounding hybrid—Maphilindo—composed of the opening syllables of the names of the three countries concerned. The meetings ended on this note of hope. President Sukarno would welcome Malaysia if the results of the United Nations inquiry favoured the plan. Yet those who had studied his career could have foretold that there were storms to come. For all his emotional variations, he had shown over the years remarkable persistence in pursuing the objectives dictated by ambition for his country.

# CHAPTER FIFTEEN

# The Storm Breaks

The British authorities agreed, however reluctantly, to the new inquiry by the United Nations in their Borneo territories, to which the Tunku had in effect committed both governments. The Secretary-General had estimated that he would need six weeks for the investigation and his team arrived in Sarawak on 16 August, only eleven days after the end of the Manila meeting. It soon became clear, however, that the exercise was to be turned by Indonesia into a major source of controversy. At the request of the Malayan Government, and after consultation with U Thant, Britain agreed to permit a small group of observers from each of the three countries to accompany the United Nations teams. Just before the inquiry should have started, Indonesia tried to insist on sending a large group of thirty. The argument which ensued over numbers was not settled for another ten days and the Indonesian and Philippine observer teams did not reach Borneo until some time after the inquiry had begun. This was developed into a source of grievance on their side. Even the Secretary-General was inclined to lay some blame at Britain's door. In his report[1] published after the inquiry he complained that 'a more congenial atmosphere would have been achieved if the necessary facilities [for observers] had been granted more promptly by the administering authority'. He also indicated some annoyance at the fact that, three days after the inquiry started, the Malayan Government, with the concurrence of Britain, Singapore, Sabah, and Sarawak, announced that Malaysia would be established on 16 September. He remarked that the 'misunderstanding, confusion, and even resentment', which this caused among the other parties to the Manila agreement could have been avoided if the date had been fixed after his conclusions had been reached and made known.[2] The principal reason given by the Malayan

[1] *United Nations Malaysia Mission Report*, Final Conclusions, p. iii.
[2] Ibid., p. ii.

Government for action which could be interpreted as less than courteous towards the Secretary-General, was that U Thant had stated that he expected to complete his task by 14 September. The British Government pointed out that it was essential to set the earliest date consistent with the Secretary-General's timetable 'in view of the disquieting effect which continued uncertainty would be bound to create'. It also drew attention to the 'numerous processes', independent of the United Nations inquiry which had been employed to ascertain the wishes of the people.

U Thant's conclusions were in fact announced on 14 September and were favourable to proceeding with the new federation. They stated that the concept of Malaysia had been widely and intensively debated and was a major issue in the elections in the two territories; that the elections had been freely and impartially held, and that a 'sizeable majority' of the people in Sabah and Sarawak wished to join Malaysia. He considered that this majority sought independence through freely chosen association with other peoples in their region with whom they felt 'ties of ethnic association, heritage, language, religion, culture, economic relationship and ideals and objectives'. The emergence of dependent territories to self-government as independent sovereign states or autonomous components of larger units had always been one of the purposes of the Charter. According to Antara, the government news agency, the leader of the Indonesian observers declared himself convinced, on returning to Djakarta, of the impartiality of the United Nations inquiry. Nevertheless, on 15 September, the day before the new federation was due to be established, Indonesia declared that it would not recognize Malaysia, which it regarded as 'illegal'. It would raise objections to the report of the United Nations mission and seek to obtain 'a correction of the flaws' in its assessment. The Philippines followed the lead of Indonesia in not recognizing Malaysia. Both countries broke off diplomatic relations with Kuala Lumpur.

Meanwhile, some internal tensions had preceded the inauguration of the new regime. Singapore, Sarawak, and North Borneo had objected to the postponement of Malaysia Day. On the date originally settled, 31 August, Prime Minister Lee proclaimed Singapore's sovereignty in foreign relations and defence pending the inauguration of Malaysia when powers in these fields would pass to the federal Government. The Malayan authorities did not appreciate this superfluous and unconstitutional gesture of independent action. It appears to have been one of Lee Kuan-Yew's periodic exhibitions of impatient cleverness in his dealings with Kuala Lumpur which were to bedevil Singapore's relations with the federal leaders. Sarawak and Sabah also marked 31 August in less controversial fashion by celebrating the entry into force of the new state constitutions and a ministerial system, that is, government by ministers supported by an elected majority in the legislatures. The persons chosen to be Chief Ministers, with the support of the local Alliance parties, were Stephen Ningkan, an Iban, in Sarawak; and Donald Stephens (the former Chairman of the Malaysia Solidarity Consultative Committee) who was half Australian and half Dusun, in Sabah. Neither of these persons was to enjoy easy relations with the Tunku. They do not appear to have been personally congenial to him. He had, indeed, endeavoured to persuade the British authorities not to select the former. He was also concerned that the central government and its leaders should have appropriate influence and authority in these distant associated territories. Shortly before Malaysia Day, he was faced with Ningkan's insistence on the appointment of another distinguished Iban as Governor of Sarawak. This was Temenggong Jugah, a principal chief of the Ibans who, despite his lack of letters, was a powerful political figure in the Alliance Party. The Tunku objected that an understanding had been reached that, if the Chief Minister was a non-Malay, the Governor should be a Malay. This was denied by the Sarawak Alliance, but the Tunku's decision prevailed. A Malay was appointed Governor, Temenggong Jugah being consoled with the duties of Minister for Sarawak Affairs in the federal cabinet. One further note of discord came from the opposition Pan-Malayan Islamic Party which dominated the state of Kelantan,[1] was strongly Malay nationalist, and disposed to favour Indonesia. Under their influence, the state of Kelantan sought an injunction in the High Court of Malaya to restrain the Malayan Government from bringing Malaysia into effect. They used an argument which ignored the whole

[1] See p. 113.

basis of evolution of the federation, namely that, Kelantan being a sovereign state, only the Sultan could make treaties on its
behalf. It was also allegedly unlawful and unconstitutional for
the Malayan Parliament to legislate for Kelantan in any matter
within the legislative competence of the state. The Court dismissed the suit on the grounds that in fact nothing in the
constitution required consultation with the state governments
or Rulers before the Malaysia agreement was signed.

Malaysia was ceremonially proclaimed just after midnight on
16–17 September. Henceforward only in the State of Brunei
and the colony of Hong Kong were true remains of Britain's
once extensive presence in southern and eastern Asia to be
found. So determined an anti-colonialist as President Sukarno
should logically have rejoiced at the swiftness and completeness
with which British 'oppression' of Asian peoples had been concluded. Yet other factors and calculations induced less welcoming reactions.

It is thought by many that, at this late stage in an exhausting
career, some of President Sukarno's more extreme policies were
inspired by his Foreign Minister and First Deputy Prime
Minister, Dr. Subandrio, who appears to have been a protagonist of the influence of the Indonesian Communist Party,
the P.K.I. This key figure in the Indonesian regime had
acquired a decisive ascendancy in the government intelligence
organization. This had set up an effective network in Malaya,
Singapore, and the Borneo territories, functioning through the
Indonesian Embassy and consular offices. Personally agreeable,
shrewd, adroit, sophisticated, well-tailored, he had a forceful
and intelligent wife who played her own public role and voiced
with feminine aggressiveness the polemics of the régime. Dr.
Subandrio knew the West well, having at one time been Ambassador in London. He may have believed that this made him
an expert in probing Britain's weaknesses. If, during the
Malaysia dispute, the President was at times prepared to
consider compromise, he may well have been diverted from it
by such counsellors. It can, however, be doubted whether, with
his visions of Greater Indonesia, Sukarno could ever genuinely
have accepted Malaysia. It is possible to interpret his encouragement of the United Nations inquiry and his fair words
at the Manila conference as a manœuvre which might serve

to place his potential adversaries in the wrong by demonstrating that he had been willing to accept a conciliatory and constructive solution. In any event, in September Indonesia's rejection of Malaysia was accompanied in Djakarta by a series of violations of the immunities and courtesies traditionally protecting foreign diplomatic and consular officers and their p remises. The only practical defence against such action wouldlie in a reciprocal overriding of the diplomatic privilege of the representatives of the offending country in the capital of the inju red nation. Yet such a departure from recognized standards of intercourse is never normally admissible and (with one minor exception) was not adopted by Britain or Malaysia in this case.

On 12 September, before the United Nations report appeared, but after the date for Malaysia had been fixed, the flag on the British Consulate at Surabaya was forcibly replaced by the Indonesian flag. On 16 September the Malaysian and British Consulates at Medan in Sumatra were largely destroyed. In Djakarta, in the absence of adequate police protection, the Malaysian and British Embassies were attacked by mobs. At the latter, the flag was violated, the Ambassador's car burned, the personnel stoned, and extensive damage done to the premises. These events took place in the part of the city most conspicuous to foreign visitors—just opposite the principal hotel. Attention was directed to the attack by the British Assistant Military Attaché who, disregarding missiles, marched up and down the courtyard playing the bagpipes. This gesture of defiance appears to have infuriated the raiders and those behind them by making them lose face in front of what was in effect an international audience. Dr. Subandrio affected to deplore the damage but expressed understanding of Indonesian indignation over 'the formation of Malaysia which is not in accordance with the Manila Summit Conference'. On 18 September, the offices of the British Embassy were burned and sacked. British homes, including those of the Embassy staff, and other British property such as the British Club, were wrecked and looted. The operations were similar to, but more serious than, those to which the Dutch had been exposed in 1957. They were carefully planned and centrally directed, and the failure to provide effective protection demonstrates the connivance of the authorities. Indeed the National Front—the

Youth Front of which was admittedly involved in the outrages
—had a Government Minister as its Secretary-General. It had
previously served the purposes of the Indonesian Government
in the campaign for the take-over of West Irian. In the present
incidents, the attackers themselves would have been unable to
distinguish between someone American, Australian, or British.
Yet only British houses were visited, the assailants being trans-
ported in trucks and provided with lists of their addresses. They
were so trained and controlled that they terrorized and destroyed property without doing serious bodily harm to individuals. In breach of all diplomatic procedure, the British
Ambassador was invited to report his movements. He was
threatened with eviction from his house and denied access to
the Embassy offices. There, such documents as had escaped
safe custody had been seized and an unsuccessful attempt made
by Indonesians to open the strong-room with safe-breaking
tools. The Embassy archives it contained could only be removed
by the Ambassador after he had forced an entrance to the
ruined building in the company of diplomatic colleagues. One
sequel to the violence in Djakarta was some damage to the
Indonesian Embassy in Kuala Lumpur.

During the disturbances, a number of British firms were
taken over by the local trade unions. This met with official disapproval and, on 20 September, President Sukarno ordered
that all British firms should be placed in the charge of government departments 'in the interests of their own safety'. In view
of the importance of oil production, the Shell Oil Company's
refinery at Pladju in Sumatra was handed back to European
management. Most other British firms, however, remained
under Indonesian control. Even with a prospect of some eventual compensation, the exclusion of efficient business management and loss of profits made this tantamount to a major confiscation of Britain's substantial interests in the country in
banking, insurance, import and export trade, and in tea, rubber, coffee, and palm oil estates. Economic measures amounting
to a total boycott were also taken against Malaysia, which was
not in future to receive shipments of Indonesian oil and natural
gas. Malaysian rubber-milling interests in Sumatra were
seized. Indonesian tin concentrates were to be sent to Europe
for processing instead of to Penang. Landing rights were re-

fused to Malayan Airways, telegraphic communications cut, and penalties, envisaging in some cases the death sentence, imposed for listening to Radio Malaysia.

There was small comfort for the Philippines in the United Nations approval of Malaysia and its sequel. Their claim to Sabah was not strictly affected, for at the Manila conference they had expressly reserved their rights in the event of the formation of Malaysia. In their official publicity the Philippines authorities continued to suggest that they were preoccupied over the possibility of Chinese communist subversion on their borders by reason of the large Chinese element in Malaysia. In any event it is clear that they had followed with some reluctance Djakarta's forceful lead in refusing diplomatic recognition to the new federation. There was no hooliganism in Manila, official comment was moderate and there was a general feeling that the U.N. report would have eventually to be accepted. They had proposed to Kuala Lumpur something less than Indonesia's complete rupture of contact, namely the maintenance of consular[1] relations. The Malaysian Government at first declined but some time later accepted this proposal.

Military Confrontation soon became a serious issue. Like the hostile propaganda campaign, it had been in progress long before Malaysia Day and had persisted even during the friendly exchanges in Tokyo and Manila. Along the nearly thousand mile border in Borneo there had been a spell of comparative calm after the suppression of the Brunei revolt. But between April and September 1963 there was a series of guerilla type, hit and run assaults on points in Sarawak and Sabah with appreciable casualties. Few of Azahari's 'National Army of North Kalimantan' had escaped after the rebel defeat and

---

[1] Diplomatic relations imply the recognition of the legitimacy of the government and head of state to which an Ambassador is accredited, and with which he is empowered to negotiate. Consular officers can deal with day to day practical problems, such as the difficulties of their nationals, shipping, trade, etc. They do not represent their government and have no powers to negotiate on its behalf. Their presence equally does not imply recognition of the legitimacy of the régime in the country in which they function. Today this distinction is sometimes obscured by the fact that the Foreign Service includes both diplomatic and consular officers and that the same person may perform these different duties alternately, or even at the same time.

Azahari, having failed, soon ceased to enjoy more than limited help from the Indonesian authorities. Yet most of these attacks were ascribed to his 'army'. They seem in fact to have been conducted partly by regular Indonesian forces and partly by 'volunteers', many of them Chinese communists from Sarawak. The latter decided to resort to armed insurrection early in January 1963, and members of their clandestine communist organization (C.C.O.) went over to Indonesian territory for military training. Captured Indonesians often tried to identify themselves as members of Azahari's 'army' or of the Sarawak United People's Party. On 21 September, after the outbreaks in Djakarta, the Indonesian Government adopted a more purposeful attitude and set up a special 'Operational Command for Crushing Malaysia'. More 'volunteers' were encouraged to come forward from the various parts of the Archipelago.

On 25 September, the Indonesian Defence Minister, General Nasution, stated publicly that Indonesia was training guerillas to liberate 'North Kalimantan' from the 'neo-colonialists'. His attitude was a significant change from the cordial relations which had earlier developed between him and the commanders of the British Commonwealth forces in Singapore. A Sumatran of moderate views regarded with some reserve by the President, he had seemed to them and others one of the constructive elements in the regime whom it might be profitable to cultivate and support. Though there was some doubt whether Nasution had the ruthless strength of character necessary to prevail against a genius in political manœuvre, it was hoped that he might help to counter-balance Sukarno's more disturbing policies, inspired in part by the P.K.I. which was coming increasingly under Peking domination. In this belief, Indonesia had been liberally supplied with Western arms to which the Soviet Union had added ample supplies of its own. Some training had also been given to Indonesian troops by Commonwealth forces in the area. Britain once more found herself (as in the days of the Malayan Emergency) fighting an enemy whom she had instructed in her ways.

Meanwhile, the Kuala Lumpur government had set up a Malaysian Defence Council. The British Commonwealth Secretary had assured the Tunku that Britain would help to defend Malaysia's independence and integrity. Shortly after-

wards, the top British naval authorities conferred with the
Malaysians on sea defence. The Prime Ministers of Australia
and New Zealand declared their support. Their troops would
help to defend Malaysia, with those of Britain, as part of the
Commonwealth Strategic Reserve. The Australian leader
emphasized the importance of Malaysia to the 'zone in which
we live'. There were 6,000 British Commonwealth troops
defending northern Borneo by the end of September. These
included alongside the Malaysians, Australians, New Zea-
landers, and British, and units of Gurkhas from Nepal fighting
as intrepid mercenaries in the British armies as their ancestors
had done since the mid-nineteenth century.

To the simple people of Sarawak and Sabah it was all very
strange. They had just been de-colonized, yet now there were
more British around than ever before. The fallacious impression
that not so very much had changed was enhanced by the fact
that so many British officials had been retained in the government. In this respect, Brunei stood out. After the Sultan's
decision not to join Malaysia, he set about discarding most of
his Peninsula Malay officers and recruiting British officials for
numbers of the senior posts. Since the revolt, he seemed somehow to feel happier with the British than with his own people.
As political life revived, many of his younger subjects, including
those who had sympathy with the now-banned Party Rakyat,
showed signs of wanting to change the traditional order and to
reduce his prerogatives to those of a constitutional monarch.
Indeed this might have been Azahari's policy, had he managed
to associate the ruler with a successful revolution. His Highness
saw little charm in a reduced role of this character. Although he
knew that this was also the ultimate objective of the Protecting
Power, he relied on the British not to hustle the process in any
violent or unseemly manner.

The incidents along the Borneo border continued month by
month. Raiders were found as far as forty miles inside the
territory of Eastern Malaysia, as it began to be called. Occasionally they achieved surprise and some success in throwing
their opponents into disarray. The troops defending Malaysia,
under the command of a British general, were in fact at a grave
disadvantage. The government thought it best for political
reasons that aggression should be unilateral. Their forces were

discouraged from launching surprise attacks and from carrying the war into Kalimantan territory. They were deprived of the vital weapon of the initiative. While the forces on the Malaysian side were thus handicapped, the Indonesians were unhampered. For their high command the Confrontation operations were an important sequel to the West Irian campaign. It had been said of the latter that 'through adroit psychological warfare the maximum diplomatic and operational effect was extracted from a minimum of actual military activities,[1] yet West Irian had been a useful preliminary phase of training and experience for the hostilities against Malaysia. And, for the latter, the Indonesians once again made a psychological score. By repeating the ingenious euphemism 'Confrontation', they led many throughout the world to believe that what were unquestionably acts of war were really something less.

As time went by, the Indonesians relied not so much on 'volunteers' as on their regular forces, though the latter often wore volunteer uniform. The volunteers had shown some fighting spirit but were not conspicuously successful as organized military units. On the other hand, some of the best-trained Indonesian troops, including parachute and marine corps units, were assigned to Confrontation and showed military qualities which impressed their adversaries. In the early stages the Indonesians had a further temporary advantage. While they still relied mostly on local units and the measure of the threat remained unknown to Kuala Lumpur, they managed to keep expensively committed a considerably larger number of Commonwealth forces than those which they employed. This again was a picture which they skilfully projected to the world after it had ceased to be true. In fact, with the reinforcements of Indonesian regulars sent out to Borneo from the end of 1963, the numbers of actual fighting troops on each side seem to have reached approximate parity some two years later. Any small surplus on the Commonwealth side was the result of a paradox. The Indonesian lines of communications from their ports in Western and Eastern Kalimantan, especially to the central portions of the fighting line, were considerably longer and more difficult than those across the comparatively narrow area of northern Borneo. With limited resources for air transport, the

[1] *A Plot Exposed*, p. 8.

Indonesians would normally have required more numerous personnel for their military 'tail' than the Commonwealth forces. In fact they used far fewer forces on their lines of communication. Instead, they lived largely off the country on supplies commandeered from the local inhabitants and faced the resentment which this inevitably caused. Finally, in spite of all the factors which could have rendered the Indonesian operations effective, they failed in fact to achieve any conclusive success. Sooner or later the raiders were checked and dispersed and not a few were killed, wounded or captured.

For nearly three years this strange combination of vituperation and military stalemate continued. It was varied by occasional bursts of energy on the part of Indonesia and exploration by her of new avenues of overt or clandestine attack. It was a running waste of resources, a burden of expenditure, and produced no concrete results. Battle casualties were moderate, partly in view of the purely defensive role to which the Malaysian forces were restricted. Economically, it was not the defenders who suffered most. The cost was some strain on Britain, anxious to strengthen her finances by reducing the Asian commitments she retained. The Malaysian economy, and especially that of Singapore, was shaken, but buoyant enough to suffer no fundamental damage. For Indonesia, however, this was a period of progressive impoverishment. Mounting inflation debased her currency and constantly raised the cost of living for a restive population. She was far more hardly hit by the loss of exports and foreign exchange than was Malaysia which had a healthy balance of payments and a stable and readily convertible dollar.[1] A further economic set-back was the virtual ending of American aid in 1964.

During Confrontation there was a certain ambivalence about the policy and opinion of the United States. They felt kindly towards Malaysia because she was anti-Red, economically sound, and friendly to free enterprise and competitive business on the Western pattern. They sympathized with her predicament and applauded Commonwealth efforts to defend her. But with an expanding and critical commitment in Vietnam, Washington was understandably determined to resist the

[1] 1 U.S. dollar = 3 Malayan dollars, approximately.

prospect of American military involvement in this other struggle, and to lose no opportunity of promoting a settlement. At the same time, most Americans had only a limited understanding of, or feeling for, Malaysia. It had always been the concern of the British, of whose colonial practices they had not invariably approved. The British had an inconvenient reputation (however little borne out by the facts) of being smart and wily. There might be something after all in Indonesian affirmations that Malaysia was a deal which Britain had fixed so that she could continue to manipulate affairs to her imperial advantage. A factor strengthening any potential reservations was that America had a warm interest in the welfare of Indonesia as a nation for whose birth she had been largely responsible after the Dutch military actions of 1947 and 1948. Despite Djakarta's discourteous response to American generosity and manifestations of anti-Western resentment characteristic of communist influence, the American Embassy at Djakarta long seemed disposed to give President Sukarno the benefit of every possible doubt.

It was, however, not merely the communist powers who cultivated the Sukarno régime during this period of Confrontation. For Peking and Moscow, Indonesia's policy had the obvious benefit of causing the kind of economic disruption which helped to advance their cause. Indonesia's *rapprochement* with the Netherlands was less to be expected. In spite of the losses and humiliations which their country had suffered in 1957, and again with the loss of West Irian, in 1962, many Netherlands citizens reappeared in due course upon the scene and diplomatic relations were eventually resumed. The Dutch were prepared to do such business as they still could in the hope of saving some portion of their enormous investments in the country. There was also some satisfaction in returning where the British, who had supplanted them seven years earlier, had been evicted in their turn. They received encouragement from the President. He had been trained in their ways and, having triumphed over them in his fashion, saw some advantage in a new friendliness. The case of Pakistan was again surprising. She was one of the most important members of the British Commonwealth and an ally of the United States in the South East Asia Treaty Organization. Yet her relations with the Sukarno government became specially close at this time, and led to a rupture with Malaysia—like Indonesia, a fellow Muslim country. Many factors contributed: the personal prejudices of Zulfiquar Ali Bhutto, the Pakistan Minister for External Affairs, with whom Dr. Subandrio cultivated cordial relations, Pakistan's inveterate suspicion of India, her incipient friendship with India's adversary, Peking, and Peking's easy relations with Djakarta.[1]

In 1964, three attempts were made to bring Confrontation to an end. All failed. In early January, the Philippine President met President Sukarno and Dr. Subandrio in Manila and, with fair words about Maphilindo, established the basis for a later meeting of the Indonesian and Philippine leaders with the Tunku. Later in January the United States Attorney-General, Mr. Robert Kennedy, visited the Presidents of Indonesia and the Philippines and the Malaysian and British Prime Ministers on a mission from President Johnson to take this controversy 'out of the jungle . . . and put it around the conference table'. One result was a Djakarta announcement that their President had issued a cease-fire order and that first the Foreign Ministers and then the three heads of government would meet. This was swiftly followed, however, by a statement that Confrontation would continue. Prince Sihanouk of Cambodia made an almost simultaneous attempt at mediation, of which little came except a meeting in Phnom Penh between the Tunku and President Macapagal. After the Foreign Ministers met in Bangkok in February the Secretary-General of the United Nations designated the Thai Government to supervise the cease fire arrangements in Borneo. The Malaysians insisted on a preliminary withdrawal of Indonesian forces from Malaysian soil. The Indonesians, however, maintained that they had no control over such people because they were 'volunteers', though they admitted that some were regular troops detached from their forces. At the same time they insisted, not very consistently, on the need to link any guerilla withdrawal with a 'political settlement'. A 20 per cent. withdrawal might be set against a 20

[1] The Pakistan Ambassador to Indonesia told the writer in August 1965 that Singapore seemed to the Indonesians a 'dagger pointed at their territorial waters' and that Britain's relations with Indonesia would be difficult 'until she pursued a policy independent of that of the United States'.

per cent. settlement, etc. In such circumstances and after two meetings the Bangkok talks broke down in early March. A few days later Kuala Lumpur called up all male citizens between the ages of 21 and 28 for military service or civil defence. Djakarta retaliated with a Presidential order that all youths should register as volunteers, and afterwards announced that 21 million had done so. A combat brigade would be raised from these new forces and sent to Borneo to be ready to enter Malaysia in support of the 'volunteers' already in action there. On 24 March, at this crucial point in the polemics, the American Secretary of State declared that the United States would give no new aid to Indonesia until the Malaysian dispute was settled.[1] The Administration for International Development pointed out that this amounted to 'a clear decision by the United States not to give Indonesia any aid that would directly support its current policies'. On the following day at a ceremony in Djakarta at which the American Ambassador was present, the President invited the United States to 'go to hell' with their aid.

In April general elections were held in Malaysia for the Federal Parliament which gave the Alliance an even bigger majority than in 1959.[2] The Pan-Malayan Islamic Party com-

[1] Since independence Indonesia had received about equal amounts of economic assistance from the free world and the Sino-Soviet bloc. According to the official assessment of the State Department, economic and technical assistance from Western sources had amounted to about $800 million, over $671 million of it from the United States. U.S. aid to Indonesia included $244·5 million for technical co-operation and development grants and loans under the Mutual Security Program (now A.I.D.), $194·5 million in surplus agricultural commodities under Public Law 480, and $164·2 million in loans from the Export-Import Bank. Department of State Publication 7267, Far Eastern Series 121, 1963 (Fact Sheet, Indonesia), Government Printing Office, Washington, D.C.

It was estimated that at the end of March 1964, with the arrival of 40,000 tons of surplus U.S. rice, American aid to Indonesia would be virtually ended.

[2] See pp. 111 and 112. The 1964 election results, with the comparable figures for 1959 in brackets, were:

| | | |
|---|---|---|
| Alliance | 89 (73) | Seats (in Malaya) |
| P.M.I.P. | 9 (13) | ,, |
| Socialist Front | 2 (8) | ,, |
| People's Progressive Party | 2 (4) | ,, |

In place of the Party Negara, Malayan Party, and Independents, which scored 5 seats in the 1959 elections, the United Democratic Party (Dr. Lim

prehensibly lost ground. So did the Socialist Front. The former was associated in the public mind with sympathy for Indonesia and suspect, not without cause, of some connivance with the policies of Djakarta. The Party's campaign was partly financed by Indonesia, as was that of the Party Ra'ayat. The Socialist Front was also regarded as guilty of disloyalty in the face of armed attack. In general the election results signified a rallying of the country behind its government in response to Indonesian provocation. The Tunku declared after the election that this gave the Malaysians courage to face their enemies with confidence.

Meanwhile the Philippines peace offensive continued. The talks between heads of government were arranged for June, in Tokyo. Their Foreign Ministers met beforehand on the basis of an undertaking finally given by Indonesia to withdraw her forces from Sabah and Sarawak. Some movements of withdrawal were verified by Thailand and the three leaders duly met. Their talks, however, broke down on the same day over the point that had caused the failure of the Bangkok meetings. Malaysia insisted on withdrawal as a pre-condition for any political discussion. Indonesia refused. To overcome this new deadlock, President Macapagal proposed an Afro-Asian conciliation commission to recommend a solution of Malaysian-Indonesian differences. The Tunku accepted in principle, subject to the immediate cessation of hostilities. President Sukarno also agreed in principle but would give no undertaking. On his return to Kuala Lumpur the Tunku warned his people to be prepared for the worst. Indonesian attacks had continued during the cease-fire and the period of the tripartite meetings. Immediately after the breakdown of the Tokyo talks, a major assault, resulting in a six-hour battle, was launched in the extreme western, Lundu, area of Sarawak. Though this was repelled it could have been critical. The Lundu region where the border between Kalimantan and Sarawak reaches the coast was particularly vulnerable being accessible by sea as well as

Chong Eu) won 1 seat. The People's Action Party, an offshoot of the Singapore party, won 1 seat also. There were already 36 Sabah and Sarawak Alliance seats in the new Federal Parliament. After the 1964 elections the Alliance therefore mustered all together 125 of the 159 seats in Parliament, or nearly four-fifths of the total.

land. According to the Sarawak Government, Indonesian raiders had sought to set up a 'liberated' zone here with the complicity of local branches of the Sarawak United People's Party.

Confrontation was not, however, confined to Borneo. From 1963 onwards there had been captures of Malay fishing craft and other incidents in the Malacca Straits, and a series of bomb explosions in Singapore. Indonesia's intelligence activities had, as we have seen, been largely conducted through her official representatives. But after the rupture of diplomatic relations, a central organization for sabotage and guerilla training was established in the Riau Archipelago immediately south of Singapore, the nearest islands being easily visible from the city. Other training bases were set up on the islands off the Sumatra coast from which there was easy access across the Straits to the Peninsula. The Tokyo fiasco was followed by intensified Indonesian activity not only in Borneo but against Malaya and Singapore. At the end of June, the government in Kuala Lumpur announced the revival of the Security Committee which had been instrumental in defeating the communist insurrection, and the raising of a vigilante corps to help in guarding installations, reporting infiltrators, etc. In July it reported the arrest of some 150 people in Malaya and Singapore guilty of implication in Indonesian subversion. August the 17th—the Indonesian National Day—seems to have been specially chosen by President Sukarno for dramatic action. On that date, 108 Indonesian troops made a sea-borne landing at Pontian in south-western Johore, only some fifty miles from Singapore. This was the first major Indonesian incursion into Malaya itself. The objective was to establish a jungle guerilla base for the training of dissident Malaysians, in the expectation of a warm welcome and numerous recruits. Such a belief was not so wild as it might sound. A high proportion of the population of Johore was of Indonesian origin. For them, Sukarno was the man who had freed his country from the Dutch at a time when Malaya was still denied her freedom by the British. They could not be expected to appreciate the decisive character of United Nations and United States intervention after the Dutch capture of the Indonesian leaders at the end of 1948. Before the emergence of striking national figures of their own, Sukarno seemed to many Malays, and especially to those with an Indonesian background, the outstanding hero of the Malay world. His portrait was often to be found in Malay *kampong* houses. Yet even such people had become aware that in recent years Indonesia had fallen conspicuously behind Malaysia in government efficiency and economic health. They had no wish to share in the privations of the Indonesian people and they humanly resented Djakarta's arrogance and abuse. Thus, in the event, the population even in Johore encountered the Indonesians with closed ranks. Those of the invaders not dealt with by the armed forces after landing, were gradually rounded up among the swamps with the help of the local villagers. Early in September another major incursion met with a similar response. This was a parachute drop on one of the agricultural estates near Labis in the middle of Johore. The invaders were to establish a central base from which to sabotage public facilities and communication links. But there was a bad thunderstorm; the landings were over-dispersed and indifferently co-ordinated; one of the aircraft crashed and failed to arrive. Some of the supply parachutes went wide and fell into the hands of the Malayan police. Some ninety-six invaders succeeded in landing, the majority regular Indonesian paratroopers, the remainder Chinese whom they had trained. One of the captured officers explained that the base was to help in freeing the people of the country. They appreciated the fallacies in their briefing by Djakarta since, instead of being welcomed as liberators, they were turned over to the security forces when they asked some villagers for food. Thus in the later months of 1964 Confrontation reached, and passed, its peak.

# CHAPTER SIXTEEN

# The Conflict Spreads

In the summer of 1964 local elements with help from the Indonesians appear to have contributed to a disturbing growth of racial tension in Singapore. Although the island has a predominantly Chinese community, it contains more Malays— nearly a quarter of a million—than in all the Borneo territories. In July, when the local Muslims were celebrating the Prophet Mohammed's birthday, and again at the beginning of September, there were serious clashes between Malays and Chinese which caused some thirty-five deaths, hundreds of injuries and nearly a thousand arrests. Although it was suspected that certain extreme Malay nationalists from the Peninsula had helped to cause these disturbances, the federal authorities placed the blame on the former Indonesian Consul-General in Singapore. It was suggested that he had arranged to finance criminals in the Chinese secret societies to stir these troubles up. This resourceful representative had later become Ambassador in Kuala Lumpur. He and his successor in Singapore—both senior officers in the Indonesian army—had in fact been chiefly responsible, in addition to their public duties, for the complex clandestine activities of Indonesia in Malaysia. The second outbreak of communal riots had started on the day of the Indonesian parachute landings at Labis in Johore. The whole series of events led the Malaysian Government to declare a state of emergency throughout the country. It became punishable by death to carry arms without authorization. Death or life imprisonment was also inflicted for consorting with terrorists or subversive agents. The government estimated that about two and a half thousand young people from different parts of Malaysia had gone to Indonesia for training and indoctrination and had returned to their country with subversive missions. These included some two thousand from Sarawak and Sabah, three hundred from Singapore and two hundred from Malaya. The last group contained some Malays but was chiefly Chinese.

A further consequence of the attacks at Pontian and Labis was an appeal by Malaysia to the Security Council of the United Nations. Her case was conducted there by the Minister for Home Affairs and Justice, Dato Ismail. He sought the condemnation of Indonesia's 'international brigandage' and an assurance that there would be no more invasions. This led to some characteristic exchanges. The Chairman of the Council was the representative of the Soviet Union. This being a country with which Malaysia was not in diplomatic relations and one of Indonesia's main sources of military supply, he displayed small sympathy for the complainant. He ordered the removal of the exhibits of captured arms which the Malaysian delegation had produced and associated himself with the assertions of the Indonesian representative. These were to the effect that Malaysia was a creation of Britain who, with the aim of preserving her colonial domination, was chiefly responsible for the present state of affairs in Southeast Asia. The Indonesian delegation admitted that volunteers and guerillas had been operating in Malaya to help 'their brothers in the fight for freedom'. But the whole problem should, they said, be viewed in the broader context of the conflict between the new emerging countries and the 'remnants of colonialism'. The 'so-called international law of the world of colonial powers' could not be used to stop this struggle. Mr. Adlai Stevenson, on behalf of the United States, challenged any use of force outside the framework of the U.N. Charter and Indonesia's implied admission that such action was justifiable against a neighbour to whom she objected. The Soviet representative denounced America as 'the leader in the chain of criminal acts of the colonialists in Southeast Asia'. At this stage, Dato Ismail stressed that Malaysia was completely sovereign and in no way dominated by the British. She had made a purely defensive military pact with Britain, as she had every right to do. Faced with the use of force by Indonesia she had to obtain British military assistance under these arrangements. But they could be terminated when the danger no longer existed. The threat was not 'colonialism' but the 'neo-imperialism' of a big neighbour out to crush their country. An anodyne Norwegian resolution was finally put forward deploring the Indonesian operations and inviting both countries to settle their differences and refrain from violence. This was barred by a Soviet veto, though passed by all but two votes. Malaysia claimed the result as a moral victory.

As might have been expected, the Indonesians were in no way deterred by these proceedings. In both eastern and western Malaysia incidents continued in varying intensity into 1965. In the west, there were further attacks on the Johore and Malacca coasts and even as far north as the coast of Perak. There were also, for the first time, incursions on the east coast of Malaya. True to their policy of not initiating armed aggression, the Malaysian forces only retaliated by dropping leaflets. In Borneo there were many minor engagements and one major one involving heavy fighting against an Indonesian force of about 120. Killed and wounded up to the end of July 1964 were estimated in Kuala Lumpur at 105 for their forces and 363 for their opponents, of whom another two hundred had been made prisoner. In the autumn of 1964 and early 1965, Britain, Australia, and New Zealand increased their forces in the area. Australian and New Zealand troops were moved to Borneo. All three nations made training facilities and arms available to Malaysia and denied them to Indonesia. Following the Tunku's visit to the United States and Canada in the summer of 1964, both these countries offered training facilities and sent military missions to Kuala Lumpur to assess Malaysia's needs. America had cancelled her military aid to Indonesia from September 1963.

Throughout 1964 the Indonesians continued to make things hard for the British within their borders. Nearly all British enterprises had been compelled to accept Indonesian tutelage in September 1963, but British staff and managers remained. There followed a series of measures by which British management was eventually eliminated. In January the communist trade unions took over a number of British-owned plantations as well as the headquarters of the Shell Oil Company and of Unilever, another Anglo-Dutch corporation specializing in soap, detergents, and food. The unions were called to order by the authorities, and in February these and other firms were put under direct official supervision. At the same time the government disclaimed any intention of taking over foreign oil companies. Oil was too important for Indonesia to be able to afford to jeopardize efficient production. In May the British plantations with which the communist unions had interfered were placed under government control and Indonesian management. The President again chose 17 August for a dramatic declaration: on that day he announced that it would 'depend on the British standpoint *vis-à-vis* the liquidation of Malaysia' whether British firms were nationalized with compensation or confiscated without it. By the end of the month, all British companies in Indonesia had been forced to discard their European managers, except Shell which had a special agreement with the government, and Unilever which came under Dutch management. The experience of the latter was hardly more encouraging than that of the British managers who had preceded them.[1] At the end of November virtually all other British-owned commercial interests in the country were placed under full Indonesian management and control. The British government declared that this amounted to *de facto* expropriation and that compensation would be expected. The boycott of the British extended to other fields. In August a stop was put to the cultural and educational work of the British Council.

Internationally the same period brought no lifting of the clouds. Both Djakarta and Kuala Lumpur had accepted in principle the Philippine President's proposal for an Afro-Asian Conciliation Commission, to be drawn from four nations. President Sukarno had sponsored the first Afro-Asian conference, from which Malaya, still under Britain, was excluded.[2] The climate of gatherings where the Africans and Asians predominated was especially congenial to him and one of these occurred in October 1964. This was the Second Conference of

[1] The Dutch managing director informed the writer in Djakarta in August 1965 that there was little he could do. Apart from the government supervisor, the communist and other trade unions were represented on an advisory committee. The principle applied under this supervision was that, if the company made a taxable profit, this should be given to the workers as a bonus. Although the workers were required to take days and even weeks at a time off to participate in political demonstrations, they received full pay and lunch money during these periods. Comprehensibly, the company was making heavy commercial losses. Some of the minor indignities to which he was subjected (blocking his air conditioning, stopping his supplies of coffee, etc.) had their lighter side. The Islamic trade unionists objected to their Marxist colleagues that this last privation was unjust: 'even a condemned man is given a meal before execution'.

[2] See p. 126.

Non-Aligned Nations at Cairo. Before and during the conference he sought to sway African and Asian opinion against Malaysia who, in view of her attitude to the communist bloc, again did not qualify for admission. The declaration which the conference produced was, however, inconvenient from the Indonesian President's standpoint and he refrained from signing it. This stressed the classical principles of peaceful coexistence, respect for territorial integrity, and non-interference in the internal affairs of others. It also condemned the use of force in violation of the Charter. The second conference of Afro-Asian nations, to be held in Algiers in January 1965, promised him fresh opportunities. In the event this was postponed but in the month which had been set for the meeting Indonesia took another dramatic step. She withdrew from the United Nations. The General Assembly had agreed that Czechoslovakia and Malaysia should share a two-year term on the Security Council, and Malaysia's turn came in 1965. On New Year's Eve 1964, President Sukarno announced that if Malaysia took her seat Indonesia would cease to be a member. This may have been a useful pretext rather than the actual reason. He was well aware that in pursuing Confrontation Indonesia was in conflict with her U.N. obligations. In her administration of West Irian she was also required to observe special conditions imposed by the U.N. It might have seemed tempting to recover her freedom of action.

Indonesia was the first country to take such a step. At the beginning of January she abandoned not only the U.N. Organization itself but all save one of the specialized agencies functioning under its Economic and Social Council. The President declared that Indonesia did not need the help of the U.N. agencies. The Food and Agriculture Organization had shown little understanding of Indonesian agriculture, his country had 'eradicated illiteracy' without the aid of the U.N. Educational, Scientific, and Cultural Organization, etc. Indonesia withdrew not only from these but also from the U.N. Children's Fund.[1] On the other hand she continued to belong

---

[1] In announcing Indonesia's withdrawal from F.A.O., U.N.E.S.C.O. and U.N.I.C.E.F., the President expressed himself in similar terms ('to hell with your aid') to those he had employed in respect of help from the United States.

to the World Health Organization. The various health programmes, such as malaria eradication, which the W.H.O. was
carrying out in Indonesia were too valuable to be discontinued.
Peking rejoiced at Djakarta's decision and declared full support
for Confrontation. Indonesia's 100 million had joined China's
650 million outside an 'infamous' body in which 'a few powers
share the spoils'.

At this same period which saw Indonesia's departure, the
Malaysian Government appealed again to the United Nations.
It drew the attention of the Security Council to the multiplicity
of incidents—some two hundred—which had occurred during
the past year and were still continuing. A large build-up of
Indonesia's forces in Borneo and the incursions in the Malay
Peninsula might herald a special drive to defeat their country
now that Djakarta had freed itself from the legal and moral
restraints imposed by the Charter. Malaysia appealed for U.N.
help should Indonesian attacks be intensified. At the same time
she asked her allies to consider sending more troops and assistance if necessary. Internal security was also tightened. At the
end of January some key figures whom the authorities had been
watching were arrested. These included[1] the President and
Vice-President of the principal opposition group, the right-
wing Pan-Malayan Islamic Party; the Chairman of the Labour
Party; a reporter from *Utusan Melayu*, the newspaper of the
pronounced right wing of the pro-government United Malays
National Organization; and a former Minister for Agriculture.
The latter, a brother of Singapore's head of state, had also been
prominent in *Utusan Melayu*. He had become critical of the
government's policy and in particular of Malaysia's pro-
western orientation. He had also attempted to prohibit
Chinese firms from marketing agricultural produce in competition with the Malay rural co-operatives he had promoted. His
militant Malay communalism seemed a threat to the Alliance.
This had led to a clash with the Tunku and his exclusion from

[1] Dr. Burhanuddin, P.M.I.P. (see pp. 84 and 113).
  Dato Raja Abu Hanifah, P.M.I.P.
  Ishak bin Haji Mohamed (Labour Party).
  Hussain Yaacob, *Utusan Melayu*.
  Abdul Aziz bin Ishak (former Minister for Agriculture and Chairman of
the National Convention Party, a small opposition group not represented
in Parliament).

the government and U.M.N.O. in 1962. The authorities published a revealing record of the arrested men's activities.[1] They were accused of sending Malaysians to Indonesia for training in subversion, of conspiring to foment an armed revolution and of planning to set up a pro-Indonesian government-in-exile. Some had received funds from a former officer of the Indonesian Embassy who had managed to re-establish contact with them after the rupture of diplomatic relations. Two of these persons had tried, and failed, to take part in the Cairo Conference of Non-Aligned Nations on behalf of Malaysian groups disloyal to the government. In Cairo they had met the former Indonesian Ambassador to Kuala Lumpur who was largely responsible for the Indonesian espionage and subversion network in Malaysia. Another of the arrested suspects had been in touch with Indonesian representatives in Tokyo during the Olympic Games, held in the same month of October 1964, as the Cairo Conference.

The Indonesian authorities were interested in recruiting Malaysians from public life to form a shadow government under their sponsorship, ostensibly backed by a 'National Front' within the country. This last would co-ordinate subversive activities and lend colour to Indonesia's claim to liberate the people from bondage to the 'colonialists'. Indonesia hoped to secure the participation of a delegation from this 'government', and of another from Azahari's 'government of the Unitary State of North Kalimantan' purporting to represent Brunei, Sabah, and Sarawak, in the forthcoming Algiers conference of Afro-Asian nations. These could have been presented as the 'real' voice of the separate components of Malaysia had the Kuala Lumpur government sent (as it intended) an official delegation to the meeting. Once all were back in Malaysia this group of somewhat muddle-headed, diffident, and ineffective conspirators decided to try to implement the Indonesian plans. They agreed to send three 'National Front' members to Algiers where, if all went well, they might proclaim the government-in-exile with themselves as members. Unfortunately they were all short of money. Their Indonesian patrons did not produce enough in time. The police descended on them at the end of January 1965, while they were waiting

[1] *A Plot Exposed.*

for more funds. This débâcle did not prevent Djakarta from continuing their support of the government of the 'National Republic of Malaya' originally proclaimed in September 1963 on the model of Azahari's fictional government. Its headquarters were established in eastern Sumatra with the help of some minor Malay renegades. These arrests and the other government measures such as the establishment of the Defence Council and Security Committee and the declaration of a State of Emergency, had equipped the country against the internal and external threat. The government leaders also sought to tighten up and streamline the political organization supporting them and to achieve the closest possible national unity in the newly formed multi-racial state. To promote their first objective they decided in April 1965 to merge the four separate Alliance parties in Malaya, Singapore, Sabah, and Sarawak into one Malaysian Alliance Party. This was to be run by a national council on which each local party would have a membership corresponding to the size of the state's representation in the federal parliament. On the other hand they were considerably less successful in achieving their second objective of national unity through inter-racial and inter-regional understanding.

During the spring and summer of 1965 the pattern of military Confrontation continued without striking change. During this period, however, two significant trends which were profoundly to affect the future took clearer shape in Indonesia and Malaysia. The first was a progressive growth in the influence of the P.K.I., the communist party of Indonesia, and in the closeness of Djakarta's alignment with, and dependence on, Moscow and Peking. This was inevitably accompanied by further deterioration in Indonesia's relations not merely with Britain but with other western powers and in particular the United States. The other trend was increasing tension between Kuala Lumpur and Singapore. This was due chiefly to the conviction acquired by the Malay leaders that Prime Minister Lee and many ambitious Chinese whom he encouraged and inspired were seeking to dominate the new federation.

The pro-communist trend in Indonesia was marked in 1964 by an exchange of visits between Mikoyan and Subandrio, the First Deputy Prime Ministers of the Soviet Union and Indonesia. The former assured President Sukarno, when he came to

Djakarta, of Soviet support for the struggle against Malaysia. Soviet arms would continue to be supplied on a commercial basis, as they had been since 1961. Some of the aircraft and warships Russia had sent to Indonesia earlier were by no means new and of dubious quality. Indonesia had failed to meet the payments on them. The Mikoyan visit seemed partly designed to restore a cordiality which had faded. Dr. Subandrio's visit to Moscow was followed by that of General Nasution and President Sukarno. It was confirmed that the Soviet Union would continue to help Indonesia to oppose the neo-colonialists and would sell her additional equipment for her armed forces. A new military aid agreement was signed in October 1964, under which Indonesia looked forward to immediate deliveries of more Soviet aircraft.

Early in January 1965, the President banned the political party of two of his most prominent Ministers, Chaerul Saleh, the Third Deputy Prime Minister, and Adam Malik, the Minister for Trade. This was apparently at the instigation of the P.K.I. under the determined leadership of D. N. Aidit. Malik had been Ambassador to Moscow and the banned group, known as Murba (the 'party of the masses') was itself inspired by Marxist ideology. But, from the standpoint of the Peking-oriented P.K.I., it was heretical and deviationist. It purported to be independent and nationalist and advocated a special brand of Marxism based on Indonesia's needs. Later, Minister Malik was relieved of all important government responsibility. He ceased to be Minister for Trade and was relegated to the nominal duties of Minister for Co-ordination. A small, frank, able, cautious, and phlegmatic person of some charm, and a friend of General Nasution, he was to prove a force for the future. In his subsequent attitude to President Sukarno there may have been a comprehensible measure of resentment towards the man who had discarded his counsels and destroyed his political following. Unlike some of his colleagues, he displayed no subservience but became an unhesitating critic of the Presidential policies which had led their country towards economic disaster.[1]

[1] In August 1965, he indicated to the writer in Djakarta that Confrontation was something quite unnecessary. Their nation had already been created and there was no need to go on stirring up the revolutionary fires. It would

Later in January, Dr. Subandrio headed an Indonesian delegation to Peking. This visit to the rival headquarters of the communist world was for the stated purpose of discovering how much military help Indonesia could expect from China if Britain attacked her in consequence of Confrontation. It was agreed at the conclusion of his stay that there could be no peaceful co-existence between the new emerging forces and the old established ones. Peking considered President Sukarno's decision to leave the United Nations a great encouragement to the revolutionary movements of the world. Indeed a revolutionary United Nations might be set up in competition with the existing body. The latter was only capable of mischief since it was manipulated by America. If the British and United States imperialists should dare to make war on Indonesia, China would 'not sit idly by'. The visit produced mutual undertakings to develop trade and communications and contacts in the military field, an agreement for economic and technical co-operation, and a Chinese credit for nearly $100 million.

On 1 March Dr. Subandrio stressed the essential role of the communists in his country. It was wrong to condemn them. The Indonesian revolution could only be accomplished with their help as well as that of the nationalist and religious elements. The watchword was Nasakom.[1] All the best minds and abilities must be united in one patriotic national front.

A few days later it was found necessary to close down all the libraries and reading rooms of the United States Information Services in Indonesia. Considerable damage had been done in December to the American Cultural Centre and library in Djakarta and the U.S.I.S. library in Surabaya, ostensibly in protest against American policy in the Congo. In mid-February there had been a further demonstration against the library in Djakarta in condemnation of American air attacks on North

---

have been best to keep foreign experts until they had a large enough managerial class of their own, and to let foreigners continue to run some of the big enterprises for the time being. With the economic situation as grave as it was then, it would soon be necessary to get down to the humdrum task of putting the country economically to rights. He did not think, however, that President Sukarno himself would ever change his policies; he was very addicted to oratory.

[1] Another hybrid (like Maphilindo) taken from the first syllable of the three elements involved. Nasionalisme-Agama (Religion)-Komunisme.

Vietnam. This was apparently organized by the government itself, which afterwards took the library over. Not only did the police and security units do nothing effective on all these occasions, but the February demonstrators included members of the armed forces as well as of political parties, trade unions, etc. In this and other respects there was a strong similarity to the organized outbreaks against the British. In spite of extensive damage to property, no actual violence was offered to American citizens. At the end of February, the grounds of the U.S. Ambassador's house were invaded by Muslim students. This last protest was against the shooting in New York of 'Malcolm X', whom they chose to regard as 'a Muslim murdered by Americans'. At the same period all American-owned rubber plantations in Northern Sumatra were put under the management of the Indonesian Government. The American staffs were to leave the country. In March the government finally abandoned its policy of leaving foreign experts in control of oil production. The three foreign oil companies, two American (Caltex and Stanvac) and one British (Shell) were placed under the supervision and control of the Indonesian authorities. The arrangement in this case was essentially inconsequential. The foreign staffs would remain responsible for operations but would have to obey government directives.

Early in April, Washington made a determined bid to put an end to the mounting tension and bitterness engendered by the policies of Djakarta. President Johnson sent Mr. Ellsworth Bunker to see President Sukarno. Mr. Bunker, formerly prominent in the business world, had been one of America's most successful non-career Ambassadors. He had also recently been mediator in the West Irian dispute. There had been some criticism of the solution adopted for this problem as being one-sidedly in favour of Indonesia and less than equitable to the Dutch. For this reason, Mr. Bunker could expect to be *persona grata* at Djakarta. Whatever his ultimate intentions, President Sukarno was rarely at a loss for fair words on an occasion of this kind. A soothing though non-committal statement was agreed at the conclusion of the visit. This referred to the tension produced by Malaysia; such differences must not, however, be allowed to affect the friendship between the two countries.

U.S. aid programmes would be 'reviewed and revised on a continuing basis' and U.S. technical assistance to certain universities would go on. Other factors perhaps revealed more clearly the course which President Sukarno or his more radical advisers had set. The American Peace Corps was to be withdrawn from Indonesia. Furthermore, at the end of the month, all remaining foreign enterprises and property in Indonesia were put under government control. This affected French, Belgian, Swiss, and Danish interests, owners chiefly of rubber and palm oil plantations in Sumatra and elsewhere. The government's fresh move was announced as being one element n a new economic policy of greatly increased socialization and state control. In effect it ended foreign investment in Indonesia. There was a disturbing parallel between these developments and the sequel to Attorney-General Kennedy's earlier visit to President Sukarno. In each case statements of good will had been swiftly (and obviously deliberately) followed by the swift adoption of measures defying these previous assurances.

With little variation, the Nasakom régime pursued its sharply leftward and aggressive course into the summer of 1965. A series of Indonesian landings on the east coast of Malaya took place between December and the middle of the year. Foreign observers had reason to expect that 17 August, the national day, would be marked by further estrangement from the West, including the possible rupture of diplomatic relations with Britain and the United States. In the event the Presidential gesture on the day of the Republic was something less sensational. Indonesia withdrew from the World Bank and the International Monetary Fund. It is a measure of the assessment of Indonesia's degenerating economy by these conservative institutions that she had received no loans from them since originally becoming a member in 1954. At this same period preparations for further special activities were being made by the crack troops stationed by the Indonesians on their islands off Singapore. These plans were disrupted by a crisis in Djakarta at the end of September which led to many being urgently recalled. Before this happened the whole status of Singapore itself had changed. This last development had its origin in the evolution of the island and its leaders since September 1963.

A few days after the inauguration of Malaysia, the Singapore Legislative Assembly had been dissolved on the Prime Minister's advice. General elections ensued which, as he had calculated, greatly strengthened his position.[1] Having held only half the seats in the legislature when it was dissolved, his People's Action Party had now acquired a large majority. This gave him a clear mandate for the execution of his policies. On the one hand he was categorically anti-communist, since the communists were the chief threat to his power. On the other, he was strongly pro-Malaysia as an outstandingly forceful and intelligent non-Malay conceived that it should be.

As regards the danger of communist subversion, earlier in 1963 Prime Minister Lee had, as we have seen,[2] ensured the

[1] Unlike the constitutional provisions in the United States, the legislature in Britain and in many former British territories such as Malaysia does not necessarily continue until the end of its full normal term. Provided that he is supported by a majority of votes the Prime Minister can ask for a dissolution when he deems it politically advantageous to do so. Fresh elections must then take place within a short stated time. The relevant provisions in the constitution of Singapore as a state of Malaysia were typical of all such arrangements in countries following the British constitutional system: Article 49, (3) and (4): 'The Yang di-Pertuan Negara may at any time . . . dissolve the Legislative Assembly if he is advised by the Prime Minister so to do, but he shall not be obliged to act . . . unless he is satisfied that . . . the Prime Minister commands the confidence of a majority of the members. . . . The Legislative Assembly, unless sooner dissolved, shall continue for five years. . . . There shall be a general election . . . within three months after every dissolution.'

The new party distribution as compared with that before the dissolution was:

|  | New | Old |
|---|---|---|
| People's Action Party | 37 | 25 |
| Barisan Sosialis | 13 | 14 |
| Alliance Party | — | 7 |
| United People's Party | 1 | 2 |
| Independents | — | 2 |

(The P.A.P. had lost a number of the seats they won in the 1959 elections owing to the breakaway of its pro-communist and anti-Malaysia left wing to form the Barisan Sosialis in 1961. Another adverse factor had been the formation in the same year of the pro-Malaysia but anti-P.A.P. Alliance Party covering, as in Kuala Lumpur, the United Malays National Organization, the Malayan Chinese Association, and the Malayan Indian Congress.)

[2] See p. 140.

stability of his régime by drastic moves against his left-wing opponents. Over a hundred trade unionists and politicians had been arrested on the authority of the Singapore Internal Security Council, which also included a Malayan, and British representatives. A number of extremist publications were banned. The government said that this was necessary in view of the threat posed by the Brunei revolt and the attempts of the Barisan Sosialis and other communist united front organizations to sabotage Malaysia. They had supported the Brunei rebels in spite of the Singapore referendum approving Malaysia the year before.[1] They worked not merely for communist objectives but in some cases 'for other subversive ends'. They were planning to use Singapore as a Cuban-style base for a political offensive against Malaysia. If they could win control of an isolated Singapore they could abolish the Security Council and use the island as a springboard for communist revolution. After their election victory in September, the government moved to cancel the citizenship of a chief founder of Nanyang University on the grounds that he had collaborated with communists there. Strangely enough the man so charged was no proletarian intriguer but a wealthy rubber magnate named Tan Lark Sye. His case was by no means unique among the substantial figures in the world of the overseas Chinese.[2] It had wider repercussions. In this aftermath of the establishment of Malaysia the Singapore government felt emboldened to proceed against its enemies even more firmly than before. In October 1963, more trade unionists were arrested including three Barisan Sosialis members of the Legislative Assembly, and seven of the organizations affiliated to the suspect Singapore Association of Trade Unions had their registration cancelled. The government declared that those arrested had intended to use Nanyang University and Chinese middle school students to compel the government to withdraw its proceedings against Tan Lark Sye and so to provoke the police that the latter could be accused of suppressing Chinese education and culture.

[1] See p. 156.
[2] One of the great sources of strength of Chinese communism, as opposed to Russian communism, has been the national genius of the Chinese for business, finance, hard work, thrift, and the tenacious acquisition of wealth.

With his political base thus secured, Prime Minister Lee had acquired a self-confidence which sometimes outweighed his judgement. He could now plan to give substance to what he termed a Malaysian Malaysia. The essential significance of this for him and other non-Malays was the guaranteed prospect of equal rights and opportunities for all races. Ironically enough, these were the basic principles underlying Malayan Union which Britain had introduced in 1946 and to which the Chinese and other minorities in Malaya had been so indifferent at the time. Even Dato Onn, although a Malay and an opponent of the Union, had paid a not entirely disinterested tribute to this concept of racial equality.[1]

Singapore's leader now argued with logic and conviction that the existing political organization of the country on racial and communal lines was a threat to the future of Malaysia as a multi-racial nation. There should be a common loyalty and patriotism and an end to narrow, conflicting, sectional interests. He condemned what he alleged to be the attempts of the Malays,

---

The Peking régime has sought to exploit the overseas Chinese capitalists in the interests of communism. In this they have had some occasional success. Most Chinese tend to be strongly realistic and to lack doctrinaire political interests and enthusiasms. They are usually prepared to adjust themselves to the facts of power, however unpalatable. The Chinese communist authorities have been able to work upon their people's fondness for profitable dealing, and their strong family loyalties. On the one hand, for example, the two Banks of mainland China, the Bank of China and the Bank of Communications, have been ready to offer loans on easy terms to overseas Chinese keen to expand their businesses or acquire new property. Once an offer of this kind is accepted, the client is under an obligation to the communists, who can then persuade him without great difficulty that he should send his children to communist-run schools, etc. There is at the same time an overriding consciousness of blood ties between the Overseas Chinese and those in China. Most of the former are solicitous for the interests of their families living under communist rule. Apart from the traditional money remittances, they have sometimes been willing to buy special protection or favours for these families by doing some significant service to communism at the behest of Peking in the overseas communities in which they live.

The Soviet Russians have virtually no comparable groups of moneyed citizens abroad who could be prevailed upon to serve their cause for similar reasons, especially after the lapse of nearly fifty years since their communist revolution.

[1] See pp. 84 and 104.

through U.M.N.O., to continue to play a dominant role, contrary (he maintained) to the spirit of the new constitution. In May 1965 he launched a movement, with opposition support, called the Malaysian Solidarity Convention. This campaigned throughout the country for a 'Malaysian Malaysia' not identified with the supremacy and interests of any one community or race. His nimble and articulate reasoning, ready accessibility and social *savoir faire* carried weight with many sophisticated and influential persons and not least with Europeans. Such people appreciated a bluntness and dynamism and clarity of thought in tune with their own approach to problems. To some the Prime Minister seemed the man who best understood what Malaysia was, or should be. Not all of them grasped the ultimate implications of his words. He himself fully realized that, with equality of opportunity, the Chinese with their industry, shrewdness, and acquisitiveness, and nearly half the population of Malaysia,[1] could if they wished eventually gain control. In that event he as their most gifted spokesman, or one of his successors, might hope to become the leader of the whole nation.

To the Malays such a prospect was just as repugnant in 1964 as it had been eighteen years before, in 1946. Not only had they violently opposed and rejected Malayan Union. The mere fact that Dato Onn had envisaged the admission of non-Malays to their national organization had been chiefly responsible for his political downfall. In the intervening years some of the most intelligent among them had come to realize that in time the Malays, already better qualified than the Chinese in some fields, might become fully capable of competing with them in all. A point might one day be reached when, without special advantages or protection, the Malays could freely maintain the position in the country which they considered their birthright.

---

[1] The proportions for the whole of Malaysia, according to official statistics based on the census for 1961 are:

*Indigenous* people: 46·2%
   (i.e. Malays and related Muslim races and the up-country peoples)
*Chinese*: 42·2%

The *Indians and Pakistanis* form about another 10%, the remainder being classified as Others.

(Supplement on Malaysia to the *Official Year Book*, 1963, p. 11.)

But most Malays regarded this as a distant and dubious prospect. Their reaction was not reasoned, but instinctive and emotional. They absolutely rejected any such pretensions on the part of non-Malays. Malaysia was designed rather to safeguard their position than to give new opportunities to others. The inclusion of Singapore, apart from the need to forestall communist subversion, had seemed to the less open-minded an excellent opportunity 'to control all those rich Chinese'.

Such was the Malay attitude towards their rivals in general. It did not prevent much individual friendship and association between the races and incidentally more frequent intermarriage[1] than might have been expected. The Chinese were frequently adept at cementing goodwill by doing services—financial or otherwise—to their Malay friends with some expectation of future advantage for themselves. Unfortunately, in the case of Prime Minister Lee, both his personal qualities and his failings had strongly prejudiced the Malays against him. They should in all fairness have felt indebted to a man who had dealt so effectively with the communist menace on their borders. Yet his very success seemed to make them feel that he might present to them and to the whole Alliance almost as great a threat as the communists themselves. By the exacting Malay standards of courtesy and human dealings he was too clever, brusque and uncivil. They deeply resented his gibes at the 'feudal' outlook of the Malay establishment and even more an ill-judged allusion to the fact that in earlier centuries the Malays themselves had been immigrants to the Peninsula. He was at the same time strongly disliked, for different reasons, by the leaders of the Malayan Chinese Association, and particularly by its President, the Minister for Finance, Tan Siew Sin. Stories circulated among the chief figures of the Alliance, some of which may have acquired additional colour in the telling, of Lee Kuan-Yew's alleged cruelty and ruthless ambition in both his family circle and political dealings.

[1] It would normally be regarded as a grave breach of religion and custom for a Muslim to marry a non-Muslim unless the latter were converted to Islam. It is thus rare for Muslim girls to marry Chinese. It is less rare for Chinese girls to marry Muslims and be converted. There are also comparatively frequent adoptions of Chinese girls, e.g. from orphanages, into Malay families where they are brought up as Muslims, and are likely to marry into the Malay community.

For his part, Prime Minister Lee did not conceal his view that the ruling body of the M.C.A. represented essentially the rich capitalist element in the Chinese community which supported the Malays in order to advance their interests. They were, as he depicted them, renegades to the Chinese cause. The claims to equality of the non-Malays should not be allowed to go by default. This assertive and provocative line seems to have won the admiration of many of the more modest Chinese in Malaya who were glad to hear one of their race voicing unpalatable truths. But at election time such people usually chose safety by rallying to the banner of the Association and the Alliance. Regrettably for his own future, the Singapore leader with his drive and impetuousness discounted and misjudged one important prospect. This was the hope that with patience and the passage of time most of the inequalities which hampered the Chinese (though they did remarkably well in spite of them) might gradually be corrected as a greater number became citizens and their political power increased. It was precisely this quality of statesmanlike gradualness which the M.C.A. represented and to which Lee Kuan Yew was temperamentally unable to subscribe. He had been warned of the dangers of pushing the Malays too far. Yet he felt that it was essential to avoid soft compromises and to press Chinese claims firmly and without delay so that they should not be overlooked and forgotten. Perhaps this note of urgency may also have been inspired by the hope of playing a major role in his own time. In the event his policy and attitude so exasperated the Alliance leaders that they felt forced to insist on a parting of the ways even if this meant losing the advantages of keeping Singapore under federal authority. For Lee Kuan Yew himself this eventually prejudiced the chance which meant so much to him of the Chinese-guided city state of Singapore becoming the model and focus of a 'real' Malaysia and perhaps, in line with the historical tradition of British days, its senior partner.

The discord between Kuala Lumpur and Singapore rumbled on through 1964 and the first half of 1965 and at times a break seemed imminent. Britain had been one of the sponsors of Malaysia and her representatives discreetly sought to avert so grave a change of course. One sign that the federal authorities would not shrink from drastic action was the expulsion of Mr.

Alex Josey, a British journalist who had become Prime Minister Lee's principal publicity adviser. A crisis finally occurred in the summer of 1965. On 9 August it was suddenly announced that Singapore had seceded from Malaysia and had become an independent sovereign nation. It transpired that an agreement, signed on 7 August, had been concluded by the two Prime Ministers in some haste and secrecy after an interview the previous night; and a bill had been passed through the federal parliament in record time. Despite Britain's close interest, even the British High Commissioner was not informed in advance. Nor were the governments of the other former British territories, Sabah and Sarawak, which had joined Malaysia at the same time and largely on the same footing as Singapore. They also felt that they had some claim to be previously notified if not consulted. It was clear from the explanations subsequently offered by the Tunku and Prime Minister Lee that 'secession' was a euphemism. There had been nothing voluntary about Singapore's withdrawal. The Tunku acknowledged his responsibility and the Deputy Prime Minister of Singapore in writing to him candidly used the word 'expulsion'. Prime Minister Lee himself broke down in tears during the press conference he gave announcing Singapore's new status and future arrangements. The public declarations did not of course spell out with any fullness the reasons for the break. The Tunku stated that he had considered and rejected the possible alternative of repressive action against some individuals. He had hoped to make Singapore into the New York of Malaysia. But Kuala Lumpur had sought co-operation in vain from Singapore. Mr. Lee Kuan Yew and others had made acrimonious attacks on the federal government, to which they had ceased to give 'even a semblance of loyalty'. He asserted that these Singapore leaders had allowed their personal glory to override the interests of the state. Mr. Lee Kuan-Yew on the other hand blamed the break on Malay extremists who should have been called to order by the Tunku long before. Singapore would have preferred to stay in a looser federation, but secession had been forced upon her. For him this was a 'moment of anguish' since he had believed all his life in the unity of the two territories. Economic co-operation continued to be essential since nearly a quarter of Singapore's trade was with the

Peninsula and three-quarters of her water supply came from there. Without such co-operation the island would have 'to make a living by trading with the devil'. Continued collaboration in certain other fields was no less vital. Common defence arrangements were laid down in the secession agreement. There would be a joint defence council. Malaysia would help over Singapore's external defence with Singapore contributing troops of her own; and shortly after separation Singapore units were despatched to Borneo to help in checking Indonesian Confrontation. Malaysia would continue to maintain bases for her forces in Singapore. Precautions were also taken in the diplomatic field. Neither government would conclude a treaty or agreement which might be detrimental to the independence or defence of the other. As might have been foreseen, all these reserved subjects were to provide material for fresh dissension in the future.

Many of the Malays themselves doubted the wisdom of what their government had done. For once it seemed that it was they who had been precipitate. Significantly, one of the principal extremists accused by Singapore of working for the domination of the state by the federal government, Dato Syed Ja'afar Albar, resigned from his post as Secretary-General of U.M.N.O. in protest against Singapore's exclusion. This was not from any belief that Kuala Lumpur should have been more liberal and tolerant. He held that the 'verbal war' could in time have been settled and that it was dangerous to lose control of a very close neighbour whose government was dominated by a hostile party. Tun Razak, the Deputy Prime Minister of Malaysia, and other Malay leaders were convinced, on the other hand, that, just because of this hostility, separation was essential. It is still too soon to say whether the one or the other of these two conflicting standpoints will prove to have been right.

# CHAPTER SEVENTEEN

# The Turning Tide

Singapore's separation from Malaysia brought internal and external adjustments and reactions. A Republic was later proclaimed and the head of state's title changed to President. All Singapore citizens ceased to be Malaysians. There were various alterations in the Cabinet, and the Deputy Prime Minister took over all departments which had dealt with federal affairs.[1] While voicing the importance of collaboration with Malaysia, Singapore asserted her freedom of action in some minor matters and the possibility of it in major ones. A turnover tax imposed by the federal government was abolished. The communist Bank of China, which was to have been closed under an order from Kuala Lumpur, was to continue operation. In spite of its large Chinese majority, this new nation in miniature was still to be a genuinely multi-racial society. A former Indian journalist who had been Minister for Culture became Minister for Foreign Affairs. The new Minister for Law and National Development was partly European. A Malay became Minister for Culture and Social Affairs, and another, Attorney-General. Malay remained a national language and was required for all official employment. At the same time people were urged to think of themselves not as Chinese, Indians, or Malays, but as one community, the Singaporeans.

---

[1] By the end of 1965 the Singapore Cabinet had been constituted as follows:

| | |
|---|---|
| Prime Minister | Mr. Lee Kuan-Yew |
| Deputy Prime Minister | Dr. Toh Chin Chye |
| Minister for Defence and Security | Dr. Goh Keng Swee |
| Minister for Foreign Affairs | Mr. S. Rajaratnam |
| Minister for Finance | Mr. Lim Kim San |
| Minister for Law and National Development | Mr. E. W. Barker |
| Minister for Culture and Social Affairs | Inche Othman bin Wok |
| Minister for Education | Mr. Ong Pang Boon |
| Minister for Health | Mr. Yong Nyuk Lin |
| Minister for Labour | Mr. Jek Yeun Thong |

The Attorney-General was Inche Ahmad bin Mohammed Ibrahim.

Anyone stirring up communal strife would be severely punished. In spite of the set-back to his hopes and plans, Mr. Lee Kuan Yew had no intention of abandoning his concept of a Malaysian Malaysia. Even outside the fold, Singapore should become a model of what Malaysia might have been. The government would continue to tax its citizens heavily in order to develop exceptionally generous social and educational services and a genuine equality for all races. Malays from Malaysia would find that in Singapore they could enjoy greater opportunities and higher standards of living than in their own country. This realization would help to pave the way for renewed understanding, and perhaps association, with the neighbouring federation in the future.[1]

The new Foreign Minister announced that the Singapore Government would pursue a policy of non-alignment. Like Malaysia it was out of sympathy with S.E.A.T.O. The defence agreement with Britain, Australia, and New Zealand would have to be negotiated afresh. Otherwise it appeared that not much would be changed in regard to these arrangements. The naval, military, and air force bases contained some 50,000 Commonwealth troops, including Gurkhas. If Britain wished to use these bases for other purposes than the direct defence of Singapore or Malaysia, she would have to satisfy them that she was acting in their best interest. There was in fact no question of the bases being forced upon Singapore. The position was rather the reverse. The island had a positive interest in keeping them. They were economically important since they gave employment to a large segment of the population and supplied some 20 per cent. of Singapore's income. On the other hand many in Britain would have been prepared to give the bases up had it not been for the immense importance of retaining them as key factors in the global strategy of the free world[2] in Southeast Asia, the western Pacific, and the China Seas. The United Kingdom was anxiously watching its overseas expenditure and certain authoritative circles were contemplating the possibility,

---

[1] The Minister for Foreign Affairs indicated this as the general policy of his government in a talk with the writer in January 1966.

[2] The United States authorities, with their commitments in Vietnam, Laos, Thailand, and other parts of the area were strongly opposed to the abandonment of Singapore by the Commonwealth forces.

after Confrontation, of dispensing with the Singapore bases altogether, and relying instead on closer defence co-operation with Australia. Those who favoured such plans envisaged finding a substitute for Singapore in northwestern Australia (for example in the neighbourhood of Darwin), or on some island in the Indian Ocean, or in both areas.

There was inevitably some contrast in the reactions to Singapore's independence of the countries immediately concerned. The new nation was promptly recognized by Britain, Australia, New Zealand, and the United States as a preliminary to the opening of diplomatic relations. The welcome given to Singapore's new status by Washington did not deter Prime Minister Lee from displaying soon afterwards anti-American prejudice characteristic of other new nations. The Central Intelligence Agency was accused of sinister activities on the strength of some apparently genuine case of a CIA agent who had earlier tried to acquire information for money. Another and more strangely imagined complaint concerned the illness of Mrs. Lee. The Prime Minister had sought to bring to Singapore a distinguished American surgeon to give treatment to his wife. He alleged that the U.S. authorities had deliberately withheld the name of this important patient so that, instead of the specialist making a special journey to Singapore, he should be compelled instead to send his wife to America at the height of the separation crisis. The State Department had thus tried to use his request as a lever to involve him with the United States. Finally he declared that it would be a disaster if the British withdrew from Singapore and were replaced there by the Americans. Indeed, he rejected the whole idea of the United States assuming Britain's defence commitments in Southeast Asia. If, as a result of the Kuala Lumpur government bringing American troops into Malaysia there should be any question of their coming into the island as well, he would have to consider 'offering Singapore as a base to the Russians'. What worried him in this context was that the Americans had a way of backing the most vocal anti-communists. Therefore the Malay leaders would use American forces to support Malay communal interests against the Chinese in order to preserve their control. Since Prime Minister Lee was too intelligent to misjudge the benefits of the American presence in Asia, these outbursts were ascribed by some to a desire to present Singapore as a genuine anti-imperialist supporter of the Afro-Asian bloc while she was seeking membership of the United Nations.

Indonesia was delighted at this set-back to Malaysia and announced her readiness in certain circumstances to recognize the new government. Dr. Subandrio took the line that Singapore's action fully justified Djakarta's attitude to an artificial Malaysia designed to keep Britain dominant and undermine his country. If Sabah and Sarawak also became independent, good relations with all these neighbours could be restored. He added that if, with separation, Malaysia ceased to exist, Confrontation would stop. Since Malaysia visibly continued, Djakarta later announced that Confrontation would continue. Prime Minister Lee said that Singapore wished to be friends with Indonesia but that this was a delicate matter, clearly in view of the position of Kuala Lumpur. Some of the Indonesian leaders affected to be anxious about the future of Singapore. Her economic isolation might spell ruin for her, particularly when the profitable Commonwealth bases were withdrawn. Yet this withdrawal was the condition for Djakarta resuming normal trading relations. Her wisest course would be to join Indonesia.[1]

The tension which developed between Kuala Lumpur and the Borneo states following the separation of Singapore, and some later acrimony between the Malay nationalists and the

[1] This was the view indicated to the writer in Djakarta in August 1965 by Dr. Ruslan Abdulgani, the Minister for Information. The Minister did not, however, dispute the obvious rejoinder that geographic and economic facts made it inevitable that the island would in practice remain part of Malaysia in spite of its political separation, just as the Irish Republic, for the same reasons, had remained part of the British Isles. As regards the bases, he appeared personally to accept the arguments that in the Asia of the 1960s it was quite impossible to maintain such bases without the consent of the people of the country, that no compulsion was in fact being exercised to maintain the Commonwealth bases in Singapore and that, if and when the local governments were persuaded to ask for their withdrawal, they would be removed, just as the British bases had earlier been dismantled in Ceylon at the request of the Ceylonese.

The Irish analogy was later confirmed by Mr. Lee Kuan Yew in a talk with the writer in April 1966, when he said that, with separation, Singapore had exchanged the status of Northern Ireland, still part of the United Kingdom, for that of southern Ireland.

British, further encouraged Indonesian hopes that the disintegration of Malaysia and the end of Britain's special relationship with the federation might be at hand. When the new status of Singapore was announced, the Tunku stated in Parliament that relations with Sabah and Sarawak had remained excellent. The sequel did not justify this assurance. The Borneo states were freshly associated with Malaysia. There had been some delay in the process of administrative and psychological adjustment and, less than two years later, this was still incomplete. Opinion in Jesselton and Kuching was strongly concerned about the sudden expulsion from the federation of another state which had joined it as and when theirs had done, and also on special terms. They considered that they should have been consulted before a decision was taken on a vital matter of principle and practice which could seriously affect them. The Tunku, on the other hand, asserted that the central government had no obligation whatever to consult Sabah and Sarawak, now frequently designated as East Malaysia, before acting, any more than it had to consult Perlis or Pahang or the other states of Malaya. This attitude was not popular with many Borneans, conscious of their distinct status and attached to the degree of autonomy which had been the condition for their acceptance of Malaysia. They were regions with a strong individual character. Some of their leaders judged that this might be threatened by their continuance in the new federation under a central government which seemed to exact such strict compliance with its views and wishes. For the non-Muslim majority fears were revived of Malay domination inspired and enforced from Kuala Lumpur.

Paradoxically, the sharpest critic of the federal government had earlier been the strongest advocate of the association of the Borneo States with Malaysia. This was Dato Donald Stephens, the former chairman of the Malaysia Solidarity Consultative Committee,[1] leader of one of the main parties of the Sabah Alliance, and Chief Minister of Sabah from 31 August 1963 to the end of 1964. He had then been induced to relinquish this key post for the more nominal duties of Minister for Sabah Affairs in the federal Cabinet. He was replaced as Chief Minister by the former Minister for Sabah Affairs, a respected

[1] See p. 174.

Chinese Christian lawyer called Peter Loh. The Malay leaders may have hoped that he would be less self-willed and more co-operative. Stephens's party was the predominantly multi-racial United Pasokmomogun Kadazan Organization, usually known as U.P.K.O., in which his own local race, the Kadazans, played a prominent role. The other principal component of the Sabah Alliance was a party known as the United Sabah National Organization, which was essentially the local counterpart of U.M.N.O. As this suggests, U.S.N.O. was more particularly concerned with the needs and ambitions of the local Muslim and Malay elements, and with keeping Sabah aligned with the policies of Kuala Lumpur. The moving spirit behind U.S.N.O. was Tun Mustapha bin Datu Harun, a Muslim whose family had originated in the Sulu Archipelago and who had fought with the anti-Japanese guerillas in the Philippines during the war. Of limited education, he was a brave, tough, intimidating, political organizer and had been president of U.S.N.O. from 1961 until he was made head of state on the formation of Malaysia.

After the separation of Singapore, U.P.K.O. called for a re-examination of Sabah's position in Malaysia. The party considered that the state might not have the resources to become independent but that there should now be a loosening of the federal structure and greater local autonomy. Kuala Lumpur was understandably disturbed by this defiant attitude of Stephens and his followers. In 1965, Tun Mustapha had stepped down from his ceremonial post to resume an active political role. At this juncture the particular task assigned to him by the Alliance leaders in Kuala Lumpur seems to have been to give new vigour to U.S.N.O. and to guide the Sabah Alliance back into conformity with the policies of the central government. In Sarawak, the situation seemed less serious and less urgent despite local discontent. The territory had even fewer resources than Sabah and the government leaders, being certain that independent nationhood was impracticable, had no thought of leaving Malaysia. Nor did they, like Dato Stephens, demand sweeping changes. In Sarawak, such demands were confined to the opposition. They came particularly from the S.U.P.P., which had always been opposed to Sarawak joining the federation. Its pro-Peking extremists now insisted on secession. The moderates only sought greater autonomy. The moderate leader, Ong Kee Hui, who was also Mayor of Kuching and chairman of the party, took the line: 'Most of us had become reconciled to Malaysia, but if Singapore is out, why should Sarawak stay in?'

Towards the end of August 1965 the Tunku visited the Borneo states to restore loyalty and morale. He referred unflatteringly to politicians in Sabah who were 'greatly interested' in the separation of Singapore, and stressed the impracticability of separate independence. Sabah and Sarawak did not have enough votes in parliament to secede from Malaysia constitutionally and Kuala Lumpur would not tolerate any attempt to bring about separation by force. During the period of the visit, Dato Stephens was forced to resign as Minister for Sabah Affairs and a pledge was exacted from Dato Ningkan, the Chief Minister in Kuching, that Sarawak would remain in Malaysia. So far as Sabah was concerned, Stephens had apparently bowed to menacing pressure and other inducements from his political rivals led by Tun Mustapha. He announced soon afterwards that he was quitting politics for good. Yet it was evident at the end of the year that he had by no means abandoned active contact with the affairs of his party. Meanwhile the weight of U.P.K.O. in the counsels of the Alliance was greatly diminished. The influence of U.S.N.O. and the Malay-Muslim elements in the country loyal to Kuala Lumpur was henceforth in the ascendant. The non-Malays were now largely bereft of strong and effective leadership. The downfall of Dato Stephens was a further set-back to the plans of Mr. Lee Kuan Yew. Before separation, the latter seems to have entertained the idea of some form of collaboration between Singapore, Sabah, and Sarawak, supported by a multi-racial political party on the lines of the Singapore P.A.P., as a counterpoise to domination by the Alliance leadership in Kuala Lumpur. Prime Minister Lee had a considerable following among the Borneo Chinese and Dato Stephens was one of the local leaders most sympathetic to his policies. Yet Stephens had lacked the courage to align himself publicly with this controversial figure while something effective could perhaps have been achieved through such co-operation. Such plans ceased to be practical after the separation of Singapore.

The leaders of Malaysia had been disagreeably surprised by these rumblings of disaffection in the Borneo states. It was natural that they should blame others than themselves and look beyond the local leaders whom they had disciplined to those who might, they suspected, have encouraged them. In their search for scapegoats they were prompt to suspect the ex-patriate British officers still serving in important government posts under the Malaysia arrangements. Such suspicion was almost bound to be latent in any newly de-colonized territory which had had to retain in office for the time being some of those who had administered it on behalf of the imperial power. There had, however, till then, been little of this suspicion in Malaya itself. This was partly because few British officials had been retained there and also because—at least until the second world war—the British colonial government had stood firmly behind the Malay rulers and the indigenous people. British administrators had tended on the whole to treat the Peninsula as an essentially Malay country in which the other races lived in fair and comfortable conditions but on sufferance. The special position of the Malays had for years been enshrined in the constitution.

In the Borneo states, however, which were seriously short of trained administrators, British officials had been retained in many key posts. In Sarawak, the State Secretary—the head of the civil service—remained British, as did the Financial Secretary, the State Information Officer and many others both in the capital and the provincial Divisions. In Jesselton, the British had kept the posts of Attorney-General and Defence Secretary and, in the Sabah districts, all the posts of Resident (the local governor) save one. In both states the Chief Justice and the head of the police were British. It was understandable that the Tunku should have declared with some asperity that going to Sabah and Sarawak was still like visiting a British colony. Another irritant for the Malays was that in the Borneo states they were a smaller minority even than the Chinese. Although the Brooke Rajahs had tended to favour the Malays in Sarawak, there had been no special position for them tradi-tionally in either territory. After 1946, the colonial govern-ments sought to be strictly impartial. British administrators aimed on the whole at advancing the standards of the majority races—the non-Muslim up-country tribes—which had been oppressed in the past by the Brunei Malays or the Sulu Sultanate and to some extent neglected by the Rajahs and the Chartered Company. When Malaysia was established there had thus been no special status or assurance of favoured treatment for Malays in Sabah and Sarawak. The British officials retained had not been conditioned to thinking of the two territories in terms of what proved to be essentially Malay leadership from Kuala Lumpur sustained by federal officials acting locally as the observers and agents of the central government.[1] It was perhaps inevitable that the new dispensation was not entirely congenial to some of the former administrators and was at variance with the code of inter-racial impartiality in which they had been trained. When the crisis came, the Sabah leaders were in fact advised by the key British officials that there could be no question of the state seceding from Malaysia. Amongst other things they could expect no defence agreement with Britain if they did. At the same time, not all the British successfully concealed their sympathy for the U.P.K.O. view that, in the light of the treatment of Singapore, there might be a case for re-examining the terms of the Borneo states' association with Malaysia.

Two other factors tended to breed resentment towards the expatriate officials. One was that the British Government had negotiated specially favourable terms for their continued service under Malaysia. In Sarawak they were guaranteed employment for four to six years, in Sabah for as long as ten. If the services of any officer were dispensed with earlier, substantial compensation had to be paid to him out of local funds. This was proportionately higher where the guaranteed period was longer, as in Sabah, and to one or two it was tempting to seek to obtain the maximum financial benefit. The second factor was virtually confined to Sabah. This was a campaign in one organ of the press, apparently set on foot with the cognizance of the

[1] In each capital there were Federal Secretaries whose task, in principle, was to facilitate liaison and understanding between the state governments and Kuala Lumpur. Inevitably their position tended to assume more positive functions. There were also a number of federal M.A.R.A. officers concerned with rural development in the districts who were widely credited with being the eyes and ears of the federal authorities.

U.S.N.O. leaders possibly with encouragement from Kuala Lumpur. This newspaper[1] persistently questioned the motives, conduct, and general attitude of the expatriates.

At the beginning of October 1965 criticism of the British spread to Malaya itself. The Tunku publicly declared that certain high-ranking British officers[2] had been trying to split the people by inciting the non-Malays against the Malays. Their propaganda in Sabah and Sarawak had encouraged the other races to believe that the Malays were treating them as third-class citizens and seeking to oppress and dominate them. This British attitude was all the worse because the constitution of Malaysia had been drawn up by a commission under a British chairman. Although Tun Razak subsequently denied that the persons accused were in the government service, this seemed to have been chiefly designed to play the matter down. The impression left by the Tunku's candour was that it was definitely caused by the controversy in Borneo over the exclusion from Malaysia of Singapore.

As the former colonial power, Britain had on the whole been fortunate in the relations she had managed to preserve with Malaysia. They were vastly more friendly and constructive than those with many of her other former territories. Common misfortune and enforced co-operation through the Emergency and Confrontation had contributed. This was the first major unpleasantness which had occurred since independence and it was on an individual not a national plane. General cordiality seemed little affected at the time, and it was obvious that, while Confrontation continued, little would be changed. There was, however, small hope of completely eradicating the anti-British suspicion which recent events had aroused. The Malay leaders resented the mutual understanding which seemed so readily to exist between the British and Lee Kuan Yew whom

[1] The *Jesselton Daily Express*, the editor of which, a gifted Indian from Madras, had been through the Japanese occupation of Singapore and had spent many years in Indonesia (see p. 74, footnote). The *Express* supported the policies of U.S.N.O., in contrast to the *Sabah Times*, edited by the father-in-law of Dato Stephens, which normally backed U.P.K.O. A typical *Express* headline objecting to the alleged high-handedness of the remaining British was 'No Room for Autocrats'.

[2] They were stigmatized as '*hantu*' a Malay word with a rich variety of meanings, including 'ghosts', 'devils', 'secret agents' and 'evil spirits'.

they judged to be dangerous and destructive. These feelings were strengthened by the ready publicity given to the Singapore leader in the British press and the approval he seemed to enjoy in the ranks of the Labour Government and party. The tension in Borneo confirmed their conviction that the British had come to favour the non-Malays and that British colonial survivals, at least in Eastern Malaysia, would soon have to be removed. The end of Confrontation, whenever it came, would clearly put Malaysian-British friendship to a hard test.

The developments which had shaken Kuala Lumpur had cheered and stimulated the leaders in Djakarta. President Sukarno and Dr. Subandrio counted on the imminent triumph of their Malaysia policies, which were strongly supported by the Indonesian communist party. But other potentially powerful elements in Indonesia were disturbed by the growing influence of the P.K.I. They deplored the waste and probable futility of Confrontation. The communists were fully aware of the opposition they faced and appear to have decided to forestall by surprise action any move against them. The sequel profoundly affected not merely the Indonesians but the peoples of Malaysia and the whole political pattern of Southeast Asia.

On the night of 30 September to 1 October the commander of one battalion of the guard at the presidential palace in Djakarta made a bid to seize power, apparently with the support of five army battalions and of the P.K.I. It was put out that this was to prevent a group of generals from overthrowing President Sukarno 'with the connivance of the U.S. Central Intelligence Agency'. The establishment of a Revolutionary Council was announced, including Dr. Subandrio, the heads of the Navy and Air Force and some minor communists. All the first three subsequently denied that they had ever backed the insurgents. Dr. Subandrio, like many other members of the government, seems in fact to have been out of Djakarta at the time, but the Air Force leader had at one stage been heard to broadcast in support of the uprising, which was named the '30th of September Movement'. General Nasution,[1] the Defence Minister and Chief of Staff of the Armed Forces, was significantly omitted from the members of the Revolutionary Council. Aidit, the communist leader, was understood to have dis-

[1] See p. 179.

appeared, supposedly to organize insurrection in Central and Eastern Java. In the evening of 1 October it was made known that the 'Movement' had been suppressed and order restored. Six generals, including the Army Chief of Staff, were murdered by the rebels. It was also learned that they had made an attempt on the life of General Nasution which had mortally wounded his young daughter.

Although many details have remained obscure, the accounts of foreign observers[1] and the information disclosed by the government suggest that young men suspected of belonging to the P.K.I. youth organization played an important part in the insurrection. They surrounded communications centres, road junctions, and railway crossings before dawn on 1 October. Other groups in military uniform seized and assaulted the generals. General Nasution, who escaped when his house was attacked, made his way to one of the command posts but, having been injured, was taken off to hospital. At this point General Suharto, the commander of the Strategic Reserve, seized command of the situation and organized the forces which defeated the rebels in the capital. General Suharto was then officially put in charge of these operations and was subsequently given command of the Army. This officer, hitherto virtually unknown outside professional circles, had been in command of the 1962 campaign to conquer West New Guinea. A close associate of General Nasution, he shared the latter's anti-communist views. The Army soon established control of the cities, and martial law was imposed in Djakarta. But insurgent communists took up arms over wide areas of central and eastern Java, and from mid-October the government forces were heavily engaged against them. At this point, the Army seems virtually to have established its control over Indonesia.

Some doubt surrounded President Sukarno's role at the time of the coup and afterwards. On 3 October, he announced that he was safe and remained in supreme command. When these events occurred he had gone to a neighbouring airport to be ready to move elsewhere 'if anything untoward happened'. In spite of his assurances of continued leadership it was soon obvious that his authority had in fact been diminished by the

[1] Notably such responsible press correspondents as Mr. Seth S. King of the *New York Times*.

positive part which the armed forces had assumed in the making of policy. Understandably he resented this shift in the balance of power, but having long been a master of political manœuvre, he appealed for national unity and bided his time. Amongst other sweeping measures taken by the government under Army influence was the suspension of Antara, the government news agency, on the grounds that it had become so dominated by the communists that it was little more than a tool of the New China News Agency. It was later permitted to resume operations under government control. There was some slackening of Confrontation, which had been largely the personal policy of the President and his Foreign Minister, and many of the best Indonesian troops were brought back from Borneo and the areas adjoining Singapore and Malaya to enable the armed forces to deal more effectively with an incipient civil war.

October 1st 1965 and its sequel proved a day of judgement for the communists. It was also the beginning of a chain of events which was to alter the destiny of world communism in one vital area. For the third time in the history of modern Indonesia the local communist forces over-played their hand.[1] Their rashness on this occasion may well have sprung from a confidence which seemed justified to the more ardent followers of the cause. The P.K.I. had a membership of some three million, the largest of any communist party outside the Soviet Union and China. They had achieved participation in the government under President Sukarno's Nasakom scheme for the integration of nationalists, Muslims and communists. Two of their top leaders, Aidit and Lukman, had become Ministers in the Cabinet without portfolio. It was not as much as they wanted,[2] but it was a partial realization of the classical communist tactic of sharing in and penetrating a popular front in ostensible alliance with 'bourgeois' parties. They had at the same time

[1] The first abortive revolt of the communists took place in 1926–27. Their second bid for power was in 1948, at Madiun in Central Java. It was promptly crushed by the Republican Government based on Jogjakarta shortly before the second Dutch Military action. (See p. 128.)

[2] 'At the end of 1962 the P.K.I. renewed with vigor the campaign for a truly Nasakom cabinet in which the parties would have representation proportionate to their popular support.' Donald Hindley, *The Communist Party of Indonesia 1951–1963*, p. 285.

adherents in a number of key positions, including sectors of the armed forces, and, as we have seen, in the principal organ of government publicity. In these circumstances there is some doubt whether Aidit had himself taken the initiative in launching, or approving and supporting, the 30th of September Movement. His policy had seemed rather to envisage gradual progress towards a communist victory regarded by many expert western observers as almost certain. The P.K.I. participants in the coup may well have been some of his younger and more impetuous followers seizing a moment which they judged to be specially favourable. Once the outbreak had begun he had of course no option but to give it his full support where and how this might be most effective.

Miscalculations contributed to the communist disaster. On the morning of 2 October—the rebels having been defeated in Djakarta the previous evening—the local communist newspaper rashly claimed that the Movement had saved the country. Although the P.K.I. subsequently associated itself with the President's appeal for national unity, it became easy for the military leaders to pin full blame for the rising on to the P.K.I. even if some of the rebels had in fact been moved by personal ambition or greed. The upshot was a prolonged outburst of emotional vindictiveness against the communists. This seemed to reflect the accumulated hatred of the conservative and religious Indonesians for these subversive elements—a hatred previously checked by the policies of a President in whom many of his people had lost faith. There were public demonstrations calling for the banning of the communist party and its affiliated organizations and the exclusion of communists from the Cabinet. Before the end of October the Djakarta Army Commander announced the banning of the party in the Djakarta area, communist members being ordered to report to the authorities. Later, the P.K.I.'s trade union federation was also banned and the party's members of parliament suspended on the instructions of the military. Meanwhile communist premises and property were sacked and burned, suffering the fate that had so recently befallen those of the British and Americans. Large numbers of communists were arrested. As the insurrections in the provinces were crushed there followed a sickening series of massacres in various parts of the country which are thought to have claimed many innocent lives. These were directed in principle against all suspected of communism, and the Muslim youth organizations seem to have taken a prominent part. Aidit was reported dead at the end of November. Yet many of the killings appear to have been done indiscriminately and without control by the most ordinary people with grudges to repay or a belief that they were the instruments of national or divine vengeance. There were particularly savage incidents on the mainly Hindu island of Bali. Far more casualties occurred in these few weeks of the Indonesian campaign against the communists than in all the twelve years of the Malayan Emergency.[1]

The P.K.I. having become predominantly the party of Peking, the popular revulsion against the communists led to outbursts against Communist China and attacks on the local Chinese. In these last much injustice again was done. Most Indonesian Chinese—like the Chinese elsewhere in Southeast Asia—were essentially capitalists. They were traders, artisans and shopkeepers, unpopular with the Indonesians because of their hard work and success and a certain position of superiority which they had acquired under the Dutch. One consequence of Indonesian resentment was that President Sukarno a few years earlier had given them the choice of becoming citizens of the country or returning to China. This traditional jealousy and suspicion of the Chinese due to causes which had nothing to do with communism contributed to their indiscriminate victimization while the anti-communist witch hunt was on. Thus in mid-October the Chinese-owned university in Djakarta was assaulted and burned to the ground. There was at the same time a sharp deterioration in Djakarta's relations with Peking after infringements of diplomatic privilege comparable to those which had occurred during the anti-British campaign two years earlier. The office of the Chinese Commercial Counsellor in Djakarta was forcibly searched. The flag was torn down on the Chinese Consulate at Medan. Chinese property was sacked on Bali and a number of Chinese murdered on the neighbouring island of Lombok. The Peking government complained of the

[1] Estimates of the total killed vary considerably. In January 1966, President Sukarno announced this as 87,000. But some unofficial estimates were nearly twice as large. Others as high as 300,000.

'slanders and anti-Chinese outcries' in Djakarta, of 'brutal encroachment upon diplomatic immunities' and of the 'atrocities and barbarity of the racist crimes' for which the 'Indonesian right wing forces' were responsible.

The economic situation had become progressively more chaotic since the expulsion of the Dutch in 1957 and the measures against British, American, and other foreign business interests between 1963 and 1965. After these disturbances it took a new downward plunge, with mounting inflation of the currency and living costs and dwindling production and foreign exchange reserves. The currency was revalued in December. Before this, the rupiah, originally equivalent to the Dutch guilder at $2\frac{3}{4}$ to the U.S. dollar, had declined to a black market rate of 30,000 to 40,000 to the dollar. One new rupiah was substituted for 1,000 old ones, but the new currency started to lose its value almost immediately since none of the fundamental ills of the economy had been cured. The authorities cast around for remedies and punished profiteers but little improvement was achieved. At the beginning of 1966 the government was faced with a new threat. There were large-scale protest demonstrations by Indonesian students. Active as pace-makers in politics, in the Asian and Latin American tradition, the students were specially embittered by the rise in transport costs which made it hard for them to get to their studies. They had also, it was understood, received encouragement and organizational training from elements in or near the government which disapproved of some of its policies. These included the Minister for Co-ordination, Adam Malik.

Despite the new power of the armed forces and the Minister for Defence, and some waning of Presidential prestige, the government continued ostensibly to function much on the old lines. In particular Dr. Subandrio, though under some suspicion by reason of his regard for the P.K.I., was still in the saddle as First Deputy Prime Minister and Minister for Foreign Affairs. At the first Cabinet meeting after the coup it was Dr. Subandrio who read the President's plausible and disarming statement appealing for national unity. This promised to deal with those involved in the uprising and to seek a political settlement. As the months went by, however, no political settlement emerged and the President showed that he was still able to assert his capricious aggressiveness towards the west. American press correspondents were expelled in January for having, it was said, given a distorted picture of Indonesian affairs.

The basic problem was that what had happened was only half a revolution. A fluid and restless situation had been created which had to move forward or backward before settling down. Had the latter occurred, much might have reverted to what it was before October. In fact, more drastic changes were to come and it was these rather than the original upheaval which so changed the future of Southeast Asia. It will be convenient to deal with these developments before returning to the course of events in Malaysia which they so profoundly affected.

One of President Sukarno's methods of patronage was the multiplication of ministers. He had surrounded himself with nearly a hundred. In mid-December an inner Cabinet or Supreme Operational Command of three was created to carry out government business directly under the President. The senior member of the triumvirate was General Nasution who thus took over the second executive post after the President and became more powerful than Dr. Subandrio, the First Deputy Prime Minister. The other two members were the Sultan of Jogjakarta, another friend of General Nasution, and Dr. Ruslan Abdulgani, who had been Minister for Information.[1] The former, an earlier Defence Minister in the 1950s, was the last hereditary Sultan left in Indonesia. He was also one of the very few persons of princely rank to have retained prestige, authority and position. Not long after the student demonstrations in January 1966, the President sought to reassert his authority and give fresh vigour to his personal policies. He seems to have judged that this had become so necessary that he could afford to risk a trial of strength with the Army leader who had undermined his power and with the restive and presumptuous students. In a surprise Cabinet re-shuffle on 21 February General Nasution was dropped from the government, but Dr. Subandrio retained. The inner Cabinet was renamed the Crush Malaysia Command.

There was no adverse reaction from the dismissed General and it was at first widely thought that the President's manœuvre had restored his full authority and the influence of Dr. Suban-

[1] See p. 212, footnote.

drio. General Suharto, who remained in command of the Army, promised that it would prosecute Confrontation against Malaysia under the President's leadership. The students, however, decided the next phase apparently with some discreet assistance from political and military elements opposed to Sukarno. In fresh demonstrations they protested violently against the change and sought the return of General Nasution and the dismissal of all Ministers suspected of being pro-communist or responsible for Indonesia's economic ills. They surrounded the President's palace to prevent the new Ministers from being sworn in. On the following day, a Presidential order banned demonstrations and the Students' Action Front. This was ignored even by the police and troops and huge protest crowds attended the funeral of a student who had been killed. Early in March determined and persistent demonstrations by students and school children recurred which lasted for ten days. The young people who came out on the streets had been educated in the quasi-mystical doctrines of national regeneration through revolution which their President had proclaimed. Many still believed, or wanted to believe, in his epic slogans and articles of faith. But they had awakened to the dangers and deprivations of the régime and the futility of empty exhortations. In his failure to provide good government and his tenderness for communism they felt that their leader had betrayed his own ideals. Yet an aura still surrounded his name and, at this stage, most of their venom was directed against the man they believed to be his evil genius. The Foreign Minister was pilloried as the 'dog of Peking'. 'Hang Subandrio' was scrawled and shouted about the town. Although the President decreed the closing of the University of Indonesia, the students continued to use it as a base. The troops again disregarded the Presidential orders, as it later appeared with the encouragement of their leaders, and made no attempt to evict them. The demonstrators broke into and temporarily occupied the Ministries of Foreign Affairs and Education. They also assaulted the New China News Agency and Chinese Foreign Service premises. In a diversionary movement by left wing elements some damage was done to the American Embassy as well.

On 13 March it was announced that General Suharto had been instructed by the President to take all necessary measures for the safety and stability of the government. The General himself afterwards reported the complete banning of the communist party, and invited the nation to put its trust in the armed forces which would continue the Indonesian revolution in a spirit of anti-feudalism, anti-colonialism, and anti-capitalism. He referred respectfully to Dr. Sukarno and the affection for him of the Indonesian people. Yet it became clear that the President had been faced with an ultimatum by the armed forces and that General Suharto had taken well-planned and forceful action to forestall a similar move by Dr. Subandrio. Despite Sukarno's own declarations that his authority was still supreme, Indonesia and the rest of Southeast Asia were soon aware that a new course had been set and that major policy decisions in Djakarta now lay in other hands. Five days later Dr. Subandrio and fifteen other Ministers, including some of the President's leading supporters, were arrested. The inner Cabinet was again reconstituted as a presidium of six, in which the three principal protagonists of the new régime, as additional deputy Prime Ministers, were given all the vital responsibilities. The three survivors of the former régime, although nominally senior, were relegated to minor tasks. Thus the Sultan of Jogjakarta was to supervise economic, financial, and development matters; and General Suharto defence and security. Adam Malik became the new Minister for Foreign Affairs and supervisor of virtually all the ministries of political importance, including Home Affairs, Information, Education, Religion, Justice, Labour, and Health. General Nasution became a Minister again in charge, under the President, of the Crush Malaysia Command. The numbers in the full Cabinet were drastically reduced. Elections were to be held for a new parliament. The Indonesian Foreign Service was purged of Dr. Subandrio's disciples. The commander of the palace guard and one of the P.K.I. leaders were condemned to death for their part in the September insurrection. Not all disturbances were over by this stage. Anti-Peking incidents continued and there was a major attack on the Chinese Embassy in April in which diplomatic staff were hurt. The protests of Communist China became shriller. They spoke of hooligans having spent the night on official premises 'carousing, rioting, dancing the twist, singing bawdy songs and behaving bestially'.

Such outrages had been 'engineered by the Indonesian Government . . . to rupture the relations between the two countries'.

Thus Indonesia's problem remained unsolved and new ones had reared their heads. Yet all moderate elements rejoiced at the ending of the long period of uncertainty and civil strife, the settlement of the internal power struggle and the inauguration of this new phase of firm, and different, rule. Indonesia's neighbours, particularly the two related nations of Malaysia and the Philippines, and Malaysia's unacknowledged partner, Singapore, had suffered from President Sukarno's caprices at the height of his power. All had fought major engagements against attempted communist domination. They had followed every move in the Indonesian struggle as if it had been a contest of their own. It has been necessary to describe this at some length just because they were so keenly conscious that the outcome might prove decisive for their future.

# CHAPTER EIGHTEEN

# The Balance-Sheet of Unrest

In the story of the federation we have reached the events sketched broadly in our introductory chapter. They formed a curious sequel to imperial rule, an artificial and unstable pattern, full of paradox and potentialities for change. Malaysia was a nation newly created and enfranchised which had turned its back on colonial domination, was irked by its survivals, suspicious of any hint of tutelage and impatient to shape its future in a way uniquely its own. Yet Confrontation, like the Emergency a few years back, had made it dependent for survival on outside support and principally on help from the former imperial power. Whatever courtesies the situation might demand, this was bound to be implicitly wounding to its pride. It was an obligation to be shed when possible. Meanwhile it need receive only the most muted acknowledgement. Once the danger was past, the consciousness of this debt was likely to render the Malaysians acutely, and even disagreeably, sensitive in their relations with their Commonwealth allies and particularly with Britain. They would judge that, in defending Malaysia, these allies were acting, not unselfishly, but essentially in their own interests. In the case of Australia and New Zealand this was largely true. The Australian Prime Minister[1] had declared that they were supporting Malaysia largely because Southeast Asia was the zone in which their peoples lived. With Britain the situation was very different. Her own territory was not implicated geographically or strategically. Her interests in the area were primarily trade, mining and the plantation industries. Her investments in these were very considerable. Yet the cost of the military assistance she furnished to Malaysia, and of the local establishments on which it was based, more than offset all the profits she derived from her commercial and industrial stake. Some of the disillusioned British claimed that from the standpoint purely of the balance-

[1] See p. 180.

sheet it would have profited Britain at the time of Confrontation if Southeast Asia, with all British interests and investments, had disappeared under the sea. Her help to Malaysia was not, then, purely a matter of selfish interest. It was an awkward burden incurred chiefly because it would have been dishonourable not to do so. On the one hand a failure to help would have been a breach of faith towards a country whose existence she had sponsored and guaranteed. On the other, it would have been unjust to the United States, heavily committed without British military aid in resisting the expansion of communism in Vietnam. During the first two years of Confrontation fresh communist advances were in the offing with the expected triumph of the P.K.I. in Indonesia. It could be argued that what had fallen to Britain's lot was her equitable share in the common cause of holding communism back and of preserving order, stability, and the right to self-determination in Southeast Asia. Once communism had been defeated in Indonesia Britain's intervention presented itself in different terms. It continued, however, to be essential so long as Malaysia was contested and attacked.

The transformation which began in Indonesia in October 1965 had little immediate and direct effect on Malaysia and Singapore. Even before this Confrontation was beginning to wear thin and there had been some easing of the military operations. There were no more landings on the Malay Peninsula after June. The earlier ones had, as we have seen, all failed through indifferent planning, ill-luck, and lack of local support, though some had achieved surprise and even limited initial success. The assault on Malaya planned from the neighbouring islands for the Indonesian national day in August never materialized and, after the disturbances in Djakarta, many of the best troops were brought home. From 1 October there was a lull of several months. Considerable forces continued to face each other across the Borneo border, but there was a lowering of quality on the Indonesian side as certain of their elite units came to be needed elsewhere. There were a number of minor exchanges but virtually no major engagements.

As the anti-communist struggle in Indonesia progressed and Djakarta's relations with Peking became more strained, a tendency developed for the more vocal role in Confrontation to be taken over by Communist China. This was a natural development from the co-operation with the Indonesian guerillas in Borneo of Chinese Communist volunteers through a clandestine organization based principally on Sarawak. In February, 1966, the New China News Agency hailed a National Liberation League and a National Liberation Army of Malaya headed by P. V. Sarma, a Malayan renegade of Indian origin. The League was modelled on the National Liberation Front in Vietnam, the parent body of the Viet Cong, and on the Thailand Patriotic Front which fostered communist insurrection in that country. The Front had inspired the outbreaks in northeastern Thailand; the communists were also active in the south. For Malaysia, a sinister reminder of past and future risk was the reported renewal of operations by Ch'in P'eng. This former leader of the communist forces during the twelve-year Emergency in Malaya was known to have under him a small hard core of guerilla terrorists, trained in the experience of those days, in the jungle areas near the Thai-Malay border. Totally defeated as he had been in Malaya, he could find new hope in the emergence elsewhere in Thailand of a fresh focus of communism stimulated from Hanoi and Peking. If the communist cause advanced in Thailand, perhaps the chapter in Malaya could be re-opened. The soldiers of Mao in China had after all had many set-backs before their final victory.

Nevertheless for the moment, whatever the uncertainties in Borneo, Malaya herself was unpropitious soil for communism. She had few of the weaknesses on which it thrives and which had so nearly given it victory in Indonesia. 'Colonialist oppression' was a dead issue for all except the communist hard core. In spite of inter-racial bickering, the country was strong politically, with a well-co-ordinated, practically effective administrative and legal system, and constitutional guarantees. For these Britain could claim a credit acknowledged by the most nationalist Malayans. Under Britain's most characteristic legacy, the parliamentary system, the ruling coalition could, it was true, hope to remain almost indefinitely in power. Yet this was still rule by consent, based on free elections, and the federation was one of the very few working democracies in Asia. The opposition could freely make its voice heard and offer criticism and counsel to the government which was sometimes heeded. Security was tight. After years of danger, the police and intelligence organizations were alert, efficient and, when necessary, ruthless. Of final importance was the remarkable prosperity which the country had attained and preserved in spite of all the adverse factors of the past twenty years. From being reduced to a subsistence economy under the Japanese occupation, the average standard of living of the Malayans had risen until it was second in Asia only to that of their former conquerors. There were great inequalities, ranging from the poverty of Malay peasants in remote kampongs[1], and the modest earnings of Indian labourers, to the bourgeois comfort of many town-dwellers of all races and the affluence of the enterprising few. But there existed a comparatively numerous middle class whose ranks were easily accessible to those below through the operation of a prudently regulated system of largely free-enterprise capitalism. This and an ordered, reliable, structure of government were key factors in social stability in Malaya, as elsewhere. They were at the same time a powerful antidote to the Marxist doctrines of class war and owner-exploitation which had such attraction for the hungry and confused.

By the end of 1965, Malaysia had survived with remarkable resilience the economic impact of over two years of Confronta-

[1] Scientifically managed estates, especially those devoted to rubber and palm oil, are one of Malaya's principal sources of wealth. These, however, are largely owned or managed by Europeans, Chinese, or Indians. The smallholder agriculture of the rural Malays, the politically dominant group, tends to be far more conservative and less productive. A very high national rate of population increase (some 3·2% per annum) has produced overcrowding, under-employment, and consequent impoverishment in some rural areas. As Professor Fisk has pointed out in a recent study of the rural economy and rural development of Malaya (*The Political Economy of Independent Malaya*, Edited by T. H. Silcock and E. K. Fisk, pp. 163–94), the problem has been aggravated by the fragmentation of holdings into very small units as a result of Islamic inheritance laws and other causes; and by the aggregation of economically unprofitable fractions into larger units under absentee landlords with small concern for the welfare of their tenants or share croppers, or for the permanent improvement of the soil. These factors amongst others have retarded the success of the government's campaign to raise the standards of the rural Malays. Fortunately Malaya is spared the agonizing population pressures of India. Her total population is still small in proportion to her size and she still has vast areas of land which can be rendered cultivable, at a cost.

tion and of the recent separation from Singapore, which had
been somewhat more seriously affected by both. This was
largely due to a series of sensible government plans. When
independence came in 1957, Malaya was in the middle of her
first five-year plan. A second followed in 1960, a third, known
as the first Malaysia plan, in 1965, to cover the period 1966–
1970. The buoyancy of the economy was also a consequence of
the ability of the private sector to operate without undue
official interference. At the same time Malaysia was fortunate
in that much of the financial and military burden of Confrontation fell, not upon herself, but upon her Commonwealth
allies, Britain, Australia, and New Zealand, and notably upon
the first. As a result of Indonesia's ban on trade, much of the
traditional movement of imports and exports between the two
areas had been diverted, perhaps permanently, into other
channels. Indonesian tin was one example. Instead of being
sent as formerly to Malaysian smelters, this now went largely
to the Netherlands, to the prejudice of Malaysia's earnings from
tin exports.[1] In spite of all such factors, 1965 proved rather unexpectedly to be an excellent economic year for Malaysia. Both
the gross national, and the gross domestic, product rose by
comparison with 1964, the rate of growth being considerably
greater than that foreseen in the first Malaysia plan.[2] There
were more savings, more domestic capital for investment, an
impressive trade surplus and a substantial increase in foreign
exchange reserves. One factor in these trade figures had been
increased rice production, stimulated by government measures
and a good season. The harvest of 1965 had reduced imports by
giving the country 65 per cent. of its domestic needs against
60 per cent. the year before. The trade surplus had also been
helped by increased production for export in many important
sectors, by good tin prices and temporarily encouraging rubber
prices. The question of price was of course capital in the case

[1] 'Excess capacity already existed in the (Malaysian) smelters due to the
ending of Indonesian supplies in 1964, and this . . . inevitably affected net
tin export earnings. Indonesian supplies of tin-in-concentrates have gone
largely to the Netherlands since the beginning of Confrontation and it is
unlikely that there will be a complete reversal in this.' *Economic Review of
Malaysia, Singapore and Brunei*, No. 2, 1966, The Economist Intelligence
Unit, London, p. 15.

[2] *Economic Review*, p. 9.

of these two staples of the Malaysian economy. In the case of the first, production was declining as more tin deposits were used up without new ones being found. Rubber yields were increasing through scientific re-planting, and Malaysian natural rubber had managed to sustain competition with synthetic rubber, the production of which tended to keep prices down. Yet both tin and rubber prices, although supervised under international arrangements, were also depressed from time to time by sales from official U.S. stockpiles, a frequent source of grievance between Kuala Lumpur and Washington.

Fortunately for the health of her economy, Malaysia had successfully diversified her agriculture and rendered herself less dependent on rubber as the traditionally dominant crop. Palm oil, more profitable even than rubber, was becoming steadily more important and exports of it had more than doubled since 1964. Malaysia had also increased her production and export of pineapples, timber, coconut derivatives, and pepper. Major projects for agricultural expansion launched by the government gave great promise for the future. One was an irrigation scheme based on the Muda river in Kedah which would permit double-cropping on rice land and bring fresh areas into cultivation. Another was the conversion to agricultural production of a huge block of jungle forest in Pahang known as the Jengka Triangle. This was one of the very few areas of rich volcanic soil in the Peninsula, which had achieved remarkable agricultural wealth with a generally poor quality of land.

A basic factor contributing to a well-balanced economy had been the priority given in government planning to agricultural development and to industries based on the country's agricultural products, such as rubber and palm-oil milling, latex processing, and tea factories, or those using a high proportion of local raw materials. There were a number of local plants employing relatively simple techniques for the manufacture of foods, beverages, tobacco, furniture, textiles, leather goods, chemicals, petroleum products, and the like. There was little heavy industry, though a steel mill was projected based on the country's iron ore resources, for which Japan had long been the best customer. This was to be installed by the Japanese who were playing an increasing role in the commercial and industrial life of the country. In general, Malaysia had resisted the economic temptations of incipient nationhood. Where it had paid her best to obtain goods manufactured more cheaply and efficiently in the older industrial countries, she had usually continued to do so. There had been little of the premature and precipitate development of uneconomic local industries as a symbol of independence and new-found stature which had burdened the economies of some other new nations of Asia and Africa. In 1965, the contribution of manufacturing to the Malaysian gross domestic product was still only some 11 per cent.[1] It was particularly encouraging that the overall balance of payments had changed from a deficit in 1964 to a surplus of some U.S. $59 million in 1965.[2] This had been achieved, not only by better export earnings, but by the country's capacity to attract investment from the advanced capitalist nations through the conservative ordering of its affairs. During the year there was a substantial inflow of long term capital, most of it from private sources, but some from a loan issued in New York.[3]

In her economic as in her political life Malaysia had sought to integrate with her own traditions and objectives what she judged to be of value in the training and experience of colonial days. With a far broader economic base and richer resources, Indonesia could have emulated and indeed surpassed Malaysia's economic performance, as she had done under Dutch rule. But President Sukarno, in pursuit of his own vision, had given first priority to the destruction of the colonial past. Under their new leaders the peoples of Indonesia had become aware that prosperity had eluded them through his deliberate choice. This would imperil not only his image but possibly his whole future position as the national leader. These countries in fact sharply exemplify two major trends among new nations. There are those, usually more successful, which have assimilated and built upon the structure bequeathed by the colonial power, while bringing this firmly into line with the outlook and aspirations of their people. Others, on a wave of nationalist fervour, have devoted their efforts to expunging their alien heritage and have sometimes found reason to regret this in later moments of reckoning.

[1] *First Malaysia Plan: 1966–1970*, p. 123.
[2] *Economic Review of Malaysia, Singapore and Brunei*, No. 2, 1966, p. 12.
[3] Ibid.

Some worries inevitably overshadowed the generally robust pattern of Malaysia's economy. The exclusion of Singapore limited the effectiveness of the customs union tentatively started between the states of the federation in March 1966. The uncertainty generated by the rift also checked to some extent the expansion of private investment. Again, the government found that it had small hopes of securing the massive contributions of foreign aid on which it had counted in the first Malaysia plan on the strength of the country's highly respectable economic record. Malaysia's leaders had expected to secure about U.S. $300 million in aid grants and rather more in borrowing from abroad. This was to have financed some 42 per cent. of all public development.[1] They resented the contention of some of the wealthy nations they approached that aid should be primarily for the needy. They stressed that it was far more expensive to rescue a bankrupt or subversion-ridden country— a goal to which America had sacrificed vast sums—than to increase the potentialities of a solvent customer who could contribute to the stability of a whole area. The Minister for Finance was particularly distressed that he was unable to persuade the British authorities when he visited London to raise their modest contributions in normal aid, which were chiefly to the Borneo territories and for technical assistance. Britain had compelling reasons for this. Her balance of payments, considerably more fragile than that of her former colony, was already strained by defence aid to Malaysia and the high cost of resisting Confrontation. Knowledge of these factors did not silence criticism of Britain in Kuala Lumpur, nor arrest the phase of disenchantment which had clouded relations between the two countries since 1965.

Singapore, the chief trade centre of Southeast Asia, was hard hit commercially by Confrontation. As an entrepôt port she had always imported raw materials from the whole region such as rubber, petroleum products, pepper, coffee, copra, and timber. They were processed, sorted, graded, and re-exported to all parts of the world. In the reverse direction she received foodstuffs, machinery, textiles, and manufactured goods from Europe, America and the Far East and distributed them throughout the area. The charges for these services were a principal

[1] Ibid., pp. 12 and 13.

source of income. Indonesia had always played a major role in this two-way traffic. Its severance was a perceptible loss, as well as a major source of difficulty and confusion for the Indonesians who had tried, not very effectively, to transfer the role of entrepôt to other ports. Apart from official dealings there was the mutual loss of the lively barter trade with the neighbouring Indonesian islands many of which had adopted the Malayan dollar as their local currency in place of the questionable rupiah. During the ban, the Indonesians had found some other, direct, outlets for their exports and, as in the case of Malaysia, a number were likely to have been permanently diverted. Singapore was also hurt economically by separation. She had lost access to the customs union and common market with the states of Malaysia on which she had counted when joining the federation. Furthermore, Kuala Lumpur, like Djakarta, was now seeking to divert its trade from Singapore. This had been done with some success in the case of Malaysia's imports which required no very complicated handling, since Port Swettenham and Penang provided adequate normal services. In the case of Malaysian exports, little had changed in the first months after separation since the country's primary products were heavily dependent on Singapore's entrepôt and reprocessing facilities.[1] But Singapore risked losing this business also in the future.

By the end of 1965, however, Singapore had achieved some progress in a new direction. Her population by then approached two million, or nearly a quarter of Malaysia's, on an area of only 224 square miles. Entrepôt trade alone could not sustain so large and sophisticated a community. Since self-government in 1959 the new state had concentrated increasingly on industrialization. There was a customs tariff to raise revenue and protect local manufacturers which would have been anathema to Raffles. It was the kind of thing which had been bitterly contested when the British-Indian authorities proposed to introduce it a hundred years before. But the principle of maintaining Singapore as a free port had been upheld by the creation of a free trade zone and bonded warehouse facilities where goods could be stored for export and bulk consignments broken down, sorted and repacked.

Singapore had always had certain industries ancillary to her

[1] Ibid., p. 6.

entrepôt role. Some were linked with the processing for re-export of Southeast Asian raw materials. Others served the port, its visitors and communications, such as ship-building and repairing, engineering workshops, and plants for assembling and maintaining motor vehicles. The building industries grew with the population and the spread of urban areas. So did those concerned with food, beverages, printing and publishing, and the requirements of daily life. Light industry expanded in various fields. With the establishment of an Economic Development Board in 1961, more ambitious projects were launched. A large industrial area was established at Jurong in the south-west of the island with its own deep water harbour and railway line, designed to become eventually a new town of half a million. This could accommodate heavy as well as light industry. By the middle of 1966 some forty-four industries, there and elsewhere, including a steel mill, were in production, most with special facilities from the government as pioneer enterprises. Despite the external problems, some unemployment, and the general quietness caused by uncertainty, the rapid expansion of industry to some extent continued after separation. The building and shipping industries, amongst others, were helped by United States procurement orders for Vietnam. Although customs duties continued to be levied between Malaysia and Singapore (as they had been when Singapore was part of the federation), one of the few constructive developments in their relations was an agreement at the end of September 1965, to remove the quota restrictions on the flow between them of most of the goods they manufactured. Quotas continued to operate for goods manufactured elsewhere.

In other ways, susceptibility between the two neighbours persisted. Immigration controls were imposed on Singapore citizens entering Malaysia across the Johore causeway. One goal of Kuala Lumpur may have been to insulate to some degree the political system of Malaysia from that of Singapore. This measure seems also to have been partly due to suspicions aroused by Indonesia's hints at the time of separation, and again in April 1966, of readiness to recognize Singapore independently of Malaysia. Prime Minister Lee remarked on this last proposal that Singapore wished to be friendly with all countries, but would consult Malaysia on any matter affecting her defence. The Tunku retorted that Malaysia would never discuss recognition without Singapore being a party to such talks. He regarded this as a move by Djakarta to isolate Malaysia and use Singapore as a base against her. Singapore would have to choose between Malaysia and Indonesia. This was a choice which in the event she had small difficulty in making. Meanwhile the federal authorities insisted that they must safeguard themselves against having the Indonesian enemy 'on their doorstep'. But there may also have been an element of retaliation for the imposition of work permits for Malaysians by Singapore, in view of the local volume of unemployment. At the end of March 1966, the Tunku complained that Singapore had withdrawn without explanation from the Joint Defence Council and the Combined Operations Committee set up for mutual defence at the time of separation. He stressed that the defence and economy of Malaysia and Singapore were indivisible and that the island was still bound by the separation agreement which made Britain and Malaysia responsible for its defence. Negotiations for a new defence treaty and joint defence council followed.

Meanwhile there were signs that Confrontation might be a dwindling prospect not only militarily but politically. A new President of the Philippines, Mr. Ferdinand Marcos, took office at the end of the year. He succeeded President Macapagal who, without marked enthusiasm, had supported the policies of President Sukarno. Under the new régime, as under the old, the Philippines were to remain firmly anti-communist and aligned with the west. But even before assuming his duties the President-designate had indicated one change of course by announcing that he would resume diplomatic relations with Kuala Lumpur in 1966. The Malaysian leaders foresaw the early dissolution of the Confrontation alliance and the chance of re-vitalizing the Association of Southeast Asia, of which Manila had been a principal creator. In fact, there were many pauses and postponements before the resumption of diplomatic relations by reason of President Sukarno's persistent disapproval. President Marcos, like his predecessor, hesitated to break step with his massive neighbour. While Dr. Subandrio was still in power, during the interim period of the anti-communist drive, there were occasional signs of Djakarta being

prepared to open talks with Kuala Lumpur, but only on unacceptable terms. Thus in mid-December the Foreign Minister
spoke of Indonesia's new position of flexibility. She would be
ready to exchange views with Singapore, Sarawak, Malaya,
Brunei, and Sabah—that is as separate units—to seek a solution.
There was as yet no hint of the acceptance of Malaysia as constituted in 1963. New and far more constructive possibilities
emerged after March with the fall of Dr. Subandrio, the curb-
ing of the President's power and the victory of the moderate
triumvirate—the Sultan, General Suharto, and Adam Malik—
determined to set Indonesia on a fresh course.

President Sukarno's position as head of state and nominal
head of government was strangely anomalous. He no longer
commanded policy. He was increasingly attacked for his part
in the economic chaos and the scope he had given to the
P.K.I. To many younger people the father-figure had become
something of an elderly and mischievous bore. At public recep-
tions, under the eye of the new leaders, he seemed to foreign
observers physically reduced, hesitant and confused or boast-
fully rhetorical, a rather pathetic survival of former greatness.
Yet he still had a substantial following in certain sectors and
regions and his prestige as the virtual creator and unifier of the
nation remained indispensable to those who had in effect taken
it over. His signature was needed on documents, his formal
sanction to acts of state. This gave him a residue of power which
he exploited to evade as far as possible the role of constitutional
monarch which others were trying to thrust upon him. There
were reports of an implicit bargain whereby the new régime
would ensure that his future reputation was honoured in return
for his present acquiescence in their proposals. Yet time and
again he skilfully used his position to hold up the adoption of
policies which he resented. One of these was of course the ending of Confrontation. His Ministers could when necessary force
his hand, and override his complaints and objections. But they
were still liable to find themselves temporarily outmanœuvred
by one of Asia's most subtle politicians.

In the weeks following the change of government in Djakarta
in March 1966, there were several indications of a genuine
wish to normalize relations with Malaysia, particularly on the
part of Foreign Minister Malik. At the beginning of May he

went to Bangkok to consult the Philippine Foreign Secretary while General Suharto assured a representative of the leading Malaysian and Singapore newspaper[1] that Indonesia had no territorial ambitions. After his Bangkok talks, Mr. Malik spoke of Indonesia's desire to find a peaceful solution to the Malaysia problem in accordance with the Manila agreements of 1963, a statement for which he was subsequently upbraided by his President. The Philippine President gave the additional assurance that there were now no obstacles to the recognition of Malaysia by his country. At this same juncture, the Association of Southeast Asia also gave fresh signs of life. A Bangkok session of its joint working party recorded progress, planned meetings, and urged the implementation of new and existing projects. Some ten days later, a further sign of the new sensitiveness of the Malay leaders in their relations with Britain was their reaction to reports that the British Embassy in Djakarta had been discussing the Confrontation dispute with the local authorities. These talks were in fact concerned with an offer by Britain of emergency help to Indonesian victims of recent floods, a gesture designed in part to ease relations between London and Djakarta at this more propitious moment. Despite prompt British denials of any intention of discussing Malaysia's affairs, although Britain herself was so closely involved in Confrontation, the Tunku had seemed disposed to take the original reports at their face value. At a rally to mark the twentieth anniversary of the foundation of U.M.N.O. he proclaimed that Britain had no authority whatever to speak on Malaysia's behalf.

On 15 May, after a long cabinet meeting, President Sukarno accepted the issue of a cautious declaration to the effect that 'although Confrontation would continue' the Indonesian Government hoped for a peaceful settlement on the basis of the Manila agreements. This could be achieved through a meeting of Foreign Ministers without mediation by third parties. The President said he would be willing to meet the Tunku, who welcomed the idea but continued to be wary of possible British interference. Indonesia would, the Tunku said, be quite wrong if she thought she could coax Britain into telling Malaysia to make peace. Britain had nothing to do with Malaysia's affairs except for the defence agreement between the two countries.

[1] *The Straits Times*, Kuala Lumpur and Singapore, 2 May 1966.

On 17 May, Minister Malik still further smoothed the path to peace. He said that Indonesia would impose no rigid preconditions for ending Confrontation. She would not demand a referendum in the Borneo states since this might not be acceptable to Kuala Lumpur. Her government would 'not be upset' if these states remained in Malaysia. It was nevertheless concerned that the will of the majority there should be correctly interpreted and would welcome suggestions on how this might be done.

The Malaysian leaders declared their readiness for immediate negotiations at ministerial level. The new approach had in no sense taken them by surprise. Through the worst days of Confrontation informal and confidential contacts had been maintained between certain key figures on the Malaysian and Indonesian sides who lived with the hope of ending this feud in the Malay family. These had been seconded by the efforts of a few prominent and formerly influential Indonesians who had settled in Malaysia, some of whom, however, were suspect to Djakarta of implication in the 1958 rebellion.

On 27 May a group of senior Indonesian officers, ironically of the 'Crush Malaysia' staff, had cordial meetings in Malaya with the Tunku and Tun Razak. These included an Admiral who was head of Strategic Command and General Suharto's deputy, and the Indonesian Military Attaché in Bangkok. Although the need for mediation had earlier been disclaimed, an offer of help from Thailand was not discouraged. The Thai Prime Minister had recently been in Malaysia to discuss the possibilities of ending Confrontation and to confirm with the Tunku the plans for strengthening A.S.A. The sequel to his visit and that of the Indonesian delegation was the opening of peace talks between Tun Razak and Mr. Malik in Bangkok on 29 May. A cheerful, almost festive mood prevailed at these meetings and there were encouraging signs elsewhere. On 30 May, at the disbandment in Djakarta of an Indonesian brigade which had been operating on the Borneo border, the General in charge announced that physical and technical confrontation against a 'foreign country' was over and that a new form of confrontation had developed inside Indonesia between revolutionary and counter-revolutionary elements.

After two and a half days the Bangkok talks ended in an agreement embodied in an exchange of notes between the two

Deputy Prime Ministers. Details were withheld pending ratification by the two governments. Although the official Indonesian statement was again cautious—it merely spoke of laying the basis for practical steps to restore relations—the informal utterances on both sides were firmly sanguine. Mr. Malik said 'we are friends and will continue to be friends. There has been a meeting point . . . on all issues. Both nations fully realize that their people will benefit greatly from a normalization of relations.' It would be some time, he said, before complete normalization could be achieved. Meanwhile liaison officers would be stationed in both countries to implement what had been settled, and freedom of travel would be restored at once. He also indicated that Indonesia, Malaysia, Thailand, and the Philippines had agreed to form a 'union of co-operation', though they had not yet decided what to call it. After returning to Kuala Lumpur, Tun Razak stated that Confrontation was over for good, and that the talks had proved that all outstanding questions between Indonesia and Malaysia could be settled by negotiation. Their two peoples, of the same race and religion, would now 'come together again'. Continuous intergovernment contact would be maintained. He confirmed that an organization for regional collaboration would be set up.

In the first week of June diplomatic relations were restored between the Philippines and Malaysia; and recognition by Indonesia was conveyed to the Republic of Singapore. Prime Minister Lee subsequently assured the Tunku that Singapore would not establish diplomatic relations with Djakarta until the latter resumed such relations with Kuala Lumpur too. In welcoming the new phase the Philippine Foreign Secretary made it plain that the recognition of Malaysia did not imply any renunciation of his country's claim to Sabah. The two sides would keep in touch for the purpose of 'clarifying' the claim and discussing means of settling it to the satisfaction of both parties in accordance with the Manila agreements. They would also co-operate in eradicating smuggling, a constant fact of life between Sabah and the southern Philippine islands. He also hoped that Maphilindo would be revived. It could perhaps be fused with a reactivated A.S.A. and expanded to include other friendly Asian countries. The Philippine Secretary-General of the Southeast Asia Treaty Organization stressed that the resumption of relations with Malaysia strengthened the region against communism.

On returning to Djakarta the Foreign Minister confidently declared that, the basis for peace having been achieved, further conferences should be unnecessary. It was just a question of signing the agreement. At this point, President Sukarno elected to make his weight felt. During the talks he had made a dramatic bid for attention by claiming that he was keeping his 'mouth shut in a thousand languages' but would soon pour out his feelings as President, Commander-in-Chief, and Great Leader of the Revolution. He now showed his disapproval of the agreement by not signing it. The intentions of the new Indonesian leaders were thus formally blocked for over two months, though some progress was made in adjusting relations with their neighbours. The President continued to describe Malaysia as a British neo-colonialist and imperialist creation and to announce a conference he had long projected of all the new, emerging, anti-imperialist forces.[1] He appears to have further antagonized his Ministers by planning to dissolve the Provisional People's Consultative Congress.[2] Under the 1945 constitution this was the sovereign body, to which even the President was subordinate. These plans were promptly vetoed by General Suharto and his colleagues, though the meeting of the Congress was temporarily postponed. At the end of July the President was again overridden. At a meeting of the inner Cabinet which he seems to have attended but which was under the General's chairmanship, it was decided to endorse the Bangkok agreement. It was then signed, on 11 August, not by the President, but by the two Foreign Ministers. Tun Razak came to Djakarta for the occasion with a silver gift for the President which was not in any way reciprocated.

The agreement provided that the citizens of Sabah and Sarawak should be given the opportunity of reaffirming 'in a free and democratic manner through general elections their

[1] Two catchwords launched by President Sukarno before his policies were called in question, were: NECOLIM, standing for 'Neo-Colonialist, Colonialist and Imperialist' and CONEFO: 'Conference of the New Emerging Forces'.
[2] Madjelis Permusjawaratan Rakjat Sementara.

previous decision about their status in Malaysia'. Diplomatic relations were to be established as soon as possible and hostile acts would cease. The preamble invoked the spirit of brotherliness between two peoples bound together by history and culture from time immemorial. At a joint press conference the signatories promised economic, cultural, and military cooperation. There would be joint patrols to check piracy in the Malacca Straits, and, on the Borneo frontier, to suppress communist guerillas. A week later the President said that he now supported the agreement with Malaysia since the peoples of Sabah and Sarawak would be able to exercise 'self determination', a point on which he had allegedly insisted. He added that there would be no recognition of Malaysia until after the Borneo elections. This was quite contrary to the agreement, but he again sought to assert what power remained to him by holding up the signature of credentials for an Indonesian Ambassador to Kuala Lumpur who should have been appointed right away.

The agreement did not mention the British bases and there appeared to be a tacit and temporary acceptance by Indonesia of the *status quo*. General Suharto had earlier commented on a suggestion by Prime Minister Lee that the bases might continue for ten years. He said he was confident that Singapore would do nothing to prejudice good neighbourliness, and that Indonesia's only worry was to ensure that the bases should not be used to threaten her. Their retention was in any case clearly implied in a later statement by the Tunku that Malaysia would maintain her defence treaty with Britain. The fact that this went unchallenged marked Indonesia's transformation. It suggested a possible realization by her new leaders, as by those of Malaysia, that these relics of colonialism could make a contribution to stability in the face of militant communist subversion. A significant military adjustment marking the end of Confrontation was the appointment of a Malay General, the Deputy Chief of Staff of the Malaysian Armed Forces, as Director of Operations in East Malaysia[1] in succession to the

[1] The terms East Malaysia and West Malaysia were officially introduced for the Borneo states and the former Federation of Malaya from 5 August 1966. These designations had, however, been used unofficially for some time before this. This new regulation stipulated that the adjectives 'Malayan and 'Bornean' would no longer be used.

British General who had held this post since 1964. The latter remained as Commander of the British forces in Borneo. On the Indonesian side the 'Crush Malaysia Command' reverted to its original title of Supreme Operational Command. In welcoming the end of the dispute, the British Government announced the withdrawal over the next few months of some 10,000 British troops. The evacuation of the Australians began in August. Total casualties of the Commonwealth and Indonesia during Confrontation were estimated in the British press as 388 and 1,583 respectively.[1]

At the beginning of 1966, Southeast Asia had been in the grip of two international crises, the struggle in Vietnam and the communist-influenced contest between Indonesia and the west, of which her western-oriented neighbour Malaysia was the principal target. The eradication for the present of communist influence in Indonesia and the reconciliation of the three nations of Malay race had brought the second to a far happier conclusion than could have been foreseen a year before. This was in part achieved by the successful military opposition offered by Malaysia to Confrontation with Commonwealth support. It was also due to the realism and intelligence of those new elements in Indonesia who sought to restore their country's fortunes after twenty years of rashly rhetorical revolutionary experiments. The resultant changes had advanced for the time being the stabilization of the whole southern fringe of one of the most sensitive and vital areas of the world, in which Indonesia was the key factor. One well-informed view in the United States was that this evolution had not been determined by the support or intervention of Washington, which by September 1965 had largely given up Indonesia as a lost cause. The expanded American effort in Vietnam had in part been dictated by the domino theory, namely by the belief that a compromise with the communists there would lead to a communist victory in Indonesia and possibly in India and elsewhere. Yet the Vietnam campaign had not deterred Djakarta

---

[1] *Commonwealth:* Military Casualties: 114 killed, 181 wounded
Civilian Casualties:  36 killed,  53 wounded
4 captured

*Indonesia:* Casualties: 590 killed, 222 wounded
771 captured

from its earlier *rapprochement* with the communists nor decided its later hostility towards them. Indonesia and her neighbours now envisaged broadening the area of stability they had created, through an expanded Maphilindo with the possible inclusion of parts of former French Indo-China. The strange paradox was that it could now be argued in some quarters that the Vietnam campaign, fought for the stabilization of Southeast Asia, might prove an obstacle to the achievement of this very goal by the efforts of the Asians themselves.[1]

The short sequel to these external tensions will be considered chiefly in relation to the specific destinies of Malaysia and Singapore. But in this context the circumstances of President Sukarno are inescapably important. He had never ceased to resent the expansion and success of a country which he regarded as a natural satellite of Indonesia. The defeat of his policies was an affront to be revenged if possible. Any revival of his power remained a potential threat to Malaysia, more particularly as his determination to incorporate the Borneo territories and even the Malay Peninsula into Indonesia was a natural ambition of many of his people. The new régime had by no means renounced all of these objectives; nor was it probable that Indonesia with her potential weight and power would permanently forego the temptation to dominate her neighbours. But her new leaders were likely to rely on peaceful process rather than on force. In fact, in the second half of 1966, the President's position was further weakened by ridicule and suspicion which his public utterances did little to dispel. On the national day in August, he insisted that the Nasakom blend of nationalism, religion, and the left wing was still essential for the reconstruction of the country, though socialism could be substituted for communism since this last was banned. But this and his plans for holding a conference of the New Emerging Forces were jeered, mostly by students. On the following day the Religious Teachers Party,[2] which had been a pillar of Nasakom, repudiated his speech and demanded that the People's Congress should remove him as head of state and deprive

[1] This was the general theme of a leading article in the *New York Times* of 17 February 1966, entitled 'The Indonesian Irony'.
[2] Nahdatul Ulama.

him of all official functions. Not long afterwards, Sukarno supporters were fighting students in Bandung who had painted insulting messages, such as 'Sukarno equals Communism', around the town. In September, the second of his four wives was accused, again by students obviously prompted by their elders, of helping and financing members and organizations of the P.K.I. with the connivance of the President. Some demanded that this lady, allegedly the confidante of Aidit and Subandrio, should be brought to trial so that 'the public might learn the offences perpetrated by Bung Karno'.[1] A number of academicians also called on the President to resign and account for his actions to a military tribunal. Further discredit was cast on Sukarno's rule by the trial of the former Central Bank Minister, condemned to death in September for subversion, corruption, importing arms for the communists, and the Muslim transgression of having six wives instead of four. Later in the month the students claimed that the President was directly involved in the coup a year before and had given orders to kill the six generals.

By October there had been five death sentences for this episode. In the same month Dr. Subandrio was condemned to death for treason, after claiming that he had only done what the President wished. In December the former Commander of the Indonesian Air Force was also put on trial and faced the same sentence. According to the press, he was specifically charged with being aware of the communist plans and not preventing them, of sending a helicopter to bring the President to the coup headquarters, and another to evacuate Aidit to Central Java. Till the end of the year, however, it remained doubtful whether the death sentences would be carried out. President Sukarno's confirmation was needed and, although he had imprisoned many of his opponents, he had always shown a human reluctance to order the killing even of those who had sought to take his own life. At the same time the new masters of Indonesia may well have reckoned that this group of defeated men, with interlocking admissions, could prove a valuable instrument in completing the fall from power of a man who, with all his

[1] This abbreviated colloquialism: 'Brother Sukarno' had been used for years with affection and regard. It was now used with a less kindly note of irony.

failings, had pursued a vision of unity and greatness for his country. He had shaped the destinies of a whole generation of Asian nationalists and these, not without good reason, had now largely turned against him and were to compass within a few months his complete removal from power.

In our recent story, Confrontation and its sequel have inevitably overshadowed the whole scene. In our final chapter we shall note some of the main developments in the area during the following year and attempt an obviously fallible prediction of the future course of events. At the same time we shall seek to trace the general pattern and significance of the part played over nearly two centuries by one European power in the affairs of an Asian people.

# CHAPTER NINETEEN

# Malay Nationalism and the New Era

Throughout the Emergency and Confrontation Malaysia and Singapore had depended for survival on outside help. They ceased to do so when Confrontation ended. As we have seen, they still sought temporary reinsurance through the maintenance of the Commonwealth bases and the defence treaty with Britain, Australia, and New Zealand. But a new mood of self-assertion prevailed in the second half of 1966, above all in Kuala Lumpur, now that the country's former rulers were less pressingly required. More than ever before, Malaysian ministerial statements revealed an almost obsessive suspicion of Britain's motives. The Minister for Finance was convinced that there were political and not merely financial reasons behind Britain's refusal to give Malaysia further aid. The Minister for Information hinted that Britain's Labour government might have a special affinity with the socialist régime in Singapore. It seemed to the Alliance leaders that Britain might be trying to force Malaysia to conform to her own policy towards Singapore or to convey to Indonesia (in spite of official London statements to the contrary) that Malaysia could no longer count on British support. The government spokesman said that Malaysia must realize that Britain might not be her friend for ever. While grateful for past British help, she resented interference and Britain could not dictate to her now. She must stand on her own feet as an independent, sovereign nation. Underlying this attitude was the Malay leaders' consciousness of fresh potential strength at a time when U.M.N.O. was celebrating its twentieth successful year. The prospective solidarity of the three nations of Malay race gave them a new confidence. Working together, Indonesia, Malaysia, and the Philippines would constitute an impressive bloc of great power dimensions. It would have a population of around 140 million in which some 6 million Overseas Chinese would be faced with an overwhelming Malay preponderance.[1] Arrogant, restless, leftist, Chinese-dominated Singapore, which had sought to play a leading part in Malaysia's affairs, would be reduced to an isolated and vulnerable enclave in a Malay-dominated world.

One of U.M.N.O.'s most dynamic members of Parliament, Dr. Mahathir bin Mohamed, from the Tunku's own state of Kedah, reflected the outlook of many able young Malays. He belonged to those who might help to shape new policies in the approaching era when the training and traditions bequeathed by the colonial power to the first generation of national leaders would inevitably seem outdated.[2] In Singapore in June 1966,

[1]

| | Total Population (Year) | | Chinese Population (Year) | |
|---|---|---|---|---|
| Indonesia | 100,795,000 | 1963[a] | 2,690,000 | 1960[b] |
| Malaysia | 9,136,641 | 1964[c] | 3,245,528 | 1964 (Sabah: 1960)[c] |
| Philippines | 31,270,000 | 1964[a] | 181,626 | 1960[b] |
| | 141,201,641 | | 6,117,154 | |

[a] Demographic Year Book, U.N., 1964.   [b] Purcell, The Chinese in S.E. Asia.
[c] Statesman's Year Book, 1966/67.

[2] There has been much speculation about potential 'Young Turks' among the Malays who might one day set Malaysia upon bolder courses than those liable to be pursued by the Tunku or Tun Razak, his designated successor. But there is no organized group of such people with uniformly defined objectives, and many are not as yet in politics at all. Most are around 40 and have an outlook distinct from that of the slightly older nationalists such as Enche Senu, the Minister for Information, Melan Abdulla, the Editor of Utusan Melayu, Ja'afar Albar, the former Secretary-General of U.M.N.O. and Syed Nasir, the Director of the Malay Language Institute (Dewan Bahasa dan Pustaka).

In addition to Dr. Mahathir, some would include the following in the category of younger Malays with considerable potentialities for the future and a sensible, pragmatic approach to its problems.

Tunku Abdulla (son of the first King of Malaya and Dr. Mahathir's business partner)

Hanafiah Husain (Chairman of the Federal Agricultural Marketing Authority)

Musa bin Hitam (Assistant Secretary-General of U.M.N.O.)

Hisham Albakri (an architect, and one of the designers of the outstandingly beautiful National Mosque)

Such a list could be considerably extended. Certain circles predict that Dato Ghazali bin Shafie, the Permanent Secretary of the Ministry of External Affairs, who greatly added to his reputation in the negotiations to end Confrontation, could be a distinguished addition to the group. This would depend, however, on his being persuaded to abandon the civil service for the political field.

when reunification with Malaysia was discussed, he stressed that the Republic was a 'racial island of Chinese in a sea of Malays'. Indonesia, Malaysia, and the Philippines were basically Malay countries with strong feelings against Chinese chauvinism. Singapore's leaders would have to drop the concept of a third China. The political chasm between the two states could only be bridged by Singapore conforming to the policies of Malaysia and the 'general pattern' of Southeast Asia.

Such an attitude had wider implications for Malaysia itself. The Indonesians had hailed the end of Confrontation as 'a victory for the Malay race'. Yet it could hardly be expected that the three Malay nations would permanently co-operate on a basis of equality. Even though Djakarta's new leaders had renounced President Sukarno's more aggressive ambitions, Indonesia with her huge population and the lively intelligence of many of her people, could hardly fail to become the leader in this Malay world. It was significant and disturbing for the future that this gifted Malay should evidently prefer the prospect of Indonesian preponderance to any process of adjustment by his people to the unique requirements of their own multiracial society, one half of which was non-Malay. Should such views continue to prevail among the younger Malay nationalists, the ending of Confrontation and the initiation of some form of Maphilindo would clearly postpone to the remote future, if not indefinitely, the realization of the non-Malay goal of a 'Malaysian Malaysia' with the progressive introduction of equal rights for all races. This could cause an explosion of racial tension and stir up simmering bitterness which the communists might exploit in a new phase of activity stimulated by their marginal progress in Thailand.

The Prime Minister of Singapore remained the most active champion of the rights of the non-Malays. He firmly ignored the Tunku's invitation not to set himself up as the protector of the Chinese in Malaysia who allegedly safeguarded themselves by joining the M.C.A. Whatever economic benefits the ending of Confrontation might bring, it would involve a further setback to the cause of the immigrant races to which he had dedicated himself and his many adherents in the federation. He had clearly no intention of renouncing the struggle. The Democratic Action Party had been registered in Malaysia under the able leadership of Devan Nair, a Malayan Indian of Kerala extraction who had belonged to, and renounced, the Communist party. The D.A.P. pursued in effect the policies defended by the P.A.P. while Singapore was in Malaysia. Meanwhile, Prime Minister Lee busily sought support and approval abroad. He played a prominent part in a congress of the Socialist International in Stockholm in May. There he explained separation with the telling argument that Singapore had not joined Malaysia to have others rule her 'but to share in ruling the whole'. He visited some of the countries of Eastern Europe, signed trade agreements with Bulgaria and Poland and agreed to exchange trade missions with Czechoslovakia, Hungary, and Rumania. He stressed Singapore's need to develop relations with all her neighbours, including Communist China, and the neutrality of her foreign policy, which was paradoxically compatible with the maintenance of the British bases. These were temporarily needed for reasons of security but could be abolished when the situation in Southeast Asia radically changed. The communist world need no longer have a false image of Singapore as an anti-communist bastion and armed stronghold of British imperialism. The Prime Minister was also at some pains to cultivate the British Government, however cavalier his occasional comments on the colonial heritage.

For entirely different, indeed opposite, reasons Dr. Mahathir was himself a sharp critic of this heritage. He condemned the British for having permitted the unrestricted immigration of Chinese, even though it was essentially Chinese and European exploitation of her resources which had transformed Malaya into a modern country. In his view, Britain should have foreseen the obvious danger to the easy-going Malays of introducing into their midst a specially gifted and industrious race which had to succeed or starve. The objective of the younger Malays who shared his views was the elimination of British influence in Malaysia. This was far too strong, yet it was accepted by the present Alliance leadership.[1] In a press interview in June he advocated a gradual nationalization of Malaysia's import-export businesses as a first step towards

[1] These points were made by him in a private conversation with the writer in November 1965.

reducing British wealth in Malaysia. This was one of the first proposals from any quarter save the left wing of this common and dubious expedient of Asian nationalism which, in countries like Burma and Indonesia, had destroyed the general prosperity built up under colonial rule. Dr. Mahathir's strong anti-colonial convictions had also made him a believer in Afro-Asian solidarity and to that extent a disciple of President Sukarno. As head of the National Afro-Asian Peoples' Solidarity Organization and a recent member of the Malaysian delegation to the United Nations, he had been one of Britain's chief accusers over the failure of her policy in Rhodesia. His strictures on British rule in Malaysia posed the ethical riddle of all colonization. Could a materially advanced nation ever be justified in ordering the affairs of an alien race even if this were not purely for its own advantage, but for what it judged to be the advancement of an emerging people? This was a dilemma which had confronted America in the Philippines and elsewhere, just as it had the European powers in Asia and Africa.

As we have seen, the Alliance leaders were now prone to suspect and resent even the possibility of British partiality in Singapore and the Borneo states. In 1965 the Minister for Sabah Affairs had been eliminated for seeking greater autonomy for the state after the separation of Singapore; and his downfall had been linked with alleged intrigues on the part of British officers serving in the region. In 1966 a prolonged crisis in Sarawak led to the eventual removal of the Chief Minister, Dato Stephen Ningkan, also suspected of excessive reliance on British officials still in charge of major government departments. In the Tunku's view he was a man who 'wanted only that degree of independence for Sarawak that would allow him to be Chief Minister while in all other respects accepting the British as the masters'. In June, Dato Ningkan dismissed his Muslim Minister for Communications for allegedly plotting his overthrow 'with the backing of people outside Sarawak'. Three other Ministers resigned in protest. Two days later, at the request of a small majority of members of the Legislative Assembly in Kuching (the Council Negri), the Tunku dismissed Ningkan from the leadership of the Sarawak Alliance Party and demanded his resignation as Chief Minister, but

Dato Ningkan refused. The central government then nominated as Chief Minister another Iban, Penghulu Tawi Sli, a former school teacher who had been their candidate in preference to Ningkan at the time of the formation of Malaysia, and the Governor of Sarawak formally dismissed Ningkan. Tawi Sli formed a Cabinet at his request and entered on his duties while Ningkan sought a declaration from the Sarawak High Court that his dismissal was unconstitutional. The British acting Chief Justice found the dismissal to be null and void, since only the Council Negri could take this step through a vote of no confidence, and Ningkan resumed office. The next move of the central government was to proclaim a state of emergency in Sarawak and pass a law which altered the state constitution by giving the Governor power to call a meeting of the Council Negri. The opposition in Kuala Lumpur protested that with this legislation Sarawak once more reverted to the status of a colony. The sequel was a special meeting of the Council Negri convened by the Governor at which 25 out of 42 members then voted to dismiss Dato Ningkan, who described the proceedings as a 'mockery of democracy'. More than three months after the crisis started, Penghulu Tawi Sli was definitely sworn in as Sarawak's Chief Minister. In a subsequent letter to *The Times* of London, Dato Ningkan claimed that one main reason for this conflict had been his reluctance to speed the departure of the remaining British officials, since they were liable to be replaced, not by local people, but by Malayans from the Peninsula. In his view, the policy of Kuala Lumpur would lead to the Malayanization of the government service in Sarawak instead of to its recruitment from Borneo itself; and to Malayan domination in Sarawak. His removal did in fact lead to some abbreviation of the terms of service of the principal expatriate officers in Sarawak. He gave as the other main reason his unwillingness to agree to a request of the Tunku to hasten the introduction of Malay as the only official language.

For Malays and non-Malays, in a country of four main languages,[1] this issue tended to be charged with emotion. When Malaya became independent on 31 August 1957, with Malay as the national language, it was provided that for the time

[1] Malay, English, Chinese, and Tamil (the language of the majority of Southern Indians who form nearly 10% of the population of Malaysia).

being English would continue as a second official language, but it might cease to be one after ten years if parliament should so decree. Then, from September 1967, Malay would become the sole official language. When Malaysia was established in 1963, Malay was readily accepted as the national language for the whole federation, but English was similarly to be retained for ten years as a second official language, that is until September 1973. Dato Ningkan had merely favoured adherence to the stipulations in the original Malaysia agreement with Britain. By 1966, however, the Tunku had decided that all Malaysians would gain by the acceptance of Malay as the official language and wished to synchronize the date of its monopoly in both halves of the federation. He declared that Dato Ningkan was wrong if he supposed that the native races of Sarawak knew English better than Malay. In fact they understood Malay better than English.

In spite of his desire for the general acceptance of Malay, the Tunku assured an U.M.N.O. rally in June that the Alliance would always protect the interests of the other languages and that the schools teaching them would continue to receive government assistance. Malaysia was, he said, unique in helping languages and religions other than those of the state. The authorities had given financial support to temples and churches as well as mosques because they believed that religion was a sure weapon against communism. Their language policy was similar. They would not force Malay on other races any more than Muslims would force Islam upon those of other faiths. All they wanted, he said, was that Malaysians of non-Malay origin should accept the national language as the official language. At the same time it was clear that this requirement would be taken seriously. Already in mid-1966, well in advance of the deadline, in P.M.I.P.-dominated Kelantan those who corresponded with government departments in English were being threatened with the future return of letters not written in Malay. Later, in November, both the Tunku and Tun Razak stressed the important part which English would still play in the law courts, institutions of higher learning, and commerce. This was because English was 'a language essential for progress and international understanding'.

Emotion on both sides clouded the response to the assurances of the Alliance leaders. The Malay Language Society at the University of Malaya protested that the prominence reserved for English signified the adoption of multi-lingualism by the government, against the spirit of the constitution and the national education policy. The non-Malays were even more deeply disturbed, more perhaps than the issue warranted, since many had customarily used Malay as a *lingua franca* for communicating with the other local races and also with the British when their English was inadequate. Moreover, there was no question of any basic change in the traditional pattern of education, whereby free primary education for six years was provided in each of the country's four main languages. After this stage, in government-assisted secondary schools, the main medium of instruction had been either Malay or English since the public examinations were conducted in these two official languages. Chinese and Tamil were, however, also taught in government-assisted schools and examinations in these languages were included in the public examinations. A small fee was charged in English secondary schools, though there were a number of free places, but Malay was favoured to the extent that education in it was free of fees at all levels. According to the Malaysia Official Year Book for 1963[1], the government in this way sought to implement a policy of 'preserving and sustaining the four main cultures of the country while . . . establishing a truly national system of education in which . . . Malay shall gradually become the main medium of instruction'. In the special circumstances of Malaysia this was on the whole a generous and reasonable system. But, for the Chinese and Indians, Malay prejudice and the ambiguities in the policy and practice of the authorities were a constant source of anxiety and complaint. The Chinese Minister for Local Government and Housing, a pillar of the M.C.A., had to urge his countrymen not to abet the fanatical few who tried to insist that Chinese should be made another official language. They must face political reality and not stir up racial antipathies. The status of the Chinese language was guaranteed; it would continue to be taught with government support and used in public places and on public occasions. He also indicated how fortunate his compatriots were, since Malaysia was the only country in

[1] *Malaysia Official Year Book, 1963*, p. 397.

the world in which the Chinese could fully exercise their democratic rights.

An incidental impediment to racial harmony in this field was an element of cultural arrogance which tended to underlie the attitude of the Chinese and to some extent that of the Indians, however humble their origin. Both races were conscious of coming from countries with highly developed ancient civilizations which had contributed to the enlightenment of Southeast Asia and could claim to be superior to the culture evolved by the indigenous races in Malaysia. For this and other reasons they felt, rightly or wrongly, that they had developed into people more enterprising and capable than the politically dominant Malays. There were, moreover, other sources of controversy in the educational and practical field. One was that non-Malays with respectable English resented the prospect of having in future to pass public examinations up to a high standard in Malay. Another derived from the limitations of the Malay language itself. For all its beauties, this tended to be vague and allusive and indifferently adapted to the mechanical and scientific complexities of modern life. This problem was emphasized by the delay of the Language Institute (Dewan Bahasa) in producing a practical and effective Malay dictionary of modern scientific terms. The Chinese Dean of the Faculty of Education of the University of Malaya, amongst others, gravely doubted the wisdom and efficacy of bi-lingual tuition in Malay and English which some of the authorities were proposing to introduce in 1966, in obvious fulfilment of the general policy directive that Malay should gradually become the main medium of instruction. One consequence would be the obvious need to have all textbooks translated into Malay. Another and more serious result might be to defeat the government's fundamental objective of raising the educational standards of the Malays so that they could compete with the Chinese and Indians on equal terms. While their rivals were at pains to equip themselves in English as the most effective instrument for getting on, many young Malays fought for tuition in their own language because this offered them the easiest, though least competitive, choice. Fortunately, the sensible and moderate Malay leaders in the Alliance were fully aware of these dangers and in drawing up their language bill, passed in March

1967, showed no sign of yielding to their own extremists. The new act provided that, from 1 September 1967, Malay alone would have the legal status of an official language. It would be used by the government in its affairs as a matter of course and would be useable by the public in transactions with the government as a matter of right. The other languages were not, however, completely prohibited, parliament being authorized to continue or discontinue the use of English in the federal and state legislatures and in the law courts. In general the Head of State and other authorities could permit the continued use of English (and the other languages) where this seemed to be in the public interest. The measure gained moderate support, though it was inevitably attacked by the non-Malay opposition for sacrificing Chinese and Indian rights and by the P.M.I.P. and other extreme Malay nationalists for selling out the Malays to the immigrant races.

At the end of October Malaysia welcomed President Johnson. This was during his memorable visit to the Manila Conference on Vietnam, and to Saigon, Bangkok, and Seoul, in a journey which also for the first time brought a President of the United States officially to Australia and New Zealand. Responsible Malaysians took pride in the fact that their goodwill towards America, unlike that of many Asians, was in no sense based upon dependence. They were gravely concerned about the war in Vietnam but had no illusions about the consequences of a communist victory. They appreciated the friendship of the richest and most powerful nation in the world, but were sufficiently solvent and successful to have no claim on America for anything she did not freely choose to give.[1] At the same time, they were delighted that the President was to be followed by his economic adviser, the former President of the World Bank, Mr. Eugene Black, and a team of experts who would assess how Washington could speed up Malaysia's economic development. They were also greatly cheered by a decision of the U.S. authorities which just preceded Mr. Johnson's arrival, to limit sales of stockpile rubber and tin and thus avoid depressing the price of Malaysia's two most valuable resources. This would

[1] Representative of these views was a leading editorial in the *Straits Times* (Kuala Lumpur and Singapore) of 29 October 1966.

mean a considerable increase in the country's revenue and in such a case trade was more important and effective than aid.

The utmost was made of a twenty-hour visit in the course of which, on the official side, there were no jarring notes. Apart from the usual entertainment and ceremonial, the President talked business with the Malaysian Cabinet and was flown to Negri Sembilan to visit one of the model settlements of the Federal Land Development Authority, afterwards renamed in his honour. The accounts of discussions and speeches struck a more genuine note than was customary on such occasions. The King spoke of the fact that small nations like Malaysia now looked to America for their security and survival. Yet the Tunku stressed that the United States should not have to fill any power gap in their area. The withdrawal of British troops from Borneo would not create this, because Britain would still have her bases under the defence agreement. Moreover she would not risk leaving a vacuum when her vested interests in the region were so large. The President was also told that the free world, and in particular America, must ensure the economic recovery of Indonesia. Otherwise her people would not be able to defend themselves against the still numerous communists in their midst. The incidental problem was broached of Malaysia equipping her armed forces so as to maintain them on a war footing in the more vulnerable areas. In this context the President undertook to consider a possible easing of the terms of payment for U.S. helicopters.

The Tunku recalled the President's welcome to him in Washington in 1964 when Malaysia was commended for her choice of freedom and democracy. He deplored the prevalent ignorance of America's role in Vietnam. Malaysia's rift with Indonesia had been caused by the same communist enemy. He described Malaysia as a country with people of many racial origins, in which however only the *Bumiputra*[1] were indigenous. The other races were from countries with proud traditions which they inevitably recalled. The problem was to make all think of themselves as Malaysians with one loyalty to their country. Yet, except for a small but articulate group whose loyalty was elsewhere and who remained a threat to peace and

[1] 'Sons of the Soil,' a favourite popular phrase often used by Malay leaders for their own people.

security, Malaysia stood united today. Having weathered many storms, her people were now striving at great cost for higher standards of living. Although Malaysia looked in fact to America for help in filling the financial gaps in her development plans, this gentle hint of prospective needs was all that the President's hosts deemed appropriate to so special an occasion.

The President spoke of Malaysia as a model of what could be done by determined and farsighted men. She had shown that communist aggression could be stopped by military action and that after the struggle—even during it—economic prosperity could be won. She bore witness to the fact that the gap between rich and poor could be narrowed and the impoverished countryside made to share in the general well-being. Furthermore their nation had reached out to its neighbours and assumed a leading role in regional co-operation. Fifteen years earlier, Malaya had suffered the fate of South Vietnam. But the bright promise the country displayed today was a symbol of what the future would surely hold for her troubled neighbour. In the mood of the occasion it was right and natural that the entire credit for these achievements should have been given to those whom the President was addressing. It would have been gravely inappropriate to recall that for three-quarters of the period of the anti-communist struggle Malaya had been under colonial leadership and rule.

Almost inevitably, there was strong objection to the visit from quarters hostile to American policy and a calculated determination to cause disturbance. A riot developed near the United States Cultural Centre in one of the most conspicuous parts of the capital. The police defending the building felt compelled to fire on an attacking mob of some five hundred which refused to disperse. One young man was killed, another wounded, some twenty persons injured and over a hundred arrested. The clashes continued when the crowd turned to tearing down the American and Malaysian flags along the processional route. There were also demonstrations in a number of state capitals.

Mr. Black and his experts arrived in Malaysia in the week of the President's departure for a visit of four days. They had been assigned to survey the needs of eleven countries in South-

eastern and Eastern Asia within the general framework of
Washington's offer of $1,000 million in aid, primarily for pro-
jects of regional importance. As a member of the World Bank-
sponsored Aid to Malaysia Club, which held its initial meeting
in London in May, the United States was regarded as committed to help in financing some of the projects in the first
Malaysia Plan for 1966 to 1970, which was to cost an ambitious
total of some $2,000 million and to give special priority to the
Borneo states. External requirements for development under
the Plan would alone cost some $600 million. In the course of
his visit, Mr. Black described the Plan as excellent and Malaysia
as a very good credit risk in the eyes of the United States. His
talks were chiefly with Tun Razak, Tan Siew Sin and the other
Ministers concerned with development, and with members of
the Prime Minister's Economic Planning Unit which had earlier
been set up by an American adviser. For the first time Malaysia
put forward a formal request for American aid, one part
reportedly covering projects for direct aid, another regional
projects. In presenting their case the Malaysian leaders appear
to have stressed that, without U.S. aid, their success in syn-
chronizing development and democracy would be imperilled,
with serious consequences for the whole region. According to
the press, the government felt that the need for financial help
had never been greater in view of the prospect of lower prices
for rubber and tin, and the 'absence' of British defence assistance, a final point strangely at variance with the Tunku's
assurances to the President about the retention of the Commonwealth bases and the defence treaty. Mr. Black announced
American interest in helping Malaysia over some of the projects in her Plan, and particularly two in the transport and
communications section. The first of these was to complete the
construction of a second East–West highway between Kota
Bharu, the capital of Kelantan, and Butterworth opposite
Penang. The second was to develop Port Swettenham and the
port of Penang so that they could handle far more cargo, a
scheme which might prove marginally prejudicial to Singapore.[1] The United States would also envisage assistance to
Malaysia's plans for regional economic co-operation; and the
establishment of joint American-Malaysian industrial ventures.

[1] *First Malaysia Plan 1966–1970*, pp. 142 and 147.

Mr. Black spoke appreciatively of Malaysia's initiatives in international and regional economic co-ordination. Thus the Malaysian Centre for Development Studies had recently organized a seminar on development planning for representatives of fifteen Asian and African countries. The government had also decided to call a meeting of Southeast Asian Ministers for Transport and Communications to study common problems and embark on joint projects. In September Malaysia had supported a plan for a multilateral treaty of commerce and navigation within the framework of the Association of Southeast Asia. Despite the fair words exchanged during the American visits, some disappointment seems to have been felt in Kuala Lumpur that Washington's generosity was more readily forthcoming for regional rather than Malaysian national projects. After Malaysia, Mr. Black and his party paid a brief visit to Singapore, chiefly to discuss with Ministers there the Republic's proposals for U.S. financial help in implementing various projects under Singapore's current five year development plan. He had been anxious to complete all his surveys before the inaugural meeting in Tokyo of the Asian Development Bank on 23 November.

This was the latest of the international financial institutions created since the second world war which had made so vital a contribution to world economic stability and to raising the standards of the materially less advanced countries in the teeth of their menacing growth in population. Two of these, the World Bank and the International Monetary Fund had just been joined by Singapore as an independent state. Malaysia had shared in and benefited from them all. An agency of the World Bank, the International Finance Corporation, had made and was making, notable contributions to industrial progress in both territories through the Malaysian Industrial Development Finance Corporation and the Singapore Economic Development Board which was given expanded powers in 1966. Faced with a Malaysian tariff and a minute home base Singapore, in addition to her traditional entrepôt role, saw hope in trying to become a second Hong Kong or a microscopic Japan, processing imported raw materials to quality standards through an impressive injection of high skill and hard work. In the ideally central position chosen by Raffles's keen eye, she was giving herself fresh scope in expanding capacity for shipbuilding and oil refining, for aircraft and ship repair, and in many other fields. The Asian membership of the new development bank, which was to start operations in December, was balanced by European, Australian, and New Zealand participation. It enjoyed substantial support from the United States and the communist countries excluded themselves on the pretext that those who made the largest capital contribution would play a 'disproportionate' role. Its headquarters was at Manila and its President Japanese.

This was one further mark of the new weight and influence in Asia of a peacefully resurgent Japan, the only Asian nation to have attained first the military and then the economic status of a world power. She was fast obliterating the harsh record of her military rule and creating by business drive and growth a genuine East Asia co-prosperity sphere, the slogan invested by her soldiers with such unhappy memories. After a period of minimum assertiveness in the years immediately following the American occupation she had made her weight felt at a meeting of Asian and Pacific countries at Seoul in June 1966, sponsored by the Foreign Minister of South Korea. This had also included representatives of Australia, Nationalist China, the Philippines, New Zealand, Thailand, South Vietnam and Malaysia, and the countries in question had established the Asian and Pacific Council (ASPAC) to promote greater cooperation and solidarity among the non-communist Asian and Pacific nations. Influenced by left wing and pacifist pressure at home, and preoccupied with broadening its contacts with Peking, the Japanese Government had insisted that this pact, largely between supporters of the United States standpoint on Asia, should not have a military or ideological character. It refused to agree to strong statements on communist aggression and South Vietnam reflecting the U.S. view, or to naming Communist China and France in a condemnation of nuclear tests in the Pacific. Japan was clearly concerned to leave the door open for non-aligned and neutral countries to join the Council at a time when Indonesia had displayed some interest in the new association; and seemed to be embarking on a new role as peacemaker between east and west. Malaysia, which had been represented by her Minister for Education, Khir Johari, had shared Japan's preoccupations.

Japan now envisaged the creation of a Southeast Asian economic union, possibly to be linked later with a wider organization of common market character for the countries of the Pacific basin. This accorded with proposals put forward the following year with Djakarta's support for an economic association embracing Indonesia as well as Malaysia, Singapore, Thailand and the Philippines which, it was thought, might take the place of the narrower Association of Southeast Asia. In the still shifting situation of the area in which Britain no longer sought to play a major role, Malaysia and Singapore welcomed Japan's new status as an element of stability and strength complementary to that provided by the United States. This clearly emerged when the Japanese Foreign Minister visited Kuala Lumpur towards the end of October and produced an offer of Japanese help over the first Malaysia Plan. He was assured by the Tunku that only a strongly developed nation like Japan could take the lead in promoting Asian friendship in the political and economic field. On a subsequent visit to Singapore, the Minister concluded an agreement for the payment of compensation by Japan for the war-time excesses committed by her forces. This was to involve the payment of 50 million Malayan dollars, half as an outright grant and half as a loan on special terms. Such a settlement, still pending in the case of Malaysia, was not only a stroke of political wisdom; it offered Japan fresh economic opportunities in the area.

By the end of 1966, Malaysia's leaders could claim that she was accomplishing 'a silent revolution'. The country had a healthy economy and climate of investment and active industrial expansion despite the possibilities of severely increased taxation to fill gaps in the financing of the first Malaysia Plan. There was some criticism of Britain and insistence on the rapid substitution of qualified Malaysians for expatriates in business jobs, yet a minimum of anti-Western prejudice and, except on the left wing, little resentment of American policies. This was offset by cautious moves towards some formal relationship with the Soviet Union and Yugoslavia; and diplomatic relations with the former were established in 1967. Malaysia and Singapore were opening up new paths in education. A Fisheries Research Institute in Penang had gained some international recognition. In 1966 it was decided that a new University College, affiliated with the University of Malaya, should be started there. It would have faculties of science and architecture, and later law. Broader facilities of this kind had become essential when some eight thousand young Malaysians were liable to be studying abroad at any one time. Suggestions were also in the air for exchanging graduates between Southeast Asian countries to develop regional thinking and cohesion. The government held out the prospect of eventually having educational facilities for every child of school age throughout the country.

In other aspects of social progress, Malaysia was still inevitably somewhat behind socialist Singapore. Only in a few cases, such as the National Union of Plantation Workers, were Malaysian trade unions massive and effective. In general, the unions were too numerous and fragmented and some had only a negligible membership. The country had made encouraging progress in extending health services. In this field, whatever the shortcomings in earlier years, the colonial régime had earned high credit for its work since the Japanese occupation.[1] Under social welfare there were most of the rather basic arrangements common to all modern societies for the care of children, youths, women, handicapped persons, the old, and juvenile delinquents. Government employees received a number of comfortable fringe benefits such as free medical treatment and, for the Muslims, generous help to make the pilgrimage to Mecca. The authorities may have counted on a move by private firms to compete in the labour market by offering some matching privileges at their own expense, but they announced in March 1966, that they would be introducing a sickness insurance scheme for workers as a government measure. In general, however, Malaysia had few of the advanced benefits, such as old age

---

[1] The *Malaysia Official Year Book* for 1963 quotes the following passage from the report of the World Bank mission to Malaya in 1954: 'Not long ago, Malaya was one of the unhealthiest places in the tropics. Today it is among the healthiest, comparing favourably with many countries in the sub-tropical climates. This is one of the world's outstanding achievements of public health and medicine, a tribute to the British administrators and their medical and public health officers.' The Year Book adds: 'With the achievement of independence, the nation continues to build on the firm foundations already laid.'

pensions and unemployment insurance, characteristic of western welfare states.

The greatest pride and interest of the country's leaders lay perhaps in rural development, to be achieved not just through outside help but by stimulating initiative and self-reliance in the *kampongs*. Emphasis was given to the co-operative movement and agricultural credit and to the elimination, in what was judged to be the interest of the Malays, of the predominantly non-Malay middleman. Two new Banks (the Bank Bumiputra and the Kampong Co-operative Apex Bank), and the recently established Federal Agricultural Marketing Authority, were designed to furnish the cultivator with financial and other facilities to grow and market his produce without the intervention of the traditional Chinese intermediary. The Banks would also help them to branch out into commercial and industrial enterprises. With similar objectives the authorities invited a World Bank team to survey their agricultural credit system. They also encouraged a meeting of co-operative societies to discuss the establishment of a national co-operative organization. There continued to be some cynicism on the part of private Chinese about plans essentially designed to promote the economic competitiveness of the Malays in a manner marginally adverse to their interests. They questioned the readiness of the rural Malay to discard his traditional habits of ostentatious and uneconomic expenditure and his dependence on the prompt and flexible resources of the Chinese money-lender and entrepreneur. Yet these measures were impressively conceived. In bringing new lands to the landless and fresh sources of independent wealth within the grasp of the poor, they made a contribution to social and political stability infinitely more valuable than the achievement of purely commercial gains. Development might have been less marked had the whole field not been dominated by the man designated as the country's future leader. Tun Razak's personality was, as we have seen, a living contradiction of the facile image of the easy-going Malay. Through his quasi-military techniques of Operations Rooms and Red Books[1] he fought the sluggish ineptitudes of bureau-

[1] See p. 121. As in military planning, Operations Rooms at Federal, State, and District level were designed to give systematic visibility, through illuminated maps and diagrams, to current problems and progress. Co-

cracy for which he partly blamed the staid traditions of the
colonial power. Rural development in Borneo was a vaster
challenge than in Malaya and the central government had
responded to it generously. Before the end of the year, however, the simmering crisis in Sarawak called for the Deputy
Prime Minister's intervention in the Borneo political field.

On 12 November Tun Razak arrived in Kuching to counsel
and to warn. He was seconded by his Chinese colleague, the
Minister for Commerce, Dr. Lim Swee Aun. He announced
that Sarawak now had a good state government with which the
federal authorities could work. Development could go satis-
factorily forward. But the machinery, both of the state government and of the local Alliance party, must be improved.
Difficult times lay ahead. Elections would soon be held to the
Council Negri, to which Malaysia was committed by her agreement with Indonesia ending Confrontation. These would be the
first direct elections in East Malaysia. Earlier ones had been
indirect and on the basis of preliminary elections to the district
councils. Sarawak and Malaysia, he said, had the same
interests, and the opposition must realize that the central
government would not tolerate any forces working against
national unity. Expatriate officers were welcome to stay until
they could be replaced, if they served Malaysia loyally. If not,
they must go. He commended the help of the British and
Commonwealth forces during Confrontation. Now that was
over Malaysia had to assume her own defence. Unfortunately a
serious security threat remained, with around a thousand active
communists still at large in Sarawak. Those to whom he referred were predominantly Chinese from the clandestine
communist organization linked with the left wing of the Sarawak
United People's Party. They had been trained by the Indo-

---

ordination at the different levels, and between them, was achieved by
frequent verbal briefings. Unnecessary correspondence was discouraged.
The Red Books were massive volumes in three copies containing a series of
district maps, each separately illustrating a different phase of the rural
schemes, such as land development, water supply, schools, roads, health,
marketing, etc. One copy was kept in the District Operations Room, a
second in the State Operations Room at the state capital, a third was sent
to the National Operations Room in Kuala Lumpur. Red Books were
intended to show what needed to be done; the Operations Rooms to carry
this out.

nesians during the hostilities and had established bases on the southern frontier. Others did not put their numbers higher than 800 and for some time joint Malaysian-Indonesian teams had been working to destroy their organization. The communist peril was real, but it seemed that the federal leaders might be somewhat exaggerating it in order to stimulate, at an awkward juncture, a sense of loyalty and inter-dependence between Sarawak and themselves.

Sabah had for the present ceased to be a problem and its legislative elections were likely to be held in March 1967, Sarawak's not till some months later. The Alliance parties were working reasonably together, including U.P.K.O. the party of Donald Stephens; and there was little subversion. Tun Mustapha had assumed Stephen's former post of Minister for Sabah Affairs in the Kuala Lumpur Cabinet and under his firm political leadership and that of the Chief Minister, Peter Loh, there was a realistic adjustment to association with Malaysia for security, development capital, and administrative and technical skills. On one minor point local opinion would be overriden: with a constant shortage of labour, many Sabah employers would have liked to hire workers from Indonesia, the Philippines, Hong Kong, or Taiwan. These would be cheaper and less demanding than those from the Peninsula, who often sought an early return home. But there was still rural unemployment in the Malay states and the federal Minister for Labour was determined to promote labour migration from Malaya to Sabah.

Sarawak had the same need of Malaysia as Sabah, but forces were still active to loosen the association. Ningkan had not accepted defeat as had Stephens. He was again seeking a legal injunction to prove that his dismissal was invalid. His Sarawak National Party no longer worked with the Alliance and favoured a revision of the federal bond. His Iban followers were apparently beginning to find common ground with the Chinese in their resentment of rule from Kuala Lumpur. This was a situation which played into the hands both of the communists and of the moderate leaders of the S.U.P.P. which had always opposed Malaysia. One of the latter, Stephen Yong, declared that, if revision were not accepted, Sarawak would be expelled from the federation or would opt out. Such talk suggested a disturbing *entente* between the S.U.P.P. and Ningkan and had been one of the chief reasons for Tun Razak's visit. By the end of the year it was held in some quarters that, if any such pact should endanger an Alliance victory in the elections, these would not in fact be held. Others predicted that those in Malaya who saw in the Borneo territories a constant source of trouble and expense might accept with resignation a vote on their part for separation. Yet such an outcome was frankly improbable for many reasons. The wiser citizens of Sabah and Sarawak appreciated the financial generosity of a central government which understandably claimed ultimate control. Separate independence was impracticable and there could now be small attraction in the earlier plan of an association of all northern Borneo. Little comparable generosity could be expected from Brunei despite the funds at the Sultan's disposal. Moreover, in view of the power and influence retained by the Ruler, the prospects of democratic modernization there were not necessarily ensured by Britain's decision, announced in November, that Brunei should progressively assume full responsibility in all fields. A final warning against any such alternative would be the remembered goal of Azahari's rebellion and the increased vulnerability of northern Borneo to eventual absorption by Indonesia.

In the Borneo states a graver danger than secession was the possible spread of communist insurrection. As we have seen, this danger had also revived on the Thai-Malay border and was likely to grow or diminish with the outcome of the Vietnam war. It was clear from a White Paper issued in Kuala Lumpur in October 1966, that the Confrontation policy of the P.K.I. had been a source of strength to the communists in Malaya as it had been to those in Borneo. Some had gone from the Peninsula to Sumatra for training, as those in Sarawak had gone to Kalimantan. The 'Malayan National Liberation Army' on the border (known to the government as the Communist-Terrorist Organization) now counted, in addition to a trained force of 500–600, a youth reserve of about 1,000. Its political arm was the Malayan National Liberation League, based on Peking.[1] These forces had recently ambushed a Thai-Malaysian patrol in the area and killed two-thirds of them. But the communists

[1] See p. 231.

did not yet seem to intend another all-out armed struggle. Their new policy was an apparent compromise between this and subversion through anti-government agitation concentrating on the language issue and the struggle in Vietnam; and the infiltration of legal bodies. Visits to their border bases were arranged for certain sympathetic politicians so that these, impressed with the appearance of a liberated area and an insurrectionary force, should be disposed to work with them in united fronts. To appeal to the Chinese, they no longer, as formerly, accepted Malay as the national language but merely its 'voluntary development' as a *lingua franca*. But they were also aware that Malay hostility had been a main factor in defeating the original Emergency and sought to appeal to Muslim opinion by using the pseudo-religious arguments with which the P.K.I. had bemused the masses in Indonesia. Meanwhile rebellious activity by students, many of them from Malaysia, in one of the Singapore colleges, was exploited by left-wing extremists from Nanyang University. This was severely and effectively checked by the police who regarded it as a first move towards a major communist demonstration. At the end of November, the Tunku estimated the total number of communists in Malaysia at around 20,000, of whom perhaps half were hard core, card-carrying members of the Malayan communist party or Sarawak's clandestine communist organization. Both in Malaysia and Singapore, however, the authorities, operating under emergency regulations, had learned to deal swiftly and harshly with subversion in its initial stages. Only in new and disastrous circumstances was either country likely to fall victim to subversion. One obvious risk would be an issue to the Vietnam war favourable to Hanoi, if this should be followed by the spread of communist control in Thailand. Another would be some grave economic crisis which brought underlying resentments between the races—now cushioned by prosperity—violently to the fore.

In mid-August there were changes in Malaysia's financial and trade relations with the United Kingdom and in currency arrangements inherited from colonial days. Although Malaysia would remain in the sterling area and retain the existing value of her dollar, this would in future be quoted in gold at the equivalent of $32\frac{2}{3}$ U.S. cents instead of in sterling. Although the change was announced as providing 'flexibility' it could more realistically be attributed to rumours of the devaluation of sterling. On the following day it was stated that Malaysia's currency would be separated from that of Singapore from June 1967. The Central Bank of Malaysia and a new currency board in Singapore would issue currency of identical value in place of the Board of Currency Commissioners which for many years had covered both areas as well as the Borneo territories. Brunei was expected to have a separate currency of its own. Kuala Lumpur and Singapore would henceforth 'co-operate in monetary and banking matters to the fullest extent possible'. The advantages were obvious of a common currency backed by combined reserves for two countries which, in effect, formed part of one economic system, more particularly when Malaysia had a large favourable trade balance and Singapore normally an unfavourable balance of visible trade. There had been recent and apparently constructive discussions between them which seemed intended to preserve the common currency and a common banking system. To many, especially in Singapore, this surprise decision seemed a more serious threat to common prosperity than political separation. It was hard to explain except in terms of the general mistrust which had grown up between the two former partners and more particularly of Malaysia's reluctance to accord to Singapore the voice in the affairs of her Central Bank to which she would have become entitled had it issued currency for both states.[1] Singapore intended that her influence on Malaysia should remain considerable. This was indeed inevitable, whatever preoccupations her policies might arouse. But by the end of 1966, with all that had occurred in the past two years, there remained little serious prospect of her renewed association with Malaysia. Apart from all other considerations her government, after starting to play a highly individual part on the world stage, was becoming ill-attuned to a supporting role.

At this same juncture the Malaysian Minister for Finance

---

[1] 'We still have virtually only one economy for two countries, and we prosper or not by joint endeavour. . . . We have no common market, we shall soon have no common currency and no common banking system. We still share a little common sense, but this seems to be a wasting asset.' The *Straits Times* (Kuala Lumpur and Singapore), 18 August 1966.

announced that, to raise increased revenue for the first Malaysia Plan, Commonwealth preferential duties would be abolished on a number of imports. Britain which had been unable to help the Plan financially, would be the country most severely affected. He had earlier explained that there was no question of Malaysia leaving the Commonwealth and that this was a matter of necessity not of retaliation. Of no dramatic importance in themselves, this series of measures nevertheless marked a conclusive point. In this key area of Asia, Britain's responsibilities had been prolonged by circumstances far beyond their natural term. Some still remained. In general, however, the peoples with whom she had been so long associated had now embarked on a decisively separate destiny.

# EPILOGUE

## The Pattern and Problems of Success

1967 was to mark a phase of further consolidation in the affairs of the Malay nations, darkened, however, by the tragic intensification of the Vietnam conflict and the failure of the Djakarta triumvirate to remedy the economic ills of Indonesia which might give renewed strength to a temporarily defeated P.K.I. At the beginning of the year the incalculable Sukarno was still the nation's chief executive, though greatly reduced in power and prestige. His continuance in office inevitably tended to discourage the wealthier western nations who had suffered as a result of his policies from producing the massive financial and economic help which Indonesia's recovery demanded. In March this personal problem was resolved in a manner inimitably Indonesian. The People's Consultative Congress formally revoked the President's mandate, withdrawing after nearly twenty-two years all powers granted to him under the 1945 constitution. It also deprived him of the title of 'Great Leader of the Indonesian Revolution' and his teachings were no longer to be the guiding principles of the state. General Suharto was appointed acting President in his place pending the holding of elections for a new Congress in 1968. In taking the oath of office, administered by his former chief, General Nasution, as Chairman of the Congress, General Suharto significantly pledged himself to prevent 'all manifestations which might lead to absolutism'. Despite voices in favour of this course, the fallen President was not brought to trial; according to his successor, Sukarno had been misled and exploited by the P.K.I. The former autocrat was even permitted the continued use of the Presidential residences. From one aspect this chivalrous treatment reflected a human tolerance characteristic of the Malay races at their best. From another, it was a shrewd and cautious move. His figure still inspired belief in many simple people in the remoter parts of the country. To have publicly humiliated or destroyed a man who for a generation had been the symbol of the nation's unity might have risked at best a damaging clash of loyalties, at worst another insurrection. It was not without value even for those who had rendered him impotent that his visible presence remained.

During this recent past the western colonial powers have become the scapegoats of the emerging world, while the Asian and African empires of earlier history, or the Soviet empire of the present, mostly escape reproach. Yet the dispassionate are beginning to realize that European colonization, though sometimes harsh and unjust and occasionally destructive, was often in fact creative. In America it used to be indiscriminately condemned even though condemnation by Americans was strictly a denial of their birthright. Few paused to distinguish between the evolution of their own society, in which the colonizers were also their founding citizens in a land where there was room for all, and the pattern of European colonization in Asia where established societies were subjected to alien control. By a harsh irony it is now the United States which is branded by half the world, alongside the sinful Europeans, as arch-imperialists. This is a calumny defying all America's earnest efforts to bring order out of chaos, spread stability and raise the living standards of the backward in other lands; and to give to individuals and societies the chance to regulate their lives according to their own free choice.

Most of these goals were also those of the British Empire in its day. Even the prospect of a free choice by the peoples it ruled was accepted, perhaps reluctantly, but as something ultimately inevitable. It is often overlooked that in India, for example, where Britain also created a nation which had not formerly existed, this freedom of choice was eventually put into effect, not by any headlong retreat of the imperial power, but by mutual arrangement. Significantly, Britain's last Viceroy became, by invitation of the Indians, the first Governor-General of their independent state. Many Americans now see this kind of colonization in a new light as something not essentially and insuperably evil. In some areas they now face the task of seeking to restore by vast and not always productive expenditure of funds and human effort the sort of conditions created quietly and at moderate cost by years of trial and error under colonial rule.

Fortunately Malaysia is not one of these unhappy cases. For all her troubles during the past quarter of a century, and the problems and controversies which arise today, there have till now been few more auspicious sequels to colonization. To what extent Britain shares the credit for this with her own peoples is a matter for future history to decide. As in India, Britain came to the area essentially to trade. It was only with great caution and reluctance that the home authorities permitted their men in the field to take over the hinterland of the Straits Settlements. This was to ensure that the commerce of these ports was not hindered by surrounding chaos and to open up fresh fields of business. British control advanced step by step, with those on the spot often characteristically exceeding their instructions and committing the home government further than it wished to go. The new administrators found groups of Chinese exploiting the mineral wealth of the country under great difficulties. To the British as a commercial race in the heyday of their gospel of free trade and *laissez-faire* it was only right to encourage the entry of such persons as orderly conditions were established. The same motives brought Indians to the country as rubber became its most profitable resource. By the generally accepted standards of the time this policy was adopted as being clearly for the benefit of all.

Nevertheless, however welcome the business acumen and hard work of the Chinese and Indians, for virtually the whole of the colonial period the British invariably gave first place to the Malays. Their qualities of unhurried courtesy and good breeding, their regard for monarchy, religion, ceremonial, and tradition struck a responsive chord in all those British who set special store by gentlemanly behaviour. Between the Malays and men like Hugh Low, Frank Swettenham, and Hugh Clifford there was a warm mutual relationship. There was some paternalism in their views, an urge to set right the mediaeval abuses not uncommon in the old Malay kingdoms; and a quite unwarranted doubt whether the Malays would ever prove effective in governing themselves. Yet their affection and regard for them was deep and real. Clifford, for one, was so attracted by the harsh and disorderly but colourful and fascinating Malay life he first encountered that he gravely doubted whether Britain was right in her zeal to impose on it a dead level of modern administrative uniformity. The great majority of British colonial officers dedicated themselves essentially to understanding Malay life. As Dr. Purcell has recorded,[1] those who specialized in Chinese affairs were looked on as rather queer fish with limited prospects of promotion. Until after the second world war the non-Malays were not regarded as entitled to claim the same political privileges as the indigenous masters of the country.

Much was informal and illogical in British colonial rule. Amongst other things the British had a strong faith in the character and common sense of young men with the most summary training. At the age of twenty Clifford was sent into the wildest part of the country, Pahang, to persuade the ruler to accept British protection; and succeeded in his mission. The colonial system grew and spread and was gradually elaborated in response to changing circumstances rather than to any clear-cut objectives planned in advance. It was more easy-going, less efficient and less carefully regulated than that of the Dutch. It was more aloof than that of the French; less protectionist and far less encouraging to scholarly research than either. By forging a common bond of variable closeness within and between two disparate groups of states, and linking these with the neighbouring ports, Britain, as in India, created for the first time the elements of a nation, without perhaps fully intending to do so. This is a factor which possibly deserves to outweigh the policies resented by her Malay critics who object to the settlement of other races in their midst. In one respect her task was simpler than in India since the historically established race in all states was of one tongue, culture, and religion.

There was, however, the special complication of the immigrant races and their inferior political status. The abortive experiment of Malayan Union was meant to solve this so that the whole country (except Singapore) could move forward to independence on a basis of equal rights. One of London's reasons had been dissatisfaction with the Malay response to the Japanese invasion and appreciation of the resistance to it of

[1] On his deciding to study Chinese he was admonished in these words by a senior official of the Malayan Civil Service: 'You have ruined your career. You will never become a Governor or even a Resident. You will merely be a specialist.' Victor Purcell, *Memoirs of a Malayan Official*, p. 96.

certain groups of Chinese. Only slowly did the colonial government realize the communist purpose of the latter. The Malays'
reaction to the Japanese had been humanly motivated by
Britain's failure to defend them. They had not the same
grounds as the Chinese for exposing themselves to a bitter
struggle. They were not pro-communist and there was no blood
feud between them and the invader. They violently rejected
Britain's post-war abrogation of their superior status. The feeling of national identity took sharp and definite shape in a form
the government had not intended, namely that of continued
Malay political predominance, but with the same goal of early
independence. Britain might have been prepared to impose her
egalitarian solution by authority had the non-Malays shown
any keen interest in the unique opportunity which was offered
them. Since they did not, she compromised by launching the
federation of Malaya to which independence was given in 1957.
When this was expanded into the federation of Malaysia it was
partly to provide for the future of Britain's Borneo colonies
which had a long relationship with the Peninsula, once it was
established that most of their people genuinely favoured the
plan.

Malaysia also solved—temporarily—the problem of Singapore, whose exclusion from the post-war political structure of
Malaya had been a departure from the pre-war system made
in the interests of the Malays. At the time of the Emergency,
when Chinese insurgents were the enemy, there was a strong
revival of pro-Malay feeling among the British. It was strengthened by Confrontation and has remained unaffected by subsequent misunderstandings. Unfortunately, however, the memories of Malayan Union left in Malay minds a latent suspicion
that Britain might henceforth be disposed to favour the Chinese
at their expense. This seemed to be confirmed when the
brilliant, ambitious Prime Minister of Singapore, *persona grata*
with many British, sought to play a leading role in their affairs.
He had successfully achieved for Singapore the objective most
vital both to the Malays and the British, namely to prevent the
island from becoming a communist base. But for this rare feat
he earned scant credit with the Malays. His campaign for a
'Malaysian Malaysia' based on equal rights for all was resented
by the Alliance almost as much as Malayan Union, with which

it had a good deal in common. At the same time, his pugnacious and irreverent personality aroused in them an almost irrational antipathy which led to some measures marginally prejudicial to the great potentialities of both territories. This is one of the few flaws in Malaysia's position today which can be attributed to biased judgement on the part of leaders who have in general displayed remarkable vision and statesmanship. Other graver hazards may emerge, such as an open outbreak of inter-racial hostility and possibly another major communist insurrection. This last, however, is unlikely save in the event of adverse developments to the north and east of her borders. Reconciliation with Indonesia and the Philippines and the retreat of communism in the former has lifted some of the darkest clouds in this whole area of Southeast Asia and for the time being has largely secured Malaysia's southern flank. With the help of these neighbours and the legacy of alertness and experience from earlier crises, there is good hope that Malaysia and Singapore can continue to overcome the minor outbreaks of subversion with which they are now faced. Their own security forces should be equal to all tasks save perhaps widespread warfare, when they would still be able to count on a measure of Commonwealth support. In this context it is now clear that Australia and New Zealand will play an increasing role in the future and Britain a diminishing one in view of her economic problems. The announcement in July 1967, of the withdrawal of most of Britain's forces from Asia and the major, but not total, dismantling of the Singapore bases caused some dismay in Malaysia and Singapore at the time. This was, however, largely allayed by Britain's assurance at talks in London of her definite intention of still honouring her obligations under the defence arrangements with those countries. From the mid 1970s her contribution to the Commonwealth Strategic Reserve would take the form of a fully prepared force stationed in Britain which could be flown out to deal with any crisis without delay.

The records of the governments in Kuala Lumpur and Singapore since independence have been a striking victory over adverse circumstances. The former led a state racially divided and born during an armed struggle. Yet it was soon made evident why the fifteenth-century Sultanate of Malacca had so impressed the first European visitors with the good ordering of its affairs; and those who doubted that the Malays were gifted in the field of politics and government were confounded. The statesmanship of their leaders was finally realized by the British when the Tunku in 1955 summarily rejected the overtures of Ch'in P'eng and resisted the temptation to make a soft and popular peace which might have had disastrous consequences. In Singapore, the prophets of disaster foresaw a possible swing to communism when the P.A.P. attained power in 1959. In fact the head of this firebrand party emerged as an anti-communist leader of exceptional if disconcerting qualities. Apart from their own dissensions and an inevitable element of politics in Malaysian rural development, both governments have displayed, in trade, industry and finance, a hard-headed realism which has produced striking economic growth and imaginative planning for the future. State control has been kept to a minimum, investment attracted, and full scope given to the free enterprise of their own and foreign citizens. With substantial support from abroad they can expect considerably to surpass the careful targets of colonial days. In Western Malaysia, the Malays are increasingly participating in the wealth and economic enterprise of the country, just as the non-Malays are gradually increasing their political stake. Dr. Mahathir is himself a company director as well as a politician and member of a liberal profession. In these circumstances, should the vigorous young Malay nationalists of his quality ever come to power it is unlikely that the sweeping measures of nationalization they advocate would extend beyond some of the more profitable foreign firms. It can be hoped that in a land where there is so much native business talent, local free enterprise would continue to enjoy full opportunity. In that event the effect of such measures on economic progress might be less damaging than they have proved to be elsewhere in post-colonial Asia. Meanwhile, for Eastern Malaysia, to which much of the government's planning is directed and which has farthest to go, there are generously conceived material opportunities beyond the financial capacity of the former colonial régimes. The not unreasonable price which the state governments are required to pay is political conformity with the pattern set by Kuala Lumpur.

What is the pattern of post-colonial Malaysia in her tenth year of independence? It could perhaps be defined as parliamentary democracy with an essential element of benevolent autocracy. This last has obviously been strengthened by the emergency regulations. There was more than a hint of it in the handling of the Borneo states. It is also implicit in the present preponderance of the Malays in the political field and their control of the administration, an entrenched position keenly resented by the non-Malays. But in a well-run and prosperous country there has been until now little abuse of authority and the individual can lead an orderly life as he pleases and expect the effective protection of the law. Understandably, the Alliance régime is not unlike the colonial régime which immediately preceded it. It had a similar constitution to that of the existing federation, an elected legislature and a ministerial system which included the present national leaders. But it provided safeguards (at that time through the powers of the British High Commissioner) for the maintenance of security and of the government's authority. Such safeguards are no less vital to independent Malaysia in the unstable Asia of today. Both the Emergency and Confrontation threatened the security of the state system approved by the majority of the people. Thus from the standpoint of the Alliance which brought the nation to independence, guided it through two major crises and planned great things for its future it would be a betrayal of their duty and a grave risk to the country to allow power to slip from their grasp. It seems clear that they do not intend that this shall happen. A strict application of the rules of the parliament of Westminster, on which the Malaysian system is based, would require that any party which gained a majority of seats should form a government. Yet the opposition are convinced that even if they won the elections they would never be allowed to take office. They would be judged a national danger and, in this most improbable event, the elections would be cancelled. Here again lies a source of potential conflict for the future. Hitherto the Alliance has triumphed in a series of genuine elections. It has built up a position of impressive strength, analogous to that of the Congress party in India, where parliamentary government has survived for twenty years. In the more affluent circumstances of Malaysia a government of the present pattern might survive indefinitely. But it is a compromise at the mercy of any intensification of racial antipathies. The situation is broadly parallel in Singapore with one dominant party, the P.A.P., and equally firm leadership, but with a theoretical absence of racial discrimination. The government has also been more sharply authoritarian in dealing with opponents formerly of considerable strength and with a constant menace of subversion.

There is a popular belief that Britain is in economic decline because she has lost her empire. It is therefore tempting to examine in conclusion what value colonies of the Asian category—that is territories not of settlement but of rule over alien peoples—have had for the colonizing power. What loss, if any, has their separation meant? First, there was the intangible and evanescent element of prestige, which in the case of Britain not infrequently lapsed into the vulgar jingoism of 'painting the map red'. Then in some cases, such as India but not Malaya, lands under colonial rule could be a major source of military manpower. More importantly, colonization could be valuable in establishing control of certain areas judged important for military or economic reasons, and in some cases the command of products which were specially valuable strategically or commercially. All of these last factors were exemplified in Malaya and Singapore as a result of their key position and the strategic and commercial value of the tin and rubber of the Peninsula. The Borneo territories, for their part, offered useful ports of call and coaling stations for ships trading with China. Colonization also made possible the establishment of a stable political régime, not without some degree of coercion, usually accompanied by a campaign for the amelioration of the living standards and conditions of the people. Finally it permitted the regulation and rationalization of the economic system of the country in the way judged most sound or profitable by the colonizing power. In this way the development of trade could be accelerated and the resources of the country opened up by the creation of a favourable climate for investment and modern enterprise.

The prosperity which this process frequently produced has led to a second widely-held belief that colonies somehow filled the coffers of the mother country, which lost a valuable source of profit when they went free. It is undeniable that it was possible for a colonial power to receive considerable benefit over a longer or shorter period by the enforcement of a mercantilist system or a régime of strict monopoly such as that applied by the Dutch at different periods to the spices of the Moluccas and the cash crops of Java. Such a system was a direct consequence of a type of colonial regimentation which the Dutch themselves found it advantageous to abandon in the second half of the nineteenth century. The régime of free trade in the Straits Settlements and free enterprise in the Malay States established by Britain also produced immensely profitable results from trade, mining, and plantations. But these benefits were not exclusive to the colonial power, nor, once the local peoples had become conscious of the value of the system, did they depend on the existence of a colonial régime. As was proved by Britain's expanded trade with an independent United States and her flourishing stake in an independent Malaysia, relations with a nation that is free, unhampered by nationalist bitterness, can be considerably more profitable than those during a period of subjection.

It is not generally realized that in the long run the colonial powers were often at a disadvantage in their own territories compared with other nations. Britain and Holland had moved into their areas of Asia in the hope of being able to develop profitable trade while avoiding more than a minimum of the burden of government. In practice they found themselves compelled to push farther and farther afield in order to safeguard the vested interests which their original settlement had created. This involved costly wars and an ever more expensive bureaucratic elaboration which eventually swallowed up the profits resulting from the development of the territory and often involved the metropolis in considerable expense. Occasionally, as was demonstrated by Confrontation, this process has dragged on even when colonization has become a thing of the past.

Confrontation is unlikely to prove a precedent. The trend among most new nations of Asia and Africa is to adopt neutrality and avoid dependence on their former masters. This has spared Britain direct military involvement in, for example, the formidable conflict between India and China. In general, the freeing of the dependent empire has lightened Britain's burdens and been a source of strength. The key to her economic problems must be sought elsewhere. One of America's most distinguished economists, Mr. John Galbraith, a former Ambassador to India with close experience of the achievements and consequences of British rule in Asia, recently discussed this in an interview with the London *Observer*.[1] In his view, Britain has positively benefited from the shedding of her empire. As a result of technological, social and legislative advances producing a more equitable distribution of wealth among her people, it became profitable for them to dispose of their manufactures and invest their money at home or in other developed countries rather than in their underdeveloped overseas dependencies. Thus, by the time these territories were demanding independence, it had become economically possible, and indeed desirable, to let them have it. Had separation not come, Britain might have been saddled for generations with the burden of providing administration, aid, education, plant and capital for the emerging nations. As it was, she was enabled to perform an 'act of social morality just at the moment when it was in fact an act of pecuniary self-interest.'

We have reached the closing chapter of Britain's second phase as an imperial power. The ending of the first phase, with the loss of the American colonies nearly two hundred years ago, was received with dismay and felt as a humiliation by many at the time. Yet as the years passed the loss of empire proved in fact to be a source of revival, inspiration and new strength. This is likely to be no less true today when all the consequences of the latest evolution are revealed. The empire was an episode of moderate length in a long history, and the experience it gave and the qualities it developed have an enduring value in the heritage of many peoples. But Britain is now concluding her role in territorial expansion and overseas dominion and has set fresh courses for the future. In developing her own society within a framework of European civilization for its part in a changed world she has turned back to the essential sources of national greatness which lie not in physical power but in the achievements of the mind and spirit. Meanwhile, the conse-

[1] Interview with Mr. Kenneth Harris: The *Observer*, London, 27 November 1966.

quences of the imperial record have been widespread and unique. Some thirty-five independent national states in the world today were at one time formed or ruled by Britain. These include two of the great powers of Asia and the wealthiest and strongest nation of the western alliance, the United States, itself the sequel to Britain's most daring and successful overseas endeavour. For those British who have concerned themselves with the emerging world it is a valid source of pride that this now turns in hope to a people sharing their ideals and originating in their own traditions.

# CHRONOLOGY OF PRINCIPAL
# EVENTS CONCERNING MALAYSIA
# SINCE 1600[1]

**1600** Foundation of English East India Company.
**1602** Foundation of (Netherlands) United East India Company (V.O.C.).
**1609–1619** Ten Years Truce between Netherlands and Spain.
**1623** 'Massacre' of Amboyna.
**1641** Dutch capture Malacca from Portuguese.
**1667** Dutch capture Macassar; subsequent Bugis expansion and influence in Malay Peninsula.
**1682** English withdrawal from Bantam.
**1697** Fort William (Calcutta) founded.
**1771** Sultan of Kedah offers Penang to British.
**1786** British occupy Penang.
**1795** Cession of Malacca by Dutch to British.
**1799** V.O.C. dissolved; Netherlands Government assumes control of Dutch interests in Southeast Asia.
**1800** Cession of Province Wellesley to British in Penang.
**1810** British capture of Java; Raffles Lieutenant Governor.
**1816** Java restored to Dutch.
**1818** Malacca restored to Dutch.
**1819** Raffles occupies Singapore.
**1824** Anglo-Dutch treaty defining spheres of influence. Malacca reverts definitively to Britain.
**1824** First Burmese War.
**1826** Anglo-Thai Commercial Treaty.
**1831** Naning expedition.
**1832** Singapore becomes capital of Straits Settlements.
**1833** East India Company loses monopoly of China trade.
**1841** James Brooke becomes Rajah of Sarawak.
**1846** Cession to Britain of Labuan.
**1847** Anglo-Brunei Treaty.
**1852** Second Burmese War.
**1854** Warfare between Chinese secret societies, Singapore.

[1] With developments prolonged over several years only the starting year may be given. Months or exact dates are given only in respect of the more numerous events of recent years.

1860 British intervention in Negri Sembilan.
1862 British intervention in Larut, Perak; hostilities between Chinese tin miners and secret societies until 1874.
1862 British blockade Trengganu.
1865 Parts of North Borneo leased to American interests by Sultan of Brunei.
1867 The Straits Settlements become a Crown Colony.
1869 Opening of Suez Canal.
1871 Anglo-Dutch Treaty facilitating occupation of northern Sumatra.
1872 Britain defines policy of non-intervention in Malay states.
1873 Dutch war with Acheh begins.
1873 British proposals for intervention to restore order in Malay States.
1874 Pangkor Engagement. Appointment of James Birch as Resident, Perak.
1874 Selangor and Sungei Ujong accept British Residents.
1875 Murder of Birch.
1877-78 Overbeck and Dent receive titles to North Borneo from Sultans of Brunei and Sulu. Establishment of British North Borneo Provisional Association.
1881 British North Borneo Company receives Charter.
1882-1914 Expansion of Sarawak.
1888 Pahang brought under British protection.
1888 Brunei, Sarawak, and North Borneo brought under British protection.
1895 Negri Sembilan brought under British protection as one confederation.
1896 Establishment of Federated Malay States.
1900-1920 Rise of rubber industry.
1906 Brunei receives British Resident.
1909 Establishment of Federal Council in Malay States.
1909 Cession to Britain by Thailand of Kedah, Perlis, Kelantan and Trengganu. British advisers posted later. They become, with Johore, the Unfederated Malay States.
1914 Johore accepts British General Adviser.
1926 Communist revolt in Netherlands East Indies.
1927 Reorganization of Federal Council.
1929 Brunei discovers oil.
1940 Japan secures dominant position in Thailand.
1940 Japan secures dominant position in French Indo-China.
1941 Sarawak Constitution granted by third Rajah Brooke.
1941 Japanese occupation of Indo-China.
1941 **December** Japanese attack on Pearl Harbor.

**1941 December** Japanese attack on Malaya.

**1941 December** Japanese occupation of Hong Kong.

**1942** Japanese occupation of Malaya, Singapore, Indonesia, Philippines, Burma.

**1942** Japan's advance checked in Indian Ocean and at battles of Coral Sea and Midway.

**1944–45** Japanese defeated in Burma.

**1945 June** Allied landings on Labuan Island.

**1945 August** Atomic bombs dropped on Japan.

**1945 August** Japan surrenders.

**1945 August** Proclamation of Indonesian Republic. Promulgation of Constitution. Sukarno becomes President.

**1945 August–September** Excesses committed in Malaya by Malayan Peoples' Anti-Japanese Army.

**1945 September** Reoccupation of Malaya and Singapore. British Military Administration.

**1945 September** Reoccupation of Indo-China by British and Chinese troops. Subsequent French occupation of salient points.

**1945 September** Reoccupation of Java by British troops. Subsequent Dutch occupation of Outer Islands and parts of Java, including Djakarta and Bandung.

**1946 March** France recognizes Ho Chi Minh's Democratic Republic of Vietnam.

**1946 March** United Malays' National Organization (U.M.N.O.) founded by Dato Onn.

**1946 April** Establishment of Malayan Union after restoration of civil government. Singapore becomes a separate Crown Colony.

**1946 July** Independence of the Philippines.

**1946 July** North Borneo (Sabah) and Sarawak become Crown Colonies.

**1946 November** French bombard Haiphong; start of Vietnam war.

**1947 July** First Dutch military action in Indonesia against the nationalists.

**1948 January** Independence of Burma.

**1948 February** Establishment of Federation of Malaya.

**1948 June** Declaration of State of Emergency in Malaya. Communist insurrection begins.

**1948 September** Communist revolt at Madiun, Java, suppressed by Republican forces.

**1948 December** Second Dutch military action in Java. Capture of Republican leaders at Jogjakarta. United States and Australia request reference to U.N. Security Council.

**1949 August** Hague Conference on Indonesia.

**1949 December** United States of Indonesia established.

**1950 April** General Sir Harold Briggs appointed to co-ordinate anti-communist operations in Malaya. Subsequent inauguration of Briggs Plan.

**1950 August** New Provisional Constitution of Unitary Republic of Indonesia. Sukarno remains President, but with only moderate powers.

**1951–52** Peak of insurrection in Malaya.

**1951 August** Tunku Abdul Rahman becomes U.M.N.O. leader in Malaya.

**1951 October** Murder of British High Commissioner, Sir Henry Gurney, in Malaya.

**1952 January** General Sir Gerald Templer appointed High Commissioner and Director of Military Operations.

**1954 May** Defeat of French forces at Dien Bien Phu. Subsequent Geneva agreements rejected by Ngo Dinh Diem, new leader of South Vietnam.

**1954 June** Sir Donald MacGillivray succeeds General Sir Gerald Templer as the last colonial High Commissioner in Malaya.

**1954 September** Establishment of Southeast Asia Treaty Organization.

**1955 April** Afro-Asian Conference at Bandung, Indonesia.

**1955 April** David Marshall becomes Chief Minister of Singapore under the Rendel Constitution introducing a new Parliamentary and Ministerial system.

**1955 July** First full elections in Malaya. These give a sweeping victory to the Alliance formed by the United Malays National Organization (U.M.N.O.) and the parallel non-Malay organizations established after the war: the Malayan Chinese Association and the Malayan Indian Congress. Tunku Abdul Rahman becomes Chief Minister under the new Parliamentary and Ministerial system.

**1955 December** Abortive negotiations of Malayan and Singapore Chief Ministers with the Communist leader, Ch'in P'eng.

**1956 January** Successful negotiations in London between British authorities and Alliance representatives led by Tunku Abdul Rahman. Malaya to become independent in 1957.

**1956 May** Breakdown of talks on further self-government for Singapore. Lim Yew Hock becomes Chief Minister.

**1957 April** London talks on future of Singapore. Agreement reached.

**1957 August 31** Independence of Malaya. Commonwealth defence arrangements concluded with Britain, Australia and New Zealand.

**1957 December** Expulsion of Dutch from Indonesia. Rupture with Netherlands. Repudiation of debt to Holland.

**1958 February** Military revolt in Indonesia begins.

**1958–62** Mounting Indonesian campaign over West New Guinea (West Irian).

**1959 April** Treaty of Friendship between Indonesia and Malaya.

**1959 May** State of Singapore established with internal self-government and Malay Head of State. People's Action Party under Lee Kuan Yew victorious in elections.

**1959 June** Lee Kuan Yew becomes first Prime Minister of Singapore.

**1959 July** Reintroduction of 1945 Constitution in Indonesia, giving greater powers to President Sukarno. Transition to 'Guided Democracy' becomes effective. Evolution of Nasakom system (a government coalition of nationalists, religious groups and communists).

**1959 August** Malayan elections. Alliance victory.

**1959 September** New constitutional arrangements introduced in Brunei.

**1960 July** Official end of Emergency.

**1961 May** Malayan Prime Minister launches the Malaysia Plan by proposing the association of Malaya, Singapore, Sabah (North Borneo), Sarawak, and Brunei.

**1961 June** Extremists break away from P.A.P., Singapore, and form Barisan Sosialis.

**1961 July** Inauguration of Association of Southeast Asia (Philippines, Malaya, Thailand).

**1961 November** London approves Malaysia Plan. Joint statement by Malayan and British authorities.

**1961 December** New President of the Philippines, Diosdado Macapagal, succeeds President Carlos Garcia.

**1962 February–April** Cobbold Commission visits Borneo territories.

**1962 April–June** Formulation and presentation to Britain of Philippines claim to Sabah (North Borneo).

**1962 August** Announcement of establishment of Malaysia on 31 August 1963.

**1962 October** Transfer of West Irian to United Nations and, later, Indonesia.

**1962 December** Brunei revolt. President Sukarno declares sympathy of Indonesian people with rebels.

**1963 February** President Sukarno announces 'Confrontation' of Malaysia.

**1963 May** Tokyo 'Summit' meeting between Malayan Prime Minister and Indonesian President.

**1963 June** Brunei declines to join Malaysia.

**1963 July** Malaysia agreement signed in London.

**1963 July** Manila 'Summit'. Maphilindo Plan for association of Malaya, the Philippines, and Indonesia put forward by President Macapagal.

**1963 August–September** United Nations investigation in Borneo Territories.

**1963 September 16** Establishment of federation of Malaysia. Non-recognition by Indonesia and the Philippines. Indonesian anti-British and anti-Malaysian sabotage. Military confrontation begins. Britain, Australia, and New Zealand support Malaysia.

**1963 November** President Diem overthrown and killed in Saigon.

**1963–64** Take-over of British firms in Indonesia.

**1964 January (onwards)** Increasingly direct and massive United States commitment in Vietnam.

**1964 January** Peace approaches to President Sukarno by Philippines' President Macapagal, U.S. Attorney-General Robert Kennedy, and Prince Sihanouk of Cambodia.

**1964 March** Cancellation of most U.S. aid to Indonesia.

**1964 April** Elections in Malaysia. Alliance gains increased majority.

**1964 July** Anti-Muslim riots on Prophet's Day in Singapore.

**1964 October** Second Conference of Non-Aligned Nations in Cairo.

**1965 January** Indonesia leaves the United Nations.

**1965 January** Second Conference of Afro-Asian nations, Algiers.

**1965 February** Anti-U.S. measures in Indonesia.

**1965 March** Indonesian Foreign Minister stresses importance of communist participation in government under Nasakom system.

**1965 April** Peace mission of U.S. Ambassador Ellsworth Bunker to President Sukarno.

**1965 May** Lee Kuan Yew, Prime Minister of Singapore, launches Malaysia Solidarity Convention to promote full equality of non-Malays in Malaysia.

**1965 August** Singapore's enforced separation from Malaysia.

**1965 August** Malaysian Prime Minister visits Borneo states to discourage secessionist trends. Sabah Minister, Donald Stephens, eliminated.

**1965 September** Removal of quota restrictions but later imposition of immigration controls between Malaysia and Singapore.

**1965 September 30** Palace Guard coup in Djakarta with local communist support. Violent anti-communist campaign follows its suppression by General Suharto.

**1965 December** New Philippines President, Ferdinand Marcos, inaugurated.

**1966 February** General Nasution, Deputy Prime Minister of Indonesia dismissed by President Sukarno. Student demonstrations.

**1966 March** President Sukarno gives General Suharto wide powers. New dominant triumvirate also includes Adam Malik, Foreign Minister with responsibility for all political affairs, and the Sultan of Jogjakarta, responsible for economic affairs. Former Foreign Minister, Dr. Subandrio, and many other leading figures arrested.

**1966 May–June** Indonesian-Malaysian agreement at Bangkok to end Confrontation.

**1966 June** Resumption of diplomatic relations between the Philippines and Malaysia.

**1966 June** Measures by federal government lead to elimination of Stephen Ningkan, Chief Minister of Sarawak.

**1966 June** Establishment of Asian and Pacific Council by Australia, Nationalist China, Japan, South Korea, Malaysia, the Philippines, New Zealand, Thailand, South Vietnam.

**1966 August** Malaysian currency linked to gold rather than sterling. To be separated from Singapore currency in 1967.

**1966 August** Malaysia abolishes Commonwealth preferential duties.

**1966 September** Indonesia returns to the United Nations.

**1966 October** Trial of former Sukarno supporters in Djakarta. Death sentences.

**1966 October** President of the United States visits Australia and New Zealand.

**1966 October** Manila Conference on Vietnam attended by President of the United States.

**1966 October** President of the United States visits Malaysia.

**1966 October** Malaysian Government White Paper emphasizes continuing communist threat.

**1966 November** Eugene Black, President Johnson's Economic Adviser, visits Malaysia and Singapore to discuss local and regional aid.

**1966 November** Inauguration of Asian Development Bank.

**1967 March** Language Act makes Malay sole official language of Malaysia from September 1967.

**1967 March** President Sukarno deposed by Provisional People's Consultative Congress. General Suharto appointed acting President.

**1967 April** Establishment of diplomatic relations between Malaysia and Soviet Union.

**1967 July** Malaysian Prime Minister discusses with British government Britain's decision to withdraw most of her forces from Southeast Asia.

**1967 August** Diplomatic relations re-established between Indonesia and Malaysia.

# Bibliography[1]

## I General

ALLEN, G. C. and DONNITHORNE, A. G., *Western Enterprise in Indonesia and Malaya: A Study in Economic Development*. Mystic: Verry, 1964.

BALTZELL, E. DIGBY, *The Protestant Establishment*. London: Secker & Warburg, 1965.

BONE, ROBERT C., *Contemporary Southeast Asia*. New York: Random House, 1962.

BRACKMAN, ARNOLD C., *Southeast Asia's Second Front*. New York: Praeger, 1966.

BUSS, CLAUDE A., *Southeast Asia and the World Today*. Princeton: Van Nostrand, 1958.

BUSS, CLAUDE A., *The Arc of Crisis*. New York: Doubleday, 1961.

BUTWELL, RICHARD, *Southeast Asia Today and Tomorrow*. New York: Praeger, 1964.

CADY, JOHN F., *Southeast Asia: Its Historical Development*. New York: McGraw Hill, 1964.

CADY, JOHN F., *Thailand, Burma, Laos and Cambodia*. New Jersey: Prentice Hall, 1966.

COEDÈS, G., *The Making of Southeast Asia*. University of California Press, 1967.

CLUBB, OLIVER E., *The United States and the Sino-Soviet Bloc in Southeast Asia*. Washington, D.C.: The Brookings Institution, 1962.

DOBBY, E. H. G., *Monsoon Southeast Asia*. Chicago: Quadrangle, 1961.

DONNITHORNE, A. G., *Economic Developments Since 1937 in Eastern and Southeastern Asia and their Effects on the United Kingdom*. London: Royal Institute of International Affairs, 1950.

DURDIN, TILLMAN, *Southeast Asia*. New York: Atheneum, 1966.

ELTON, LORD, *Imperial Commonwealth*. London: Collins, 1945.

FIFIELD, RUSSELL H., *Southeast Asia in United States Policy*. New York: Praeger, 1965.

FIFIELD, RUSSELL H., *The Diplomacy of Southeast Asia*. New York, Harper, 1959.

FISHER, C. A., *Southeast Asia, A Social, Economic and Political Geography*. London: Methuen, 1964.

FITZGERALD, C. P., *The Third China*. Singapore: Donald Moore Books, 1965.

[1] Primarily intended for students and the general reader.

FURNIVALL, J. S., *Colonial Policy and Practice*. New York: New York University Press, 1956.

HALL, D. G. E., *A History of South-East Asia*. London: Macmillan, 1964.

HALL, D. G. E. (Ed.), *An Atlas of Southeast Asia*. London: Macmilan, 1964.

HANNA, WILLARD A., *Sequel to Colonialism*. New York: American Universities Field Staff, 1965.

HARRISON, BRIAN, *Southeast Asia*. London: Macmillan, 1963.

HOLLAND, W. L., *Asian Nationalism and the West*. New York: Macmillan, 1953.

HUNTER, GUY, *Southeast Asia: Race, Culture and Nation*. London: O.U.P./Institute of Race Relations, 1966.

KAHIN, G. MCTURNAN, *Governments and Politics of Southeast Asia*. Ithaca: Cornell, 1964.

KAHIN, G. MCTURNAN, *Major Governments of Asia*. Ithaca: Cornell, 1961.

MICHAEL, F. H., and TAYLOR, G. E., *The Far East in the Modern World*. New York: Henry Holt, 1964.

MILLS, L. A., *British Rule in Eastern Asia*. London: O.U.P., 1942.

OLVER, A. S. B., *Outline of British Policy in East and Southeast Asia*. London: Royal Institute of International Affairs, 1950.

OLVER, A. S. B., *S.E.A.T.O.: The Manila Treaty and Western Policy in Southeast Asia*. London: Royal Institute of International Affairs, 1956.

PURCELL, VICTOR, *The Chinese in Malaya*. London: O.U.P./Royal Institute of International Affairs, 1958.

PURCELL, VICTOR, *The Chinese in Southeast Asia*. London: O.U.P./Royal Institute of International Affairs, 2nd Ed. 1965.

PURCELL, VICTOR, *The Revolution in Southeast Asia*. London: Thames & Hudson, 1962.

ROSE, SAUL, *Britain and Southeast Asia*. Baltimore: Johns Hopkins Press, 1962.

ROSE, SAUL, *Socialism in Southeast Asia*. London: O.U.P., 1959.

STRANG, LORD, *Britain in World Affairs*. London: Faber & Deutsch, 1961.

THOMPSON, SIR ROBERT, *Defeating Communist Insurgency*. London: Chatto & Windus, 1966.

*Tripartite Summit Meeting, Manila*. Petaling Jaya: Solai Press, 1963.

VANDENBOSCH, AMRY, and BUTWELL, RICHARD, *The Changing Face of Southeast Asia*. Lexington: University of Kentucky Press.

VANDENBOSCH, AMRY, and BUTWELL, RICHARD, *Southeast Asia Among the World Powers*. Lexington: University of Kentucky Press, 1957.

VON DER MEHDEN, F. R., *Politics of the Developing Nations*. New Jersey: Prentice Hall, 1964.

WILLISTON, F. G., *Viewer's Guide to Southeast Asia*. Seattle: University of Washington, 1958.

## II Malaysia and Singapore

BASTIN, JOHN, and WINKS, ROBIN, *Malaysia: Selected Historical Readings.* Kuala Lumpur: O.U.P., 1966.

*Brunei Constitutional Documents.* Kuala Belait: The Brunei Press Ltd., 1965.

BUCKLEY, C. B., *An Anecdotal History of Old Times in Singapore.* Kuala Lumpur: University of Malaya Press, 1965.

CAMERON, JOHN, *Our Tropical Possessions in Malayan India.* Kuala Lumpur: O.U.P., 1965.

CHAPMAN, F. S., *The Jungle is Neutral.* London: Chatto & Windus, 1952.

CLIFFORD, SIR HUGH, *Stories.* Kuala Lumpur: O.U.P., 1966.

COLLIS, MAURICE, *Raffles.* London: Faber & Faber, 1966.

COUPLAND, SIR REGINALD, *Raffles of Singapore.* London: Collins, 1946.

COWAN, C. D., *Nineteenth Century Malaya: The Origins of British Political Control.* London: O.U.P., 1961.

Economist Intelligence Unit, London. *Economic Review of Malaysia, Singapore, and Brunei.* (Published annually.)

EMERSON, RUPERT, *Malaysia.* Kuala Lumpur: University of Malaya Press, 1964.

FATIMI, S. Q., *Islam Comes to Malaysia.* Singapore: Malaysia Sociological Research Institute, 1963.

*First Malaysia Plan 1966–70.* Kuala Lumpur: Government Press, 1965.

FISK, E. K., *Studies in the Rural Economy of Southeast Asia.* Singapore: Eastern Universities Press, 1964.

GEDDES, W. R., *Nine Dayak Nights.* London: O.U.P., 1961.

GINSBURG, N., and ROBERTS, C. F., *Malaya.* Seattle: University of Washington Press, 1958.

Government of the Federation of Malaysia, *A Plot Exposed.* Kuala Lumpur: Government Press, 1965. CMND 12.

GROVES, HARRY E., *The Constitution of Malaysia.* Singapore: Malaysia Publishing House, 1964.

GULLICK, J. M., *Malaya.* London: Ernest Benn, 1964.

HANNA, WILLARD A., *The Formation of Malaysia.* New York: American Universities Field Staff, 1964.

HANNA, WILLARD A., *The Separation of Singapore.* New York: American Universities Field Staff, 1965.

HILLS, A. H., Hikayat Abdullah, An Annotated Translation. Singapore: *Journal of The Malayan Branch*, Royal Asiatic Society, 1955.

HOCK, TJOA SOEI, *Institutional Background to Modern Economic and Social Development in Malaya.* Kuala Lumpur: Liu & Liu, 1963.

IBRAHIM, AHMAD, *The Status of Muslim Women in Family Law in Malaysia, Singapore, and Brunei.* Singapore: Malayan Law Journal, Ltd, 1965.

KENNEDY, J., *A History of Malaya 1400–1959.* London: Macmillan, 1962.

MACDONALD, RIGHT HONOURABLE MALCOM, *Borneo People.* New York: Knopf, 1958.

MAHAJANI, USHA, *The Role of Indian Minorities in Burma and Malaya.* Bombay: Vora, 1960.

*Malaysia Agreement.* London: H.M. Stationery Office, 1963. CMND 2094.

*Malaysia Official Year Book. (Buku Rasmi Tahunan.)* Kuala Lumpur: Government Press (Published annually).

*Malaysia Year Book 1963–64.* Kuala Lumpur: The Malay Mail; Straits Times Press.

*Malaysia-Sarawak Development Plan 1964–1968.* Kuching: Government Printing Office, 1963.

Malaysian Ministry of External Affairs, *Background to Indonesia's Policy towards Malaysia.* Kuala Lumpur: Government Printing Press, 1964.

Malaysian Ministry of External Affairs, *Malaya-Indonesian Relations 1957–1963.* Kuala Lumpur: Government Press, 1963.

*Malaysia's Case in the United Nations Security Council.* Kuala Lumpur: Government Press, 1965.

*The Militant Communist Threat to West Malaysia.* Kuala Lumpur: Government Press, 1966.

MILLER, HARRY, *Prince and Premier, A Biography of Tunku Abdul Rahman Putra Al-Haj, First Prime Minister of the Federation of Malaya.* London: Harrap, 1959.

MILLS, L. A., *Malaya: A Political and Economic Appraisal.* University of Minnesota, 1958.

MILNE, R. S., *Government and Politics in Malaysia.* Boston: Houghton Mifflin, 1967.

MONTGOMERY, MARTIN R., *History of the British Possessions in the Indian and Atlantic Oceans.* London: Whitaker, 1837.

MOORHEAD, F. J. A., *A History of Malaya and Her Neighbours.* London: Longmans Green, 1963.

MORAIS, T. V., *Who's Who in Malaya.* Kuala Lumpur: Solai Press, 1965.

MORRISON, HEDDA, *Life in a Longhouse.* Borneo Literature Bureau, 1962.

MORRISON, HEDDA, *Sarawak.* Singapore: Donald Moore Gallery, 1965.

OSBORNE, MILTON E., *Singapore and Malaysia.* Ithaca: Cornell, 1964.

PAARLBERG, DON (and others), *Policies and Measures Leading Toward Greater Diversification of the Agricultural Economy of the Federation of Malaya.* Kuala Lumpur: Government Press, 1963.

PARKINSON, G. NORTHCOTE, *British Intervention in Malaya 1867–1877.* Kuala Lumpur: University of Malaya Press, 1964.

PURCELL, VICTOR, *Malaysia.* London: Thames & Hudson, 1965.

PURCELL, VICTOR, *Memoirs of a Malayan Official.* London: Cassell, 1965.

PUTUCHEARY, T. T., *Ownership and Control in the Malayan Economy.* Singapore: Donald Moore, 1960.

PYE, LUCIAN N., *Guerilla Communism in Malaya.* Princeton: Princeton University Press, 1950.

RATNAM, K. J., *Communalism and the Political Process in Malaya.* Kuala Lumpur: University of Malaya Press, 1965.

*Report of the Commission of Enquiry, North Borneo and Sarawak.* London: H.M. Stationery Office, 1962. CMND 1794.

RUNCIMAN, SIR STEVEN, *The White Rajahs.* Cambridge University Press, 1960.

*Sabah Development Plan 1965–1970.* Government Printing Department, 1964.

*Sabah Annual Report 1963.* Jesselton, Sabah: Government Printing Department, 1964.

*Sarawak: Report for the Year 1962.* London: H.M. Stationery Office, 1963.

SILCOCK, T. H., *The Commonwealth Economy in Southeast Asia.* Durham, N.C.: Duke, 1959.

SILCOCK, T. H., and FISK, E. K., *The Political Economy of Independent Malaya.* Canberra: Australian National University, 1963.

*State of Brunei Annual Report 1963.* Kuala Belait: Brunei Press Ltd., 1965.

SLIMMING, JOHN, *In Fear of Silence.* London: Murray, 1959.

SLIMMING, JOHN, *Temiar Jungle.* London: Murray, 1958.

SWETTENHAM, SIR FRANK, *British Malaya.* London: John Lane, The Bodley Head, 1907. (Reprinted by Allen & Unwin, 1948.)

SWETTENHAM, SIR FRANK, *Footprints in Malaya.* Hutchinson, 1942.

TARLING, NICHOLAS, *Piracy and Politics in the Malay World: A Study of British Imperialism in 19th Century Southeast Asia.* Vancouver: University of British Columbia, 1965.

THOMPSON, VIRGINIA, *Post-Mortem on Malaya.* New York: Macmillan, 1943.

TILMAN, ROBERT O., *Bureaucratic Transition in Malaya.* Durham, N.C.: Duke University Commonwealth Studies Centre, 1964.

TREGONNING, K. C., *A History of Modern Sabah.* Singapore: University of Malaya Press, 1965.

*United Nations Malaysia Mission Report.* Reprinted by the Department of Information, Kuala Lumpur: Government Press, 1963.

WANG, GUNG WU, *Malaysia.* London: Pall Mall, 1964.

WELLS, GORDON, *Sabah.* Jesselton: Sabah Times Press, 1963.

WINSTEDT, SIR RICHARD, *History of Malaya.* Singapore: Marican, 1962.

WINSTEDT, SIR RICHARD, *Malaya and Its History.* London: Hutchinson, 1962.

WINSTEDT, SIR RICHARD, *The Malays: A Cultural History.* New York: Philosophical Library, 1950.

## III Indonesia and the Philippines

BASTIN, JOHN, *The Native Policies of Sir Stamford Raffles in Java and Sumatra.* London: O.U.P., 1957.

BENDA, HARRY J., and MCVEY, RUTH T., *The Communist Uprisings of 1926–1927 in Indonesia.* Ithaca: Cornell, 1960.

BENDA, HARRY J., *The Crescent and the Rising Sun. Indonesian Islam Under the Japanese Occupation 1942–1945.* Bandung and The Hague, 1958.

BENDA, HARRY J., *The Pattern of Administrative Reforms in the Closing Years of Dutch Rule in Indonesia.* New Haven: Yale University Southeast Asia Studies, 1966.

COEDÈS, G., *Les Etats Hindouisés D'Indochine et D'Indonésie.* Paris: Boccard, 1964.

CORPUZ, ONOFRE D., *The Philippines.* New Jersey: Prentice Hall, 1965.

FEITH, HERBERT, *The Decline of Constitutional Democracy in Indonesia.* Ithaca: Cornell, 1962.

FURNIVALL, J. S., *Netherlands India: A Study of Plural Economy.* Cambridge: Cambridge University Press, 1939.

HANNA, WILLARD A., *Bung Karno's Indonesia.* New York: American Universities Field Staff, 1961.

HINDLEY, DONALD, *The Communist Party of Indonesia, 1951–1963.* Berkeley: University of California Press, 1964.

KAHIN, G. MCTURNAN, *Nationalism and Revolution in Indonesia.* Ithaca: Cornell, 1952.

LEGGE, J. D., *Indonesia.* New Jersey: Prentice Hall, 1964.

MCVEY, RUTH T. (Ed.), *Indonesia.* New York: Taplinger.

MCVEY, RUTH T., *Rise of Indonesian Communism.* Ithaca: Cornell, 1965.

PALMIER, L. H., *Indonesia and the Dutch.* London: O.U.P./Institute of Race Relations, 1962.

PAUKER, GUY, *The Role of the Military in Indonesia.* Santa Monica: Rand Corporation, 1961.

RAFFLES, SIR THOMAS STAMFORD, *History of Java.* Kuala Lumpur: O.U.P., 1965.

RAVENHOLT, ALBERT, *The Philippines*. Princeton: Van Nostrand, 1962.

SOEDJATMOKO, *An Approach to Indonesian History: Towards an Open Future*. Ithaca: Cornell, 1960.

SOEDJATMOKO (and other editors), *Introduction to Indonesian Historiography*. Ithaca: Cornell, 1965.

TAYLOR, GEORGE E., *The Philippines and the United States*. New York: Praeger, 1964.

VANDENBOSCH, AMRY, *The Dutch East Indies: Its Government, Problems and Politics*.

VAN LEUR, J. C., *Indonesian Trade and Society*. The Hague and Bandung, 1955.

VLEKKE, B. H. M., *Nusantara: A History of Indonesia*. Chicago, Quadrangle, 1960.

YAMIN, MUHAMMAD, *Atlas Sedjarah*. Djakarta: Djambatan, 1956.

YAMIN, MOHAMMED, *Naskah Persiapan, Undang-Undang Dasar*. Djakarta: Djambatan, 1945.

# Index

Abdul Aziz Bin Ishak, former
Minister for Agriculture,
Chairman National
Convention Party, Malaysia,
194
Abdul Kadir Bin Shamsuddin,
Defence Secretary, Malaysia,
120
Abdul Rahman, Dato, President
of Senate, Malaysia, 118n.
Abdul Rahman, Tunku, Prime
Minister, Minister for
External Affairs and Culture,
Youth and Sports, Malaysia,
('The Tunku'), 106–7,
112–14, 118–19, 122, 124–5,
133–4, 142–4, 154, 166, 170,
171–2, 174, 184, 186, 194,
213, 215, 218, 239, 241–2,
245, 251–2, 260, 265, 271, 280;
Chief Minister, 106; language
issue, attitude to, 256; legal
career and character, 104–5;
Ningkan, objections to,
254–5; separation of Singapore,
comments on, 207; Tokyo
meeting with Sukarno, 169;
U.M.N.O., leader of, 104
(see also Malaya, Federation
of, Malaysia, federation of,
Malaysia Plan)
Abdul Razak, Tun, Deputy
Prime Minister, Minister for
Defence, National and Rural
Development, Land and
Mines, Malaysia, 112, 169,
218, 242–4, 256, 262, 268,
270; career in Pahang, 119;
character and origins,
118–19; defence policy, 119;
Operations Room, 121; rural
development policies, 120,

122; views on separation of
Singapore, 207; special
development bodies,
encouragement of, 122;
U.M.N.O., Deputy President,
120
(see also Malaya, Federation of,
Malaysia federation of)
Abdulla, Raja Muda and Sultan
of Perak, 44, 46, 48–9;
Chinese support for, 46;
exiled, 49; recognized as
Sultan, 47; requests British
protection, 46
Abdulla, Tunku, 251n.
Abdullah, Munshi, Raffles'
interpreter and teacher of
Malay, 31
Abu Hanifah, Raja, Dato,
P.M.I.P., Malaysia, 194
Acheh (see Sumatra)
Act of Union, United Kingdom,
1707, 18n.
Adam Malik, Minister for Trade,
Co-ordination, Foreign
Affairs, Indonesia, 240–2,
career and character, 197;
Confrontation, condemnation
of, 197n.; Minister for Foreign
Affairs and supervisor of all
political Ministries, 227;
Sukarno, attitude to, 197;
student demonstrations,
alleged encouragement of, 224
Administration for International
Development (A.I.D.), Aid
to Indonesia, details of, 185n.
Afro-Asian bloc, 212
Afro-Asian Conciliation
Commission, 186, 192
Afro-Asian Conference 1955, 126,
192

Afro-Asian Journalists Conference, 165
Afro-Asian Second Conference, 193, 195
Afro-Asian solidarity, 132
Agricultural Banks, Malaysia: Bank Bumiputra, 267; Kampong Co-operative Apex Bank, 267
Agriculture and Co-operatives, Malaysia, Ministry of, 125
Ahmad Boestamam, Chairman of Peoples' Party (Party Ra'ayat), 114, 168; 'President' of 'National Republic of Malaya', 196
Ahmad Ibrahim, Attorney-General Singapore, 209
Aid to Malaysia Club, 262
Aidit, D. N., P.K.I. leader, Minister in Indonesian government, 197, 248; escapes from Djakarta after 30 September coup, 220, 222; reported dead, 223
Akbar, Mogul Emperor of India, 6
Algeria, 167
Algiers: Second Afro-Asian Conference, 193, 195
Alliance of U.M.N.O., M.C.A., and M.I.C., 205; communalism a threat to, 194; electoral success, 106; government, 122; fresh blood needed, 124; independence negotiations, 105; Regional Alliance parties merged into Malaysian Alliance Party, 196; Sabah, 215
(see also Tan Tong Hye)
All Malayan Council for Joint Action, 189.
Amboyna, Massacre of, 13
(see also Moluccas)
America (see United States)
American armed forces, 80; colonies, 14, 16, 382; communities in Southeast

Asia, 222; naval victories in Pacific in World War II, 73; Peace Corps, withdrawal from Indonesia, 199; Revolution, 10, 15, 22, 25, 62, 79; Trading Company of Borneo, 64
Anglo-American Agreement of 1930, 64, 160
Anglo-Brunei Treaty of 1847, 41, 65
Anglo-Brunei Treaty of 1888, 66, 161
Anglo-Dutch Treaty of 1824, 34, 65
Anglo-Dutch Treaty of 1871, 42
Anglo-Spanish Agreement of 1885, 65
Anglo-Thai Commercial Treaty, 1826, 36
Angola, 167
Antara, Indonesian Government news agency, 167, 173; suspended, 221
Arab role in spread of Islam, 20
Asia, the colonial role in, 5-8, 13-15, 20
Asian and Pacific Council Conference at Seoul, 264
Asian Development Bank, 263-4; Japanese President, 264; Manila headquarters, 264
Asian peoples, 14, 23; society, 23
Association of Southeast Asia, (A.S.A.), 133, 158-9, 265; Multilateral Treaty of Commerce and Navigation, plan for, 263; prospect of revitalizing, 239, 241-2, 244
Atlantic exploration, 11
Australia, 19, 122, 128, 211, 233, 259, 264, 279; armed forces, 3, 135, 180, 246; Christmas and Cocos Islands acquired, 87; defence of, 72; defence of Malaya, arrangements for, 109; Malaysia, support for, 179; New South Wales, 1; Southeast Asian role, 229,

278; Asian Development
Bank, membership of, 263;
Stephens, Australian
antecedents, 174
Austrian Consul in Honkgong
(see Overbeck)
Azahari, A. M., Sheikh, 180, 196,
270; Borneo Territories, plan
for, 163, 164; Brunei revolt,
absence, 165; character and
career, 162; Indonesian
sympathies and connections,
162, 163, 167; Sultan of
Brunei, relations with, 163;
S.U.P.P., contact with, 166

Bajaus, (Sabah), 66, 78, 142
Bali (Indonesia): anti-Chinese
sabotage on, 224; killings on,
223
(see also Lombok)
Baling talks (see Ch'in P'eng)
Bandung (Indonesia): pro-and-
anti Sukarno disturbances,
248
Bangkok (Thailand), 36–7, 57,
185, 241–4, 259
Barisan Sosialis (Singapore), 137,
139, 155, 202
Barker, E. W., Singapore Minister
for Law and National
Development, 209n.
Batavia, 21, 28 (see also Djakarta)
Bateman, Dr. L., Chairman,
Rubber Fund Board, 117n.
Bau (Sarawak), 1
Belgian plantations in Indonesia,
200
Bencoolen (Fort Marlborough),
(see Sumatra)
Bendahara (see Johore, Pahang,
Perak)
Bhutto, Zulfiquar Ali, Minister for
External Affairs, Pakistan:
friendly relations with Dr.
Subandrio, 184
Birch, James, Colonial Secretary,
Singapore, and first Resident,

Perak, 43, 48–9; character
and policies, 48; murdered,
48–9
Black, Eugene, former President,
World Bank, Economic
Adviser to President Johnson,
259; Malaysia, visit to,
261–2; Singapore, visit to,
262
Borneo, British and Malaysian, 2,
34, 62, 65, 73, 79, 142, 157,
187, 191, 242, 255, 277, 282;
Azahari's plans for, 163; British
officials, retention of, 216–17;
British policy in retrospect,
216–17; common free trade
area, 146; continued
association with Malaysia,
270; continued communist
subversion, 270; Eastern
Malaya, comparison with,
142; Kalimantan border
security, 245; Malay
domination feared, 147,
150–2, 213 (see also Cobbold
Commission); Malay
population, 65, 216; other
races, 66 (see also Bajaus,
Illanuns, Kedayans, Melanaus,
Suluks); plans for association,
143, 146, 163–4; referendum
not required, 241; terms for
entry into Malaysia, 169;
Tunku, visit by, 215
(see also Sabah—North Borneo,
Sarawak)
Bose, Subhas Chandra, 75
(see also Indian National Army)
Brazil, 60
Briggs, General Sir Harold,
Co-ordinator of Operations,
Malaya, 96, 121 (see also
Emergency)
Britain, 5–8, 10, 14–15, 22, 24–5,
27–9, 31–6, 109, 131, 168,
174, 176, 182, 190, 196, 198,
206, 210, 211–12, 233, 241;
diminished role in Asia, 264,

Britain—*cont.*
279; Malaysia, good relations
with, 218–19; Malaysia,
support for, 179, 229, 269,
273, 275–6, 278–9, 282–5;
withdrawal of forces from
Asia, 279
British armed forces, 3, 25, 49,
80, 135, 166, 179, 246
British attitude to Malaysia,
173–4
British Colonial Office, 42, 44, 46,
48, 50
British colonial policies, 33–4,
61, 62, 134, 182
British communities in Malaya,
56
British Council, 192
British economic interests in
Malaya, 56
British Embassy, Djakarta, damage
to, 176, 177
British Imperial preference, 62,
273
British in Indonesia, 80, 177–8,
191, 192
British in southern Indo-China, 80
British Labour Party, 81, 88
British Royal Family, 65
British rule in Malaya:
advisers in U.F.M.S., 58
Chief Secretary becomes Federal
Secretary, 59
Chinese Protectorate, 46, 100
conference of Malay Rulers, 56
decentralization, 59
District Officers, 54
Federal Council, 56–7, 59
Federated Malay States, 55,
59–61, 82, 85
general assessment of, 62–3
Governor becomes High
Commissioner for the F.M.S.,
55
health and education facilities,
123
indirect becomes quasi-direct
rule, 56

introduction of ministerial
responsibility, 105
Malay participation in
government, 58, 61
multiplication of government
departments, 55
pragmatic pattern of, 60
post-war military administration,
81
Resident-General becomes Chief
Secretary, 57
Resident system, 46, 50–2, 54
Secretariat for Chinese affairs,
99–100
slavery, abolition of, 52
State Councils, 50, 53–4, 56–7,
59, 83
Thailand, transfer of four
Northern States,
Unfederated Malay States,
58–60, 82
village headmen, 54
British, the, 11–12, 22, 24, 26–7,
29–30, 34, 37, 177, 183, 222
Brooke Rajahs of Sarawak, 2, 67,
142; general policies, 67
Brooke, Sir Charles, 41, 64–5
Brooke Sir James, character, 41;
Chinese attack on, 41;
Consul-General in Brunei, 41;
death, 41; Governor of
Labuan, 41, 87; original
intervention, 40, 65; Rajah,
40; Singapore Court of
Enquiry, 41
Brooke, Sir Vyner, 68; Council
Negri expanded, 68; Japanese
occupation, 77; liberal
constitution, 68, 88; Supreme
Council, 68; surrender to the
Crown, 87
Brunei, 1, 20, 40–2, 133, 142, 144,
159, 175, 240; allied
re-occupation of, 87; British
Consul-General in, 66; British
High Commissioner, 154,
161–2, 165; British presence,
180; British Resident in, 66,

161; Emergency Council, 166; Japanese occupation, 78; Kuala Belait, 165; Malay officials, elimination of, 180; new constitutional arrangements, 146, 161; oil discovered, 67; Peoples' Party (Party Rakyat), 162, 165-6, 180; responsible government, 270; Sarawak expansion, 67; separate currency, 272; Seria, 165; Tutong, 165

Brunei revolt, 202; background, 161-2, 164; British forces, 165; Constitution, suspension of, 166; Indonesian reactions, 167; 'North Borneo Liberation Army', 165; outbreak, 165; rebels, punishment of, 166

Brunei, Sultan of, 1, 62, 65, 163, 166; character and policies, 154; Malaysia, declines to join, 169; Malaysia proposal, first reactions to, 154; new role, 180; oil revenues, 169; Malaysia terms, 169

Buddhist Culture, 19

Buddhist Religion, 18

Bugis (Celebes and Malaya), 23-5, 118

Bulgaria (see Singapore, modern economy)

Bunga Mas (gold and silver flowers, symbols of vassalage), 37

Bunker, Ellsworth, U.S. Ambassador: visit to Indonesia, 199

Burhanuddin, Dr., 81, 84, 194; P.M.I.P. leader, 113

Burma, 2, 73, 75, 119; annexations by Britain, 36, 54; British rule, 3; Communist subversion, 89

Burma, parliamentary government, breakdown of, 115; Republic of Burma, 76; racial origins, 17

Burma-Thailand railway, 75

Cairo: Second Conference of Non-Aligned Nations, 193, 195

Cambodia, 131n., 184

Canada, 169; Malaysian Prime Minister's visit to, 191

Catholic Church, 9, 20

Celebes (Indonesia), 23, 127, 129; Macassar, 23; Macassar Sea, 2

Ceylon, 29, 73, 115, 212n.

Chaerul Saleh, Third Deputy Prime Minister, Indonesia, 197

Champa, 131n.

Charles II, 14; establishment of American Colonies, 14; Portuguese Queen, 14; religion, 14 (see also Stuart Dynasty)

Chiang Kai-Shek, President of Nationalist China, 70

China, 7-8, 19, 20; Bank of, 110; China Seas, 2, 29, 210; Communist régime, 92; Imperial China, 18; Kapitans China, 35; Manchu Dynasty, 6; Nationalist China, 264; Peoples' Republic of China, 183; Third China, 252; Yunan, 17

China trade, 26, 32, 36, 41, 43, 282

Chinese (in Malaysia) passim

Chinese collaborators with Japanese, 73

Chinese Communist resistance movement, 73

Chinese cultural arrogance, 257

Chinese economic predominance, 54, 61

Chinese jungle squatters, 74, 96

Chinese language, 138

Chinese: Lee Kuan Yew's special role, 'Protector', 253

Chinese, Malay preponderance in Southeast Asia over, 250

Chinese, Overseas, 95
Chinese resistance in Borneo, 77
Chinese secret societies, 35, 38, 44, 189
Chinese tin miners, 37
Ch'in P'eng, Secretary-General, Malayan Communist Party, 280; abortive negotiations with, 107; Communist hard core on Thai border, 231; Hanoi and Peking, encouragement from, 231
Chins, 17
Christmas Island: transferred to Australia, 87
Churchill, Sir Winston, 98
Clarke, Sir Andrew, Governor of Straits Settlements, 44-6, 48
Clifford, J. P. M., Vice-Chairman, Federal Land Development Authority, 117n.
Clifford, Sir Hugh, Resident and Governor, 54, 276
Cobbold Commission, 143 (see also Malaysia Plan)
Cobbold, Lord, Chairman, Commission of Enquiry, Borneo Territories (see Cobbold Commission)
Cocos Islands: transferred to Australia, 87
Colonialism (Colonization), 7, 254; assimilation or rejection of the colonial heritage, 235; Britain's Empire: scope and sequel, 284, 285; dependencies, profit and loss, 282-3; Malaysia, the balance sheet, 276, 277; the new phase an economic gain?, 282-3; U.S. role and British imperial record, 275; verdict on the past, 275
Combined Operations Committee, Malaysia and Singapore, 238
Commerce and Industry, Malaysia, Ministry of (see Lim Swee Aun)
Commonwealth, British, 1, 169,

183; armed forces, 139, 179, 191; bases in Malaysia and Singapore, 210, 250, 262, 279; defence and mutual assistance agreements between Britain, Australia and New Zealand and Malaysia, 109, 132, 168, 190, 210, 246, 250, 279; future bases in Darwin and Indian Ocean, 211; Parliamentary Association, 144; preferential duties abolished by Malaysia, 272; Strategic Reserve, 109, 180, 279
Communism: Chinese versus Soviet, 203
Communist imperialism, 79
Communist insurgency, methods to defeat, 97-8 (see also Thompson, Sir Robert)
Communist Party Conference, Calcutta, 89
Communist plans in Singapore, 202
Confederation of Greater Malaya: President Macapagal sponsors, 159, 169; proposed alternative to Malaysia, 159
Confrontation, 1, 86, 98, 185, 193, 198, 218, 229, 232, 240, 242, 250, 252, 276, 281, 283; agreement to end, 242-3, 245; ambivalence of U.S. policy, 182; battle at Lundu, 186; Borneo border, military confrontation, 179-80; British firms taken over by Indonesia, 177-8, 192; casualties, 182, 191, 246, cease-fire arrangements, 184; Chinese Communist 'volunteers,' 179, 231; Commonwealth military initiative barred, 180-1; Communist subversion strengthened, 270; 'Crush Malaysia Command,' 179; declines, 188, 230, 239; Djakarta cease-fire, 184;

Djakarta's initial attitude, 158; econonomic harm, 182; efforts to end, 159, 184; exports to Malaysia and Singapore diverted, 177; fighting continued, 184; financial and military burden, 233, 236; Indonesian attacks in Malacca Straits, 187–8, 191, 200; Indonesian goal of 'liberated zone', 187; Indonesian Parachute and Marine Corps units, 181; informal contacts maintained, 242; Malaysia, Indonesian ban on communication, 178; Malaysia, Indonesian-backed shadow government and 'National Front', 195; Malaysian firms boycotted, 177; Malaysia Plan, Sukarno's suspicions of, 157, 158; Malaysia's dependence on Commonwealth support, 229; military stalemate, 182; 'neo-colonialists' vilified, 178; numbers engaged, 181–2; Peking's role, 231; regular Indonesian forces involved, 179; Singapore, continued military co-operation, 208; Sukarno's definition, 167; Vietnam war, relation to, 246; West Irian campaign, sequel to, 181; withdrawal of British and Australian forces, 246

Congo, the, 167, 198
Cowie, W. C., 68; policies of, 68–9 (see also Sabah North Borneo)
Currency: Malayan dollar, 234 (see also Spanish dollar); Malaysia-Singapore Board defunct, 272; Malaysia-Singapore currencies separated, 272; sterling, partial divorce from, 271

Czechoslovakia (see Singapore, modern economy)

Danish plantations in Indonesia, 200
Darwin (Australia), 211 (see also Commonwealth Bases)
Davidson, J. G., Resident, Selangor, 49, 52
Dayaks, land, 40, 67; Sea (Ibans), 40, 67
De Gaulle, President, 7
Democratic Action Party, Malaysia: parallel policy with P.A.P. Singapore, 253 (see also Devan Nair)
Dent, Alfred, 64–5, 68, 160
Dent brothers, 64
Devan Nair, leader of Democratic Action Party, 253
Development Administration Unit (see Malaya, Federation of)
Dia Udin, Tunku, Viceroy of Selangor, 47–8
Dinding Island: ceded to Britain, 37
Djakarta (Indonesia), 3, 132, 163, 165, 183, 200, 226–7, 230, 239–40, 243–4, 247; Chinese University destroyed, 223, 224; violations of diplomatic immunity in, 175–6, 211, 218–19, 223
Domesday book, 8
Drake, Sir Francis, 10
Dusun (see also Kadazan), 150, 174
Dutch campaign to conquer Acheh, 42
Dutch colonial policy, 28
Dutch colonies, 29, 64
Dutch culture system, 62
Dutch economic and financial stake in Indonesia, 128
Dutch ethical system in Indonesia, 62
Dutch Governor-General Coen, 13
Dutch in Southeast Asia, 2, 11–15, 20–2, 24–6, 28–31, 34, 36, 127, 176, 187, 223–4, 282

Dutch military actions in
Indonesia, 127, 183
Dutch negotiations with Indonesian
nationalists, 109, 127
Dutch policy, U.N. reactions to,
128
Dutch re-occupation of Indonesia,
127
Dutch spice trade monopoly,
22–3, 32
(see also Netherlands, The)

Economic Planning Unit, 262
(see also Malaya, Federation
of)
Education, Malaysia, 54, 58;
Malay language policy, effect
of, 256–7; new institutions,
266
Elizabeth I, 12 (see also Tudor
Dynasty)
Elizabethan Age, 9, 14
Emergency, the, 123, 134, 179,
219, 223, 230–1, 251, 262,
276, 279, 281; Briggs plan,
96, 98; communist campaign,
change of emphasis, 99;
communist effectiveness,
limitations of, 94; communist
forces, strength of, 91–2;
communist guerilla tactics and
strategy, 93–4; communist
terrorists, hard core on Thai
border, 110; communist hopes
for the future, 110; communist
methods of subversion, 92–3;
communist reliance on Chinese
squatters, 93–4; communist
victory in China, effect of,
92; Emergency Regulations,
95; final phase: official
ending, 106, 109, 270;
government military
operations, 93, 95, 121;
independence, the key to
success, 106; key conspirators
not arrested, 89–90; New
Villages, 96, 98, 101;

preparations for, 89–90; rural
Malays reaction to New
Villages, 97; uncommitted
Chinese, sufferings of, 95;
'White' areas, 101
(see also Gurney, Templer)
England, 8–9, 11, 13–14, 125 (see
also Britain, United Kingdom)
English East India Company,
10–11, 13–16, 25–7, 29, 31,
34–5, 37; monopoly of
China trade lost, 39; Straits
Settlements, proposed
abandonment of free trade, 39
English Levant Company, 10
European colonial rule in Asia, 64
European impact upon Asia, 24–5
European interest in Malaya and
Singapore, 39, 43
European membership of Asian
Development Bank, 263
External Affairs, Ministry of,
Malaysia, 122; Permanent
Secretary of, 125 (see also
Muhammad Ghazali)

Far Eastern trade increased by
Suez Canal, 42
Farquhar, R. J., Military
Governor of Malacca, 29
Federal Agricultural Marketing
Authority, 251n., 267
(see also Hanafiah Husain)
Federal Land Development
Authority, Malaysia
(F.L.D.A.), 121, 260
(see also Clifford, J. P. M.,
Malaya, Federation of)
Federation Regiment, 94, 99
Fenner, Sir Claude (Inspector-
General of Police, Malaysia),
117n.
Ferguson, C. G., Special Adviser
on Rural Affairs, Malaysia,
121
Fitch, Ralph, 10
Food and Agriculture Organization
(F.A.O.) (see United Nations)

Fort Marlborough (*see* Sumatra, Bencoolen)

Fort St. George (*see* India, Madras)

Fort William (*see* India, Calcutta)

France, 6, 9–10, 15, 71; defeat by Germany, 43

free trade, Britain's sponsorship of, 32, 62

free world, global strategy of, 210

French armed forces, 25

French colonies, 64, 110

French imperialism, 29

French in Indo-China, 43, 71, 247

French plantations in Indonesia, 200

French Revolution and consequences, 22, 24, 28, 79

Galbraith, John, Professor, Harvard University, former U.S. Ambassador to India, 284

Garcia, Carlos P., President of the Philippines, 133 (*see also* A.S.A.)

Genoese, 9

Gent, Sir Edward, Governor and High Commissioner, Malaya, 91

George Washington University, 159

Germany, 7, 71; ambitions in Asia, 43–4; Gestapo, 73; occupation of Western Europe, 71

Ghana (Gold Coast), 134

Gladstone, 6n.

Goa, 20

Goh Keng Swee, Minister for Defence and Security, Singapore, 209n.

Gujeratis (*see* Indians)

Gurkhas, 3, 164, 180, 210 (*see also* Nepal)

Gurney, Sir Henry, High Commissioner, Malaya, 91, 102; murdered, 98, 120

Hague Conference on Indonesia, 128

Hanafiah Husain, Chairman, Federal Agricultural Marketing Authority, 251n.

Hanoi (North Vietnam), 231

Hastings, Marquis of, Governor-General of India, 29–32

Hastings, Warren, Governor-General of India, 16

Hatta, Mohammad, Vice-President of Indonesia, leader of Muslim Masjumi Party, 127

Health, Ministry of, Malaysia, 124; services, extension of, 266

Henry VIII, 9 (*see also* Tudor Dynasty)

Hindu ceremonial, 18

Hindu Culture, 18

Hindu Religion, 17, 18

Hindu resistance to Muslims, 15

Hisham Albakri, architect, 251n.

Holland (*see* Netherlands, The)

Hong Kong, 49, 64, 68, 140, 150–1, 175, 269

Hudson's Bay Company, 14

Hundred Years' War, the, 15

Hungary (*see* Singapore, modern economy)

Hussain Yaacob (*Utusan Melayu*), 194

Illanuns, 66, 142

Independence of Malaya Party, 102–4 (*see also* Onn)

India, 8–9, 14–15, 18, 21–2, 25, 34–5, 42, 49, 119, 183, 281; Bay of Bengal, 2, 26; Bengal, 2, 16; Bombay, 13–14, 16, 25; Calcutta (Fort William), 13, 16, 29–30, 35, 39; Congress party, 281; defence of, 43; Madras (Fort St. George), 13, 16, 25–6; Masulipatam, 13; Mogul Empire, 15; Surat, 13, 15

Indian culture, 18, 257

Indian Empire, 14, 36

Indian mutiny, 39

Indian National Army, 75
Indian Ocean, 11, 20, 211
Indian Parliamentary system, 115–16
Indian prisoners of Japanese, 75
Indian religious influence on
  Southeast Asia, 17–18
Indian social organization, 6
Indian statecraft, 18
Indian textiles, 20
Indians: Gujeratis, 19; Tamils, 27,
  60
Indians in Malaysia passim
Indonesia, 1, 13, 17, 20, 22–3, 69,
  75, 119, 131, 162, 177,
  182–3, 185, 235, 243, 245,
  260, 269; American aid to,
  182, 200; anti-Malaysia
  propaganda, 173; Britain and
  U.S., bad relations with, 196;
  British Commonwealth bases,
  tacit acceptance of, 245;
  British Council work stopped,
  192; British economic interests
  in, 130; British firms,
  measures against, 192, 224;
  Brunei rebels, support for,
  167; Chinese diplomatic
  immunities, violations of, 224,
  226, 228; Chinese military,
  economic and technical aid,
  198; C.I.A. accused, 219;
  communist subversion, 89, 196,
  220–3 (see also Indonesian
  Communist Party—P.K.I.);
  'Crush Malaysia Command'
  reverts to Supreme
  Operational Command, 246;
  death sentences, 228, 248;
  economic ills, 182, 224, 237,
  274; elections promised, 227;
  flood help offered by Britain,
  241; General Suharto restores
  order, 219, 226; Greater
  Indonesia, 131, 163, 175;
  Inner Cabinet, 224, 227;
  Kuala Lumpur, rupture
  with, 173; Malaya, treaty
  of friendship with, 132;

Malaysia, non-recognition of,
  173; Malaysia, normalization
  of relations, 240;
  Malaysian P.M.I.P. and
  Party Ra'ayat, support for,
  194; military revolt, 179;
  murder of generals, 220;
  Netherlands, rapprochement
  with, 183; new leadership
  plans, 247, 252–3; oil
  companies, 199; other foreign
  enterprises taken over, 200;
  Pakistan, relations with, 183;
  Peace Corps withdrawn, 200;
  Peking and local Chinese,
  attacks on, 223–4; People's
  Consultative Congress deposes
  Sukarno, 274; Peoples'
  Republic of China, exchange
  of visits, 198; P.K.I. revival
  possible, 274; Security Council,
  allegations before, 190;
  separation of Singapore and
  Malaysia, elation, 212, 218;
  September 30, 1965, coup in
  Djakarta, 200, 219–20, 222;
  Singapore, possible separate
  deal with, 239; Soviet support,
  assurance of, 197; Soviet
  Union, exchange of visits
  with, 196; Subandrio attacked,
  226; subversion danger:
  joint operations with
  Malaysia, 268; Suharto Acting
  President, 274; Sukarno
  overridden by Suharto, 245;
  unfinished revolution, the
  224; United Nations,
  withdrawal from, 192–3,
  198; United States of
  Indonesia, 128; U.S.
  plantations taken over, 198,
  224; U.S. policy a paradox?,
  247; University of Indonesia
  closed, 226; World Bank and
  International Monetary Fund,
  withdrawal from, 200
(see also Confrontation)

Indonesian Air Force Commander,
    death sentence, 248
Indonesian ambitions in Malaysia,
    81
Indonesian Archipelago, 10, 13,
    17, 34, 126
Indonesian armed forces, 167
Indonesian attitude to Afro-Asian
    Conciliation Commission,
    192
Indonesian attitude to Borneo
    States, 242
Indonesian Central Bank Minister,
    death sentence, 248
Indonesian clandestine activities
    in Malaysia, 189, 194–5
Indonesian Communist Party
    (P.K.I.), 129–30, 168, 175,
    179, 196, 218, 224, 229, 271,
    273; Aidit and Lukman
    Government Ministers, 221;
    anti-communist sabotage and
    massacres, 222; casualties,
    223; membership, 221;
    over-confidence, 222;
    Party completely banned,
    227; P.K.I. and Trade Union
    Federation partially banned,
    222; P.K.I. Parliament
    members suspended, 222
Indonesian Constitution of 1945,
    129, 244
Indonesian 'Constructivists' from
    Sumatra, 127
Indonesian debt to Netherlands,
    repudiation of, 129
Indonesian expulsion of Dutch,
    129, 224
Indonesian flexibility over
    Confrontation, 240
Indonesian Foreign Service purged,
    227
Indonesian immigration into
    Malaysia, 3, 126
Indonesian Masjumi (moderate
    Muslim) Party (see Hatta)
Indonesian Military Attaché,
    Bangkok, 242

Indonesian Nahdatul Ulama
    (Muslim Teachers' Party),
    129; demands Sukarno's
    removal, 248
    (see also Nasakom)
Indonesian National Front, 177
Indonesian nationalist
    government, 76–7, 80, 187
Indonesian Nationalist Party
    (P.N.I.), 129
Indonesian Provisional People's
    Consultative Congress, 244,
    247, 274
Indonesian refusal to join A.S.A.,
    133
Indonesian Republic, 80, 126, 129
Indonesian Revolution, Sukarno's
    concept, 59
Indonesian Revolutionary Council
    announced, 219
Indonesian Socialist Party, 129
    (see also Sjahrir)
Indonesian-Soviet military aid
    agreement, 197
Indonesian Strategic Command,
    242
Indonesian student demonstrations,
    223, 225–6
Indonesian Students' Action
    Front banned, 226
Indonesian superiority, sense of,
    131, 133
Indonesian tin exports, 232
Indonesian troops withdrawn
    from Confrontation, 221
Indonesian volunteers, 167, 184
Information and Broadcasting,
    Ministry of, Malaysia, 125
    (see also Senu)
Internal Security, Ministry of,
    Malaysia, 122
International Finance Corporation,
    (see United Nations, Malaysia,
    Singapore)
International Monetary Fund
    (see United Nations, Malaysia,
    Singapore)
Ireland, 8n., 212n.

Irian (see New Guinea)

Ishak bin Haji Mohamed (Labour Party), 194

Islam, 17–21, 66; pilgrimage to Mecca, 266

Ismail, Dato, later Tun, Minister for Home Affairs and Justice, Malaysia, 118; Ambassador to U.S. and representative at U.N. 118; career, character, and policies, 122; racial equality, liberal attitude to, 123; U.N. Security Council, presents Malaysia's case, 190

Ismail, Sultan of Perak, 46–9

James I, 11, 12 (see also Stuart Dynasty)

Japan, 7, 9; advance into British Borneo and Burma, 73; advance into Philippines, Indonesia, New Guinea, Pacific Islands, 72–3; advances in China, 71; advisory Malay council, creates, 76; alliance with Britain, 70; alliance with Germany and Italy, 71; ambitions in China and Pacific, 70; annexation of Korea, 70; A.S.P.A.C. role, 264; attack on Malaya, 71 attack on U.S. at Pearl Harbor, 71; Borneo territories, policy in, 77; Burmese and Indonesian nationalism encouraged, 76–7; combined administration of Sumatra and Malaya, 76; conquest of Manchuria, 70; defeat in Burma, 80; defeat of China, 70; defeat of Russia, 70; dominant in French Indo-China, 71; dominant in Thailand, 71; Geneva Convention, disregard of, 72; Greater East Asia Co-Prosperity Sphere, 73;

Great Power status, rise to, 70; Imperial House, 72; installation of steel mill in Malaysia, 234; Kempeitai, 73; Liberal opposition, 72; Malays, attitude to, 75; Malaysian economy, interest in, 73; Mandate for German Pacific Islands, 70; military authorities' economic mismanagement, 75; military predominance in government, 70; naval defeat of Britain, 71; naval disparity with U.S. and Britain, 70; new economic plans for Southeast Asia, 264; plans against Britain and United States, 70; policies towards the defeated peoples, 72–3; racial antipathies encouraged, 76; seafaring traditions, 9; Shinto religion, 70; surrender, 80; victimization of Chinese in Malaya, 73; weight and influence in Asia, 264

Japanese occupation of Southeast Asia, 35, 51, 60, 68, 74, 131, 276; consequences of, 79; Foreign Minister's visit to Kuala Lumpur, 264; occupation of Malaya, 71–2; reparations, 264

Java (Indonesia), 13, 18–20, 28–9, 128, 336; Bantam, 13, 16, 19; Communist revolt at Madiun, 128, 221n., Java Sea, 126

Javanese qualities and influence, 19–20, 131

Jek Yeun Thong, Singapore Minister for Labour, 209n.

Jengka Triangle (Pahang) (see Malaysian agricultural resources)

Jervois, Sir William, Governor of the Straits Settlements, 48

Jesselton (Sabah), 78, 88

Jogjakarta (Java), 221n.; Sultan of, role in Indonesian government, 225, 227 (*see also* Indonesia, Inner Cabinet; Triumvirate, Indonesia)

Johnson, Lyndon B., President of the United States, 184, 199; Australia visit, 259-60; economic adviser to, 259; hostile demonstrations against, 262; Korea visit, 259; Malaysia visit, 259, 260; New Zealand visit, 259; Thailand visit, 259; tribute to Malaysia, 260; Vietnam visit, 259

Johore, Malaysia, 21, 23-4, 29, 31, 38, 49, 60, 96, 103, 122, 189; Bendahara of (later Sultan of Pahang), 38, 49; British General Adviser, 79; Indonesian population of, 187; Johore Causeway, 239; Johore Empire (Riau, Lingga, Johore, Singapore, and Pahang), 30-1, 38; pride in Malaysia's progress, 188; resistance to invader, 188 (*see also* Confrontation); Socialist Front, strength in, 113; Sultan Husain of, 30, 38; sympathy for Sukarno, 187; Temenggongs (later Sultans) of, 30, 38, 49

Joint Defence Council, Malaysia-Singapore, 239

Josey, Alex, Adviser to Lee Kuan Yew, Singapore, 140; expelled from Malaysia, 207

Jugah, Temenggong, Minister for Sarawak Affairs, 174; (*see also* Sarawak)

Jurong (*see* Singapore, modern economy)

Kachins, 17n.

Kadazans, 150 (*see also* Dusuns)

Kalabakan (Sabah), 3

Kalimantan (Indonesian Borneo), 1, 142; coastal border with Sarawak, 186; 'National Army of North', 178; 'Revolutionary State' of, 164; proposed 'Unitary State' of, 163, 195

Karens, 17n.

Kedah (Malaysia), 17, 21, 24-7, 36-7, 50, 104, 234; transferred to British Malaya from Thailand, 57

Kedayans, 66

Kelabits, 66

Kelantan (Malaysia), 1, 37, 39, 50, 94, 174, 256; Kota Bharu, 262; P.M.I.P. strong in, 113; transferred to British Malaya from Thailand, 57

Kennedy, Robert, U.S. Attorney-General, Senator: visits to Confrontation protagonists, 184, 200

Kenyahs, 66-7

Keppel, Admiral, 40 (*see also* Royal Navy)

Khaw Kai Boh, Minister for Local Government and Housing, Malaysia, 257

Khir Johari, Mohammed, Minister for Agriculture and Cooperatives, Malaysia; career and character, 125; Malaysia's representative at A.S.P.A.C. Conference, 264

Korea; Seoul A.S.P.A.C. Conference at, 264; visit of President Johnson, 261; Korean War, 97

Kuala Belait (*see* Brunei)

Kuala Lumpur (Malaysia), 4, 52, 173-4, 189, 218, 223, 237, 240-1, 255, 261, 269, 279; damage to Indonesian Embassy, 177; National Museum in, 101

Labis (Johore): Indonesian
    parachute attack on, 188–90
    (*see also* Confrontation)
Labour, Ministry of, Malaysia, 124
Labour Party, Malaysia; arrest of
    Chairman, 195;
    (*see also* Lim Kean Siew)
Labuan, Island of, Borneo, 34,
    49, 142; Allied landings, 78;
    ceded to Britain, 41, 65;
    separated from Singapore, 87
Lancaster, James, 10
Land and Mines, Ministry of,
    Malaysia, 122
Larut (Perak), 38, 46, 53;
    disturbance by Chinese tin
    miners, 44; Mantri of, 44–6, 49
Lawas (*see* Sarawak)
Lee Kuan Yew, Prime Minister of
    Singapore, 106, 137, 155, 196,
    201, 209, 218, 239, 243, 253,
    278; advocates association with
    Malaya, 137; ambitions for
    Chinese predominance, 205;
    anti-American prejudice,
    211–12; antipathies aroused
    by, 205; arguments in favour
    of Malaysia, 156; bid for a
    'Malaysian Malaysia', 204,
    209–10; campaign against left
    wing opponents, 201–3;
    continued collaboration
    with Malaysia, 208;
    criticisms of M.C.A.,
    206; dissensions between him
    and Kuala Lumpur leaders,
    138, 173, 279; following
    among Borneo Chinese, 215;
    influence among the 'small'
    Chinese, 206; launches
    Malaysian Solidarity
    Convention, 204; Malay
    extremists blamed for
    separation, 207;
    Mrs. Lee's illness, 211;
    opposition to U.M.N.O.'s
    policies, 204; popu-
    larity with Europeans, 203,

279; reaction to Stephens'
    downfall, 215; severe measures
    against communist subversion,
    139
Legal system; in British dependent
    territories, 33, 53; in Dutch
    colonies, 53; in French
    colonies, 53; rule of law, 123
Levant, 11, 13
Light, Francis, 25–7
Limbang (*see* Sarawak)
Lim Chin Siong, leader of
    Barisan Sosialis, 137, 140
Lim Chong Eu, Dr., Founder of
    United Democratic Party,
    112–13
Lim Kean Siew, Secretary-General
    of Labour Party, 114; his
    family, 114
    (*see also* Labour Party, Socialist
    Front)
Lim Kim San, Minister for Finance,
    Singapore, 209n.
Lim Swee Aun, Minister for
    Commerce and Industry,
    Malaysia, 120, 269
Lim Yew Hock, Chief Minister of
    Singapore, 135, 138
Lingga (Indonesia), 23, 30–1
    (*see also* Johore Empire)
Little Englanders, 6n.
Local Government and Housing,
    Malaysia, Ministry of, 257
Loh, Peter, Minister for Sabah
    Affairs and Chief Minister of
    Sabah, 213, 265
Lombok (Indonesia), 287
London, 1, 12, 39, 50, 60, 144;
    Kew Gardens, 60; *Times*, 255
Low Countries (*see* Netherlands)
Low, Sir Hugh (Resident, Perak),
    49, 52–3, 142n., 276
Lukman, P.K.I. leader, Minister
    in Indonesian Government,
    221
Lundu (Sarawak), 186
    (*see also* Confrontation)
Lutong (Sarawak), 78

Macapagal, Diosdado, President of the Philippines, 158, 168, 170–1, 239; efforts to end Confrontation, 184; preoccupations over Malaysia Plan, 159; proposes Afro-Asian Conciliation Commission, 186, 192

MacDonald, Right Honourable Malcolm, U.K. Commissioner General in Southeast Asia, 91, 99

MacGillivray, Sir Donald, Deputy High Commissioner and High Commissioner, Malaya, 99, 105

MacMichael, Sir Harold, 83 (see also Malayan Union)

Mahathir bin Mohamed, Dr., 251, 280; Afro-Asian solidarity, protagonist of, 253; anti-British views, 253; attitude to Singapore, 252

Majapahit, Empire of, 19, 80

Majlis Amanah Ra'ayat Bumiputra, (M.A.R.A.: Council of Trust for the Indigenous People), 121, 125, 217n. (see also Malaya, Federation of)

Malacca, 19–23, 28–9, 31–6, 47, 82, 86, 102, 191; Chamber of Commerce, 56; Naning expedition, 36; Straits of, 1, 15, 18–19, 21, 29, 31, 126, 131n., 187, 245; Sultanate of, 20–3, 29

Malay Bumiputra (Sons of the Soil), 260

Malay capacity for modern progress, 123

Malay character and claims to priority, 121

Malay College, Kuala Kangsar (Perak), 118

Malay communalism, 194

Malay co-operatives, rural, 194

Malay land reservations, 83

Malay language: attitude of non-Malays, 256; bill passed, 257, 258; limitations of, 258; Malay Language Institute (Dewan Bahasa Dan Pustaka), 257; official status in Borneo, 254; official status in Singapore, 137; similar to Indonesian language, 132; tension over issue, 255–8

Malay leadership, potential 'Young Turks', 251n.

Malay Nationalist Party, 81, 84, 113

Malay nations, prospects for, 274

Malay Peninsula, 2, 4, 16–22, 24, 34, 187

Malay race; membership conditions, 66, 141n.

Malay Regiment, 94, 103

Malay relations with Chinese, 203–6

Malay Rulers, conference of, 85, 163; powers, 46 55–6; succession changes, 76

Malay rural development (see Rural Development, Malaysia)

Malay States, 20–2, 25, 39, 56, 282; Britain's reluctance to intervene in, 35, 43; eventual intervention, 43; intervention policy defined, 45; Thai suzerainty in, 19, 37–8, 49

Malay titles, 118n.

Malaya, 17, 24, 34, 131–3, 159, 189, 195, 240; economic progress, 60; finance, 54, 56; health, 55, 56, 61; immigration, 54; investment in, 54; modernization, 56, 61–2; nationalism, 77; National Liberation League and National Liberation Army, 230, 271; political parties, 81; population, 54–6, 86, 121n., 132n.; railways, 54–5; relation to Sumatra, 132, 157; roads, 54; Treaty of Friendship with Indonesia, 132;

Malaya—*cont.*
  unpropitious for Communism,
  231
Malaya, Federation of, 2, 276, 281;
  anti-Communist foreign policy,
  110; citizenship, 85, 109;
  Commonwealth defence
  arrangements, 109;
  Communist sabotage, 88;
  concessions to Malay standpoint, 85; consequences of
  Brunei revolt, 166;
  constitution, 107;
  Development Administration
  Unit, 122; division of powers,
  109; durability of government,
  86, 123, 124; Economic
  Planning Unit, 122, 262;
  elections, 1959, 112; elective
  Monarchy, 107, 108;
  establishment of, 85;
  government personalities,
  117–125; government
  resentment of independent
  municipalities, 115; growth in
  non-Malay electorate, 111;
  independence, 107, 109;
  inter-racial pattern, 111;
  Judiciary, 123; opposition
  debarred from power, 115,
  116; opposition groups, 112,
  113, 114, 115; Pakistan,
  relations with, 111;
  parliamentary and
  ministerial system, 108;
  pattern of the future, 116;
  post-independence problems,
  117; retention of British
  officials, 117; revival of State
  powers, 85; Rural and
  Industrial Development
  Authority, 120, 121, 124;
  State of Emergency declared,
  89; State Rulers, changed
  position, 108; view of
  Southeast Asia Treaty
  Organization, 110, 111
  (*see also* Commerce and Industry,

  External Affairs, Health,
  Internal Security, Labour,
  Land and Mines, National
  and Rural Development,
  Posts and
  Telecommunications,
  Public Works)
Malayan Chinese Association
  (M.C.A.), 99, 102, 112, 253;
  objections to Singapore Prime
  Minister, 205
Malayan Civil Service, 97, 121,
  123; reform of, 42, 122
Malayan Communist Party, 74,
  81, 89; Secretary-General
  (Ch'in P'eng), 106
Malayan Democratic Union, 81
Malayan Historical Association,
  101
Malayan Indian Congress, 102,
  124; support from trade
  unions, 113
Malayan National Union of
  Plantation Workers, 103n.,
  (*see also* P. P. Narayanan, Trade
  Unions)
Malayan Peoples' Anti-Japanese
  Army, 74, 80–1, 89, 92
Malayan Races Liberation Army,
  93; British weapons and
  training, 93
  (*see also* Malayan Peoples'
  Anti-Japanese Army)
Malayan Union, 104, 277;
  attitude of non-Malays, 83–4;
  citizenship provisions, 82–3;
  loss of Malay special rights,
  83; reasons for, 82–3;
  reduction in Sultans' powers,
  83; similar goals to those of
  'Malaysian Malaysia', 203;
  system and application of, 82
Malaysia, 1, 182; armed forces, 3,
  179; East Malaysia, 213, 219,
  307n., Greater Malaysia, 168;
  West Malaysia, 245n.
Malaysia, federation of, 176, 196,
  239–46, 268–9, 276, 283

Afro-Asian Conciliation
Commission, attitude to, 192
agricultural prosperity, 231
Alliance, entrenched position,
281
anti-Western prejudice minimal,
265
arrest of pro-Indonesian
subversives, 187, 194
Asian and Pacific Council,
membership of, 264
Australian and New Zealand
support, 180, 264
British offer to Indonesia
misunderstood, 241
British support, 180, 261-2
Central Bank, 272
colonial structure, assimilation
of, 235
colonial survivals in E.
Malaysia, 218
communist subversion threat,
270-1, 279
consular relations with
Philippines, 178
criticism of British, 216-17,
265, 278
Defence Council established,
179, 196
doubts about wisdom of
Singapore separation, 208
East-West Highway, 262
elections 1964, 117n., 185n.
English, retention of, 256
estates and smallholder
problems, 232n.
Federal Secretaries, 217n., 218,
250
former colonial régime,
resemblance to 280
free enterprise maintained, 233
general call-up, 185
immigration controls imposed
on Singapore, 239
Indonesia accused of 'Neo-
imperialism', 248
King's speech to President
Johnson, 260

main languages and cultures,
255n., 256
Malay General Director of
Operations, East Malaysia,
246
Malay hostility to Lee Kuan
Yew, 204-5, 278
Malay leadership, present
trends, 251n., 280
M.C.A. continued support for
Alliance, 206
Marxist indoctrination, antidotes
to, 232
non-Malays, British attitude to,
218, 227-8
non-Malays, improving
prospects of, 206
population conditions and
statistics, 204, 232n., 251n.
pro-Indonesian volunteers, 190
Proclamation of Malaysia, 175
post-Confrontation mood, 250
racial tensions, risk of
explosion, 253
reactions to Indonesian crisis,
228
security and government
authority, measures to safeguard, 187, 281
separation of Singapore, 206-8
silent revolution, the, 265
Social Welfare, 266
State of Emergency revived, 189
strength of inherited traditions,
231
Tunku and Razak meet
Indonesians, 241
Tunku's speech to President
Johnson, 260
U.N. Security Council, appeals
to, 190, 193, 194
U.S. aid, 259, 260-2
vigilante corps raised, 187
(see also Malay language)
Malaysia, Modern Economy, the;
aid, Japanese 264; aid,
Malaysia's claims and needs,
235, 236; American-

Malaysia, Modern Economy, the
 —*cont.*
 Malaysian joint industrial
 ventures, 263; British aid
 contribution, lack of resented,
 236, 248; Centre for
 Development Studies, 262;
 development and diversification of agriculture, 234;
 economic impact of
 Confrontation and
 separation from Singapore,
 233, 235; favourable trade
 and financial factors, 233–4;
 foreign investment, 235;
 gross national and gross
 domestic product 233; growth
 and imaginative planning,
 280; imperial preference
 abolished, 273; Indonesia's
 divergent path, 235; iron and
 steel, 234; Industrial
 Development Finance
 Corporation, 263; Malay
 economic participation
 increasing, 280; manufacturing
 still a minor factor, 235;
 surplus balance of
 payments, 235; tin and rubber
 developments, 234.
Malaysia plan; Borneo
 communists reject, 147;
 Borneo territories, decision to
 consult, 143; Borneo territories
 faith in Britain and Tunku,
 151; Borneo territories,
 general background, 147;
 Borneo territories, special
 Malaysia provisions, 152–3;
 Britain's readiness to
 co-operate, 142-3; colonial
 governments' encouragement
 of Malaysia, 147–8; dates for
 establishment of Malaysia,
 153, 169, 172; federal
 parliament, distribution of
 Borneo seats, 151n.; Inter-
 Governmental Committee, 1,
 164, 169; London talks, 144;
 Malaysia constitution, 152;
 Malaysia, early formation of,
 152; Malaysia plan favoured,
 151; Malaysia Solidarity
 Consultative Committee, 144,
 147–8, 174, 213; motives
 and objectives, 133–4;
 prospective balance of Malays
 and non-Malays, 141; racial
 controversy, 147; racial
 harmony produced by colonial
 rule, 148–9; recommendations
 for Borneo approved in
 London and Kuala Lumpur,
 153, 164; regional association,
 reservations, 152; Sabah-
 North Borneo background,
 150; Sarawak background,
 149–50; signature of
 Malaysia Agreement, 171;
 Singapore's need for special
 degree of autonomy, 143;
 Tunku announces, 133;
 unique character of, 156
 (*see also* Cobbold Commission)
Malaysian agricultural resources;
 coconut derivatives, 234;
 coffee, 60; Jengka Triangle,
 234; Muda River irrigation
 scheme, 234; palm oil, 7, 234;
 pepper, 234; pineapples, 234
 (*see also* rubber, Sabah, Sarawak,
 timber)
Malaysian Department of
 Aborigines, 94
Malaysian Development Plans:
 First Five Year Plan, 120,
 233; First Malaysia Plan, 233,
 265; Second Five Year Plan,
 233
Malaysian Home Guard, 3, 94, 97
'Malaysian Malaysia', 5, 203, 210
 278; Lee Kuan Yew
 champions, 278; Young
 Malay Nationalists object to,
 251n.
Malaysian Police Service, 89–90, 93

Malaysian Solidarity Convention, 204
'Malcolm X' (*see* Muslim protests against U.S. policies)
Manila (Phillippines), 239; Manila Agreements, 171–2, 241, 243; Manila Conference on Vietnam, 259; Manila Declaration, 170–1; Manila meetings on Malaysia, 168–70, 175–6, 178
Maoris, 9
Mao Tse Tung, Chairman of the Chinese Communist Party, 231
Maphilindo (*see* Southeast Asia Regional Projects)
Marco Polo, 19
Marcos, Ferdinand, President of the Philippines, 239–41; announces resumption of diplomatic relations with Malaysia, 239
Marlborough, Duke of, 10
Marshall, David, Chief Minister of Singapore, 106, 135
Maryland (*see* United States of America)
Mataram (Java), 19
Medan (Sumatra), 176, 223
Melanaus, 66
Melan bin Abdulla, Editor of *Utusan Melayu*, 125, 251n.
mercantilist system of trade, 22
Mikoyan, Anastas, First Deputy Prime Minister of Soviet Union, 196–7 (*see also* Indonesia)
Minangkabaus (Sumatra and Negri Sembilan, Malaysia), 23–4
Minto, Lord, Governor-General of India, 28–9
Miri (*see* Sarawak)
Mogul Empire 15
Mohammed, the Prophet's Birthday riots, 189
Moluccas (Indonesia), 2, 11–13, 283; Amboyna, 13; Ternate, 11

Moore, General Sir Rodney, Chief of Armed Forces Staff, Malaysia, 117n.
Moscow; alignment with Djakarta, 196
Moses, Charles Lee, 64
Mountbatten, Admiral Lord Louis (later Earl), 74, 80
Muda River (Kedah), (*see* Malaysian agricultural resources)
Muhammad Ghazali bin Shafie, Dato, Permanent Secretary, Ministry of External Affairs, Malaysia, 125; education and character, 126; Indonesian connections, 126; membership, Cobbold Commission, 144
multi-racial society, creation of, in Malaya, 38; Singapore's approach to, 209
Murba ('Party of the Masses', Indonesia), banned, 197
Muruts, 66
Musa bin Hitam, Assistant Secretary-General, U.M.N.O., 251n.
Muslim protests against U.S. policies, 198
Muslim religious education, 61
Muslim youth organizations, Indonesia, 223
Mustapha bin Datu Harun, Tun, Head of State Sabah, later President of U.S.N.O., 214, 269; alignment with federal government, 215; character and policies, 214

Naning (*see* Malacca)
Nanyang University, 36, 139, 202; student disturbances at, 271
Napoleon, I, 71
Narathiwat (*see* Thailand)
Narayanan, P. P., Secretary-General, National Union of Plantation Workers, 103n.

Nasakom (coalition of nationalist, religious and communist elements in Indonesia), 198. 200, 221, 247

Nasution, A. H., General, Indonesian Minister for Defence, 127, 179; character, policy and background, 180; dismissed, 226; escapes attack, 220; Inner Cabinet, member of, 226; recalled as Minister, 227; visit to Moscow, 197

National Afro-Asian Peoples' Solidarity Organization, Malaysia, 254 (*see also* Mahathir)

National and Rural Development, Ministry of, Malaysia, 120

National Convention Party, Malaysia (*see* Abdul Aziz bin Ishak)

National (Negara) Party, Malaysia, 104

Navigation Acts, 8n.

Negri Sembilan (Malaysia), 23, 38, 51, 54, 260; elects supreme ruler, 54; Sungei Ujong, 47, 49–51

Neo-Colonialism, 132, 245; Malaysia accused of, 167, 245 (*see also* Sukarno)

Nepal, 1

Netherlands (The Low Countries), 9–13, 24, 28–9, 32, 34, 233n., 283

Netherlands Borneo (Kalimantan), 66

Netherlands East Indies, 14, 29

Netherlands Government, 22, 34

Netherlands-Indonesian *rapprochement*, 183

Netherlands States-General, 128

New China News Agency, 221, 231; offices attacked by students, 226

'New Emerging Forces,' 170, 198; Conference of (Conefo), 245, 247, 248 (*see also* Manila Declaration, Sukarno)

New England (*see* United States of America)

New Guinea, West (Netherlands New Guinea, West Irian), 128, 167, 177, 183, 220; transfer to Indonesia, 130, 158, 193, transfer to United Nations, 130

New York (*see* United States of America)

New Zealand, 211, 229, 233, 259, 264, 279; armed forces, 3, 135, 180; arrangements for support of Malaya, 109, 180; Asian Development Bank, membership of, 264; Auckland, 1; Southeast Asian role, 279

Ningkan, Stephen (Chief Minister of Sarawak), 174, 254–6, 270; alleged excessive reliance on British, 254; appeal to high court, 255; called to order, 215; Kuala Lumpur, criticism of, 254; Sarawak cabinet crisis, 255

Non-aligned nations, second conference of, 192–3, 195; final declaration, 193

Norman Kings, 8, 15

Olympic games (*see* Tokyo)

Ong Eng Guan, Mayor of Singapore, 137

Ong Kee Hui, Chairman of S.U.P.P. and Mayor of Kuching, 215

Ong Pang Boon, Singapore Minister for Education, 209n.

Onn bin Ja'afar, Dato, Chief Minister of Johore, founder and leader of United Malays National Organization, 84, 104, 119–20, 122, 204

Othman bin Wok, Singapore Minister for Culture and Social Affairs, 209n.

Ord, Sir Harry, Governor of Straits Settlements, 42, 45–6; policy in Larut, 44

Overbeck, Baron von, Austrian Consul in Hongkong, 64–5, 160

Pahang (Malaysia), 23, 31, 38, 50, 54, 60, 118, 213, 234; accepts British Resident, 54; Bendahara of Johore becomes Sultan of, 50 (see also Johore Empire)

Pakistan, 111, 119; breakdown of parliamentary government, 115; friendship with Indonesia, 183; rupture with Malaysia, 184

Palembang (see Sumatra)

Pangkor Island (off Perak); ceded to Britain, 37; Engagement, 46; meeting, 45; significance of Pangkor policy, 47

Pan-Malayan Islamic Party, 112, 256; arrest of President and Vice-President, 194; election campaign, 186; links with Indonesia favoured, 113; loses control of Trengganu, 113; loses ground in 1964 elections, 185; opposes Malaysia, 174; policies of, 113

Partindo, Indonesia, 163

Pasai (see Sumatra)

Patani (see Thailand)

Peking, 183, 214, 223, 230, 253; increasing influence on Indonesia, 195–6; protest against diplomatic violations, 223, 226–7; supports Confrontation, 193

Pelaez, Emmanuel, Vice-President and Foreign Minister of the Philippines, 168–70, 241, 243

Penang (Malaysia), 1, 16, 26–8, 30, 33, 35–7, 44, 49–50, 58, 82, 86, 237; agriculture, 27; Butterworth, 262; Chief Minister, 143; Fisheries Research Institute, 265; legal system, 27, 35; port development, 262; Presidency of India, 27; Province Wellesley, 27; Socialist Front strength in, 113; trade, 28

Pennsylvania (see United States of America)

People's Action Party, Singapore, 106, 134, 136, 155, 253, 180, 282; dominant party, 137; extremist manoeuvres create Barisan Sosialis, 137–8; Lee Kuan Yew a moderate, 137; strengthened after Malaysia, 201

People's Party (Party Ra'ayat), Malaysia, 113, 114; support from Indonesia, 186 (see also Ahmad Boestamam, Socialist Front)

People's Progressive Party, Malaysia, main support from Perak, 114–15

People's United Front (Putera), 84

Perak (Malaysia), 21, 38–9, 49–50, 52, 124, 191; British and Thai policy towards, 37; Dato Bendahara of, 48n., disrupted succession, 44–5, 48–9; Ipoh, 114; Kinta Valley, 114; Maharajah Lela, 48–9; Resident system in, 49, 52–4

Perlis (Malaysia), 37, 50, 76n., 213; transferred to British Malaya from Thailand, 57

Perry, Commodore, 70 (see also Japan)

Persian Gulf, 19

Philip II, King of Spain, 11

Philippines, 2, 12n., 62, 69, 75, 126, 133, 160, 168, 178, 214, 239, 243, 254, 264, 269; independence, 65, 160; moderate attitude to Malaysia, 178;

Philippines—*cont.*
non-recognition of
Malaysia, 173; official
relations with Malaysia, 178,
243; peace offensive, 184, 186;
reactions to Indonesian crisis,
227; rupture with Kuala
Lumpur, 174; Secretary-
General of S.E.A.T.O., 243;
smuggling, 243
Philippines claim to Sabah, 158,
159, 170, 171, 178; Britain's
title previously unshaken, 160;
formal presentation of claim,
159; London talks, 159; no
renunciation of, 243; original
grant by Sultan of Sulu, 160;
Philippines and British
arguments, 161, 168, 177;
Philippines Congress support,
159; United States encouragement of, 160
Phnom Penh (Cambodia); meeting
of Malaysian Prime Minister
and Philippines President,
184
Pickering, W. A., First Protector
of Chinese, 46
piracy, 22–3, 40–1, 47
Pladju (Sumatra), 177
Poland (*see* Singapore, Modern
Economy)
Pontian (Johore, Malaysia);
Indonesian attack on, 187,
190
(*see also* Confrontation)
Port Swettenham, 190, 262
Portugal, 9–12
Portuguese, 11, 21, 23–4, 28
Protestant role in imperial
expansion, 9
Province Wellesley (*see* Penang)
Public Works, Posts and
Telecommunications, Ministry
of, Malaysia, 124
Purcell, Victor, Dr., former
Protector of Chinese, 99–100,
277

Raffles, Sir Thomas Stamford,
28, 73n., 131, 237; History
of Java, 33; in Bencoolen, 29;
in Java 28–9; in Malacca, 28;
in Penang, 28; in Singapore,
30–3; minute on education,
33; policies, 33–4
Rajaratnam S., Foreign Minister
of Singapore, 209n.
Ramanath, K. R., Editor, *Sabah
Daily Express*, 74n., 218n.
Rendel, Sir George (*see* Singapore)
Rhodesia, 254
Riau Archipelago, (Indonesia), 24,
29–31, 38, 187 (*see also* Johore
Empire)
Roman Empire, 8
Royal Engineers, 44, 48
Royal Navy: operations in
Sarawak, 41; operations in
Selangor, 47
Rubber industry in Malaysia,
general, 4, 60, 69
Rumania (*see* Singapore, Modern
Economy)
Rural and Industrial Development
Authority (R.I.D.A.),
Malaya (*see* Malaya,
Federation of; Rural
Development, Malaysia,
M.A.R.A.; F.L.D.A.)
Rural Development, Malaysia, 61;
agricultural credit, 267;
Borneo development and the
federal government, 268;
contribution to stability, 267;
co-operative movement, 267;
elimination of non-Malay
middleman, 267; kampong
initiative stimulated, 267;
land, wider distribution of,
267; Operations Rooms and
Red Books, 267n.
(*see also* R.I.D.A., M.A.R.A.,
Abdul Razak, Ferguson,
F.L.D.A., Federal
Agricultural Marketing
Authority)

Rusk, Dean, United States
Secretary of State:
announces end of U.S. aid to
Indonesia, 185
Ruslan Abdulgani, Indonesian
Minister for Information;
member of Inner Cabinet,
225; recommends Singapore
joining Indonesia, 212n.
Russian imperialism, 8, 79
Russian Revolution, 79
(*see also* Soviet Union)

Sabah (North Borneo), 2, 20, 64,
133, 144, 160, 163, 189, 196,
207, 212, 215, 217, 240, 244;
abolition of slavery, 66;
administratiove problems, 68;
Allied re-occupation, 87
anti-Japanese uprising, 77
British North Borneo
(Chartered) Company, 65, 68,
87; British North Borneo
Provisional Association, 65;
brought under British
protection, 66; constitutional
progress more limited than
in Sarawak, 146; continued
British presence, 216;
Crown Colony, 88–9, 145,
146; Daily Express, 74n.,
218n., death march from
Sandakan, 78; discontent
with separation of Singapore,
212; economic resources,
69–70, effect of Brunei revolt,
164; elections favour
Malaysia, 168–9; Japanese
control from interior, 77;
Kimanis Bay settlement, 44;
impending elections, 268;
labour problems, 268–9;
Labuan detached and
re-attached, 87; links with
Philippines guerillas, 77;
objections to postponement of
Malaysia Day, 174; obstacles
to association with Sarawak,

147; population distribution,
150n., 151; Stephens
becomes Chief Minister, 174;
United Nations inquiry, 170;
Weston, 165
St. Francis Xavier, 20
Sambanthan V. T. Dato, Minister
for Public Works, Posts and
Telecommunications;
background and career, 124
Sandakan (Sabah), 78, 88, 150
Sarawak (Borneo), 2, 10, 40, 67–70
77, 87, 133, 144, 159, 186,
189, 196, 207, 212, 215, 218,
240, 244, 254; Alliance Party,
174, 254; Allied re-occupation,
87; anti-Japanese operations,
77; Baram Basin annexed
from Brunei, 65; brought
under British protection, 66;
Chinese subversion, 98;
Clandestine Communist
Organization (C.C.O.), 179;
constitutional progress, 146;
continued British presence,
180; Council Negri convened
by Governor, 255; Crown
Colony, 87, 145, 146;
demand for revision of federal
ties, 214; effect of Brunei
revolt, 164; elections, 149;
frontiers extended to
Bintulu, 41; head hunting, 77;
Iban-Chinese understanding,
269; impending elections,
268; Jugah, Temenggong,
174; Kuching, 38, 41, 87;
Lawas, 165; Limbang, 166;
local Communist threat, 268;
Lundu (*see* Confrontation);
Lutong, 78; Malay Governor
appointed, 174; Malaysia
favoured, 169, 170; mineral
resources, 67; Miri, 78;
Museum, 77; Ningkan,
Chief Minister, 174, 254–5;
North Borneo, obstacles to
association, 147; oil, 78, 165;

Sarawak (Borneo)—*cont.*
opposition warned, 268;
pepper, 67; political crisis
revives, 269; population
distribution, 149n.;
postponement of Malaysia
Day, objections, 173; Razak
and Lim Swee Aun in
Kuching, 268; separation of
Singapore, resentment, 212;
state constitution altered, 255;
Tawi Sli, Chief Minister, 255;
United Nations' inquiry,
172–3
(*see also* Brooke, Dayaks,
Kayans, Kelabits, Kenyahs,
Melanaus, etc.)
Sarawak National Party, 269
(*see also* Ningkan)
Sarawak United People's Party
(S.U.P.P.), 149, 214, 270;
Chinese frustrations breed
subversion, 149; contact with
Azahari, 165; federal ties,
demands revision of, 269;
help to Indonesians, 187;
moderate leadership masks
clandestine communist links,
149, 268
(*see also* Ong Kee Hui, Stephen
Yong)
Sarma P. V., 231
(*see also* Malaya National
Liberation League and
National Liberation Army)
Satun (*see* Thailand)
Scandinavians, 9
Scott, Sir Robert, United
Kingdom Commissioner-
General in South-east Asia,
136n.
Sea Gypsies, 19
Sebatik (Borneo), 2
Seenivasagam brothers (D. R. and
S. P., founders of People's
Progressive Party, Malaysia)
S. P. Seenivasagam, Mayor of
Ipoh, 154

Selangor (Malaysia), 24–5, 37,
44–5, 47, 49–50, 54; Klang,
54; Socialist Front strength
in, 113
Selkirk, Earl of, United Kingdom
Commissioner-General in
South-east Asia, 136n., 164
Senu bin Abdul Rahman, Minister
for Information and
Broadcasting, Malaysia, 251n.;
career and character,
124–5
Seoul (*see* Korea)
Seria (*see* Brunei)
Shakespeare, age of, 6
Shans, 17n.
Shell Oil Company, 191;
installation at Seria (Brunei),
165; Sumatra refinery, 177
Sicily, King of, 9
Sihanouk, H.R.H. Prince, Head of
State of Cambodia; efforts to
end Confrontation, 184
Singapore, 2, 4, 18, 23, 29–51
*passim*, 55, 60, 66, 134, 159,
189, 196, 215, 233, 238–9,
245, 252, 262, 278–80, 282
Alliance, 138
association with Malaya, 140
authoritarian leadership, 282
Britain's continuing
responsibilities, 136
Chambers of Commerce, role
of, 87, 88
Chinese settlement, 33
Christmas and Cocos Islands
transferred to Australia, 87
Commonwealth bases, 210, 278
Commonwealth Parliamentary
Association, 144
communism, 338–41
communist bloc, relations with,
253
Constitution, 87–8, 135–6
corruption, elimination of, 140
Currency Board, 272
declaration of temporary
sovereignty, 173

Defence and Security Council, 135
education problems, 110, 138, 140, 202
elections, 201
Emergency, the, 89, 103
independent policies and government, 209
Indonesian crisis, reactions to, 228
Internal Security Council, 136, 202
joint defence with Malaysia, 207, 239
Labour Front, 106
Malay Head of State, 135
Malays in, 189, 210
Malaysia, prospects for re-association with, 210, 272
Malaysia, relations with, 196
Malaysia, separation from, 207-8
Malaysian bases retained, 208
multi-racial society, goals for, 209
non-alignment in international relations, 210
People's Alliance, 138
progress to self-government, 105, 135
racial disturbances (see Mohammed, the Prophet's Birthday)
reactions to Malaysia plan, 134, 154-6, 173
recognition of independence, 211, 244
referendum, 156
Republic, 209
separate British colony, 82-3, 86
social and educational services, 210, 266
socialism, 140
trade, industry, investment, 35, 139
trade unions, 202, 266
traditional economic activities, resumed, 86
United Nations membership, 212

(see also Johore Empire, Josey, Lee Kuan Yew, Lim Yew Hock, Marshall, Nanyang University, People's Action Party)
Singapore, Modern Economy, the, Economic Development Board, 238, 263; Five Year Development Plan, 263; free trade zone, 237; growth through imaginative planning, 280; Hong Kong or Japanese pattern of development, 263-4; impact of Confrontation and separation, 232, 236; Indonesian boycott of entrepôt trade, 237; industrialization, progress of, 237; International Monetary Fund, membership of, 263; Jurong industrial area, 238; local barter trade, 237; Malaysia's diversion of trade, 237, 238; Malaysian Customs Union and prospective Common Market, no access to, 236; population and area, 237; processing and re-export of raw materials, 236; quotas with Malaysia, removal of, 238; trade links with Bulgaria, Czechoslovakia, Hungary, Poland, Rumania, 253; United States aid, 263 (see also United States Vietnam procurement orders); World Bank, membership of, 263
Sjahrir, Sutan, leader of Socialist Party and Prime Minister of Indonesia, 127
Socialist Front (Malaysia), 113, 168; composition and policy, 113-14; Labour Party, 113; loses ground, 186; Parliamentary leader, 114; People's Party (Party Ra'ayat), 113

Socialist International: Stockholm meeting, 253
Soedjatmoko, Indonesian publisher, 127n.
South Africa, 29
Southeast Asia Command, 74 (*see also* Mountbatten)
South-east Asia Regional Projects; associations of Malay races, 250; Japanese economic plans, 265; Maphilindo, 171, 243, 247, 252; student exchanges, 266; transport and communications, 263; union of co-operation, 243; United States financial assistance, 261 (*see also* Macapagal, A.S.A.)
South-east Asia Treaty Organization, 110–11, 133, 168, 244
Soviet Union, 71, 179, 183, 191, 273; Chairmanship of Security Council, 190; denounces United States support for 'Colonialists', 190; Malaysia, diplomatic relations with, 265; World Power status, 79 (*see also* Moscow, Russian Imperialism, Russian Revolution)
Spain, 9–12, 160
Spanish–American War, 65
Spanish campaign to conquer southern Philippines, 43
Spanish colonial system, 62, 64
Spanish dollar, 26n.
Spanish sovereignty over Sultanate of Sulu, 62
Speedy, Captain, Assistant Resident, Larut, 48; recruited by Mantri of Larut, 44
Spice Islands (*see* Moluccas)
Srivijaya, Maritime Empire of, 18–19, 29, 80
Stephens, Donald, Chief Minister of Sabah, later Minister for Sabah Affairs, 174, 213, 269;

character and policies, 214; resignation, 215, 254
Stevenson, Adlai, U.S. Ambassador to United Nations: challenges Indonesian arguments, 190
Straits Settlements (Singapore, Penang, Malacca), 35–9, 44–5, 86, 283; a separate Crown Colony, 40, 42; Legislative Council, 42; Straits Association, London, 42
Stuart Dynasty, 8n., 12, 14 (*see also* James I, Charles II)
Subandrio, Dr., Deputy Prime Minister and Foreign Minister of Indonesia, 158, 169, 176, 184, 219, 221, 225, 239; arrested, 227; character, career, and policy, 175; condemned to death, 248; condones communist role in Indonesia, 198; Confrontation pronouncements, 273; continues in office, 225; 'Dog of Peking', 226; Moscow visit, 196, 197; Peking visit, 198
Suez Canal, 35, 42
Suharto, General, Commander of Strategic Reserve, later, Army Commander, Minister for Defence and acting President, Indonesia, 220, 226, 241–2, 245, 274; forestalls Subandrio, 227, in charge of defence and security, 226
Sukarno, President of Indonesia ('Bung Karno'), 1, 76, 79–80, 126, 130–1, 163, 175, 184–6, 219, 223, 225, 228, 239; anomalous position, 240; Bangkok Agreement unsigned, 244; Britain, attitude to, 157, 158; British interests, campaign against, 192; Brunei revolt, attitude to, 166; capture by Dutch, 127; communist

aid sought, 126; colonial heritage, rejection of, 235; deposition, 274; Djakarta coup, attitude to, 220, 248; 'Guided Democracy', 129; humane qualities, 248; Jacobin strain, 127; Malaya, attitude to, 131–2, 157–8; Malaysia, policy towards, 170–1, 241, 245, 247; Moscow visit, 197; nationalist policies, 79, 170; Netherlands, relations with, 183; Non-Aligned Nations Conference, attitude to, 192; Pan-Malay ambitions, 80; partial eclipse, 248; P.K.I. and Peking influence on, 179, 248; Provisional People's Consultative Congress, threat to dissolve, 244; racial antecedents, 79; receives lenient treatment, 272; Tokyo meeting with Tunku, 169; ultimatum by armed forces, 227; United States of America, relations with, 183, 186

Sulu (Philippines), 160, 161, 214
Sulu Archipelago, 65
Sulu Sea, 2
Sulu, Sultan of, 64–5, 160–2
Suluks, 66, 77, 142
Sumatra (Indonesia), 13, 18, 20–1, 23, 34, 127–9, 167, 187; Acheh, 21, 56; Bencoolen (Fort Marlborough), 13, 29; Palembang, 18–20; Pasai, 19
Sunda Straits, 18
Surabaya (Java), 80, 176
Swettenham, Sir Frank, 42, 46, 52–3, 55–6, 276; Assistant Resident, Selangor, 47; escapes after Birch's murder, 49; Resident-General, Kuala Lumpur, 55; opposition to Malayan Union, 82
Swiss plantations in Indonesia, 200

Syed Ja'afar Albar, Dato, Secretary-General of U.M.N.O., 251n.; opposition to separation of Singapore, 208
Syed Nasir, Director of Malay Language Institute (Dewan Bahasa dan Pustaka), 251n.

Taiping (Perak), 39
Taiping rebellion in China, 38
Taiwan, 269
Tamils (see Indians)
Tan Chee Koon, Dr., Socialist Front, Malaysia, 114; relations with government, 114
Tan Cheng Lock (Sir Cheng Lock Tan), founder of Malayan Chinese Association, 102, 112, 118n.
Tan Lark Sye, 202 (see also Nanyang University)
Tan Siew Sin, Minister for Finance, Malaysia, 102, 112, 118, 262; criticism of Britain, 236; differences with Prime Minister of Singapore, 205 (see also Tan Cheng Lock, Malayan Chinese Association)
Tan Tong Hye, Senator and Honorary Secretary of Alliance, 124n.
Tawau (Sabah), 1–3, 150
Tawi Sli, Penghulu, (see Sarawak)
Temenggong (see Johore)
Temiar (Malayan aborigines), 94
Templer, Field-Marshal Sir Gerald, High Commissioner, Malaya, and later Chief of Imperial General Staff, 99, 105, 121
Ten Years' Anglo-Dutch Truce, 12
Ternate (see Moluccas)
Thai Buddhism, 59
Thai mediation to end Confrontation, 242
Thai Prime Minister in Malaysia, 242

Thai suzerainty in Malay
    Peninsula, 19
Thailand, 17, 24, 36–7, 50, 57,
    71, 133, 243, 259, 264;
    assimilationist policies, 58–9;
    Britain abandons
    extraterritorality, 57;
    communist subversion, 231,
    270; Confrontation, efforts to
    end, 184; Malay irredentist
    claims, 113; Malay provinces
    (Patani, Yala, Narathiwat,
    Satun), 59; Patriotic Front,
    231; railway loan, 57; super-
    vision of cease fire, 184, 186
Thais, 17, 19, 23, 26–7, 37
Thant, U, Secretary-General of
    United Nations, 170, 172–3,
    184
Thompson, Sir Robert, former
    Defence Secretary, Malaya,
    and Head of British Advisory
    Mission, Vietnam, 97n., 98,
    117n., 119
Thomson, Sir James, Chief Justice
    of Malaya and Lord
    President of the Courts of
    Malaysia, 117n.
timber resources of Malaysia, 234
timber resources of Sabah (North
    Borneo), 69
timber resources of Sarawak, 69
tin resources of Malaya, 4, 37, 54
Tokugawa, Marquis, Director of
    Singapore Museum during
    Japanese occupation, 73n.
Toh Chin Chye, Deputy Prime
    Minister of Singapore, 209n.
Tokyo Olympic Games, 195
Tokyo 'Summit' Meetings, 169,
    186–7
Tordesillas, Treaty of, 12n.
Torrey, Joseph, 64
    (see also Sabah (North Borneo)
'trade follows the flag' doctrine, 15
Trade Unions, Malaysia, 81;
    moderates support Malayan
    Indian Congress, 113; National

Union of Plantation Workers,
    103n., 266 shortcomings, 266;
    Templer's encouragement of,
    102
Trengganu (Malaysia), 24, 37,
    39, 50, 57–8; P.M.I.P. strong
    in, 113; transferred to British
    Malaya from Thailand, 57
Trinidad, 169
Triumvirate, Indonesia, 240
    (see also Joggjakarta, Sultan of,
    Suharto, Malik)
Truman, Harry S., President of the
    United States, 160
    (see also Philippines)
Tudor Age, 9
Tudor Dynasty, 8n., 12
    (see also Henry VIII and
    Elizabeth I)
Tumasik (see Singapore)
Turkish (Ottoman) Empire, 10
Turks (Ottoman), 8
Turtle Islands: returned to
    Philippines, 159
Tutong (see Brunei)

Unilever, 191
United Democratic Party, 112
    (see also Lim Chong Eu)
United Dutch East India
    Company (V.O.C.), 10, 12,
    14, 22–3
United Kingdom Commissioner-
    General in Southeast Asia,
    91, 164, 166
    (see also MacDonald, Scott,
    Selkirk)
United Kingdom defence
    co-operation with Australia,
    210
United Kingdom financial
    stringency, 210, 279
United Kingdom withdrawal from
    Singapore bases, 211
    (see also Britain, British)
United Malays National
    Organization (U.M.N.O.),
    84, 102, 104, 122, 194, 204,

241, 250–1; resignation of Ja'afar Albar as Secretary-General, 208

United Nations, 122, 168, 187, 198, 254; Charter, 190, 193; Children's Fund, 193; Economic and Social Council, 193; Educational, Scientific and Cultural Organization, 193; Food and Agriculture Organization, 193; General Assembly, 193; Indonesian withdrawal from, 193; International Finance Corporation, 263; International Monetary Fund, 200, 263; Norwegian resolution on Confrontation, 190; Peking's suggestions for reform of, 198; Security Council, 128, 190, 193; Soviet veto, 191; West Irian responsibility for, 130; World Bank, 200, 263, 267; World Health Organization, 194

United Nations Inquiry in Borneo Territories, 170–2, 175; Malaysia, approval of, 173; observers, 172; report, 172–3,

United Pasokmomogun Kadazan Organization (U.P.K.O.), Sabah, 214, 217; advocates greater local autonomy, 214; influence diminished, 215 (see also Stephens)

United Sabah National Organization (U.S.N.O.), Sabah, 213; influence increased, 215 (see also U.M.N.O., Mustapha, Tun)

United States of America, 7, 10, 43, 120n., 122, 160, 182–3, 187, 196, 211, 236, 254, 259–62, 283, 284, 285; aid wasted, 236; alleged imperialism, 126; Asian Development Bank, membership of, 264; British colonial policies, suspicion of, 182; Central Intelligence Organization, 211; Commonwealth bases, attitude to, 210n.; criticism by Lee Kuan Yew, 212; diplomatic violations, victim of, 198, 226, 261; Indonesia, attitude to, 182–3; Malaysian Prime Minister's visit, 191; Malaysia problem, doubts, 182; Maryland, 9, Netherlands, attitude to, 128; New England, 9; New York, 6; Pennsylvania, 9; policies in Congo and Vietnam, 198; press correspondents expelled from Indonesia, 225; tin and rubber stockpiles, 234, 259; Vietnam involvement, 182, 229, 247; Vietnam procurement orders, 238–9

University of Malaya: Faculty of Education, 258; Malay Language Society, 257

Utrecht, Peace of, 10

*Utusan Melayu*, Malay nationalist newspaper, 125; arrest of reporter, 194

Victoria, Queen, 65

Vietnam, 3, 109, 182, 199, 230, 238, 259, 260, 264, 271, 274; British advisory mission, 98; communist subversion, 89, 95; domino theory, 247; National Liberation Front, 230; strategic hamlets, 98; War, relation to Malaysia, 110, 246; Vietcong, 110, 231

V.O.C., (Vereenigde Oostindische Compagnie) (see United Dutch East India Company)

Wales, 8n., 9, 125

Wallace Bay Timber Company (Sabah), 3

Washington Treaties, 70

W.A.S.P.S. (White Anglo-Saxon
    Protestants), 6
Weld, Sir Frederick, Governor of
    the Straits Settlements, 54
Westminster Parliamentary System,
    115
Weston (*see* Sabah)
Westphalia, Treaty of, 11
White Anglo-Saxon Protestants
    (*see* W.A.S.P.S.)
women, status of in Southeast
    Asia, 18
Wong, Pow Nee, Chief Minister of
    Penang, 144
Wong, Dr. Ruth, Dean of the
    Faculty of Education,
    University of Malaya, 258
World Bank (International Bank
    for Reconstruction and

Development) (*see* Indonesia,
    Malaysia, Singapore, United
    Nations)
World Health Organization
    (W.H.O.) (*see* United Nations)

Yala (*see* Thailand)
Yong Nyuk Lin, Singapore
    Minister for Health, 209n.
Yong, Stephen, S.U.P.P.,
    Sarawak, 269
Yusof bin Ishak, Tun, Head of
    State, later President, of
    Singapore, 136, 209
Yusuf, Raja, Regent and Sultan of
    Perak, 46, 49

Zaini, 164, 166 (*see also* Azahari,
    Brunei revolt)

# Maps

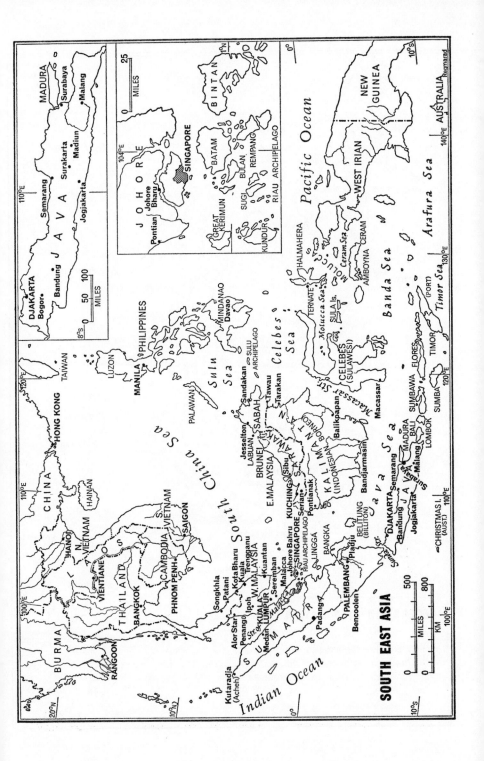

SOUTH EAST ASIA

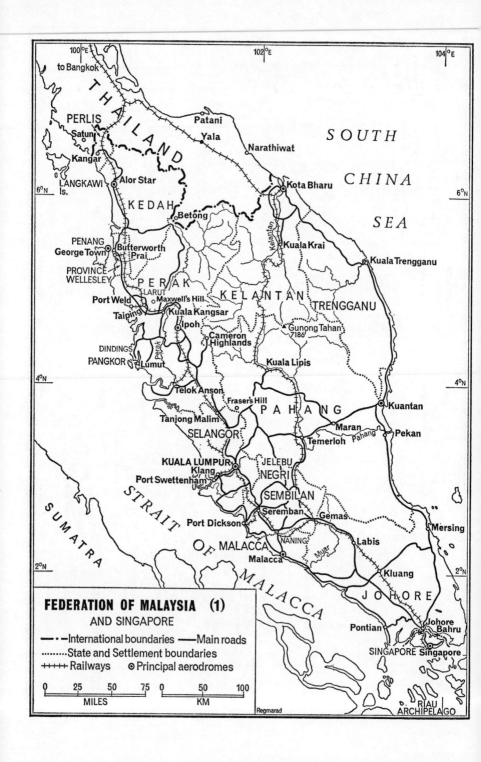

FEDERATION OF MALAYSIA (1)
AND SINGAPORE

— · —International boundaries —— Main roads
·········· State and Settlement boundaries
+++++ Railways ⊙ Principal aerodromes

0  25  50  75  0  50  100
MILES          KM

Regmarad

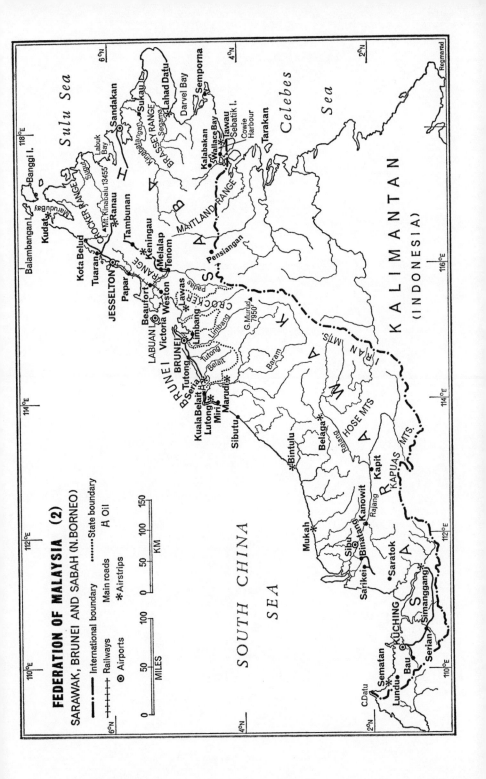

# FEDERATION OF MALAYSIA (2)

SARAWAK, BRUNEI AND SABAH (N.BORNEO)

— International boundary
+++++ Railways
◎ Airports
——— Main roads
⚹ Airstrips
······ State boundary
⧌ Oil